Refusals to License Intellectual Property

Testing the Limits of Law and Economics

Ian Eagles and Louise Longdin

·HART·
PUBLISHING

OXFORD AND PORTLAND, OREGON
2011

Published in the United Kingdom by Hart Publishing Ltd
16C Worcester Place, Oxford, OX1 2JW
Telephone: +44 (0)1865 517530
Fax: +44 (0)1865 510710
E-mail: mail@hartpub.co.uk
Website: http://www.hartpub.co.uk

Published in North America (US and Canada) by
Hart Publishing
c/o International Specialized Book Services
920 NE 58th Avenue, Suite 300
Portland, OR 97213–3786
USA
Tel: +1 503 287 3093 or toll-free: (1) 800 944 6190
Fax: +1 503 280 8832
E-mail: orders@isbs.com
Website: http://www.isbs.com

© Ian Eagles and Louise Longdin 2011

Ian Eagles and Louise Longdin have asserted their right under the Copyright, Designs and Patents Act 1988, to be identified as the authors of this work.

All rights reserved. No part of this publication may be reproduced, stored in a retrieval system, or transmitted, in any form or by any means, without the prior permission of Hart Publishing, or as expressly permitted by law or under the terms agreed with the appropriate reprographic rights organisation. Enquiries concerning reproduction which may not be covered by the above should be addressed to Hart Publishing Ltd at the address above.

British Library Cataloguing in Publication Data

Data Available

ISBN: 978-1-84113-873-2

Typeset by Columns Design XML Ltd, Reading
Printed and bound in Great Britain by
TJ International Ltd, Padstow, Cornwall

Preface

Refusals to license intellectual property provide an interesting testing-ground for those who would wish to see a greater interaction between law and economics. Usually the problem they face is that of feeding the results of their scholarship into judicial and regulatory processes in the absence (in most jurisdictions) of any formal machinery for doing so, and with judges and regulators often unfamiliar with this particular mode of reasoning (at least outside the United States). Economic analysis rarely figures in intellectual property litigation even at the appellate level, and cases are seldom lost or won for want of an economics input. None of this applies to competition proceedings. Here the symbiosis between law and economics is both unremarkable and continuous. Economist witnesses are familiar figures in the courtroom, and the language of economics is scattered throughout the judgments of even the highest courts. Indeed the trend in competition law is toward more economics not less, not merely during the adjudicative process but also at the doctrinal level. Jurisdictions are more and more moving towards case-by-case analysis and away from *per se* liability. It is therefore all the more surprising that the seemingly fruitful symbiosis between the two disciplines should begin to falter when judges and regulators are asked to determine the appropriate relationship between intellectual property rights and competition rules. In this particular corner of competition policy there is an observable tendency for courts and enforcement agencies to abandon economic analysis for a series of black-letter exceptions to otherwise generally applicable (and equally black-letter) rules.

This partial roll-back of economics-based rules of reason is not a retreat into the behavioural prohibitions and presumptions of anti-competitive vice that once characterised whole areas of United States competition law, and of which traces still linger both there and in other jurisdictions. This time, the move is in the direction of a presumption of pro-competitive virtue, or even, on occasion, a complete exemption from liability for intellectual property dealings. The move is accelerated when it is a unilateral (meaning for our purposes non-collusive) refusal to license that is in issue. The explanations usually offered for this retreat from case-specific economic analysis rest upon a series of empirically unsupported assumptions about the role of competition regulation and intellectual property in a market economy. Responsibility for this empirical underfeeding has to be shared between lawyers and economists. These are, however, not moral lapses. They are due to conflicting starting assumptions and divergent methodologies. These things surface not only in relation to refusals to license, but in other areas of competition law as well. We have chosen to focus on refusals to license because the subject points up these issues in a particularly stark way. That there have always been limits to the successful interaction of law and economics in framing competition policy cannot be denied. The refusals to license debate allows these limits to be explored within a reasonably narrow factual compass. What needs to be stressed, however, is that these limits cannot be analysed properly merely by looking at the competition side of the equation. The objectives, assumptions and methodologies of intellectual property lawyers also need to be put under the law and economics microscope. We hope this book will go some way towards doing all these things.

Summary Contents

Preface	v
Contents	ix
Table of Cases	xv
Table of Legislation	xxiii
1 Framing the Analysis	1
2 The Uneasy Cohabitation of Law and Economics in Competition Regimes	23
3 Fault Lines in Competition Policy	35
4 Intellectual Property and Competition Policy: Constructing the Interface	76
5 Refusals to License in the United States	122
6 Europe's Exceptional Circumstances Test	150
7 Refusals to License in Australia and New Zealand: Parsing the Hints and Silences	181
8 Canada: Legislative Solutions and Regulatory Bypasses	210
9 Reintegrating Law and Economics: Perfecting the Art of the Possible	233
Bibliography	240
Index	257

Contents

Preface	v
Summary Contents	vii
Table of Cases	xv
Table of Legislation	xxiii

1 Framing the Analysis 1
   1.1 The Nature of the Problem 1
   1.2 The Scheme of the Book 2
   1.3 The Distractions of Terminology 3
      1.3.1 'Intellectual property', 'intellectual property right' and 'refusal to license' 4
      1.3.2 'Regulator' and 'regulation' 5
      1.3.3 'Competition', 'antitrust', 'abuse of market power' and 'monopolisation' 5
   1.4 Two Bad Ideas Converge 6
   1.5 The Ideal Competition Regime 6
   1.6 Rhetorical Dead Ends and Red Herrings 10
      1.6.1 Ownership carries with it the right to exclude others from the thing owned 10
      1.6.2 What the State has expressly granted it shall not take back by stealth 12
      1.6.3 Intellectual property owners must be free to choose their licensees 13
      1.6.4 Coerced licensing is confiscation 15
      1.6.5 Regulatory intervention is justified only in the case of marginal or weak intellectual property rights 16
      1.6.6 Under-regulation is always and everywhere better than over-regulation 17
      1.6.7 The need for competition scrutiny diminishes when there is a parallel regulatory regime and intellectual property provides such a regime 18
      1.6.8 Compulsory licensing discourages investment in innovation and creativity 18
   1.7 The Incomplete Globalisation of Competition Policy 20

2 The Uneasy Cohabitation of Law and Economics in Competition Regimes 23
   2.1 Empiricism versus Formalism 23
   2.2 The Uneven Reception of Economics across Jurisdictions 24

		2.2.1	The rule of reason and economics in United States case law	24
		2.2.2	The delayed take-up of economics in Europe	25
		2.2.3	Economics legislatively mandated or excluded: Canada, Australia and New Zealand	26
	2.3	The Inherent Indeterminism of Economics		27
	2.4	Judicial Exits from Indeterminate Economics		29
		2.4.1	Deference to the regulator	29
		2.4.2	Manipulating the onus and standard of proof	30
		2.4.3	Deference to business autonomy or expertise	30
	2.5	Modes of Absorbing Economics		31
	2.6	Choosing Between the False Positive and the False Negative		32
3	Fault Lines in Competition Policy			35
	3.1	A Taxonomy of Competition Rules		35
	3.2	Disentangling Fact and Law in Competition Cases		36
		3.2.1	Rules or prophecies?	37
		3.2.2	Proof and presumption in competition cases	37
	3.3	The Role of Markets in the Refusal to License Debate		40
		3.3.1	Defining markets and delimiting rights are not the same thing	41
		3.3.2	Substitutability and intellectual property	41
		3.3.3	How many markets? How many rights?	42
		3.3.4	Special rules for special markets?	47
		3.3.5	Standard setting and standard capture	50
		3.3.6	Mandated interoperability	51
	3.4	Efficiency and Consumers: Centre Stage or at the Margins?		52
		3.4.1	Efficiency: goal or fall-back defence?	53
		3.4.2	The three faces of efficiency	53
		3.4.3	Whose welfare matters?	54
	3.5	Probability, Intent and Outcome		57
	3.6	The Uncertain Role of Barriers to Entry in Competition Analysis		58
		3.6.1	Measurement or categorisation	59
		3.6.2	Structural versus strategic barriers	60
	3.7	The Ever-receding Perfect Remedy		61
		3.7.1	Remedial objectives in competition cases	62
		3.7.2	Structural remedies: nuclear deterrent or conventional weapon?	62
		3.7.3	Judicial recoil from the role of quasi regulator	66
		3.7.4	Pricing coerced access	67
		3.7.5	Court-created supervisory structures: assisting whom—court or regulator?	69
		3.7.6	Retrospective assessment of efficacy	70

	3.7.7	Reasoning backward from remedy to breach	71
	3.7.8	Multi-purpose monetary remedies	74

4 Intellectual Property and Competition Policy: Constructing the Interface 76
   4.1 Privilege, Punishment and Neutrality 76
   4.2 Winners and Losers in the Intellectual Property Game 77
      4.2.1 Innovators, creators and owners 77
      4.2.2 Competitors as innovators 78
      4.2.3 Users and consumers 78
      4.2.4 Dispersed contributors to innovative efficiency 79
   4.3 The Magic of Names: 'Property', 'Regulation' and 'Monopoly' 79
      4.3.1 Property's necessary ambiguities 80
      4.3.2 Is intellectual property really the same as other property and does it matter? 82
      4.3.3 Property versus regulation: a false polarity 83
      4.3.4 Legal versus economic monopolies 84
   4.4 Slicing the Intellectual Property Pie 85
      4.4.1 The juristic form of the right 85
      4.4.2 Matching rule to rationale 88
      4.4.3 Different jurisdictions slice the pie differently 90
      4.4.4 Paracopyright and privatised regulation 91
   4.5 Intellectual Property's Lopsided Relationship with Competition Policy 92
      4.5.1 Intellectual property's internal competition controls 92
      4.5.2 Ranking rights in terms of utility and vulnerability 96
      4.5.3 One size fits all 97
      4.5.4 Intellectual property and barriers to entry 98
   4.6 The Contested Economics of Intellectual Property 101
      4.6.1 The economics of rights justification 101
      4.6.2 The economics of rights expansion 102
      4.6.3 Cheering on the expansion 105
      4.6.4 Worried bystanders and prophets of doom 108
   4.7 The Erosion of Intellectual Property's Own Limiting Mechanisms 110
      4.7.1 Towards the fully protectable idea 111
      4.7.2 Cutting the link between signifier and reputation 112
      4.7.3 Effort and investment protected *per se* 113
      4.7.4 Widening the copyright infringement net 115
      4.7.5 Restricting follow-on innovation and creativity 116
   4.8 Pushing at the Time/Space Envelope 117
      4.8.1 Extending the term of the right 117
      4.8.2 Towards the inexhaustible right 119
      4.8.3 Exporting over-protection 121

5	Refusals to License in the United States	122
	5.1 The Fragmentation of United States Monopolisation Law	122
	5.2 The Push-Me-Pull-You Intellectual Property–Antitrust Relationship	123
	5.3 The Interrupted Journey Towards Regulatory Neutrality	125
	5.4 The Right to Refuse and Essential Facilities in United States Antitrust Law	126
	5.4.1 Expansion and refinement of the essential facilities doctrine	127
	5.4.2 The *Colgate* principle	131
	5.4.3 The significance of fair dealing	132
	5.4.4 The *Trinko* retreat: squeezing the life out of essential facilities	134
	5.5 The Continuing Problem of Constructive Refusal and Margin Squeeze	137
	5.6 Spare Parts and After Markets: A Dead End?	138
	5.7 Variation across the Intellectual Property Spectrum: Uneven Treatment of Patents and Copyright	141
	5.8 Parallel Jurisprudence on Abuse of Rights	144
	5.9 The Uncertain Line between Action and Inaction in US Law	147
	5.10 A Summary of Judicial Responses to Refusals to License in United States Courts	148
6	Europe's Exceptional Circumstances Test	150
	6.1 Soft and Hard Law in Europe	150
	6.2 Hallmarks of European Refusals Jurisprudence	152
	6.2.1 The nexus between market power and ownership of intellectual property right	152
	6.2.2 Close and enduring embrace of the essential facilities doctrine	153
	6.2.3 Leveraging theory and the multiple markets debate in Europe	156
	6.2.4 Entrenchment of the need for objective justification	157
	6.3 Refusals to Supply Tangibles	159
	6.4 Refusals to Supply Intangibles	160
	6.5 Refusals to License Intellectual Property	161
	6.5.1 The emergence of the concept of exceptional circumstances	161
	6.5.2 Judicial refinement of the concept of exceptionality	163
	6.5.3 National treatment of refusals to license intellectual property	166
	6.6 *Oscar Bronner*: Anomaly or Path Through the Woods?	168
	6.7 Euro *Microsoft*	170
	6.8 Little Guidance from the *Guidance*	176

7	Refusals to License in Australia and New Zealand: Parsing the Hints and Silences	181
	7.1 Convergence and its Limits	181
	7.2 Taking Advantage of Market Power	182
	7.2.1 The statutory provisions	182
	7.2.2 Australia: many roads home	183
	7.2.3 New Zealand: one test to rule them all	189
	7.3 Feeding Intellectual Property into the Legislative Mix	196
	7.3.1 The legislated line between action and inaction in relation to intellectual property in Australia and New Zealand	196
	7.3.2 Judicial hints and silences in Australia	197
	7.3.3 A New Zealand oddity: section 36(3) of the Commerce Act	205
	7.3.4 Restraint of trade and breach of confidence preserved by statute	208
8	Canada: Legislative Solutions and Regulatory Bypasses	210
	8.1 A Three Pronged Legislative Assault	210
	8.2 Enforcement and Adjudication	211
	8.3 Section 75: Refusals to Deal	211
	8.4 Section 79: General and Specific Prohibitions	217
	8.5 Section 32: Special Remedies for Abuse of Intellectual Property Rights	223
	8.6 The Patent Assignment Cases	225
	8.7 The Competition Bureau's Enforcement Guidelines	228
	8.7.1 *Intellectual Property Enforcement Guidelines* (2000)	228
	8.7.2 *Draft Enforcement Guidelines on Abuse of Dominance*	229
	8.8 Compulsory Licensing Under Intellectual Property Statutes in Canada	231
9	Reintegrating Law and Economics: Perfecting the Art of the Possible	233
	9.1 The Case for Neutrality Restated	233
	9.2 Intellectual Property and Competition Policy: Rebuilding the Interface	233
	9.2.1 Setting limits to competition policy	234
	9.2.2 The inadequacy of intellectual property's internal controls	234
	9.2.3 The choices for courts and regulators	235
	9.3 Failed Black-Letter Exits from the Refusal to License Impasse	235
	9.3.1 Essential facilities, the right to refuse and exceptional circumstances: non-solutions to non-problems	236
	9.3.2 The ranking of rights: unworkable and distracting	236
	9.4 The Perils of Legislative Intervention	237

9.5 The Shifting of Competition Law's Internal Markers 238
9.6 Reducing the Empirical Deficit 238

Bibliography 240
Index 257

Table of Cases

Australia

Allied Mills Industrial v TPC (1981) FCA 11; 34 ALR 105. 94
ASX Operations Pty Ltd v Pont Data Australia Pty Ltd [1990] FCA 515; (1991) ATPR 41–069; 97 ALR 515. 199–200
Australasian Performing Rights Association Ltd v Ceridale Pty Ltd [1990] FCA 516; (1991) ATPR ¶41–074. 197
Australian Competition and Consumer Commission v Australian Safeway Stores Pty Ltd [2003] FCAFC 149; (2003) ATPR 41–935. 186
Australian Competition and Consumer Commission v Boral Ltd [1999] FCA 1318; (1999) 166 ALR 410. 188
Australian Competition and Consumer Commission v Boral Ltd (2001) FCA 30 41
Autodesk v Dyason (No 2) [1993] HCA 6. 111
Boral Besser Masonry Ltd v Australian Competition and Consumer Commission [2003] HCA 5; 215 CLR 374. 185
Broderbund Software Inc v Computermate Products Australia Pty Ltd [1991] FCA 563; (1992) ATPR 41–155 201
Children's Television Workshop Inc v Woolworths (NSW) Ltd [1981] RPC 187; [1981] NSWLR 273. 112
Dais Studio Pty Ltd v Bullet Creative Pty Ltd [2007] FCA 2054. 111
Federal Commissioner of Taxation v United Aircraft Corporation [1943] HCA 50; (1943) 68 CLR 525. 86
General Newspaper Pty Ltd v Telstra (formerly Australian & Overseas Telecommunications Corp Ltd) [1993] FCA 473; (1993) ATPR 41–274. 188
Hallstroms Pty Ltd v Federal Commissioner of Taxation [1946] HCA 34; (1946) 72 CLR 634 40
Hogan v Koala Dundee Pty Ltd [1988] FCA 33; 83 ALR 187. 112
Melway Publishing Pty Limited v Robert Hicks Limited [1999] FCA 664 and [2001] HCA 13; (2001) 205 CLR 1. .... 185–8, 191, 197
NT Power Generation v Power and Water Authority [2002] FCAFC 302 and [2004] HCA 48; (2004) 219 CLR 90. .... 18, 84, 185, 187, 203
Pacific Dunlop Ltd v Hogan [1989] FCA 185; 87 ALR 14. 112
Pacific Film Laboratories Pty Ltd v FCT [1970] HCA 36; 121 CLR 151. 120
Queensland Wire Industries Pty Ltd v Broken Hill Pty Co Ltd [1989] HCA 6; (1989) 167 CLR 177. .... 8, 60, 184
R v Federal Court of Australia; Ex Parte Pilkington ACI (Operations) Pty Ltd [1978] HCA 60; (1978) 142 CLR 113. 62
Regents Pty Ltd v Subaru (Australia) Pty Ltd [1998] FCA 730; (1998) 84 FCR 218.
Rural Press Ltd v Australian Competition and Consumer Commission [2003] HCA 75; (2003) 216 CLR 53. 201
Telstra Corporation Limited v Phone Directories Company Pty Ltd [2010] FCA 44 (Affirmed [2010] FCAFC 149). 11, 200
Welcome Real-Time SA v Catuity Inc [2001] FCA 445; 51 IPR 327. 111

xvi   TABLE OF CASES

Canada

B-Filer Inc v The Bank of Nova Scotia CT-2005–006 (2006) Comp Trib 42. 212
Canada (Commissioner of Competition) v Superior Propane Inc 2001 FCA 104. 228
Canada (Director of Investigation and Research) v Bank of Montreal ('Interac')
    CT-1995–002 Doc 93a: Reasons for Order; [1996] 68 CPR (3d) 527. 210
Canada (Director of Investigation and Research) v Chrysler Canada Ltd CT-1988–004;
    Doc 185a: Reasons and Order; [1989] 27 CPR 3d 1 (Comp Trib); 1989 CPR LEXIS
    1741. 214–15
Canada (Director of Investigation and Research) v NutraSweet Co CT-1989–002 Doc 176a:
    Reasons and Order; (1990) 32 CPR (3d) 1. 219
Canada (Director of Investigation and Research) v Warner Music Canada Ltd ('Warner')
    CT-1997–003 Doc 22: Reasons and Order; [1997] 78 CPR 3d 321. .... 216–17, 225
Canada (Director of Investigation and Research) v Xerox Canada Inc ('Xerox Canada')
    CT-1989–004 Doc 88a; [1990] 33 CPR 3d 83. 214–16
Commissioner of Competition v The Canadian Real Estate Association CT-2010–002 Doc
    75: Consent Agreement registered 25 October 1010. 210
Compo Co v Blue Crest Music Inc [1980] 1 SCR 357. 83
Eli Lilly and Co v Apotex Inc (2005) FCA 361. .... 226, 227
MacDonald v Vapor Canada Ltd [1977] 2 SCR 134. 218
Molnlycke AB v Kimberly-Clark of Canada [1991] 36 CPR 3d 493. 225–6
Nowegijick v The Queen [1983] 1 SCR 29. 228
Re Gauntlet Energy Corp Ltd [2003] ABQB 718; [2004] WWR 373. 80
Sarco Co Inc v Sarco Canada Ltd [1969] 2 Ex CR 190. 232
Sears Canada Inc v Parfums Christian Dior Canada Inc and Parfums Givenchy Canada
    Ltd CT-2007–001 Doc 30: Reasons for Order; (2007) Comp Trib 6; 2007 CACT 6
    (CanLII). 213
Torpharm Inc v Canada (Commissioner of Patents) 2004 FC 673. .... 93, 232

EU

Boosey v Hawkes: [1987] OJ L286/36; [1988] 4 CMLR 67. .... 158, 214, 230
British Horse Racing Board v William Hill Organisation Case C-203/02 [2002] ECR
    I-10415. 20
British Midlands/Aer Lingus [1992] OJ L96; [1993] 4 CMLR 596. 154
British Petroleum v European Commission Case 77/77 [1978] ECR 1513. 158
Centre Belge d'Etudes du Marché-Télémarketing SA (CBEM) v Compagnie
    Luxembourgeoise de Télédiffusion (CLT) Case 311/84 [1985] ECR 3261; [1986] 2
    CMLR 558. 156
CICCRA & Maxicar v Renault Case 53/87 [1988] ECR 6039; [1990] 4 CMLR 265. ... 161
Clearstream Banking AG v Clearstream International SA Case T-301/04 [2009] ECR
    II-3155; [2009] 5 CMLR 24. 160–1
Compagnie Maritime Belge Transport SA v European Commission Joined Cases C-395/96
    P and C-396/96 P [2000] ECR I-1365. 155
Deutsche Post AG Case COMP/C-1/36.915 [2001] OJ L331. 164
European Commission v French Republic Joined Cases 92 & 93/87 [1989] ECR 405. 67
European Commission v International Business Machines [1984] 3 CMLR 14. 162

Fixtures Marketing Ltd v Organismos Prognostikon Agonon Podosfairou (OPAP) AE Case
C-444/02 [2004] ECR I-10549. 20
Fixtures Marketing Ltd v Oy Veikkaus Ab C-46/02 [2004] ECR I-10365. 20
Fixtures Marketing Ltd v Svenska Spel AB C-338/02 [2004] ECR I-10497. 20
Flughafen Frankfurt/Main AG [1998] OJ L72/30 [1998] 4 CMLR 779. 154
Hoffmann-La Roche & Co v European Commission Case 85/76 [1979] ECR 461. 153
ICI and Commercial Solvents v European Commission Joined Cases 6/73 and 7/73 [1974]
ECR 223; [1974] 1 CMLR 309. .... 159, 163, 168, 214
IMS Health GmbH v NDC Health GmbH Case C-418/01 [2004] ECR I-5039; [2004] 4
CMLR 28. .... 11–14, 20, 153, 221
ITT Promedia NV v European Commission Case T-111/96 [1998] ECR II-2937. 155
Liptons Cash Registers v Hugin [1978] OJ L22/23; [1978] 1 CMLR D19. 158
London- European Airways v Sabena [1988] OJ L317/47; [1989] 4 CMLR 662. 160
Merck-Principi Attivi, Case A364, Decision of June 15, 2005, Case A364, IAA Bulletin n
23/2005, p 7. .... 68, 166
Metropole Television (M6) v European Commission Case T-112/99 [2001] II-2459; [2001]
All ER (D) 37. 35
Michelin v European Commission Case T-203/01 [2003] ECR II-4071. .... 57, 60
Microsoft Corporation v European Commission Case T-201/04 [2007] ECR II-3601; 5
CMLR 11. .... 13, 29, 36, 87, 151, 170, 216
Ministere Public v Tournier Case 395/87 [1989] ECR 2521. 158
Morlaix (Port of Roscoff) [1995] CMLR 177. 153
Orange-Book-Standard Case KZR 39/06 (2009) BGH (German Federal Supreme
Court). 166
Oscar Bronner v Mediaprint Zeitung und Zeitschriftenverlag GmbH Case C-7/97 [1998]
ECR I-7791; [1999] 4 CMLR 112. .... 9, 13, 151, 155, 157, 163, 168–70, 177,
203, 216, 224
Österreichische Postsparkasse AG and Bank für Arbeit and *Wirtschaft AG v European
Commission* Joined Cases T-213/01 and T-214/01 [2006] ECR II-1601 56
Port of Rødby [1994] OJ L55/52. 153
Radio Telefis Eirean and Independent Television Publications v European Commission
('*Magill*') (1995) Joined cases C-241/91 P and C-242/91 P [1995] ECR I-743; 4
CMLR 718. .... 12, 41, 117, 155, 221
Sea Containers/Stena Sealink 94/19 [1994] OJ L15/8; [1994] 4 CMLR 84.
Sealink/B & I—Holyhead [1992] 5 CMLR 255. .... 8, 155
SGL Carbon AG v European Commission Case C-308/04 P [2006] ECR I-5977. .... 8, 67
Standard-Spundfass Case KZR 40/02 (2004) BGH (German Federal Supreme
Court). 166
*Synetairismos Farmakopoion Aitolias & Akarnanias (Syfait) and others v GlaxoSmithKline
AEVE* Case C-53/03 [2005] ECR I-4609. 158
Tiercé Ladbroke SA v European Commission Case T-504/93 [1997] ECR II-923. 154,
163
T-Mobile Netherlands BV & Others Case C-8/08 [2009] ECR I-4529. 151
United Brands Co and United Brands Continental BV v European Commission Case 27/76
[1978] ECR 207. .... 2, 60, 153, 157
Volvo v Erik Veng (UK Ltd) Case 238/87 [1988] ECR 6211; [1989] 4 CMLR 122. 14,
153, 161, 201

NZ

Barson Computers (NZ) Ltd v John Gilbert and Co Ltd (1984) 4 IPR 533. 120
Carter Holt Harvey Building Products Group Limited v Commerce Commission [2004]
    UKPC 37; [2006] 1 NZLR 145. .... 191, 195
Commerce Commission v Telecom Corporation of New Zealand Limited ('0867') [2010]
    NZSC 111. 188-9
Dennison Manufacturing Co v Alfred Holt and Co Ltd (1987) 10 IPR 612. 94
Direct Ltd v Best Buy Ltd [1992] 2 NZLR 723. 113
Electricity Corporation v Geotherm Energy [1992] 2 NZLR 641. 206-8
Fisher and Paykel Ltd. v Commerce Commission [1990] 2 NZLR 730. 106
Land Transport Safety Authority of New Zealand v Glogau [1999] 1 NZLR 261. 114
Magic Millions Ltd v Wrightson Bloodstock Ltd [1990] 1 NZLR 731. 43
Mono Pumps (New Zealand) Ltd v Karinya Industries (1986) 7 IPR 25 94
Neumegen v Neumegen [1998] 3 NZLR 310. 113
Phonographic Performances (NZ) Ltd v Radioworks Ltd [2010] NZCOP 1. 3
Plix Products Ltd v Frank M Winstone Ltd (1984) 3 IPR 390. .... 112, 115
Port Nelson Ltd v Commerce Commission [1996] 3 NZLR 554. .... 9, 57, 181, 201
Telecom Corporation of New Zealand Limited v Clear Communications Limited [1994]
    UKPC 36; [1994] CLC 1312; [1995] 1 NZLR 385. ...... 66, 84, 132, 135, 191-5, 207-9
The University of Waikato v Benchmarking Services Ltd (2004) 8 NZBLC 101. 114
Villa Maria Wines v Montana Wines Ltd [1984] 2 NZLR 422. 113

Singapore

Global Yellow Pages Ltd v Promedia Directories Ltd [2010] SGHC 97. 3

UK

Allnutt v Inglis (1810) 12 East 527. 127
Attheraces v British Horse Racing Board Ltd [2005] EWHC 3015 (Ch); [2007] EWCA Civ
    38. .... 20, 68, 156, 165, 179
British Leyland v Armstrong, Patents Ltd [1986] AC 577. 94
Chaplin v Hicks [1911] 2 KB 786. 61
EI du Pont de Nemours & Co and Op Graphics (Holography) Ltd Case CP/1761/02 (2003)
    OFT CA98/07/2003. 163
EMI Music Publishing Ltd v Papathanassiou [1993] EMLR 306. 115
Francis Day and Hunter Ltd v Bron [1963] Ch 587. 115
Herbert Morris Ltd v Saxelby [1916] 1 AC 688. 86
House of Spring Garden Ltd v Point Blank Ltd [1983] FSR 213; [1984] IR 611. 115
Initial Services Ltd v Putteril [1968] 1QB 396. 94
L B Plastics Ltd v Swish Products Ltd [1979] RPC 551. 115
Nova Productions Ltd v Mazooma Games Ltd [2007] EWCA Civ 219. 111
Phillips Electronics v Ingman Ltd [1998] EWHC Patents 321; [1999] FSR 112. 13
R v Morris [1984] UKHL 1; AC 320. 80
Regent Oil Co Ltd v Strick [1965] 3 ALL ER 174. 39
Rolls Royce Ltd v Jeffrey [1962] 1 ALL ER 801. 86

Shepherd Homes Ltd v Sandham [1971] 1 Ch 340. 71
Software Cellular Network Limited v T-Mobile (UK) Ltd [2007] EWHC 1790
   (Ch). 155, 160
Solar Thomson Engineering Co v Barton [1997] RPC 537. 94
South Yorkshire Transport Ltd v Monopolies and Merger Commission [1993] 1 ALL ER
   289. 39
Waterlow Directories v Reed Information (1990) 20 IPR 493; [1992] FSR 409. 115

US

Abbott Laboratories v Brennan 952 F 2d 1346 (Fed Cir 1991). 141
Abkco Music Inc v Harrison's Music Ltd 722 F 2d 988 (2nd Cir 1983). 115
Alaska Airlines v United Airlines 948 F 2d 536 (9th Cir 1991). 136
Alcatel USA Inc v DGI Technologies Inc 166 F 3d 772 (5th Cir 1999). 45, 146
ASCAP v Showtime/The Movie Channel 912 F 2d 563 (2nd Cir 1990). 69
Aspen Skiing Co v Aspen Highlands Skiing Corp 738 F 2d 1509 (10th Cir 1984); 472 US
   585 (1985). 13–14
Associated Press v United States 326 US 1 (1945). 127
AT &T v Excel Communications 172 F 3d 1352 (Fed Cir 1999). 111
Beard v Parkview Hospital 912 F 2d 138 (6th Cir 1990). 220
Bell Atlantic Corp v Twomby 550 US 544 (2007). 136
Bellsouth Advertising v Donnelley 719 F Supp 1551 (S D Fla 1988), reversed 999 F 2d
   1436 (11th Cir 1993). 130–1
Berkey Photo Inc v Eastman Kodak 603 F 2d 263 (2nd Cir 1979); cert denied, 444 US
   1093 (1980) 74
Broadcast Music Inc v Columbia Broadcasting System 441 US 1 (1979). 35, 125
Brown Shoe Co v US 370 US 294 (1962). 10
Brulotte v Thys Co 379 US 29 (1964). 144
Brunswick Corp v Riegel Textile Corp 752 F 2d 261 (7th Cir 1985). 72
Byars v Bluff City News Co 609 F 2d 843 (6th Cir 1979). 129
Chamberlain Group Inc v Skylink Technologies Inc 381 F 3d 1178 (Fed Cir 2004). . 146–7,
   218
Chicago Board of Trade v United States 246 US 231 (1917). 35
City of Anaheim v Southern California Edison Co 955 F 2d 1373 (9th Cir 1992). 130
Continental TV Inc v GTE Sylvania 433 US 36 (1977). 125
Covad Communications Co v BellSouth Corp 374 F 3d 1044 (11th Cir 2004). 134, 149
Credit Suisse v Billing 551 US 264 (2007). 84
Data General Corporation v Grumman Systems Support Corporation 36 F 3d 1147 (1st Cir
   1994). 137, 143
Directory Sales Management Corporation v Ohio Bell (1987) 833 F 2d 606. 220
Eastman Kodak v Image Technical Services 504 US 451 (1992) ('*Kodak I*'). 37, 133–4,
   201, 211
ebay v MercExchange 547 US 388 (2006); 126 S Ct 1837. .... 68, 82
Eldred v Ashcroft 537 US 186 (2003). 118
Feist Publications Inc v Rural Telephone Service Co 499 US 340 (1991). 11, 13, 200
Ferguson v Greater Pocatello Chamber of Commerce Inc 848 F 2d 976 (9th Cir
   1988). 130
FTC v Indiana Federation of Dentists 476 US 447 (1986). 35

Gaste v Kaiserman 863 F 2d 1061 (2nd Cir 1988). 115
Haelan Laboratories v Topps Chewing Gum Inc 202 F 2d 866 (2nd Cir 1953). 86
Harper and Row v Nation Enterprises 471 US 539 (1985). 108
Hartford Empire Co v US 323 US 386 (1945). 67, 69
Hecht v Pro-Football Inc 570 F 2d 982 (DC Cir 1977). 128
Hudson's Bay Co v American Legend Co-op 651 F Supp 819 (DNJ 1986). 137
Hutchins v Zoll Medical Corporation 492 F 3d 1377 (Fed Cir 2007). 111
Illinois Tool Works Inc v Independent Ink Inc 547 US 28 (2006); 126 S Ct 1281
    (2006). 14, 140–1, 145, 147, 152, 204, 206, 221, 226
Image Technical Services Inc v Eastman Kodak Co ('Kodak II') 125 F 3d 1195 (9th Cir
    1997). 134
In Re Independent Services Organization Antitrust Litigation 203 F 3d 1322 (Fed Cir
    2000). 13
Intergraph Corporation v Intel Corporation 3 F Supp 2d 1255 (N D Ala 1998); 195 F 3d
    1346 (Fed Cir 1999). 129, 131, 133
International News Service v Associated Press 248 US 215 (1918). 89, 114
International Salt Co v United States 332 US 392 (1947). 14, 71, 145
Jefferson Parish Hospital District No 2 v Hyde 466 US 2 (1984). 145, 220
Kellog Co v National Biscuit Co 303 US 111 (1938). 86
LA Land Co v Brunswick Corp 6 F 3d 1422 (9th Cir 1993). 59
Lasercomb America v Reynolds 911 F 2d 970 (4th Cir 1990). 146
Lexmark International Inc v Static Control Components Inc 387 F 3d 522 (6th Cir 2004).
    146–7
LinkLine Communications Inc v SBC California Inc 503 F 3d 876 (9th Cir 2007). 138
Lorain Journal v United States 342 US 143 (1951). 148
MCI Communications Corporation v AT & T 708 F 2d 1081 (7th Cir 1983). . 128–30, 136
Mercoid Corporation v Mid-Continent Investment Co 320 US 661 (1944). 144
Metronet Services Corporation v US West Communications 329 F 3d 986 (9th Cir 2003).
    .... 130, 134, 137
Mitsubishi Motors Corp v Soler Chrysler-Plymouth Inc 473 US 614 (1985). 21
Monsanto Co v Spray-Rite Service Corp 465 US 752 (1984). 23
Morris Communications Corporation v Professional Golf Association 364 F 3d 1288 (11th
    Cir 2004). 136, 137, 149
Morton Salt Co v GS Suppiger Co 314 US 488 (1942). 14, 144
Motion Picture Patents Co v Universal Film Manufacturing Co 243 US 502 (1917).
NCAA v Board of Regents 468 US 85 (1984). 123, 125
Nelson v PRN Productions Ltd 873 F 2d 1141 (8th Cir 1989). 115
New York Mercantile Exchange Inc v Intercontinental Exchange Inc 323 F Supp 2d 559
    (SDNY 2004). 135
Nobody in Particular Presents v Clear Channel Communications 311 F Supp 2d 1048 (D
    Colo 2004). 149
Northern Telecom v Datapoint 908 F 2d 931 (Fed Cir 1990). 116
Novell Inc v CPU Dist Inc, US Dist Lexis 9952 (S D Texas, May 12 2000). 147
Otter Tail Power Co v United States 410 US 366 (1973). 128, 129
Pacific Bell Telephone Co v Linkline Communications Inc 555 US 07–512 (2008); 129 S Ct
    1109 (2009). 130
Paddock Publications Inc v Chicago Tribune Co 103 F 3d 42, 44 (7th Cir 1996); cert
    denied, 520 US 1265 (1997). 127

Paladin Associates Inc v Montana Power Co 97 F Supp 2d 1013 (D Mont 2000); 328 F 3d 1145 (9th Cir 2003). 130
Peter Pan Fabrics Inc v Martin Weiner Corp 274 F 2d 487 (2nd Cir 1960). 112
Qwest Corporation v MetroNet Services Corporation (formerly *US West Communications*) 540 US 1147 (2004); 124 S Ct 1144 (2004). 137
Rambus v Federal Trade Commission 522 F 3d 456 (DC Cir 2008). 51, 148
Re Independent Service Organisations Antitrust Litigation ('*CSU v Xerox*') 203 F 3d 1322 (Fed Cir 2000). 100, 141, 214
Robinson v Magovern 688 F 2d 824 (3rd Cir 1982). 136
Roche Products v Bolar Pharmaceutical Co 733 F 2d 858 (Fed Cir 1984). 116
Rockford Map Publishers Inc v Directory Service Co of Colorado 768 F 2d 145 (7th Cir 1985). 120
Ruckelhaus v Monsanto 467 US 986 (1984). 80
Sega Enterprises Ltd v Accolade Ltd 977 F 2d 1510 (9th Cir 1992). 45, 146
Senza Gel Corp v Seiffhart 803 F 2d 661 (Fed Cir 1986). 144
Siegel v Chicken Delight 448 F 2d, 43 (9th Cir 1971). 126
Smith v Chanel 402 F 2d 562; 159 USPQ 338 (1968). 113
Sony Corp v Universal City Studios 464 US 417 (1984). 108
Sony Electronics v Soundview Technologies 157 F Supp 2d 180 (D Conn 2001). 51
Spectrum Sports Inc v McQuillan 506 US 447 (1993). 135
Standard Oil of New Jersey v United States 221 US 1 (1911). 25, 35
*State Street Bank & Trust v Signature Financial Group*149 F 3d 1368 (Fed Cir 1998). 111
Sun Dun Inc v Coca-Cola Co 740 F Supp 381 (D Md 1990). 137
United States v Aluminum Corp of America 148 F 2d 416 (2nd Cir 1945). 21
United States v ASCAP 981 F Supp 201 (SDNY 1997). 68
United States v Colgate & Co 250 US 300 (1919). 14, 131–2, 135, 154, 188
United States v E I du Pont de Nemours & Co 351 US 377 (1956). 69
United States v General Electric 115 F Supp 835 (DNJ 1953). 69
United States v Goss 803 F 2d 638 (11th Cir 1986). 120
United States v Grinnell Corp 384 US 563 (1966). 71
United States v Kansas City Star Co 240 F 2d 643 (8th Cir 1957). 63
United States v Loew's Inc 371 US 38 (1962). 14, 142, 145
United States v Microsoft Corporation 158 FRD 318 (DDC 1995). 46
United States v Microsoft Corporation 980 F Supp 537 (DDC 1997); affirmed 147 F 3d 935 (DC Cir 1998). 46
United States v Microsoft Corporation 84 F Supp 2d 9 (DDC 1999). 60
United States v Microsoft Corporation 253 F 3d 34 (DC Cir 2001). .. 11, 13, 49, 59, 60, 63, 71, 73, 124, 126, 207
United States v National Lead Co 332 US 319 (1947). 69
United States v Paramount Pictures 334 US 131 (1942). 65
United States v Terminal Railroad Association 224 US 383 (1912). 8, 126–7, 129, 134
United States v United Shoe Machinery Corp 110 F Supp 295 (D Mass 1953); affirmed 391 US 244 (1968). 65
Verizon Communications Inc v Law Offices of Curtis V Trinko, LLP 540 US 398 (2004). 14, 18, 30, 36, 66, 74, 134–8,, 140, 149, 153, 157, 202, 204

Warner/Chappel Disc Inc v Pilz Compact Disc Inc 52 USPQ 2d (BNA) 1942 (E D Pa 1999). 147
Warner-Lambert Pharmaceutical Co v John J Reynolds Inc 178 F Supp 655 (SDNY 1959); affirmed 280 F 2d 197 (2nd Cir 1960). 118
WGN Continental Broadcasting Co v United Video Inc 693 F 2d 662 (7th Cir 1982). .. 120
Whelan Associates Inc v Jaslow Dental Laboratory 797 F 2d 1222 (3rd Cir 1986). 111
Wholesale Stationers v Pacific Stationery 472 US 284 (1985). 35
Zenith Radio Corp v Hazeltine Research Inc 395 US 100 (1969). 70

Table of Legislation

International Treaties and Conventions

Berne Convention for the Protection of Literary and Artistic Works 1886 223
General Agreement on Tariffs and Trade (GATT) 1947 18
Marrakesh Agreement 1994
    Annex 1C 18
Trade-Related Aspects of Intellectual property Rights (TRIPS) 1994 .... 18, 21, 93
    Art 6 120
    Art 8(2) 21, 224
    Art 31 92
    Art 39(2) 90
    Art 40(2) 21
World Intellectual Property Organisation Copyright Treaty (WCT) 1996 91
    Art 11 218

European Treaties

European Patent Convention 1973
    Art 54 111
Treaty of Maastricht 1992 150
Treaty on the Functioning of the European Union (TFEU) (Treaty of Lisbon) 2007 1, 150, 151
    Art 101 (ex Art 81 EC) 9, 35, 46, 56, 196
    (1) 196
    Art 102 (ex Art 82 EC) 3, 9, 26, 35, 40, 45, 46, 150, 151, 155, 156, 159–62, 164, 166, 169, 170,
    172, 174, 177, 180–83, 230, 237
    (b) 163, 173

European Secondary Legislation

Regulations

Reg 1/2003 Competition Regulation [2003] OJ L1/1
    Recital 12 64
    Art 7(1) 64
Reg 139/2004 Merger Regulation [2004] OJ L24/1 25
Reg 772/2004 Technology Transfer Block Exemption Regulation [2004] OJ L123/11 .... 1, 12, 196

Directives

Dir 89/104 Trade Mark Directive [1989] OJ L40/1
    Art 4(4)(a) 113
    Art 5(2) 113
Dir 91/250 Directive on the Legal Protection of Computer Programs [1991] OJ L122/42 ...... 51, 171
    Art 6 96
Dir 96/9 Directive on the Legal Protection of Databases [1996] OJ L77/20 .... 11, 114, 165
Dir 2001/29 Copyright Directive [2001] OJ L167/10 .... 13, 91

Notices

Guidance on the Commission's Enforcement Priorities in Applying [Art 102 TFEU] to Abusive
    Exclusionary Conduct by Dominant Undertakings (Guidance Communication) [2009] OJ
    C45/7 .... 26, 53, 56, 150–52, 176–78, 180

para 3 151
para 5 .... 159, 178
para 19 .... 177, 178
para 22 177
para 29 158
para 71 178
para 75 152
para 78 176
para 81 176
para 83 155
para 84 .... 157, 177
Guidelines on the Applicability of Art 81 of the Treaty to Horizontal Cooperation Agreements
   [2001] OJ C3/2 25
Guidelines on the Application of Art 81 of the Treaty to Technology Transfer Agreements [2004] OJ
   C101/2
   para 5 178
Guidelines on the Application of Art 81(3) of the Treaty [2004] OJ C101/97
   para 13 178
Guidelines on the Assessment of Horizontal Mergers under the Council Regulation on the Control
   of Concentrations between Undertakings [2004] OJ C31/5
   para 8 178
Guidelines on the Assessment of Non-Horizontal Mergers under the Council Regulation on the
   Control of Concentrations between Undertakings [2008] OJ C265/6
   para 10 178
Guidelines on Vertical Restraints [2000] OJ C291/1 25
   para 7 178

Domestic law

Australia

Competition and Consumer Act 2010 (Cth) .... s 4M208, 209
   s 18 205
   s 44B 66
   s 45(2) 196
   s 46 .... 182–88, 197, 198, 200–04
      (1) 45
      (4)(c) 204
      (6A) 189
      (7) 183
   s 46A 181
   s 51(1) 200
      (3) 196, 204
   s 80 62
   sch 2 .... 89, 205
Patents Act 1990 (Cth)
   s 128 101
   s 133(2)(b) 92
   s 134(2)(b) 92
Securities Industry Act 1980 199
Trade Practices Act 1974 (Cth) 182
   s 46(1)(b) 200
      (k) 199
   s 52 205
Trade Practices Amendment (Australian Consumer Law) Act (No 2) 2010 92

Canada

Combines Investigation Act 1910
  s 22 225
Competition Act 1985 (C-34) (consolidated 2011) 140, 210, 213, 228, 231
  s 32 .... 210, 211, 216, 223–25, 228, 229, 231
    (1) 223
    (3) 224
  s 45 225–27
    (1) 226
  s 75 .... 210, 211–17, 222–24
    (1) 211–13
      (a) 213
      (2) 213
      (3) 211
  s 77 220
  s 78 .... 217, 229
    (1)(a) 217
      (e) 217
      (g) 217
  s 79 .... 210, 211, 217–23, 226, 229
    (1) 217
    (4) 219
    (5) 216, 217, 219, 221, 222, 227
  s 92 229
  s 96(1) 214
  s 103(1) 211
  s 104(1) 210
Interpretation Act 1985 (RS 1985, c I-21)
  s 2 218
  s 35(1) 218
Patent Act 1985 (RSC 1985, c P-4)
  s 50 227
  s 65(1) 231
    (a)–(c) 231
    (2) 92, 231, 232
      (c) 231, 232
      (d) 231, 232
      (e) 231
      (f) 231
  s 66 231
  s 67 232
  s 68 232
Trade Marks Act 1985 (RSC 1985, c T-13) 221
  s 50(1) 221

Guidelines

Enforcement Guidelines on the Abuse of Dominance Provisions (ss 78 and 79 of the Competition
  Act) (Abuse Guidelines) 2001 .... 229, 230
    paras 10–13 230
Intellectual Property Enforcement Guidelines 2000 .... 140, 212, 227–29
  para 4.2.1 .... 227, 228
  para 4.2.2 228
Merger Guidelines 228

Germany

Act against Restraints of Competition (*Gesetz gegen Wettbewerbsbeschränkungen*) (GWB) (as amended 2005) 159
   s 19(4) 166
      (4) 154

Ireland

Competition Act 2002
   s 5 154

New Zealand

Commerce Act 1986 207
   Pt IV 84, 195
   s 4(1) 21
   s 7 .... 208, 209
      (1) 208
      (2) 209
   s 27 .... 181, 196
   s 36 .... 181–83, 190, 192, 195, 208
      (1) 209
      (2) 45, 182, 191, 192, 206
      (3) 205–08, 209, 222
   s 36A 181
   s 36B 183
   s 45 .... 196, 205
Copyright Act 1994
   s 14(1) 83
   ss 205–24 93
   s 226D(3) 52
Copyright (New Technologies) Amendment Act 2008 205
Designs Act 1953
   s 14 92
Fair Trading Act 1986 205
   s 9 89
Layout Designs Act 1994
   s 39(1) 83
Patents Act 1953
   s 24 115
   s 46 92
   s 74 101
   s 85(2) 101
Personal Property Securities Act 1999
   s 16 80
Plant Variety Rights Act 1987
   s 21 92
Trade Marks Act 2002
   s 9 83

United Kingdom

Statutes

Competition Act 1998 (c 41)
  s 18(1) 161
Copyright Act 1709 (c 21) 83
Copyright, Designs and Patents Act 1988 (c 48) 94
  Pt I Ch 8 93
  s 1(1) 83
Patents Act 1977 (c 37)
  s 48A(1) 92
Statute of Monopolies Act 1623 (c 3) 83
Trade Marks Act 1994 (c 26)
  s 10(6) 113

Statutory instruments

Copyright and Rights in Databases Regulations 1997 (SI 1997/3022) 90

United States

Antitrust Procedures and Penalties Act (Tunney Act) 15 USC §16 71
Copyright Act 1976 .... 110, 143
Copyright Law 17 USC
  §106(3) 142
  §107 51
Digital Millennium Copyright Act (DMCA) 1998 146
  §1201(c)(1) 91
Patent Act 1952 124
Patent Law 35 USC
  §261 83
  §271(d) 124, 145
Patent Misuse Reform Act 1988 124
Restatement (Third) of Unfair Competition §46 (1995) 86
Sherman Act 1890, ch 647, 26 Stat 209, 15 USC §§1–7 .... 25, 124, 127, 143
  §1 .... 25, 136, 196
  § 2 .... 3, 14, 25, 63, 72, 122, 124, 126, 135, 136, 138, 141, 150, 181, 204, 226, 237
'Sonny Bono' Copyright Extension Act 1998 118
Telecommunications Act 1996 .... 135, 137, 204
Trade Mark Act 1946 (Lanham Act) 15 USC §22 89
Trade Mark Dilution Act 1996 15 USC §1125 (c) 113
Trade Mark Technical and Conforming Amendment Act 2010 113

Guidelines

Antitrust Guidelines for the Licensing of Intellectual Property 1995 .... 93, 147
  para 2.2 140

1

Framing the Analysis

1.1 THE NATURE OF THE PROBLEM

Finding the appropriate legal mechanism through which to mediate the interaction of intellectual property rights and competition values is a problem that at various times, and with varying degrees of urgency, has confronted policy makers, courts and regulators in more than one OECD economy. When the holders of these rights take active steps to exploit them by licensing or assigning them to others, the conceptual uncertainty surrounding the construction of the interface between the two areas of law is, to some degree, masked by the existence in most jurisdictions of legislative exemptions, administrative guidelines and safe harbours that grant such dealings varying degrees of special treatment.[1] Where, however, the right owner simply sits tight and either actively or constructively[2] *refuses to license* the right to actual or perceived competitors (or more remotely

---

[1] See, eg, Commission Regulation No 772/2004/EC of 27 April 2004 on the application of Art 101(3) of the Treaty on the Functioning of the European Union (TFEU) (ex Art 81(3) EC before the Treaty of Lisbon came into force in December 2009) to categories of technology transfer agreements. ('Technology Transfer Block Exemption' [2004] OJ L123/11.) It is not intended to re-open the case for special treatment for proactive licensing arrangements in this book. Specific exemptions or safe harbours are simply too entrenched in the competition law of most jurisdictions to be easily shifted. Nor do we propose to traverse their content in detail in what follows. As to the reasons why this imbalance might have come about, see Eagles, I, 'Intellectual Property and Competition Policy: The Case for Neutrality' in CER Rickett and GW Austin (eds), *International Intellectual Property Law and the Common Law World* (Oxford, Hart Publishing, 2000) 285. Differential treatment, however, does bear directly on the refusal to license debate in one very important respect. Because the line it draws between dealing and non-dealing is both hard to justify in policy terms and often difficult to draw in practice, rational explanations as to why the two should be treated differently are hard to find.

[2] A constructive refusal to license will occur when an intellectual property owner offers to supply but makes available only a lesser or substandard version of a protected process or product, or asks for royalties that are unfair, unreasonable or discriminatory (see discussion of 'RAND' or 'FRAND' royalties at 3.7.4 below). In the case of computer software, a refusal to license may also be inferred if there is a denial of access to information that could potentially effect full technical interoperability between technological products or systems. Constructive refusals are not to be confused with conditional refusals to license intellectual property which may occur if, eg, access to patent A is withheld unless the access seeking party agrees to sign up for patents X, Y and Z which it may not want, or to other certain limitations on its conduct under some kind of tying, bundling or exclusive arrangement.

2 FRAMING THE ANALYSIS

those who deal or wish to deal with such competitors[3]*)*, the potential conflict between competition policy and intellectual property law has not been (and in some jurisdictions cannot lawfully be) disguised or softened in this way. The tug of war between right holders, competitors and consumers as to how putatively anti-competitive refusals to license might be approached is thus both more visible and more urgently in need of a set of guiding principles. In an ideal world such guiding principles would minimise forensic uncertainty and maximise economically defensible outcomes in individual cases. They would also be indifferent as to whether market power was sustained or exercised through tangible or intangible property, or indeed any other form of business advantage (proprietary or otherwise). To what extent these objectives are simultaneously attainable, and which should give way if they are not, are issues with which many competition regimes have had to grapple and with which, by and large, they are still grappling. Refusals to license intellectual property are thus not only important in themselves, they also place under the spotlight issues whose resolution is important to the internal coherence of competition law as a whole.

1.2 THE SCHEME OF THE BOOK

Anyone writing on this subject has to come to terms with the inescapable reality that in a world in which goods and services are freely traded across borders, real markets seldom correspond with the boundaries of any single legal system, and that any proffered solution to the refusal to license problem needs to be as workable and effective *across* jurisdictions (statutory language permitting) as *within* them. This immediately presents the writers with a problem of selection and organisation. Which jurisdictions should be surveyed, and how to make sense of the survey once conducted?[4] Individual jurisdictions may throw up isolated examples of refusals to license which, however significant in their time and place, provide scant material from which to extrapolate a trend or pin down

---

[3] Indeed one of the first European refusal to deal cases involved a reprisal situation. In Case 27/76 *United Brands Co and United Brands Continental BV v European Commission* [1978] ECR 207, a dominant firm's abrupt termination of an existing supply arrangement was found anti-competitive although the supply cut was not to a rival but rather to an entity that had cooperated with that rival to the displeasure of the dominant firm.

[4] The *Report on the Analysis of Refusal to Deal with a Rival under Unilateral Conduct Laws* prepared by the International Competition Network Unilateral Conduct Working Group (ICNUCWG) and presented at the 9th Annual Conference of the ICN Istanbul, April 2010 provides a useful mine of factual information gleaned from responses to a standardised questionnaire submitted by competition authorities and non-governmental advisors in 43 jurisdictions. The ICNUWG Report is available at <www.international competition network. org/uploads/library/doc616.pdf>, and the original questionnaire and individual responses are available at <www.internationalcompetitionnetwork.org/working-groups/current/unilateral/ questionnaires-responses/refusal-deal.aspx>.

an analytical approach.[5] Given that selection is both inescapable and inevitably arbitrary, we have chosen to make a virtue of necessity by concentrating on five jurisdictions, each possessing a sufficient body of case law or detailed enough legislative provisions to make trans-jurisdictional comparisons meaningful. The jurisdictions chosen are Australia, Canada, New Zealand, the European Union and the United States. We have, however, assumed that the last two competition regimes are better known outside their home jurisdiction than the first three, and have adjusted the level of detail accordingly. It is most emphatically not our intention in these pages to venture upon a reprise of the many excellent books and articles on Article 102 TFEU and section 2 of the Sherman Act.

If our trans-jurisdictional analysis is to work, however, it is important that our analytic framework should precede rather than follow detailed expositions of the law in the jurisdictions selected. With that in mind, we have organised our material by commencing in chapters one to four with the identification of the economic issues surrounding refusals to license intellectual property, and examining various policy choices when it is sought to convert these into legal rules. We then proceed, in chapters five through to eight, to survey the treatment of the problem in particular jurisdictions. In chapter nine, by way of conclusion, we offer some solutions and reject others.

1.3 THE DISTRACTIONS OF TERMINOLOGY

One of the unfortunate features of the refusals to license debate (especially when conducted across jurisdictions) is that the language used by courts and commentators can sometimes muddy the waters in unintended but nevertheless unhelpful ways. Most commonly this occurs when a particular term used by a writer or decision maker to signify concept A can be (and sometimes is) understood by other participants in the debate to stand for the sometimes antithetical concept

---

[5] See, eg, *Global Yellow Pages Ltd v Promedia Directories Ltd* [2010] SGHC 97, in which the High Court of Singapore in a copyright infringement action struck out the defendant's claim, by way of defence, that the plaintiff had refused to license the copyrighted works in question in a non-discriminatory way, referring the issue to Singapore's competition authority to be dealt with separately instead of considering it under the fair dealing provisions of the copyright statute. A somewhat similar fact situation came before the New Zealand Copyright Tribunal in *Phonographic Performances (NZ) Ltd v Radioworks Ltd* [2010] NZCOP 1, but that authority declined to adjudicate on any competition concerns raised by the refusal because it perceived itself to lack formal jurisdiction to do so. See also the constructive refusal to deal case successfully pursued by the Polish Office of Competition and Consumer Protection (UOKiK) mentioned in that authority's response of 4 November 2009 to the ICNUCWG's *Questionnaire* (see n 4 above). In that case a firm that had created a software platform for regional offices of the National Health Service was found to have acted anti-competitively when it subsequently thwarted competitors also wishing to provide patient management software from achieving full interoperability with its platform, by not providing all the necessary technical information in a timely fashion.

B. Most of the time, in most competition contexts, this is distracting rather than misleading. (It also tends to afflict lawyers more than economists, although the latter are not entirely immune; witness the loaded way in which 'consumer welfare' is used by some economists.) Where slippery words and phrases distort the analysis we address the issue in context and in detail. This does not happen very often. Of less immediate concern, but even so potentially disconcerting, are individual authorial idiosyncrasies. To minimise the effect of these, we think it useful simply to declare—Humpty Dumpty[6] fashion—what we think we mean by certain key words and phrases used throughout the book.

1.3.1 'Intellectual property', 'intellectual property right' and 'refusal to license'

The term 'intellectual property right' is used in what follows as shorthand for both proprietary and non-proprietary rules, except in those instances where the distinction leads to different legislative or judicial treatment in competition contexts. In such cases we use Professor Cornish's term 'allied rights'[7] to refer to those non-proprietary obligations (or, as the Americans term them, liability rules) which sustain intellectual innovation and artistic creation while falling short of 'true' property rights (as usually conceived). We also accept that the term 'refusal to license' is not altogether apposite in cases when what is in issue may be nothing more than an advance indication that an unlicensed act will be treated as an infringement and responded to accordingly. Even mere silence in the face of a competitor's demands we would, in some contexts, consider to be a refusal.

---

[6] See Carroll, L (1871), *Through the Looking Glass and What Alice Found There* (ch 6, Millennium Fulcrum Edition 1.7, at <www.gutenberg.org/files/12/12-h/12-h.htm>):
'I don't know what you mean by "glory,"' Alice said.
Humpty Dumpty smiled contemptuously. 'Of course you don't—till I tell you. I meant "there's a nice knock-down argument for you!"'
'But "glory" doesn't mean "a nice knock-down argument,"' Alice objected.
'When I use a word,' Humpty Dumpty said in rather a scornful tone, 'it means just what I choose it to mean—neither more nor less.'
'The question is,' said Alice, 'whether you can make words mean so many different things.'
'The question is,' said Humpty Dumpty, 'which is to be master—that's all.'
[7] See Cornish, W, Llewelyn, D, and Aplin, T, *Intellectual Property: Patents, Copyrights, Trademarks & Allied Rights*, 7th edn (London, Sweet & Maxwell, 2010).

1.3.2 'Regulator' and 'regulation'

'Regulator' and 'regulation' are terms freighted with inevitable imprecision.[8] Many (but not all) law and economics scholars reserve their use for those forms of public law intervention in the market that proceed by way of direct control over such things as prices and access fees. This form of regulation usually relates to a particular sector of the economy—most notably in what are generally referred to as public utilities.[9] We have chosen to call this *direct* regulation. Absent this qualifier, 'regulation', for the purposes of this book, also embraces the ordinary processes of competition law enforcement. 'Regulator' then becomes a generic term for any enforcement agency or body, other than a court or tribunal, charged with bringing about competitive outcomes, or maintaining or fostering competitive conditions in a market. Our confessedly broad-brush usage necessarily ignores a great many fine institutional and structural distinctions, and does not seek to pinpoint the regulator's exact place on a spectrum of judicial and administrative roles. 'Regulation' can also be used more widely, as well as more narrowly. Thus intellectual property may be viewed both historically and conceptually as a form of State intervention in the economy, sharing many of the social goals of competition law. While this particular *aperçu* is important in demystifying and hence de-privileging intellectual property (in competition terms), the usage is too idiosyncratic to be offered without qualification or explanation and so we do this where appropriate. (In this context there is of course no regulator. The situation is not too different from that obtaining when competition law is privately enforced.)

1.3.3 'Competition', 'antitrust', 'abuse of market power' and 'monopolisation'

'Antitrust law' and 'competition law' are used synonymously in this book, although strictly speaking the use of 'antitrust' should be confined to discussion of United States law. The same qualification applies equally to 'monopolisation' and 'abuse [or misuse] of market power'.

---

[8] For a valiant attempt to bring some conceptual clarity to both terms, see Selznick, P, 'Focusing Organisational Research on Regulation' in R Noll (ed), *Regulatory Policy in the Social Sciences* (Berkeley, University of California Press, 1985).

[9] Some jurisdictions may have fall-back price control mechanisms operating across the whole economy, as is the case in New Zealand.

1.4 TWO BAD IDEAS CONVERGE

One of the factors clouding the refusals to license debate is that it takes place at the intersection of two deeply flawed ideas. The first of these is the notion that unilateral[10] refusals to act by holders of market power should be judged more leniently (if indeed they should be judged at all) by courts and competition authorities than overt acts by those same holders. Or, to put it another way, coercing a party with substantial market power into a relationship with rivals or potential rivals is inherently wrong and should be avoided wherever possible. The second equally unfounded notion is that dealings (or in this case non-dealings) in intellectual property are (or should be) to a greater or lesser degree privileged in competition cases compared with dealings or non-dealings in anything else.

Both of these statements (for they are no more than that) are normative. They seek to tell us about the proper shape of legal rules. Those rules are not plucked out of thin air, however. They rest, or at least purport to rest, on what economists have to say about the risks of over- (and less often under-) regulation, and the effect of both of these things on innovation and investment. The trouble is that conversations of economists on these subjects are also curiously normative, often disconnected from any empirically demonstrable reality. It is therefore not that surprising that some members of both professions are sometimes inclined to treat these propositions as free-standing statements of the obvious, quarantined off from the rest of competition law without any felt need for apology or justification.

1.5 THE IDEAL COMPETITION REGIME

The discussion that follows is based on a very different set of normative principles about what an ideal competition regime should look like.[11] Underpinning these principles is the concept of regulatory neutrality, under which competition enforcement operates even-handedly across all sectors of the economy and all forms of business activity. If an economic justification needs to be found for regulatory neutrality, it is best sought in a particular application of investment displacement theory, under which the shielding of intellectual property dealings (or non-dealings) from competition scrutiny and the favouring of inaction over action has the potential arbitrarily to suck investment out of one form of

---

[10] Collective refusals to license raise very different issues. See Richman, BD, 'The Antitrust Reputation Mechanisms: Institutional Economics and Concerted Refusals to Deal' (2009) 95 *Virginia Law Review* 325. Of course an ostensibly collective arrangement may be a unilateral act of *force majeure* in disguise, an issue we touch on below at 5.4.4.

[11] The discussion has its origins in a paper given by the writers at the 3rd Law and Economics of Intellectual Property and Information Technology Conference at Queen Mary College Centre for Commercial Legal Studies, University of London, 5–6 July 2007.

economic activity and into another for reasons of legal form rather than efficiency. We, however, would prefer to rest the case for regulatory neutrality (Rawlsian fashion) on the need to preserve the integrity of the legal system by ensuring that regulatory intervention commands the widest possible degree of support amongst market players before it is applied to them, and without the need for any ability on their part to predict their own future behaviour. Neutrality is not, we would stress, a cure-all for all competition ills. One could imagine a regime in which courts and regulators came to share the scepticism of some commentators as to the efficacy of restrictions on the unilateral exercise of market power in general. There would then be neutrality in the sense that refusals to license would become part of a wider problem (or evidence of a non-problem), but that is not the book we are writing. Our aim is not to lay down a blueprint for the harmonisation of substantive rules across jurisdictions (an unattainable objective given the political difficulties attending amendments of core legislative provisions in the United States and Europe, and one that the World Trade Organisation (WTO) has now formally abandoned[12]). Still less do we suggest that the application of similar principles (economics-based or otherwise) will inevitably lead to similar regulatory outcomes on the same or similar facts.[13] Our objective is the much more modest one of distilling from judges' and regulators' decisions in selected jurisdictions a list of *desiderata* on which most commentators could agree even if individual competition regimes fall short in detail—for the purposes of discussion. Such a list would look something like this:

a) Competition law necessarily elevates substance over form. Dominant market players should not be able to game the regulatory system by manipulating bright-line rules. Indeed, bright-line rules are to be preferred to rules of reason only where the transaction costs avoided by adopting them are both large and easily demonstrable. This remains true whether or not the bright-line rule in question imposes or deflects liability. Shifting the onus of proof by adopting presumptions of vice or virtue for particular transactions merely disguises the choice between substance and form. It does not eliminate it.

b) To be effective, competition law needs to be able to cut across private law rights and obligations, whether those rights and obligations be based in contract or property. There can be no private law shields against regulatory

---

[12] See Manne GA, and Weinberger, S, 'International Signals: The Political Dimension of International Competition Harmonization' SSRN Paper Series (10 August 2009), available at <http://papers.ssrn.com/sol3/papers.cfm?abstract_id=1448223>, for a detailed explanation of why attempts to adopt international norms for competition law have eluded the WTO (in contrast to a much readier pursuit of those norms in the intellectual property area).

[13] As to why this might be, see Heyer, K, 'A World of Uncertainty and the Globalisation of Antitrust' (2005) 72 *Antitrust Law Journal* 375.

action.[14] Opinions may differ as to whether there should be a self-denying presumption by regulators as to their ability to get things right or the need to recognise that temporarily anti-competitive situations may self-correct over time. These are matters on which competition regimes (and economists) may rationally disagree. What all agree on, however, is that there will be occasions on which private ordering has to give way to administrative action. To hold otherwise would be to render competition law entirely nugatory; indeed it would question the need for its very existence.[15] Deference to property rights becomes especially problematical when the boundaries of the property right are themselves unclear,[16] or if their content varies across jurisdictions between which goods and services are traded freely.

c) All economic activity should equally be grist to the regulator's mill. It is not the role of competition law to play favourites and prefer one business strategy or structure over another.[17] From this it follows that neither property in general nor particular forms of property should confer any immunity or advantage on owners when used as instruments of market power. Conversely, market advantages which cannot be propertised (or which have yet to be propertised) should not be treated less gently by competition regulators than those instruments of market power to which the law grants property status.

d) High-technology markets and industries based on creative content do not need to be subjected to more (or less) onerous competition rules than dealings or refusals to deal in fence posts[18] or access to bridges,[19] ports[20] or

---

[14] As the Court of Justice pointed out in Case C-308/04 P *SGL Carbon AG v European Commission* [2006] ECR I-5977, the freedom to conduct business and the right to property are necessarily subject to public interest restrictions in the context of competition law enforcement.

[15] Not that all such questioning should be dismissed as irrational or unnecessary. Market economies can function perfectly well without competition law. This, however, is of little assistance to those charged with enforcing or complying with such a law once in place.

[16] Hovencamp, H, 'Innovation and the Domain of Competition Policy' (2008) 60 *Alabama Law Review* 103 at 123.

[17] It is generally supposed that a competition policy that favoured vertical integration over vertical dealings would be counter-productive. Thus, patent pooling between independent undertakings should not lead to different regulatory outcomes than attempts by single firms to buy up rivals' patents. If it be accepted that ex ante merger control and the ex post facto regulation of anti-competitive conduct should be aligned in such a way so as to discourage undertakings from favouring or disfavouring integration and acquisition over contractual and licensing arrangements, then it follows that the same logic should be applied to the unilateral exercise or non-exercise of particular forms of market power.

[18] The product refused by one competitor to another in *Queensland Wire Industries Pty Ltd v Broken Hill Proprietary Co Ltd* [1989] HCA 6, (1989) 167 CLR 177. See discussion of this decision of the High Court of Australia at 7.2.2 below.

[19] *United States v Terminal Railroad Association* 224 US 383 (1912). See 5.4 below.

[20] *Sealink/B & I—Holyhead* [1992] 5 CMLR 225 and 22nd Annual Report on Competition Policy (1992) at para 219; and Case 94/19 *Sea Containers/Stena Sealink* [1994] OJ L15/8, 4 CMLR 84. See ch 6 below. The 22nd Annual Report may be downloaded from <http://bookshop.europa.eu/>.

print distribution networks.[21] It has never been the function of competition regulation to direct investment to any particular form of economic activity, and it is a measure of its failure if it does.

e) Competition regimes may draw the line between rules of reason and strict liability in different places and by different means but, once drawn, that line should not need to be moved again in order to accommodate particular types of market or particular categories of property. Similarly, while there may be room for doubt as to the efficacy of probing anti-competitive intent in competition cases,[22] and a consequential preference for tests of liability based on proof of anti-competitive outcomes, such doubts should not resonate more or less loudly just because the alleged source of market power, or the mechanism for its misuse, is an intellectual property right.[23]

f) Regulatory outcomes should not depend upon the *form* of the conduct complained of. This means that when assessing putative abuses of market power, action on the part of the supposed perpetrator is not presumptively more virtuous or more vicious than inaction.[24]

---

[21] Case C-7/97 *Oscar Bronner v Mediaprint Zeitung und Zeitschriftenverlag GmbH* [1998] ECR I-7791, [1999] 4 CMLR 112, analysed in ch 6 below.

[22] The ICNUCWG Report (n 4 above), at pp 14–15, notes, in relation to the questionnaire concerning the role of intent motivating refusals to deal, that only four countries (Costa Rica, Korea, New Zealand, Taiwan; fn 51) require evidence of anti-competitive intent; cf the European Commission and many more countries (France, Finland, Germany, Israel, Japan, Jersey, Lithuania, The Netherlands, Romania, Singapore, Sweden, Turkey, United Kingdom, United States; fn 48) indicated that while they do not expressly require anti-competitive intent to support an infringement claim, evidence of its existence might go some way towards supporting a finding that a refusal resulted in an anti-competitive effect.

[23] There is an observable tendency amongst some commentators and competition law reformers to minimise the downside of what are rightly seen as overly expansive *per se* rules, or tests based on unrealistically purposive or rhetorical statements of intent, by walling off intellectual property dealings and non-dealings from their operation. For an example of this kind of thinking at work, see the Australian Intellectual Property and Competition Law Review Committee's Final Report (the 'Ergas Committee'), *Review of Intellectual Property Legislation under the Competition Principles Agreement*, Commonwealth of Australia (September 2000). In the present writers' view this simply diverts the debate by delaying the reopening of across-the-board discussions as to the appropriateness of particular *per se* rules (those relating to tying and resale price maintenance are two pertinent examples) or the usefulness of intent-based tests in competition law generally. The Final Report of the Ergas Committee, together with copies of submissions, original 'Issues Paper' and other related information, is available at <www.ipaustralia.gov.au/about/ipcr.shtml#final>.

[24] The line between action and inaction is not neatly co-extensive with the distinction between multilateral and unilateral liability. The latter is often legislatively mandated in the manner of Arts 101 and 102 TFEU, but even this distinction is not as solid as it may appear, witness Court of Justice (ex ECJ) jurisprudence on collective dominance or coerced tying or bundling under Art 102 TFEU. A similar blurring of the lines may be seen in those jurisdictions in which the statutory language attributes anti-competitive intent to one of several parties to a multilateral arrangement. See *Port Nelson Ltd v Commerce Commission* [1996] 3 NZLR 554 and an analysis of the case in Eagles, I, 'Of Ports, Pilots and Predation: New Zealand Courts Reassess Some Competition Fundamentals' (1996) 17 *European Competition Law Review* 462. The

10 FRAMING THE ANALYSIS

g) Economic opinion may be divided on predicting particular market outcomes from particular market behaviours, or the effect of regulatory intervention in particular cases. Such divisions only rarely and accidentally coincide with the jurisprudential categorisations of the instruments through which market power is sought to be exercised.
h) Competition law exists to protect the competitive process—not individuals, nor the collective interests of consumers or producers.[25] Any of these persons may be the indirect beneficiary of regulatory activity, but that is not the aim of the exercise. Neither is the substantive objective of protecting competition in any way diminished by the evidentiary truth that in particular cases outcomes which are not passed on to consumers may be neither substantial nor sustainable.

1.6 RHETORICAL DEAD ENDS AND RED HERRINGS

The refusals to license debate is all too frequently clouded by resort to rhetorical exaggeration and distortion, usually in the form of punchy sound bites that glide easily over the complexity of the issues involved. Sometimes these incisive one-liners will be unproven in the sense that they rest on empirically untested assumptions. As such they are no more than attempts to hijack the refusal to license debate before it has even begun. (Indeed, the claims made will often be so broad as to be beyond easy empirical verification by anyone.) On other occasions the rhetorical posturing may be true as far as it goes but is of no assistance in resolving the policy choices a judge or regulator is being asked to make. Set out below are the most commonly asserted of these fallacies and red herrings.

1.6.1 Ownership carries with it the right to exclude others from the thing owned

As a statement of one of the key indicia of property this is unexceptional enough, although not all might agree that it is property's defining attribute and opinions may differ as to whether it is a precondition or a consequence of property status. When invoked in a competition context, however, it becomes a claim for an absolute right to use one's property entirely free of regulatory constraints. Such, for example, was the basis for Microsoft's claim in *United States v Microsoft*

---

unilateral versus multilateral divide is also relevant to the refusals to license debate only to the extent that it affects the application of a block exemption or statutory exclusion of liability.

[25] *Brown Shoe Co v US* 370 US 294 (1962).

Corporation[26] that it was free to impose whatever restrictions it liked on computer hardware manufacturers because the computers operated Microsoft's software in which Microsoft had copyright and other forms of intellectual property right.[27] Once intellectual property rights had been acquired, so the argument went, their subsequent exercise by Microsoft could not give rise to antitrust liability. So large a claim invited rejection on the obvious ground that, once allowed, it could not be confined to any particular type of property. Rejected it duly was by the seven-strong District of Columbia Court of Appeals, who rather mordaciously pointed out that the next step for litigants would be to argue 'that use of one's personal property such as a baseball bat cannot give rise to tort liability'.[28] The Court might well have added that acceptance of such arguments would introduce an economically irrational distinction into competition law under which those liability rules allowed to shelter under the intellectual 'property' umbrella are subjected to the full rigours of competition scrutiny, while anti-competitive actions involving the exercise or non-exercise of 'true' proprietary rights would be to a greater or lesser degree protected against that same scrutiny. The distinction would also be unworkable when the property status of a right is challenged, as it is in many jurisdictions in relation to trade secrets and other valuable forms of information.[29] Again, when the property status of a right varies across jurisdictions (as it often does[30]) then competition outcomes would also vary even when the matters complained of spanned jurisdictional boundaries and concerned the actions or non-actions of a single corporate.

---

[26] *United States v Microsoft Corporation* ('*Microsoft*') 253 F 3d 34 (DC Cir 2001). Microsoft's justifications for integration are discussed in II-B(2)b, at p 66.

[27] Similar arguments were advanced in Case C-418/01 *IMS Health GmbH v NDC Health GmbH* ('*IMS Health*') [2004] ECR I-5039, 4 CMLR 28.

[28] *US v Microsoft*, n 26 above, at p 62, section II-B(1)b: Microsoft's justifications for the license restrictions.

[29] As it certainly is in English law and that of most Commonwealth jurisdictions, resting as it does on the insecure jurisprudential foundations of breach of confidence and giving rise to the question of whether judges in common law jurisdictions can still create (or recognise) new forms of property.

[30] Eg, in New Zealand and most European jurisdictions, including the United Kingdom, databases are property rights whether they happen to be copyrightable or protected under specially enacted *sui generis* rules under the Directive on the Legal Protection of Databases 96/9/EC [1996] OJ L77/20, 11 March 1996. In the United States and Australia, by contrast, databases and low authorship forms of compilation can slip through the 'property' door only if they meet the higher originality threshold set for copyright works by *Feist Publications Inc v Rural Telephone Service Co* ('*Feist*') 499 US 340 (1991) and *Telstra Corporation Limited v Phone Directories Company Pty Ltd* [2010] FCA 44, aff'd [2010] FCAFC 149, respectively. This is a hurdle at which many such products would fall in these two jurisdictions.

1.6.2 What the State has expressly granted it shall not take back by stealth

This statement is a more refined version of the 'property is privileged' argument. It is based on the assumption that because intellectual property takes the form of an express legislative grant of a bundle of rights exclusive to the right holder, only the legislature can remove what it has explicitly bestowed, a function which it is not for the courts or regulators to usurp. Sometimes referred to as the 'scope of grant' principle, this view of things allows the boundaries of the right to determine the jurisdiction of both court and regulator. What the right owner or licensee does or refuses to do within the four square walls of the right cannot therefore be challenged on competition grounds.

'Scope of grant' theories rest on two logical fallacies. The first takes the unexceptionable (but in the past sometimes forgotten) truth that the legal monopoly represented by an intellectual property right does not always represent market power, and inverts that truth so that it becomes the empirically untested proposition that intellectual property can *never* do so. Economic and legal monopolies need not coincide to reinforce each other, either within or across markets. The second fallacy is a legal one. By inflating the principle of *generalis non specialibus non derogant* into a rule of invariable and rigid application, its proponents argue that regulatory intervention is excluded as a matter of law. An express legislative grant, they would say, requires an equally express revocation. Absent such revocation, the competition regulator must observe the statutory 'keep out' sign. The obvious difficulty with this line of reasoning is that it characterises intellectual property statutes as 'general' and competition jurisdiction as 'special'. This is to prejudge the position. Competition statutes are not noticeably more or less 'general' in their terms than intellectual property statutes.

As well as being conceptually flawed, the scope of grant approach also has enforcement downsides. The principle is the logic on which the European Union Technology Transfer Block Exemption[31] rests, and it also underlies statutory exemptions for proactive licensing arrangements in some countries such as Canada and New Zealand. If applied to *refusals* to license it would effectively grant refusers immunity from competition scrutiny, provided they were acting within the confines of an identifiable statutory right. If correct it would mean that much European jurisprudence on the subject[32] could be explained (as indeed some commentators have argued[33]) only by positing a distinction

---

[31] [2004] OJ L123/11, see n 1 above.

[32] See the analysis at 6.2.3 below of Joined Cases C-241/91 P and C-242/91 P *Radio Telefis Eireann and Independent Television Publications v European Commission* ('*Magill*') [1995] ECR I-743, 4 CMLR 718; and *IMS Health*, n 27 above.

[33] Ong, B, 'Anti-competitive Refusals to Grant Copyright Licences: Reflections on the *IMS Saga*' [2004] *European Competition Law Review* 505 at 507. See also the same author's 'Building Brick Barricades and Other Barriers to Entry: Abusing a Dominant Position by Refusing to

between the information contained in a copyright work (unprotectable facts and hence falling outside the grant) and the work itself (the way in which those facts are expressed or arranged and thus within the grant). This way of thinking can have no application outside this narrow copyright context.

While scope of grant arguments in their pure form have had some judicial enthusiasts, they are rare.[34] This may be because scope of grant theories require, in common law jurisdictions at any rate, a distinction to be made between statutory grants and judge-made rules. This would mean that refusals to license unpatented know-how would be governed by different competition rules from those governing refusals to license patents or copyright, a distinction based on no discernible policy grounds and particularly inconvenient when both surface in the same litigation (as indeed happened in the European *Microsoft* proceedings[35]). Adherence to such notions would also allow national intellectual property laws to have the last word on behaviour which is transnational in scope (a matter of some importance in Europe where originality thresholds in copyright are still a matter for national law, the Copyright Directive notwithstanding).[36]

1.6.3 Intellectual property owners must be free to choose their licensees

Here the banner being waved is freedom of contract not proprietary absolutism,[37] but the effect is the same: an attempt to elevate private right over regulatory objectives. The freedom to choose one's business associates, it is true, is a fundamental attribute of free markets. From this it follows that a firm is perfectly justified in rejecting the advances of a competitor who seeks access to technological or commercial advantages the firm has built up by its own efforts.

License Intellectual Property Rights' [2005] *European Competition Law Review* 215. Implicit here is a distinction between the right to use or consume a work outside the grant and the right to copy it.

[34] While the US Federal Circuit has intimated that a substantial role may exist for 'scope of grant' in *In Re Independent Services Organization Antitrust Litigation* 203 F 3d 1322 (Fed Cir 2000), a more considered rejection of 'scope of grant' as an absolute defence is to be found in *Microsoft*, n 26 above. In the EU, courts have preferred to treat 'scope of grant' not as a substantive exemption in itself but more as an evidentiary presumption, although the strength of that presumption may vary (cf *Magill*, n 32 above, with *Oscar Bronner*, n 21 above). See also *Phillips Electronics v Ingman Ltd* [1998] EWHC Patents 321, [1999] FSR 112.

[35] Case T-201/04 *Microsoft Corporation v European Commission* ('Euro Microsoft') [2007] ECR II-3601, 5 CMLR 11.

[36] Directive 2001/29/EC on the harmonisation of certain aspects of copyright and related rights in the information society, [2001] OJ L167. It is by no means evident, eg, that the 'brick structure' to which access was refused in *IMS Health*, n 27 above, would have been given protection in all Member States. Indeed, its copyright status in German law was by no means assured. Ironically, under US law, the law of both the parties involved in the case, the brick structure was unlikely to have been protected: see *Feist*, n 30 above.

[37] See, eg, *Aspen Skiing Co v Aspen Highlands Skiing Corp* 472 US 585 (1985) at 601, discussed in ch 5 below, in which it was unsuccessfully waved by way of defence.

The market, however, must be competitive. When it is not, ordinary competition principles require that such behaviour be scrutinised. Invoking freedom of contract as an absolute right in this situation is simply another disguised claim for complete freedom from regulatory intervention, and as such must fail on the same grounds as the two preceding claims.

Sometimes, however, the freedom to choose argument is presented in the weaker form of a presumption against coerced licensing. There are two versions of the presumption, one evidentiary and one remedial. The evidentiary rule is the perfectly valid proposition that proof of a refusal to license and nothing more does not in itself demonstrate either the existence of market power or any unlawful use of that power. It is in the latter, wholly unremarkable sense that freedom to choose has been taken up by the Court of Justice as the starting point for dissecting the refusals to deal cases discussed in chapter six.[38] A similar logic lies behind the United States Supreme Court's rejection in *Illinois Tool Works v Independent Ink Inc*[39] of the once prevalent assumption that breaches of section 2 of the Sherman Act could be established simply by pointing to the mere exercise or threatened exercise of the powers that a patent confers.[40] Used in this way the evidentiary rule is a salutary corrective to the claims previously put forward (and sometimes accepted[41]) by parties seeking to use regulatory intervention as a backdoor route to a compulsory licence even where the intellectual property statute in question made no provision for such things and no anti-competitive outcomes could be demonstrated. The evidentiary rule is simply a warning against over-extended inferences based on too little information. There is no reason, therefore, to confine its application to refusals to license intellectual property. It is equally pertinent to any refusal to deal by a firm with market power.[42]

The remedial rule is rather different. It assumes that judges should be reluctant to order access to complex technologies or business systems if such an order is likely to outstrip the court's ability to supervise that order effectively on an ongoing basis. It also assumes that fixing the price of access in such cases will require skills that courts and enforcement agencies do not routinely possess. These problems can be overstated, as we demonstrate in chapter three; and even

---

[38] Case 238/87 *Volvo v Erik Veng (UK Ltd)* [1988] ECR 6211; *Magill*, n 32 above; and *IMS Health*, n 27 above.

[39] *Illinois Tool Works v Independent Ink Inc* 547 US 28 (2006).

[40] The presumption that patents confer market power on their holders arose outside the antitrust context as part of the patent misuse doctrine and migrated to antitrust law in *International Salt Co v United States* 332 US 392 (1947). See also *Morton Salt Co v GS Suppiger Co* 314 US 488 (1942) and *United States v Loew's Inc* 371 US 38 (1962).

[41] *Verizon Communications Inc v Law Offices of Curtis V Trinko LLP* ('*Trinko*') 540 US 398 (2004) may be explained this way rather than as an endorsement of earlier arguments that dominant firms had the absolute right to refuse to deal at all, see *United States v Colgate & Co* 250 US 300 (1919) at 307; cf *Aspen Skiing*, n 37 above.

[42] As the US Supreme Court demonstrated in *Trinko*, n 41 above. See discussion at 5.4.4 below.

if this were not the case, they are by no means confined to licences of intellectual property. Similar difficulties are likely to be experienced whenever access is sought to unregulated or partially regulated public utilities.

Again, not all court-ordered licensing is complex, as the seminal European *Magill* case[43] demonstrates. Neither does the line between complex and simple remedies correspond to that between intellectual property and other rights, still less to that between action and inaction. The court's supervisory role may also be delegated to independent experts (jurisdictional obstacles permitting). And we should not forget that injunctive relief is not always the only remedy sought.[44] In jurisdictions where compensatory damages, disgorgement and civil penalties are a normal part of the remedial scene, the supervisory problem may be less acute. Remedial difficulties need to be dealt with as and when they arise. To assume that they are always and forever present converts a potential remedial problem into a permanently available substantive shield. Ruling whole suites of remedies out in advance is effectively to disarm the judge or enforcement agency.

1.6.4 Coerced licensing is confiscation

This notion equates coerced licensing by courts and regulators with compulsory taking. Ordering licensing in particular circumstances to achieve a stated, and by definition limited, regulatory aim is assumed to deprive the right in question of all economic utility. The reference to confiscation is a rhetorical flourish on property-based arguments and can easily be dismissed. A more nuanced version of this thesis depicts regulatory action as a general assault on the right which makes it useless to the right holder in economic terms. It implies that such licences are to be had on demand and ignores the need of aspiring licensees first to demonstrate both the existence of market power and its misuse. (In most jurisdictions the latter requirement may be rebutted by pointing either to a positive, in the form of an alternative business explanation for the refusal to license, or a negative, showing that even a non-dominant firm would not or could not refuse to license without adverse commercial consequences.) It also assumes that courts and regulators are incapable of fine-tuning the compulsory licence so as to minimise interference with the dominant firm's activities. Remedial caution is one thing, remedial abdication is another. Judges can do no more than their inevitably imperfect best as they struggle to balance cure against harm when fashioning remedies, something that they have long been accustomed to doing in other competition law contexts. To assume that intervention will

---

[43] *Magill*, n 32 above.
[44] Frischmann, B and Waller, SW, 'The Essential Nature of Infrastructure or the Infrastructural Nature of Essential Facilities' (unpublished paper, 2007) at pp 41, 43 and 51. Available at <www.luc.edu/law/academics/special/center/antitrust/pdfs/frischmann_waller_article_31107.pdf>.

16 FRAMING THE ANALYSIS

fatally (and by implication unfairly) damage the dominant firm is simply an extrapolation from the frequently repeated but empirically unsupported 'under-regulation is always better than over-regulation' mantra discussed below.[45]

1.6.5 Regulatory intervention is justified only in the case of marginal or weak intellectual property rights

Sometimes the case for or against regulatory intervention in refusal to license cases is made by positing a hierarchy of rights. It is said courts and regulators should be more reluctant to interfere with 'strong' rights than with 'weak' ones,[46] and that the remedy of coerced licensing is more easily justified towards the 'weak' end of the spectrum.[47] 'Weak' in this context can refer to intellectual property rights that, while initially easily asserted or granted, are prone to invalidation through re-examination or litigation, an outcome courts in competition proceedings are not particularly well placed to assess in advance of such an attack being actually mounted. There are competing concepts of 'weakness' moreover. Sometimes it is assumed that some particular forms of intellectual property are entitled to less protection against competition than others. Thus copyright is envisaged as being less privileged than patents,[48] a mode of analysis that slices the intellectual property pie formally rather than functionally and which we criticise in chapter four.[49] A slightly different approach is that courts are more justified in mandating a licence if the claim for intellectual property

---

[45] See 1.6.6 below.
[46] See, eg, the suggestion of AG Gulmann in *Magill* that the finding that a refusal to share television listings was an abuse of dominance could be justified as the listings might not merit copyright protection since they lacked a creative element. *Magill*, n 32 above, AG Opinion, at paras 15–16, 118–27 and 134–41.
[47] American courts seem to have reached this point by accident rather than by analysis as a temporary resting point in the dismantling of abuse of rights principles, see discussion at 5.7 below.
[48] A common justification here is that these different privileges are reflected in the different terms of exclusive protection granted to patents and copyrights. Patents prohibit others from making and selling patented inventions for a relatively short period of time, after which the public interest in gaining access to the inventions prevails over inventors' rights to recoup their research and development expenses and profit from exploitation of the invention. Copyright, by contrast, does not exclude others from using ideas contained in a work, only the particular *expression* of those ideas. Thus, absent any exclusivity in the ideas *per se*, the term of protection in a copyrighted work (in most jurisdictions generally life of the author plus 50 or 70 years) is much longer than in the case of patents (20 years).
[49] This purely formal hierarchy has been criticised by some commentators who would prefer to see all categories of intellectual property rights as theoretically equal, with 'strength' or 'weakness' depending directly upon a right's financial worth to the holder in the market(s) in question. (See, eg, Devlin, A, Jacobs, M and Peixoto, B, 'Success, Dominance and Interoperabilty' (2009) 84 *Indiana Law Journal* 1157 at 1188.) This formulation comes with its own set of problems.

protection is marginal under whatever national law applies.[50] This makes sense only in relation to self-constituting rights (copyright, layout designs and trade secrets) rather than those depending on formalities and created by express grant (patents and registered trade marks). Yet another argument currently gaining some traction (especially where a duty to grant access or a compulsory licence is being considered) is that when the intellectual property in question is used in network systems[51] it may merit less protection against competition scrutiny than in other contexts.[52]

The problem that all of these arguments share is that they cannot be tested without reopening the policy reasons for granting intellectual property rights in the first place, something that proponents of these arguments are usually deeply reluctant to do. The arguments can also be turned on their heads. As Lemley puts it, 'when intellectual property laws are strong, antitrust laws should also be strong and vice versa'.[53]

1.6.6 Under-regulation is always and everywhere better than over-regulation

This is the belief that because courts and regulators will always be acting on less than perfect information, the risks attached to a false negative must always be assumed to be greater than those attached to a false positive (or, as it is sometimes put, type one errors are worse than type two errors).[54] As pointed up by the recent collapse of global financial markets, this is by no means an immutable truth. The risk, like all risks associated with regulation, has to be assessed, not baldly asserted.[55] The factors bearing on that assessment are discussed in chapter two. The likelihood of over-protection when intellectual property rights are expanded in scope or duration also needs to be placed on the risk assessment scales, a topic we take up in chapter four.

---

[50] As discussed in ch 6, the *Magill/IMS* line of cases is sometimes explained in this way.

[51] Such as sophisticated computer systems evolved through multiuser participation and dependent upon cooperation for their continued efficient operation.

[52] See, eg, Lang, JT, 'Compulsory Licensing of Intellectual Property in European Antitrust Law', Department of Justice/Federal Trade Commission Hearings, Washington DC, May 2002.

[53] Lemley, MA, 'A New Balance between IP and Antitrust' (2007) 13 *Southwestern Journal of Law and Trade in the Americas* 1 at 18.

[54] Judge Easterbrook, wearing his commentator's hat, described the choice thus: 'If the court errs by condemning a beneficial practice, the benefits may be lost for good. Any other firm that uses the condemned practice faces sanctions in the name of *stare decisis*, no matter what the benefits. If the court errs by permitting a deleterious practice, though, the welfare loss decreases over time. Monopoly is self-destructive. Monopoly prices eventually attract entry.' Easterbrook, FH, 'The Limits of Antitrust' (1984) 63 *Texas Law Review* 1.

[55] On the relationship between risk and regulation generally, see Lee, M, 'Beyond Safety? The Broadening Scope of Risk Regulation' [2009] *Current Legal Problems* 242.

1.6.7 The need for competition scrutiny diminishes when there is a parallel regulatory regime and intellectual property provides such a regime

This is the reverse of the 'property is sacrosanct' argument. It accurately acknowledges that the 'propertiness' of intellectual property is an historical accident masking what is in fact a series of rival regulatory regimes, each with its own set of policy objectives and internal competition controls of varying degrees of efficacy.

While the notion of intellectual property as a regulatory regime in its own right has a demonstrable appeal, that alone cannot act as a shield against competition scrutiny for two reasons. The first is that if rival regulatory regimes are to be kept apart, this is best achieved by direct legislative buffering rather than relying on the vagaries of discretionary relief. In the absence of a coherent set of principles justifying intervention or non-intervention across regulatory boundaries, remedial restraint, on one side of the regulatory boundary only, can easily slide over into a permanent conferring of de facto immunity.[56] Again where the legislature has directly mandated that the two systems are to co-exist, remedial reluctance should, one imagines, be harder, not easier, to justify.

The second objection to this way of thinking bears more directly on the subject of this book. If intellectual property is an alternative system of regulation, its internal mechanisms for avoiding over-protection are seldom designed with preservation of the competitive process in mind and are often weakened by imperfectly articulated justifications for a robust public domain, issues that we take up in chapter four.

1.6.8 Compulsory licensing discourages investment in innovation and creativity

Unlike the formalistic and normative assertions considered so far, this is an argument in theory capable of empirical justification and, again in theory, capable of being absorbed into an economics-based rule of reason. It also has an automatic resonance with intellectual property lawyers in a post-TRIPS world.[57] The effect of competition enforcement on innovation cannot be assessed in the

---

[56] This has become a particular problem in the United States, as lower courts seek to come to terms with the decision of the Supreme Court in *Trinko*, n 41 above. See discussion at 5.3 below. Contrast this with the decision of the High Court of Australia in *NT Power Generation v Power and Water Authority* [2004] HCA 48, 219 CLR 90 in ch 7 below.

[57] The Trade-Related Aspects of Intellectual Property Rights ('TRIPS') Agreement of the Uruguay Round of the General Agreement on Tariffs and Trade (GATT) is set out in Annex 1C to the Marrakesh Agreement; it was signed on 15 April 1994 and is monitored and enforced through the WTO. TRIPS stipulates minimum standards relating to the form, scope, duration and enforcement of intellectual property rights for all WTO members.

abstract,[58] however. We need to remind ourselves once again that we are talking here about an occasional regulatory intervention, not a general right to a compulsory licence available on demand to all comers. It is the potentially chilling effect of a particular amount of regulatory intervention on a particular defendant's incentive to innovate in a particular product market that needs to be investigated. In relation to this much more circumscribed question, the evidence has to be gathered and evaluated, and in most competition regimes this is an obligation which falls upon the defendant once an anti-competitive outcome or intent has been proven.[59] Even if a defendant manages to fulfil this onus in relation to a particular product, this has to be set against the incentives to innovate or create in relation to its other products if it is allowed to continue its proven anti-competitive behaviour.[60] Indeed, a defendant's decision to introduce a particular technological or business innovation may precede (and therefore may be presumed to outlast) its refusal to license in any particular case.[61] Objective justification or legitimate business explanations do not pull only in an exculpatory direction. It could be argued, of course, that it is the impact of coerced licensing on the innovative activities of *all* firms, not just those of the dominant firm, that should be looked at. It can be expected, however, that any risk aversion generated in the mind of third parties contemplating whether to innovate would vary inversely with their distance from the event or industry under scrutiny. Where these third parties are building (or proposing to build) on the dominant firm's innovations, this argument has some force.[62] In other cases the connection between the two is too remote to count for much.

---

[58] Such empirical evidence as exists suggests that the link between coerced licensing and the licensor's incentive to invest in research and development is extremely tenuous. See Scherer, FM, 'The Innovation Lottery' in RC Dreyfuss *et al* (eds), *Expanding the Boundaries of Intellectual Property: Innovation Policy for the Knowledge Society* (Oxford, Oxford University Press, 2001), pointing out that compulsory patent licensing imposed as part of over 100 antitrust settlements appeared to have little or no impact on the defendant's research and development investments. See also Scherer, FM, 'Does Antitrust Compromise Technological Efficiency?' (1989) 15 *Eastern Economic Journal* 1.

[59] Eg, as seen in Euro *Microsoft*, n 35 above, at para 711. The General Court found Microsoft had not discharged the burden of showing that objective justification existed for its refusal to disclose interoperability information. Its assertions on this score were undercut by the fact that it had already made some disclosures of its source code for its own purposes. There are good reasons for placing the onus on the party resisting access. In most cases the level of investment required to introduce the information in the first place or to improve upon it later is a matter that is peculiarly within the knowledge of that party. For a contrary view see van Rooijen, A, 'The Role of Investments in Refusals to Deal' (2008) 31 *World Competition* 63.

[60] Euro *Microsoft*, n 35 above, para 724.

[61] *Ibid*. Ritter, C, 'Refusal to Deal and Essential Facilities: Does Intellectual Property Require Special Deference to Tangible Property?' (2005) 28 *World Competition* 281 at 296. Shelanski, HA, 'Unilateral Refusals to Deal in Intellectual and Other Property' (2009) 76 *Antitrust Law Journal* 369.

[62] See, eg the 2009 Final Report of the Centre of European Policy Studies, *Treatment of Exclusionary Abuses under Art 82 [Art 102 TFEU] of the EC Treaty: Comments on the European Commission's Guidance Paper* at para 12. In the view of the writers of that Report, the *Guidance*

We also need to remember that not all innovation is efficient; indeed, it may sometimes be introduced with the aim of thwarting competition in mind.[63] Neither can the value of the innovation to the innovator (still less to society) simply be equated with the value of the original investment.[64] The investment may have been made anyway, whether or not the end product was protected against appropriation.[65] More importantly, since the scope of legal protection conferred on a particular piece of innovation may bear no relation to the investment needed to conjure it up, any calculation of lost investment would have to take into account the dead weight loss caused by over-protection in the first place. These are all specific questions of fact that cannot be bypassed simply by posing the question at a higher level of abstraction.[66]

1.7 THE INCOMPLETE GLOBALISATION OF COMPETITION POLICY

It is in the nature of a comparative study such as ours that it should seek to compare the comparable. There are, however, different legislative histories, different wordings and different traditions of statutory interpretation. All of these can skew an economics-based analysis. Insights from economics can smooth out these bumps but cannot eliminate them. While courts have often been creative in these matters, the words of the statute do sometimes intrude and cannot entirely be ignored.

---

falls short of backing that argument, since they note the Commission would 'consider claims [by way of defence] by [a] dominant undertaking that its own innovation will be negatively affected by [an imposed] obligation to supply, or by the structural changes in the market conditions that imposing such an obligation will bring about, including the development of follow-on innovation by competitors.'

[63] See Merges, RP and Nelson, RR, 'On the Complex Economics of Patent Scope' (1990) 90 *Columbia Law Review* 839 for general discussion of the effect of blocking patents on innovation and market protection, as well as Dogan, SL and Lemley, MA, 'Antitrust Law and Regulatory Gaming' (2009) 87 *Texas Law Review* 685 for a particular account of the phenomenon of 'product hopping' in the pharmaceutical industry (whereby firms at the end of a patent term sometimes deliberately switch the mode of administering a drug from, say, a tablet to a capsule).

[64] This is particularly true in the case of network industries: van Rooijen, n 59 above.

[65] As was found to be the case in *Attheraces v British Horse Racing Board Ltd* [2007] EWCA Civ 38 in line with the decision of the European Court of Justice (ECJ) in Case C-203/02 *British Horse Racing Board v William Hill Organisation* [2002] ECR I-10415; Case C-46/02 *Fixtures Marketing Ltd v Oy Veikkaus Ab* [2004] ECR I-10365; Case C-338/02 *Fixtures Marketing Ltd v Svenska Spel AB* [2004] ECR I-10497; Case C-444/02 *Fixtures Marketing Ltd v Organismos Prognostikon Agonon Podosfairou AE (OPAP)* [2004] ECR I-10549. (All cases were decided together by the ECJ, 9 November 2004.) Arguably, it could also have been the case on the facts of *IMS Health,* n 27 above. Such little empirical evidence as there is suggests that the prospect of compulsory licensing has little or no effect on investment decisions. See Scherer, FM, 'The Effect of Conservative Economic Analysis on US Antitrust' in R Pitofsky (ed), *How the Chicago School Overshot the Mark* (Oxford, Oxford University Press, 2008) 30 at 37.

[66] van Rooijen, n 59 above, at 80.

Competition law has been much less successful than intellectual property law in leaping borders. Conflicts-of-law rules in all jurisdictions treat it as part of public law, even when it is sought to be enforced through private litigation.[67] There can thus be no escape from the *lex fori*. Even when it is sought to give the *lex fori* some extraterritorial reach,[68] it is easily fended off by evidential 'shield' laws in the jurisdictions in which the anti-competitive conduct is said to have occurred. Efforts to harmonise the content of competition law have not borne much fruit either. The TRIPS Agreement has generally been content to focus on the trade-distorting aspects of various forms of State aid to industry. Within this minimalist framework, States are free to construct their competition regimes largely as they please,[69] even engaging in regulatory races to the bottom if they perceive that this gives them an advantage in securing inward investment. Such cross-border unity as exists tends to come from the direct input of economists into the legal process. (There is a thriving international trade in expert witnesses.) Despite the role of economics as a trans-jurisdictional language, the speed and extent of economic take-up differs across jurisdictions.[70] Much will depend on how risk-averse judges and regulators are to false positives or false negatives.[71] It is not our contention that cross-border harmonisation of refusals to license laws is an objective to be pursued for its own sake. For the present writers, the lessons of divergence are lessons about how and why competition law and economics can be integrated, and the limits of that integration. Where national economies are unequal in their size and global reach, convergence will either not happen at all or be imposed in unequal bargaining tussles. Where national economies are equal, the most interventionist regulatory regime will

---

[67] Parties can sometimes avoid particular jurisdictions through suitably drafted arbitration clauses. This gives them no choice as to the applicable law. *Mitsubishi Motors Corp v Soler Chrysler-Plymouth Inc* 473 US 614 (1985).

[68] Either by projecting the boundaries of the market across borders, or through extending the provisions of the competition statute to conduct, which although external to the jurisdiction, affects competition or markets within it, eg Commerce Act 1986 (NZ), s 4(1). See also *United States v Aluminum Corp of America* 148 F 2d 416 (2nd Cir 1945) at 443.

[69] TRIPS, at Art 8(2), notes that '[a]ppropriate measures, provided that they are consistent with the provisions of this Agreement, may be needed to prevent the abuse of intellectual property rights by right holders or the resort to practices which unreasonably restrain trade or adversely affect the international transfer of technology.' At Art 40(2) TRIPS then allows Members to 'specify in their legislation licensing practices or conditions that may in particular cases constitute an abuse of intellectual property rights having an adverse effect on competition in the relevant market', suggesting that appropriate measures may include, eg, exclusive grant-back conditions, conditions preventing challenges to validity and coercive package licensing.

[70] Lianos, I, 'Lost in Translation? Towards a Theory of Economic Transplants' (2009) 62 *Current Legal Problems* 346 at 389.

[71] *Ibid*.

win, as multinationals will seldom find it worthwhile to offer jurisdictionally-specific products in technologically-innovative industries.[72]

---

[72] Heyer, n 13 above; Blumenthal, W, 'The Challenge of Sovereignty and the Mechanisms of Convergence' (2004) 72 *Antitrust Law Journal* 267.

2

The Uneasy Cohabitation of Law and Economics in Competition Regimes

2.1 EMPIRICISM VERSUS FORMALISM

Competition policy has always had to steer a wary course between economic rationality and justiciability. There is thus a tension in all competition regimes between prescription and analysis, the wish to provide certainty by condemning (or increasingly often, blessing in advance) nominated forms of business behaviour versus the desire to fit regulatory responses as closely as possible to the circumstances of particular cases. The first approach, which we may call *formalist*, assumes without further proof that particular economic outcomes (be these desirable or undesirable) follow so frequently from particular acts or omissions that the transaction costs associated with investigating the link between the two in each and every case are not worth incurring. The second approach, which could usefully be dubbed *empiricist*, requires a case-by-case showing of anti-competitive purpose or effect.[1]

The tension between empiricism and formalism is not a question of law versus economics. Bright-line rules, where possible, should be justified on economic grounds before they become part of regulatory practice. As part of this process, the transaction costs attached to over- and under-regulation need to be assessed properly. Once a bright-line rule is in place, however, economics is effectively banished from the courtroom. Conversely, it has to be admitted that much of the economic evidence given in competition cases will seem peculiarly indeterminate to the trier of fact, partly because of the ex ante nature of the questions economic witnesses are required to answer, partly because of a lack of consensus among economists as to the conclusions to be drawn from such facts as can be proven, and partly due to the important but easily blurred distinction between deductive and inductive reasoning that lies at the heart of everything economists say and think. The point that needs to be emphasised here is that while this often means that fact finding in competition cases has to be done in the face of an empirical deficit, this also applies (if less visibly) to the adoption of bright-line rules. Bright-line rules do not fill factual *lacunae*, they ignore them.

---

[1] *Monsanto Co v Spray-Rite Service Corp* 465 US 752 (1984) at 761.

2.2 THE UNEVEN RECEPTION OF ECONOMICS ACROSS JURISDICTIONS

While the language of economics provides a convenient and seemingly ubiquitous *lingua franca* in which competition lawyers can converse easily across jurisdictional boundaries, we need to remember that the openness of individual competition regimes to economic reasoning has evolved over time at different speeds and within different legislative frameworks. There is also the lingering persistence of non-economic values in competition policy everywhere,[2] a persistence that provides periodic opportunities for a legislatively driven populist resurgence. The different rates of economic take-up are the product of different views as to how (and how far) legal and economic thought processes can properly be made to mesh in the application of what are, in the end, legal rules. These differences owe as much to history and politics as to logic. All feed into the way in which individual jurisdictions treat refusals to license.

2.2.1 The rule of reason and economics in United States case law

In the earliest period of antitrust history, a period in which economic analysis played little or no part, the *rule of reason* became established as the appropriate mechanism for assessing anti-competitiveness. Despite its present-day centrality in the internal taxonomies of competition laws around the world, the concept of a rule of reason has always been rather fluid. In some contexts it means no more than that when such a rule applies, antitrust liability is fault-based rather than absolute. More usually it purports to describe a process or a methodology in which judges remain free to mould liability to the circumstances of individual cases in the pursuit of relatively diffuse goals such as 'competition' or 'efficiency.' When invoked in this way it is invariably counterpoised against its supposed opposite, the *per se* rule, a not entirely apposite dichotomy, at least in relation to United States antitrust law. There is nothing, however, about the concept of a rule of reason that mandates an economic input into either its formulation or application.

Employment of the concept of the rule of reason in judicial decision making long pre-dated the routine acceptance of economic evidence as a guide to factual outcomes or the content of legal rules. Rather than being the handmaiden of economics, the rule of reason was in its earliest manifestations simply a mechanism for defending freedom of contract. It was first invoked by the United States

---

[2] Sullivan, L, 'Economics and More Humanistic Disciplines: What are the Sources of Wisdom for Antitrust?' (1977) 125 *University of Pennsylvania Law Review* 1214.

Supreme Court in *Standard Oil of New Jersey v United States*[3] to read down the otherwise bald and seemingly uncompromising prohibition set out in section 1 of the Sherman Act. By this means, the expression 'every restraint in trade is illegal' was softened into 'every *unreasonable* restraint in trade is illegal': a methodology taken directly from common law notions of restraint of trade which, at this early stage of antitrust law, the judges imagined themselves to still be applying. In time, the rule of reason made the passage to section 2 of the Sherman Act, again without much in the way of a direct contribution from economics.[4]

2.2.2 The delayed take-up of economics in Europe

In contrast to the United States, where different economic models and methodologies have, one after another, cut a swathe through its antitrust law, European competition law regimes have by and large managed to avoid economics-driven oscillations in enforcement policy. Courts and regulators in the European Union continued for several decades to apply an approach[5] based on formalistic categories of permitted (or not permitted) behaviour,[6] an approach that to its critics seem to be as much concerned with the impact of that conduct on individual competitors as with its effect on the competitive process as a whole. They remained, until relatively recently, unreceptive to the infiltration of economic theories of any school.[7]

It is only in the last decade or so that it can be said that economists and economic theory have gained a firm foothold in the decision making of the European Commission itself. The formal appointment in 2004 of a Chief

---

[3] *Standard Oil of New Jersey v United States* 221 US 1 (1911). The Supreme Court noted the legislature intended the 'standard of reason' as applied at common law should be used to assess whether particular acts were within the Sherman Act's prohibitions.

[4] At the time of its introduction many, if not most, US economists opposed the Sherman Act because they thought trusts or concentrations of market power were normal and eradicable. See Hovencamp, H, 'United States Competition Policy in Crisis: 1890–1955' (2009) 94 *Minnesota Law Review* 311 at 320, 321 and 329. While most economists at the time also considered such trusts were necessary for economies of scale and efficiency gains, what they had in mind was efficiency in the productive rather than allocative sense. See Scherer, FM, 'Efficiency, Fairness, and the Early Contributions of Economists to the Antitrust Debate' (1990) 29 *Washburn Law Journal* 243 at 247.

[5] See 2.4.1 below.

[6] As manifested in the European Commission's *Guidelines* on *Vertical Restraints* [2000] OJ C291/1; *Horizontal Cooperation Agreements* [2001] OJ C3/2; and *Merger Regulation* [2004] OJ L24/1.

[7] Kallaugher, J, 'Existence, Exercise and Exceptional Circumstances for a more Economic Approach to IP Issues under Art 102 TFEU' in S Anderman and A Ezrachi (eds), *Intellectual Property and Competition Law: New Frontiers* (Oxford, Oxford University Press, 2011) 113 at 115.

Economist to the Commission and an increasing reliance on purportedly 'scientific' market-measuring tools such as the Herfindahl–Hirshman Index in the Commission's analysis of market power[8] have been followed by the announced integration by the Commission of more econometric analysis into abuse cases (including refusals) via various soft law initiatives.[9] These signal the adoption by the Commission of a more 'effects-based' approach to enforcement, one under which concepts such as 'economic efficiency' and 'consumer welfare' are intended to play an increasing part in assessing anti-competitive harm. Given that both concepts are fraught with ambiguities,[10] this effects-based approach is yet to be properly tested in the courts. Neither is it clear that the Court of Justice or the General Court is entirely persuaded by these new perspectives.

2.2.3 Economics legislatively mandated or excluded: Canada, Australia and New Zealand

Courts and regulators in our other three jurisdictions have been blessed (or cursed) with a degree of legislated detail that simultaneously limits and reinforces the economic element in their decision making. Thus while on one hand legislators have been happy to pick up[11] economic terms of art such as 'market', 'consumer' and 'efficiency', and thereby leave would-be interpreters to choose among competing theories on these subjects, they have also not hesitated on occasion to seek to insert a particularly economic viewpoint into the legislation, generating some fairly creative statutory interpretation in response. The line between *per se* rules and rules of reason in these jurisdictions is laid down in the statute itself. Limitations and exemptions for particular types of activity are also legislatively mandated, particularly in relation to intellectual property. In Canada and New Zealand there are also provisions laying down the objectives of the competition statute which further seek to tie the courts' hands in various ways. The end result of this close legislative attention, however, turns out not to be

---

[8] The Index was first devised in the 1940s by Herfindahl and Hirshman acting independently. The latter used it to gauge the extent to which Nazi Germany was increasing its political power via its trading arrangements.

[9] The latest of these is the communication *Guidance on the Commission's Enforcement Priorities in Applying [Article 102 TFEU] to Abusive Exclusionary Conduct by Dominant Undertakings*, issued 3 December 2008 and formally adopted by the European Commission on 9 February 2009. It eventuated after a lengthy consultation process in which the Commission reviewed its methodology and approach to dominance and abuse of dominance under Art 102 TFEU (ex Art 82 EC). The aim of the review was 'to evaluate policy, to assess how it could be made more effective and to define ways in which [the Commission] might make it more transparent'. The *Guidance Communication* addresses the specific abuses of exclusive dealing, tying and bundling, predation, refusal to supply and margin squeeze. See discussion in ch 6.

[10] See discussion at 3.4.1–3.4.3 below.

[11] This is not always as straightforward as it might seem. Economic terms may be picked up in one part of the statute but omitted from another, leaving courts to parse the silence.

greater clarity but rather a raft of illogical distinctions that few economists of whatever stripe would be able to endorse or justify.

2.3 THE INHERENT INDETERMINISM OF ECONOMICS

While the modern rule of reason relies heavily on economic analysis to move its operation beyond mere judicial hunch, there are still occasions on which lawyers and economists appear to be talking past each other when the results of that analysis are fed into the mincer of legal and regulatory processes. The reasons for these mutual misperceptions are not hard to find. They arise from the fact that, while the logic of economics appears to be unified, its conclusions are actually based on two quite different forms of reasoning. The first is *inductive*; proceeding by way of the 'last hypothesis standing' methodology of all sciences (hard and soft) in which empirical evidence is gathered and sifted not to demonstrate that 'X is true' but that 'X has yet to be proven untrue'. Economics' second mode is *deductive*; reasoning down logically from stated assumptions, a process usually presented mathematically in the form of a model. In its inductive aspect, economics is not markedly more developed or rigorous than other behavioural sciences. It is the deductive side that both gives economics its rigour and limits its ability to provide definitive once-and-for-all answers to the factual and hard legal questions thrown up by competition proceedings, questions which require immediate answers with little or no time for empirical or statistical analysis before or during a formal hearing or investigation. This empirical shortfall would be there even if all economists were to agree on predicted outcomes (which they largely do not) and methodology (where they tend to). It is scarcely surprising, then, that disputes as to theory in competition cases tend to take the form of a battle between the current starting assumptions or past predictive reliability of competing models.[12] In theory, it should be possible to bring induction and deduction together by using the former to test the latter as predictions against actual outcomes. For reasons that are as much cultural as methodological, this seldom happens outside the courtroom, much less within it.[13] Erecting and

---

[12] Indeed some Chicago economists would say that testing assumptions is both undoable and pointless; see Friedman, M, *Essays in Positive Economics* (Chicago, Chicago University Press, 1975) at 40. Only predictive power matters. Since most competition regimes have few mechanisms for revisiting cases when predicted outcomes are later shown not to have occurred, this warning is of less value in practical terms than it might be.

[13] Assessments of predictive accuracy outside the courtroom of necessity look back. Competition cases require courts and regulators to both look backwards and forwards, and to factor in the effect of regulatory intervention as well. Conversely, if intellectual property is fenced off from such intervention, prediction becomes both impossible and irrelevant. The result can be a certain foreshortening of thought processes in the courtroom; Brunt, M, 'Antitrust in the Courts: The Role of Economics and Economists' in M Brunt (ed), *Economic Essays in Australian*

demolishing models is what most economists do most of the time (such activity providing a surer path to career advancement, as a public choice theorist would no doubt observe). Empirical studies tend to be on a smaller (and thus more easily assailable) scale than the models which they seek to test. Conducting them is therefore not without professional risk.

One of the consequences of elevating the forensic use of models in this way is the marginalisation of that which is not easily modelled. As one commentator has pointed out, the propensity of modern industrial economics to emphasise internal logical consistency and internal rule following[14] is both a symptom of its disconnect from the other behavioural sciences and a 'response to the lack of a secure empirical base'.[15] That which is formalised or susceptible to formalisation can be discussed; that which is neither remains at the margins of economic discourse even when economists agree on its importance. Thus discussions of innovative efficiency (a concept with too many variables to be as easily applied as its more mathematically tractable allocative and productive brethren) lack the rigour of other areas of economics, leading those who engage in such discussions to resort to a great deal of assertion and counter-assertion. This matters greatly, for example, when it comes to assessing competing claims that coerced licensing will or will not result in a loss of efficiency.

It is against this backdrop that the predilection of economists for graphs and equations must be viewed. The mathematics is there 'to ensure precision and openness to scrutiny for logical errors'.[16] It is part of the chain of deduction. It is not there to fill in empirical holes. Indeed its presence can sometimes mask them, especially to an economically untrained judicial eye. As long as their internal logic holds up, models can be attacked and undermined effectively only by challenging the assumptions on which they are based. These contested starting-points are precisely where the economic consensus is most likely to break down.[17] They can also shift in periods of market failure.[18]

---

and New Zealand Competition Law (The Hague, Kluwer, 2003) 356 at 359. This is perhaps forgivable. The alternative of listing every presumption can be a great consumer of court time. Fact gathering can of course occur at both the deductive and inductive stages. *Ibid*.

[14] The internal rules of economics in no way resemble legal rules. Legal reasoning has its deductive moments, but its normal methodology is an extended form of argument by analogy, a modus which most economists would scorn as supremely illogical. This can lead to a certain amount of talking at cross-purposes.

[15] Lianos, I, 'Lost in Translation? Towards a Theory of Economic Transplants' (2009) 62 *Current Legal Problems* 346 at 355.

[16] *Ibid*, at 354.

[17] *Ibid*, at 369.

[18] See, eg, Posner, RA, *A Failure of Capitalism: The Crisis of '08 and the Descent into Depression* (Cambridge MA, Harvard University Press, 2009), in which Judge Posner resiles, calling for more effective oversight of the financial industry in the wake of the global financial crisis of 2008.

2.4 JUDICIAL EXITS FROM INDETERMINATE ECONOMICS

Faced with disharmony among economists, how might courts react? A range of responses is possible. They can elevate the interests of one set of stakeholders (say consumers or investors) over another, thus pre-empting debates about whether competition policy is, or should be, distributive. They can characterise the decision to intervene as 'exceptional' and thus hope to marginalise any gaps in the economic consensus.[19] They can retreat to the words of the statute where these hint (and there is seldom more than a hint, given that the legislation will often pre-date reception of economic reasoning as a normal part of competition analysis in the jurisdiction in question) at a preference for one theory over another, sometimes parsing the words of the legislature in unlikely ways to embrace (or avoid capture by) a particular economic viewpoint. They can refuse a remedy on the grounds that whatever the economics says about the substantive decision, the solution proposed by one or other party is beyond its ability to enforce (where, say, the price of access eludes easy estimation). They can give themselves room to disown their decision at some future date should the economics become less disharmonious than it appeared to be at the operative time, by presenting the issue as context specific rather than as one requiring the creation or prior acknowledgement of the existence of a more widely applicable rule. Such allegedly fact dependent decisions can then be dismissed in future cases as being of limited or no precedential value, and the economic debate can thereby be kept open (both in the courtroom and beyond[20]).

All of these techniques are perfectly legitimate forms of legal reasoning with parallels in areas of law other than competition policy and areas of professional expertise other than economics. There are other avoidance techniques, however, that have a more immediate resonance within the refusals to license debate. They are explored below.

2.4.1 Deference to the regulator

This has two aspects. The first is the general reluctance to second-guess complex findings of fact by competition authorities, the sort of hands-off approach adopted by the General Court in *Microsoft v European Commission*.[21] This will usually but not always work against the dominant firm. The second form of

---

[19] In so far as these are meant to reassure by pointing out that coerced licensing is such a rare event that it will have little impact on incentives to innovate in general then such warnings do no harm. As explanations as to when and why such coerced licensing might be justified in particular cases they can be used to mask sloppy thinking.

[20] 'Preserving "variety" in the marketplace for ideas', as Lianos puts it, n 15 above, at 382.

[21] Case T-201/04 *Microsoft Corporation v European Commission* ('Euro *Microsoft*') [2007] ECR II-3601, 5 CMLR 11.

deference is that displayed by the United States Supreme Court in *Verizon Communications Inc v Law Offices of Curtis V Trinko LLP*,[22] in which the reviewing court refuses (as a matter of discretion not law[23]) to apply ordinary competition principles where there is a parallel system of industry-specific regulation. Here the beneficiaries will often be the ineffectively regulated holder of market power.[24] If intellectual property rights are regarded as a form of regulation (as they can be), the benefit of such an approach will adhere to the right holder.[25]

2.4.2 Manipulating the onus and standard of proof

In their ordinary lives outside the courtroom economists will usually be indifferent as to who has to prove what. Empirical deficits are simply there for the filling by those who have the interest and the skills. Litigation under a rule of reason requires that an empirical hole be filled by someone, and that someone is the person bearing the onus of proof. Issues may be subdivided by shifting the onus. The legal mechanism used is the presumption.

2.4.3 Deference to business autonomy or expertise

This is the concept known as 'objective justification' in Europe and as 'legitimate business explanation' elsewhere. It is based on the premise that courts and regulators should not seek to second-guess business decisions without good reason. It can enter the debate at different points. Sometimes it is used to reject accusations of anti-competitive intent or purpose. It may also be a way of backing away from a prediction of anti-competitive outcomes that might otherwise be inferred on the facts or used to give an exculpatory twist to an inculpatory principle.[26]

---

[22] *Verizon Communications Inc v Law Offices of Curtis V Trinko LLP* 540 US 398 (2004).
[23] The doctrine of pre-emption was not applied in *Trinko*, *ibid*. See discussion at 5.4.4 below.
[24] For a critique of the opportunities for gaming this gives incumbent firms, see Dogan, SL and Lemley, MA, 'Antitrust Law and Regulatory Gaming' (2009) 87 *Texas Law Review* 685.
[25] For a discussion of intellectual property as a disguised and clumsy form of regulation, see 4.3.3 below.
[26] Most notably in relation to the softening of the essential facilities doctrine, see chs 5 and 6 below.

2.5 MODES OF ABSORBING ECONOMICS

As long as the conclusions of economists are presented to them as an exercise in fact finding, courts and regulators have no particular need to evolve new techniques for dealing with them. Where, however, economic analysis is brought to bear on the content of a legal rule the position is different. Here the synergy is two-way. Economics alters the shape of the law, it is true, but when this happens the nature of the debate among economists is itself subtly altered in its turn. In some jurisdictions this occurs when phrases with particular resonance for economists (and generally understood among economic disputants) are picked up by the legislature and incorporated into the competition statute. Sometimes the phrase in question will form part of the legal test (for example, 'market' and 'market power'), but even here the addition of qualifiers (such as 'substantial') or probability tests (such as 'likely') will introduce levels of meaning not present in economic discourse before the term is absorbed into the statute. On other occasions the statute will recognise the concept by naming it but give no indication of how it is to be used.[27] All of these mechanisms may be found in the competition legislation of Australia, Canada and New Zealand. In Europe and the United States, by contrast, the economic analysis enters judicial thought processes without much in the way of a legislative prompt. Two things may then occur. The economics can remain in the realm of fact, so that while there is judicial acceptance of one theory over another for the purposes of resolving a particular case, that theory never solidifies into a precedent for resolving like cases. Alternatively, if a theory does set hard, any later rethinking on the part of economists may simply be edited out by judges unwilling to stray too far thereafter from *stare decisis*. Paradoxically, the now embedded theory then feeds back into the internal economics debate as a logical given and ends up 'freezing it a particular moment of its evolution'.[28] Winning the economic debate by judicial fiat may be flattering to the winner, but the implications of economists using courts to say 'please take this theory and make it law' should not always be assumed to be good for the health of the discipline.

Regulators are of course less free to shape the law than judges. When they do so, it is usually via guidelines and safe harbours; so-called soft law. Here the economics can operate largely untroubled by problems of precedent.[29] Guidelines too may of course be absorbed into the law,[30] when judges decide to defer to the regulator.

---

[27] Recognition may be even more cryptic, as where the statute accepts the possibility of leveraging in the abstract but goes no further.

[28] Lianos, n 15 above, at 370.

[29] Fox, E, 'The 1982 Merger Guidelines: When Economists are Kings?' (1983) 71 *California Law Review* 281.

[30] Lianos, n 15 above, at 375. According to Lianos, such absorption and change has occurred with concepts such as market power and barriers to entry; *ibid*, at 384. The phenomenon may

2.6 CHOOSING BETWEEN THE FALSE POSITIVE AND THE FALSE NEGATIVE

One issue that has a long history in competition law and which forms the (often unstated) major premise in debates between different schools of economic thought is whether it is better for regulators, given that they are often acting on less than perfect information, to err on the side of under- or over-regulating. This is the famous choice between false positive and false negative (or, as some would frame the question, the choice between type one and type two errors). Long a staple of economic debate, it has now become part of the judicial lexicon, especially in the United States where it is increasingly used as a case breaker.[31]

Proponents of this viewpoint are really running two quite distinct arguments. The first is that false positives are more likely once the regulator decides to intervene. The second is that false positives are more damaging (or in Chicago terms, more costly) than false negatives. The first point is true but trite. Doing nothing does, it is true, eliminate type one errors entirely, but it poses instead the much harder question: Why regulate at all? The statement is more apt to paralyse regulators than assist them. The second bears closer examination. As a warning against over-confidence on the part of the regulator, it is salutary. It is, however, one thing to say that the risk of getting things wrong may be higher when the regulator is being asked to act on incomplete information, but that is (or should be) a spur towards ensuring the information is as complete as it can be, not an invitation to shirk the task of looking for it. Some uncertainty may be the inevitable by-product of a case-by-case rule of reason, but presuming that the conduct complained of is harmless in each and every case carries with it its own set of risks. Those risks cannot be wished away by solemnly intoning, in round Posnerian tones, that successful firms should not be punished for their success or that firms with market power should be free to compete like anyone else.

Often overlooked in this debate is the issue of scale. If failure to intervene has the capacity to entrench monopoly in wide areas of the economy then that has to be balanced against what might be a relatively small degree of regulatory tinkering. Looked at this way, the European notion of super dominance (much decried by some commentators) can be seen as a useful attempt to rebalance the debate.[32] Thus, the emphasis by the General Court, in its decision in *Microsoft v*

---

also surface as a contest of methodologies, witness the sometimes linear approach of courts to market definition and market power in which the former must precede the latter when compared with the way in which economists describe how the two concepts interact. This does not of course rule out any convergence between the two approaches; *ibid*, at 387.

[31] The false positive versus false negative is present in European cases but is usually invoked in a coded way.

[32] The point we seek to make here is that the extent of dominance cannot be ignored in the false negative versus false positive tug-of-war. It is not suggested that the concept of 'super dominance' is in any sense a precise analytical tool, or that there is a precise dominance tipping-point with fixed regulatory responses on either side of it.

European Commission,[33] on the scale of Microsoft's market power may be seen as a salutary reminder that the problem of scale is real and cannot simply be eliminated by taking refuge in inflated fears of the false positive. The use of intellectual property rights to back market power raises issues of scale in a different way. An intellectual property right that is broader in scope or longer in duration than can be justified on the grounds of innovative efficiency may, issues of substitutability apart, confer a greater degree of market power on its holder than would otherwise be the case. In such cases the uncertain risk of over-regulation has to be weighed against the reality of over-protection.

Also often overlooked in the flight from the false positive is the reversibility issue, ie will continuation of the practice complained of be hard to put into reverse through behavioural remedies[34] if ignored now. (This is particularly important where the dominant firm has captured the industry standard.[35])

Again, even if uncertainty cannot be eliminated entirely, it can be compensated for (by over-pricing access, for example). And we should not assume that the courts and regulators are incapable of remedial finesse. Remedies that drove a dominant firm out of the market entirely, or froze all its research and development indefinitely,[36] are the stuff of neoclassical fantasy in which deranged regulators stalk the world seeking out businesses to ruin. Real-world remedies can be much more precisely targeted, and are also able to be adjusted over time (for example, by allowing the dominant firm to apply for a variation of the order should conditions change, or making orders subject to a sunset clause[37]).

Preferences for false negatives or false positives are really disguised ideological preferences for less or more regulation.[38] That is why they so easily morph into presumptions of virtue, or calls for immunity from regulatory scrutiny for particular kinds of conduct. Such calls should be ignored unless they can be backed empirically. Until that happens regulators should always be free to balance the risks and consequences of making a type one or a type two error in a given case. Neither should be ruled in or out of court in advance. It is one thing to conclude that type one is worse than type two in a given situation, after weighing all the relevant factors bearing on the decision (including those of scale and reversibility), but quite another to say that this is always and inevitably so. For

---

[33] See Euro *Microsoft*, n 21 above.
[34] Structural remedies can, of course, put anything into reverse, but the cure may be worse than the disease.
[35] See 3.4.5 below.
[36] Crocioni, P, 'Leveraging of Market Power in Emerging Markets: A Review of Cases, Literature and a Suggested Framework' [2008] *Journal of Competition Law and Economics* 449 at 512.
[37] *Ibid.* That means that the regulator should have some idea of the remedy it wants at the outset.
[38] For an unusually frank espousal of this viewpoint, see McChesney, FS, 'Easterbrook on Errors' (2010) 6 *Journal of Competition Law and Economics* 11. For McChesney, the obstacles to the repeal of US antitrust law are political not economic.

that is to pre-empt the debate permanently and irrevocably. Regulatory perfection is unattainable and evidentiary uncertainty is always with us. There is no 'just right' solution.[39] In hindsight regulators will always be seen to have overstated or understated the importance of one factor or another. Striking the balance ex ante is difficult, but struck it must be. Over-enthusiastic waving of the false positive shroud does little to assist regulators in that task.

Refusals to license introduce a further destabilising element into the type one versus type two debate. The degree of protection conferred by the intellectual property right in question, and the relationship between that degree of protection and innovative efficiency, can set a type two error in stone by matching it to the duration of the right and projecting it far into the future.

---

[39] For an attempt to find one, see Ahlborn, C, Evans, DS and Padilla, AJ, 'The Logic & Limits of the "Exceptional Circumstances Test" in *Magill* and *IMS Health*' (2005) 28 *Fordham International Law Journal* 1109. The choices laid out for regulators by these authors depend on a priori assumptions about the weight to be given to the risk of a false positive.

3

Fault Lines in Competition Policy

3.1 A TAXONOMY OF COMPETITION RULES

Competition rules can take a variety of forms, each displaying varying degrees of receptiveness to the input of economists. These legal taxonomies vary in detail across legal systems. Despite the differences, the following broad distinctions hold true:

a) Liability-*creating* as opposed to liability-*denying* rules.[1]
b) Rules in which economic evidence or analysis is constrained only by broadly-framed behavioural prohibitions of undesired outcomes, as against rules which forbid particular conduct by describing it in detail and in which economic analysis plays no part in establishing liability in a given case.[2] The former are usually described as rules of *reason*, the latter as *per se* rules, an

---

[1] Liability-denying rules take two forms: statutory exemptions for a particular type of activity; and discretionary safe harbours, which provide refuge against some forms of liability and which are usually applied by administrative or prosecutorial agencies under minimal statutory guidance but stiffened by agency issued guidelines. Block exemptions in European law occupy an intermediate ground.

[2] The imposition of *per se* liability is usually justified both in terms of the magnitude of the harm the proscribed conduct does to competition and the unlikelihood of demonstrating sufficient counterbalancing pro-competitive benefits flowing from that conduct. See *Standard Oil of New Jersey v United States* 221 US 1 (1911) and the remarks of Brandeis J in *Chicago Board of Trade v United States* 246 US 231 (1917) at 239. The distinction between *per se* rules and rules of reason is blurred by the existence of 'quick look' methodologies that subject particular behaviour to less than full competition scrutiny without prohibiting it entirely. Further confusion is introduced when courts allow pro-competitive explanations for breaches they nevertheless describe as *per se* (see *Wholesale Stationers v Pacific Stationery* 472 US 284 (1985); *NCAA v Board of Regents* 468 US 85 (1984) at 101; and *Broadcast Music Inc v Columbia Broadcasting System* 441 US 1 (1979) at 8) or summarily exclude such explanations in the course of a supposedly rule-of-reason approach, as in *FTC v Indiana Federation of Dentists* 476 US 447 (1986) at 459 (equally the product of judicial inventiveness). The *per se* rule of reason dichotomy in European law has to be teased out of the words of Art 101 TFEU and, more problematically, Art 102 TFEU rather than judicially constructed from the policy of an otherwise enigmatic statute as in the United States. Again while European judges have sometimes been reluctant to embrace American terminology in this context, they have been much less hesitant about adopting the pro- and anti-competitive balancing that characterises a rule of reason. See the Court of Justice's decision in Case T-112/99 *Metropole Television (M6) v European Commission* [2001] II-2459, [2001] All ER (D) 37.

over-simplified dichotomy which is not always as rigid as this classification would suggest.[3]
c) Heads of liability that depend on proof of actual or likely anti-competitive *intent* versus those that work by way of assessing anti-competitive *outcomes*.[4]
d) Rules that are *evidentiary* or remedial in their effect as distinct from those that are *substantive*.
e) Rules that strike at *collective* misconduct versus those that focus on *unilateral* acts or omissions.[5]

All of these distinctions affect the design and legal relevance of economic analysis in different ways. None of them, however, distinguishes between particular economic activities or forms of investment, or between action and inaction.

3.2 DISENTANGLING FACT AND LAW IN COMPETITION CASES

The line between fact and law (never as clear-cut as common lawyers would like to think) is more blurred in competition cases than in most other areas of law. The line can become fuzzier still when common law and civilian modes of reasoning meet (or fail to meet). Thus, common lawyers, when perusing the General Court's decision in *Microsoft Corporation v European Commission* ('Euro Microsoft')[6] find it difficult to discern the rule-making wood for the myriad factual trees, where civilians (because they tend to look askance at too overt a usurpation of the legislator's role) would see the primacy of fact-finding over rule-making displayed in the General Court's decision as perfectly normal. This blurring of fact and law, while visible in judicial decisions on both sides of the Atlantic, tends to assume different forms in Europe and the United States. In the United States it may be seen in the use of judge-made presumptions that obscure the invisible privileging of one economic viewpoint over another. In Europe there is a tendency on the part of the courts to describe the need to interfere with private law rights as being in some sense extraordinary, a regrettable but rare necessity to be resorted to only when an unlikely combination of seldom

---

[3] Hovencamp, H, *The Antitrust Experience: Principle and Execution* (Cambridge MA, Harvard University Press, 2005) at 308.

[4] These can be (and usually are) combined in the same provision, not always expressly. (They play an equivocal and subsidiary role in US antitrust law, not being liability-creating in themselves, but may nevertheless negative an otherwise pro-competitive outcome or explanation.) Intent-based tests of liability may have been given a new lease of life (albeit only negatively) in *Verizon Communications Inc v Law Offices of Curtis V Trinko LLP* ('*Trinko*') 540 US 398 (2004). See Schoen, FX, 'Exclusionary Conduct after *Trinko*' (2005) 80 *New York University Law Review* 1625 at 1648.

[5] Refusals to license may be either. They may also be instigated by licensees as well as licensors.

[6] Case T-201/04 *Microsoft Corporation v European Commission* [2007] ECR II-3601, 5 CMLR 11.

occurring facts is present in the case before them. Both techniques have the capacity to divert attention from the underlying economic issues. Both therefore have a direct bearing on how these jurisdictions treat refusals to license.

3.2.1 Rules or prophecies?

When courts describe the likelihood of intervention as being 'rare' or a case as 'exceptional',[7] they are, on the face of it, doing no more than predicting factual outcomes on a quasi statistical but wholly unscientific basis. Predictions can too readily morph into rules, however, when used to explain why the court's approach to refusals to license intellectual property diverges from its approach to other forms of property. Nothing remarkable in this, it might be thought, just the normal mechanism by which judges make law (relatively overtly in common law legal systems these days, more covertly in civil law ones). When used in a series of cases over a short time frame, however, the technique can bestow unwarranted legal significance on the facts of the first case in which the exceptionality principle happens to be invoked. While the presence or absence of these facts may or may not have economic significance, that is not something that can be debated in later judicial decisions. The first case off the block can thus, purely fortuitously, put the economics into a legal straitjacket.

3.2.2 Proof and presumption in competition cases

In competition law, as in other legal contexts, confusion often arises when courts do not adequately distinguish between a constitutive element of a legal rule and the way in which the existence of that particular element is to be proven on the facts. Given the seeming intractability of much economic evidence, judges are sometimes tempted to remove the particular matter at issue from the rule of reason and treat it not as a question of fact but as an unformulated question of law, employing for this purpose various 'presumptions' as a kind of verbal shorthand for dispensing with the need to identify the process of legal reasoning by which they have arrived at their conclusions.[8] Thus presumptions are often

---

[7] 'Exceptionality' is of course the basis of the Court of Justice's jurisprudence on refusals to license copyright works, as discussed in ch 6 below.

[8] Indeed the US Supreme Court has expressly delivered strong advice against the practice in *Eastman Kodak v Image Technical Services* ('*Kodak I*') 504 US 451 (1992) at 466–67, warning that 'legal presumptions that rest on formalistic distinctions rather than actual market realities are generally disfavored in antitrust law'. The Court also reminded itself and the lower courts that it 'preferred to resolve antitrust claims on a case-by-case basis', focusing on the 'particular facts disclosed by the record'; *ibid*, at 467. Regrettably, this prudent warning has since then often been ignored both by lower courts and the Supreme Court itself.

invoked by lower courts in the United States in antitrust cases to provide an exit from the impasse of indeterminate or contested economic theory. It is not always clear, however, what judges imagine themselves to be doing in these cases. The language of presumption can be (and in competition cases often is) applied in very different ways. Historically, the use of presumptions has been a way of 'softening' a *per se* rule that has proved overly interventionist. As such it may be seen as an intermediate stage in the transition to a full rule of reason. Once the case-by-case approach is in place, however, courts will sometimes be daunted by the complexity of the factual inquiry with which they have landed themselves and seek to revive the presumption again, but this time as one of legality rather than one of illegality. Whether the presumption is one of virtue or of vice, its function in these cases is to paper over cracks in the economics.

The presumption of competitive virtue suggested by courts in relation to some kinds of transactions[9] needs to be set against the general move away from presumptions of anti-competitive harm when assessing liability. It is not obvious that one form of presumption is better than the other. These presumptions of virtue seem to rest on another presupposition (often unstated): a presumption against any regulatory intervention at all. This makes them a stalking horse for the assumption that type one errors are in all circumstances to be avoided. If framed as remedial recognition of the law of unintended consequences or a general warning against drawing unwarranted evidentiary conclusions from particular types of economic activity, the presumption of virtue is harmless, if misleading. When presented as a substantive shield, however, it gives rise to two further questions: first, when is it to be applied; and, secondly, if it is, why should it operate more strongly when intellectual property is involved than in other cases?[10]

A frequent source of confusion in these cases is that it is not always clear whether judges are talking about the burden of proving facts[11] or assessing ex

---

[9] See, eg, Turney, J, 'Defining the Limits of the EU Essential Facilities Doctrine on Intellectual Property Rights: The Primacy of Securing Optimal Innovation' (2005) 3 *Northwestern Journal of Technology & Intellectual Property* 179. As Turney's argument runs, if the essential facilities doctrine is primarily used as a tool to allow free access to intellectual property rights which are not deserving of protection, it will also capture rights which have a beneficial purpose for innovative efficiency and ultimately consumers. Thus, Turney says, even were abuses of intellectual property occasionally to occur, the beneficial effects of dynamic research and development would outweigh the negative effects of imperfect competition because, after all, one of the key aims of competition policy is also to increase innovation.

[10] Given the indeterminate nature of much of the economics of intellectual property, this means that policy will be upended by process, usually in an unexplored fashion. See Kobayashi, BK, 'Spilled Ink or Economic Progress: The Supreme Court Decision in *Illinois Tool v Independent Ink*' (2008) 53 *Antitrust Bulletin* 5 at 17, for an analysis of this phenomenon in the context of tying. The same point may be made in relation to refusals to license.

[11] The distinction between 'persuasive' and 'evidential' burdens so beloved of common lawyers is of little relevance in competition cases, in which debates tend to centre on the conclusions to be drawn from undisputed facts rather than on the proof of those facts themselves.

ante a party's success or failure in persuading a court to adopt its submissions as to the content or applicability of a legal rule. This is wrong-headed. Courts and regulators must be assumed to know and accurately apply the law. There is (or should be) no such thing as the onus of proving the applicability or content of a legal rule.[12] That reasonable minds may differ as to the application of the rule, or that there is such a thing as regulatory leeway in its interpretation when it comes to be considered by an appellate or reviewing body, in no way detracts from this principle.[13]

Useful guidance may be found here from the way in which judges in some jurisdictions have put presumptions to work in tax cases when required to distinguish between expenditure on account of revenue and outgoings of a capital nature. Here, courts have by and large insisted that any presumption emerges *a posteriori* from proven facts rather than laid down *in futuro*. Used in this way, the term 'presumption' is merely a way of tracing the manner in which the decision has been arrived at and is not necessarily of assistance in other circumstances.[14] A clear distinction is thus made between judicial observations that the presence or absence of a particular fact or factor resulted in the case being placed in a particular legal category, and the very different situation obtaining where that presence or absence is presumed without investigation or factual inquiry.

The real difficulty with presumptions comes when they are used not as a short-cut for establishing what economists can agree on but in order to mask the lack of consensus among them. When used in this way the shorthand of presumptive liability or non-liability ensures that the party bearing the onus of proof will lose.[15] Given the indeterminate nature of much of industrial economics, this means that policy is being upended by process, all the worse for being done in an unexplored way. A more rational basis on which to construct a presumption would be to ask who is most likely to have the information necessary to prove the anti-competitive harm under investigation[16] (a mode of

---

[12] As to the uneasy balance between fact and law in this context, see Lianos, I, 'Judging Economists: Economic Expertise in Competition Law Litigation' in I Lianos and I Kokkoris (eds), *The Reform of EC Competition Law* (The Netherlands, Kluwer, 2010) 185. For a contrary view see Elhauge, E, 'The Failed Resurrection of the Single Monopoly Profit Theory' (2010) 6 *Competition Policy International* 155 at 160, where he argues that empirical evidence should be required to shift an existing precedent. In our view the problem arises when a particular economic theory becomes entrenched in the law as a 'rule'. We would prefer to view such 'precedents' as no more than findings of fact in the first place. Professor Elhauge is entirely right, however, in his insistence on the need for empirical evidence.

[13] *South Yorkshire Transport Ltd v Monopolies and Merger Commission* [1993] 1 All ER 289 at 298.

[14] *Regent Oil Co Ltd v Strick* [1965] 3 All ER 174 at 201, per Lord Wilberforce.

[15] Blair, RD, 'The Economics of the Roberts Court: An Introduction' (2008) 53 *Antitrust Bulletin* 1 at 4.

[16] Akman, P, 'Consumer Welfare and Article 82 EC: Practice and Rhetoric' (2009) 32 *World Competition* 71 at 79, fn 40. See also Elhauge, n 12 above, at 156 and 167.

allocating the evidentiary burden and the onus of proof on a particular issue that can be seen at work in the General Court's decision in *Microsoft*[17]). Viewed in this way, the presumption becomes a kind of regulatory version of private law's *res ipsa loquitur*. Such an approach would be more productive than simply treating presumptions as a kind of halfway house between economics as fact and economics as law, with no empirical justification as to why this particular stopping point has been chosen or why the journey has been embarked upon in the first place.

Jurisdictions differ as to the freedom with which they allow courts to create (and withdraw) presumptions (be they presumptions of vice or virtue) in competition cases. In the United States presumptions are almost entirely judge-made.[18] In Australia and New Zealand the existence or absence of presumptions is generally seen as the province of the legislature, while in the European Union presumptions tend to take the form of minatory observations that departures from previously expounded case law are to be regarded as rare.[19]

In sum, the authors are not attempting here to point courts towards the right economic answer but rather to show that disputes among economists cannot be bridged simply by manipulating the onus of proof.[20]

3.3 THE ROLE OF MARKETS IN THE REFUSAL TO LICENSE DEBATE

Issues of market definition and market power and the role of product substitutability loom large in the refusal to license debate. Unresolved doctrinal disputes over these core concepts prove singularly troublesome when the boundaries of rights and markets are conflated, or when right holders project (or fail to project) market power across those boundaries. Equally problematic are attempts to rank markets in terms of modernity or technical sophistication when justifying (or decrying) regulatory intervention.

---

[17] Euro *Microsoft*, n 6 above, para 688. The General Court imposed on the dominant undertaking Microsoft the evidentiary burden of demonstrating that its conduct was objectively justified, but reserved to the Commission the role of establishing whether or not the evidence with which it was supplied allowed for a finding that there had been no abuse. For a more detailed discussion see ch 6.

[18] Indeed flexibility even extends to judicial adjustment of the line between *per se* rules and rules of reason.

[19] Precedential flexibility can later be restored by holding out the possibility of a later return to the actual words of Art 102 TFEU.

[20] Once again there is a lesson to be drawn from taxation jurisprudence. Better simply to state what positive factor or factors in each given previous case has or have led to the assignment of expenditure to capital or income after the event rather than as a guide to future cases. See *Hallstroms Pty Ltd v Federal Commissioner of Taxation* [1946] HCA 34, (1946) 72 CLR 634 at 646, per Dixon J.

THE ROLE OF MARKETS IN THE REFUSAL TO LICENSE DEBATE   41

3.3.1   Defining markets and delimiting rights are not the same thing

Markets are the fundamental construct around which competition law is built.[21] Potentially anti-competitive outcomes are not assessed in the abstract but in terms of particular products or regions. Product markets are groupings of outputs (demand side) or inputs (supply side) that are substitutable for each other. Geographic markets assume an invisible boundary across which it will not pay to move or provide competing goods or services. Limitations on the jurisdictional reach of individual competition regimes (all have some) will turn these invisible lines into real borders, setting purely legal limits to market definition which ignore both the reality of free trade and the distance-defying possibilities of cyberspace. All of this can sometimes look rather like the process whereby the reach of intellectual property rights is set by limitations on protectable subject matter, territorial allocation of licences and the principle of national treatment. The resemblance is purely superficial, however. Delimiting rights is a question of law, defining markets is a question of fact. Confusing the two distorts the debate. Rights and markets coincide only by accident.[22] From this two things follow. Right owners and licensees who step outside the boundaries of their right should not, from that fact alone, be presumed to be acting anti-competitively. Conversely, staying religiously within those confines cannot be assumed to confer immunity from regulatory intervention. (Neither should we ignore the often circular nature of the interrelationship between market definition and market power.[23])

3.3.2   Substitutability and intellectual property

Any economics-based analysis of the role of intellectual property in competition policy has to take account of substitutability. On the demand side, this means that regard must be had to whether ordinary goods or services unprotected by intellectual property are as attractive to consumers as those that are so protected. On the supply side, the issue is whether competitors can invent or create around

---

[21] See generally Baker, JB, 'Market Definition: An Analytical Overview' (2007) 74 *Antitrust Law Journal* 129.

[22] The more narrowly a market is defined, the more likely this accidental convergence is to occur. See, eg, Joined Cases C-241/91 P and C-242/91 P *Radio Telefis Eireann and Independent Television Publications v European Commission* ('*Magill*') [1995] ECR I-743, and *Kodak I*, n 8 above, at 481.

[23] See, eg, the decision of the Full Federal Court in *Australian Competition and Consumer Council v Boral Ltd* [2001] FCA 30, in which Merkel J reasoned backwards to deduce the defendant had possessed market power because it had been able to act anti-competitively by engaging in predatory pricing.

the intellectual property right within a reasonable time frame without infringing it. Hypotheticals in these cases tend to take one of the following forms:

a) Would there be substitutable alternatives even if the intellectual property right in question had never existed?
b) Is it the intellectual property right that is preventing actual or potential substitution?

Both are, of course, different ways of putting the same question, and both may be resolved by pointing to real evidence of past substitution or, more problematically, speculation as to future substitution using the SSNIP[24] test and the like. What makes this particularly difficult in the case of products protected by intellectual property is the time frame. Intellectual property can delay substitution as well as preventing it outright, but constructing a model of the latter will always be easier than arriving at a formula capable of pinpointing exactly when during the life of the right, substitution becomes probable.

3.3.3 How many markets? How many rights?

Compounding the confusion between right and market is the fact that more than one market and more than one set of rights may be under the regulatory microscope in a given case. Take, for example, the classic spare parts or after-sales service case, in which component or service A goes into the making or supporting of product B. The issue here is whether there are separate markets A and B or a single market AB, because consumers build the costs of servicing or spare parts into their initial cost calculation. A and B may or may not be covered by intellectual property rights, and those rights may be either wider or narrower than either market. (B may be the subject of a patent, A, a design right and AB, a trade mark.) Allegations of anti-competitive behaviour in such cases usually take the form of tying product A to product B. When this happens, either the tie itself or the refusal to allow competitors to bypass the tie may become the subject of competition proceedings. This can cause problems when the tie and the refusal are covered by different rules, and where the application of those rules varies according to whether an intellectual property right is involved or not. The tying claim may be defended by the argument that there is only a single market AB. That defence may, in its turn, be sidestepped by the argument that competitors are being locked out of the market for the now composite product by refusal to license intellectual property rights protecting either the part or the whole.

A somewhat different state of affairs arises when a formula or a piece of information (again possibly covered by an intellectual property right, or possibly

---

[24] A test for market definition, SSNIP is an abbreviation for a 'small but significant and non-transitory increase in price.'

not) is being used in market A to produce a good or service X, but is also capable of being utilised in market B to produce a different good or service Y. In such a case, A is variously described as the 'upstream' or primary market and B as the 'downstream' or secondary market. Market B may be actual (where the technology or process is licensed to some downstream market players but not others) or hypothetical (where, for example, the right holder is vertically integrated and feels no need to license to anyone but a potential demand for a licence does exist). In such cases, it may not always be clear whether this hypothetical market is in the upstream product or process, or the rights that protect it. There is nothing inherently implausible about a market for rights, but competition cases are rarely argued that way. Complicating matters further is the dubious concept of a submarket. In some jurisdictions, most notably the United States, courts sometimes treat these as markets in their own right.[25] In other jurisdictions, a submarket merely pinpoints the source of market power within a market.[26] Either approach can be misleading if the 'submarket' and the intellectual property right are given the same borders.

Multiple markets and multiple rights pose two quite distinct kinds of problem for courts and regulators. The first arises when market power is claimed to have been leveraged from one market to another. The second occurs when it is sought to stand this argument on its head by arguing that only when there is leveraging can a competition problem involving intellectual property arise. The first problem is a debate among economists. The second is an artificial truncation of that debate imposed by lawyers.

(a)   *The leveraging debate*

The form of words used in competition legislation to strike down actual or attempted abuses of market power is open-textured enough to embrace at least the theoretical possibility that market power can be projected from one market into another. Sometimes, as in the Australian and New Zealand statutes, the leveraging door is expressly left open. More usually the spectre of anti-competitive leveraging can only be inferred *sub silentio* from the legislation's failure to locate either the prescribed behaviour, or its intended or actual consequences within the confines of a particular market (jurisdictional boundaries apart). Whether and when cross-market leverage is sustainable or even theoretically possible is a subject on which economists differ. Chicago School theorists in particular are sceptical that vertical leverage can ever make economic sense. Why, they ask, would a firm that was dominant in upstream market A not simply extract monopoly profits in that market rather than try the chancier exercise of projecting its power into downstream market B where, as they

---

[25] An approach that prompts the immediate and obvious response: 'Might not one of these markets (whole or part) be wrongly defined for the purpose for which it being used?'
[26] *Magic Millions Ltd v Wrightson Bloodstock Ltd* [1990] 1 NZLR 731.

surmise, it can extract additional profits only at the cost of losing them in market A? On this view of things, there is only one monopoly profit to be had, and it will be taken where it is most easily earned. Indeed some commentators would go further by positing that leveraging is not only pointless but will also decrease the dominant firm's own profits overall if it engages in it.[27] While generally raised in the context of tying, bundling and vertical mergers, the single monopoly profit theory may also be invoked in the context of refusals to deal or license.

Other analysts, while conceding that such self-destructive outcomes can occur when dominant firms attempt to leverage in this way, refuse to extrapolate from possibility to universal rule. There are, they say, some circumstances in which vertical leveraging of market power is perfectly rational.[28] This is especially likely to be the case when the downstream market is itself not competitive for some reason.[29] It may also make sense when (as often occurs where intellectual property rights are involved) the upstream market is proportionally small relative to the size of the downstream market.[30] These possibilities should at least be investigated, they suggest, not simply brushed aside with a priori assumptions about perfect competition or costless entry and exit. (Indeed for some post-Chicago thinkers, leveraging can be the mechanism whereby strategic barriers are erected in the first place.[31])

Other critics point out that the single monopoly profit theory assumes too easily that power in the upstream market is impregnable. If it is in fact vulnerable then firms active in market B could try to get a foothold in market A, thus giving a firm dominant in the latter market every reason to frighten them off while its power lasts, or better still bluff would-be entrants out of both markets.[32] The

---

[27] Stigler, G, 'United States v Loews Inc: A Note on Block Booking' [1963] Supreme Court Review 152 at 153; Bork, RH, The Antitrust Paradox: A Policy At War With Itself (New York, The Free Press, 1993) at 374.

[28] See discussion in Candedub, A, 'Trinko and Re-Grounding the Refusal to Deal Doctrine' (2005) 66 University of Pittsburgh Law Review 821.

[29] Whinston, MD, 'Tying, Foreclosure and Exclusion' (1990) 80 American Economic Review 837.

[30] This is Merges' theory of disproportionate leverage, see Merges, RP, 'Who Owns the Charles River Bridge? Intellectual Property and Competition in the Software Industry' (1999) UC Berkeley Public Law and Legal Theory Working Paper Series No 15 at <www.law.berkeley.edu/files/criver.pdf>. See also Arora, A, 'Refusals to License: A Transaction Based Perspective', available at <http://www.ftc.gov/opp/intellect/020501arora1.pdf>, and Crocioni, P, 'Leveraging of Market Power in Emerging Markets: A Review of Cases, Literature and a Suggested Framework' (2008) Journal of Competition Law & Economics 449 at 489. See also Elhauge, n 12 above.

[31] Crocioni calls this 'dynamic leveraging' (Crocioni, n 30 above, at 461). As he points out, the ultimate aim of such 'dynamic leveraging' may be to dissuade potential entrants from eroding the dominant firm's market power in the upstream market at some future stage, rather than a mere desire to foreclose the downstream market alone. (Both motivations may be present in a given case.)

[32] Salop, DC, 'Economic Analysis of Exclusionary Vertical Conduct: Where Chicago has Overshot the Mark' in R Pitofsky (ed), How the Chicago School Overshot the Mark (New York, Oxford University Press, 2008) 141 at 147.

theory is similarly flawed, such critics say, where the withheld input has dual uses[33] or the dominant firm is trying to evade regulation in the upstream market.[34] (An example of the latter relevant to refusals to license would be where a dominant copyright owner was seeking to avoid the application of the fair use rules, or to resile from open-source protocols to which it had previously agreed.) To focus solely on the profit forgone and ignore the wish to see off competing technologies is to address only half the problem.[35]

Whatever the outcome of these debates,[36] two points need to be made concerning them. The first is that courts in most jurisdictions accept that leverage can occur, and nowhere has it been definitively ruled that it cannot.[37] The second is that the real problem with the single monopoly profit theory is an evidentiary one. That is to say, even if one accepts that a rational monopolist will take the best and easiest route to profit, how is one to assess what is meant by profit in these cases? Bundling, tying and even refusals to deal can both increase or reduce price, or limit or expand choice depending on the circumstances. In such situations the temptation to avoid this difficulty by resorting to all or nothing leveraging theory becomes correspondingly greater as the available evidence on cost or quality becomes exiguous and ambiguous. Such temptation should be resisted. Evidential difficulties are part and parcel of the case-by-case analysis through which any rule of reason has to operate.[38]

The leverage debate becomes even more complicated when an intellectual property right enters the picture. It is not always accurate, for example, to assume (as Chicago thinkers do when they postulate a 'single profit' approach to leveraging) that the dominant firm will always be operating directly in the upstream market. Here too, it may be dealing through licensees to capture the supposed single profit. In such cases expanding output in the upstream market

---

[33] *Ibid*, at 146.
[34] *Ibid*, at 147.
[35] Hovencamp, n 3 above, at 35.
[36] See Schmalensee, R, 'Thoughts on the Chicago Legacy on Antitrust' in Pitofsky (ed), n 32 above, 11 at 15 ff for a good history of the debate.
[37] For the US position see *Sega Enterprises Ltd v Accolade Ltd* 977 F 2d 1510 (9th Cir 1992) at 1526; *Alcatel USA Inc v DGI Technologies Inc* 166 F 3d 772 (5th Cir 1999). (While both these cases involved leveraging and intellectual property rights, neither involved the direct application of antitrust law. *Sega* concerned the application of the fair use defence in copyright law and *Alcatel* was an abuse of copyright case.) Leverage analysis is part of Art 102 TFEU jurisprudence in the European Union. In some jurisdictions the possibility of successful leverage is acknowledged in the statutory language used. See Commerce Act 1986 (NZ), s 36(2); Competition and Consumer Act 2010 (Cth), s 46(1). Acceptance of the single monopoly profit theory inevitably carries with it acceptance of *per se* legality as the appropriate legal standard, see Elhauge, E, 'Tying, Bundled Discounts and the Death of the Single Monopoly Theory' (2009) 123 *Harvard Law Review* 397. This is not (or not yet) the law in any of the jurisdictions studied in this book.
[38] As to how a rule of reason analysis of leverage might be conducted in a particular case, see Lévêque, F, 'Innovation, Leveraging and Essential Facilities: Interoperability, Licensing and the EU Microsoft Case' in F Lévêque and HA Shelanski (eds), *Antitrust, Patents and Copyright: EU and US Perspectives* (Cheltenham, Edward Elgar, 2005).

would detract from the margin to be extracted by artificially restricting the supply of licences.[39] One should be wary of the fallacy of *requiring* a showing of leverage (and with it the presence of two markets) in refusals to license cases. This can encourage forensic gaming, by tempting parties to treat separate products as one for litigation purposes.[40]

(b) Leveraging as a condition precedent for regulatory intervention

A very different stance on leveraging is evidenced in later European cases on refusals to license.[41] Here both the existence (actual or hypothetical) of two markets and actual leveraging or attempted leveraging across them have to be demonstrated before the court or regulator will even begin to look behind the refusal. Not only is leveraging rational in this scenario, its exercise is a mandatory fetter on what the court or regulator can decide. This self-denying ordinance takes two forms. The first is jurisdictional, so that the regulator's scrutiny stops at the boundaries of the right and the right owner's powers are not interfered with (for example, the existence/exercise dichotomy that is a feature of much Article 101 and 102 TFEU jurisprudence[42]). The second response (and now the prevailing one under the exceptional circumstances test applied to these cases under Article 102 TFEU) is remedial. The refusal may be contested in exceptional circumstances, but any order made should not extend to allowing competitors to compete directly with the right holder in the upstream market, that is, the intellectual property right should be bypassed only to the extent necessary to ensure effective competition in the downstream market and in the downstream market alone.[43]

---

[39] See Crocioni, n 30 above, at 460; Rey, P and Tirole, J, 'A Primer on Foreclosure' in M Armstrong and R Porter (eds), *Handbook of Industrial Organisation*, vol III (Oxford, North Holland, 2007) at 2145–220.

[40] This process may be seen at work in the litigation arising from a consent decree under which Microsoft agreed to end certain volume discounts and, more importantly, not to tie the sales of other products to Windows 95: *United States v Microsoft Corporation* 158 FRD 318 (DDC 1995). The Justice Department alleged that by tying Internet Explorer to Windows, Microsoft had breached the consent order. Microsoft contended that there was no breach because Internet Explorer was not a stand-alone program but an integrated part of Windows, a contention which after an initial setback in the form of an interlocutory injunction (see *United States v Microsoft Corporation* 980 F Supp 537 (DDC 1997)) was upheld on appeal by the DC Circuit: 147 F 3d 935 (DC Cir 1998). See also the unsuccessful arguments advanced by Kodak in *Kodak I*, n 8 above.

[41] These cases are discussed in some detail in ch 6.

[42] The New Zealand statutory provisions may also be read as making this distinction, see discussion below at 7.3.3.

[43] Some pronouncements of European courts can be read more restrictively, so that the power to go behind the right may be exercised only to prevent complete foreclosure of the downstream market, hence the concern of the General Court in Euro *Microsoft*, n 6 above, that the source code not be disclosed in the course of Microsoft complying with the order to allow interoperability. See 6.7 below.

Both of these approaches are manifestations of the scope of grant theories. Empirical evidence to support them is lacking. They are purely black-letter attempts to limit what courts and regulators can do to interfere with intellectual property rights. They have no equivalents in the sphere of tangible property.

3.3.4 Special rules for special markets?

Another of the issues dividing law and economics scholars is whether the likelihood of acquiring or misusing market power is present to a greater or lesser degree in particular kinds of markets. The industries most commonly singled out for this bending (or even, it is sometimes suggested, abrogation) of rules previously regarded as being of general application tend to be those associated with the tendentiously named 'new', 'innovative' or 'emerging' economy[44] often built around the development and application of various kinds of digital technology. Interest in the supposed 'specialness' of these industries has in part been driven by the positions taken by Microsoft and its opponents in competition cases on both sides of the Atlantic over the last two decades.

How different in fact are these markets from other markets, and what implications might such a difference have for competition enforcement? The first of these questions is easy enough to answer. High-technology industries do have some distinguishing features. Choice, market differentiation and product function are apt to be more important than price in such markets,[45] and substitutability therefore correspondingly harder to pin down.[46] They are also often characterised by network effects,[47] whereby the value that individual consumers place on adopting or subscribing to a particular product or service increases commensurately with the number of consumers who adopt or subscribe to it. Network effects mean relatively high switching costs that can sometimes discourage consumers from embracing competing technology that they might in other

---

[44] A terminology that is already beginning to look rather dated and which begs more questions than it answers. Just how 'innovative' many Internet-based technologies really are remains open to debate.

[45] Hovencamp, n 3 above; Ramello, GB, 'Copyright and Antitrust Issues' in W Gordon and R Watt (eds), *The Economics of Copyright* (Cheltenham, Edward Elgar, 2003) 118 at 121.

[46] Ramello, n 45 above, at 124.

[47] This is the 'more the merrier' notion that technologies based on connectedness become increasingly more compelling and valuable as more and more people use them. See Eagles, I and Longdin, L, 'The Microsoft Appeal: Different Rules for Different Markets?' (2001) 7 *New Zealand Business Law Quarterly* 296 at 300; Katz, ML and Shapiro, C, 'Network Externalities, Competition and Compatibility' (1985) 75 *American Economic Review* 424; and Katz, ML and Shapiro, C, 'Systems Competition and Network Effects' (1994) 8 *Journal of Economic Perspective* 93 at 95.

circumstances find more technically useful and/or cost-effective.[48] The resultant tipping of the market in favour of the dominant firm can be both swift and total. This in turn can lead to a high degree of path dependence, under which inefficient products cannot easily be displaced by more efficient ones. (Particularly so, when a dominant player's standards have become de facto industry standards.[49])

Putting aside for the moment problems of proving that any of these things has occurred in a particular case (and such problems can be formidable[50]), how should competition policy react to these where they can be shown to exist? It is at this point that the economic consensus starts to fray, and fray badly. Three possible responses may be found in the literature (and to a much more limited extent in the decisions of those few courts and regulators who have had occasion to consider the problem). There are those who believe that high-technology markets are more likely to self-correct (and self-correct more quickly) than low-technology ones, thus both requiring less regulatory intervention in the first place and making such intervention more problematical if resorted to. Buttressing these views is the notion that market power is only a temporary phenomenon in these industries if the system itself can be bypassed.[51] Often accompanying these theories is the idea of an 'innovation market' that dwells on competition

---

[48] See Crocioni, n 30 above, at 471; and Arezzo, E, 'Intellectual property rights at the crossroad between monopolization and abuse of dominant position: American and European approaches compared' (2006) 24 *John Marshall Journal of Computer & Information Law* 455.

[49] Crocioni, n 30 above, at 451. This is simply a highly contextual application of the scale and reversibility principle discussed in ch 2. The risk of false negatives in such cases is correspondingly high. Despite his recognition of the importance of both factors in emerging markets, Crocioni nevertheless takes the view that the risks of over-regulation are escalated in such markets.

[50] Demonstrating that an alternative technology that consumers have not in fact taken up would have been more innovative than that actually adopted is never going to be easy. Neither does it follow that a technological improvement is always dynamically efficient. See Veljanovski, CG, 'Competition Law Issues in the Computer Industry: An Economist's Perspective' (2003) 3 *Queensland University of Technology Law and Justice Journal* 48; Liebowitz, SJ and Margolis, SE, *Winners, Losers and Microsoft: Competition and Antitrust in High Technology* (Oakland CA, Independent Institute, 1999) at 138.

[51] See McKenzie, R, *Trust on Trial: How the Microsoft Case is Reframing the Rules of Competition* (Cambridge MA, Perseus, 2000); Alborn, C, Evans DS and Padilla, AJ, 'Competition Policy in the New Economy: Is European Competition Law Up to the Challenge?' (2001) 22 *European Competition Law Review* 156; Newberg, JA, 'Antitrust for the Economy of Ideas: The Logic of Technology Markets' (2000) 14 *Harvard Journal of Law & Technology* 83; Minda, G, 'Antitrust Regulatability and the New Digital Economy: A Proposal for Integrating Hard and Soft Regulation' (2001) 46 *Antitrust Bulletin* 439; Elhauge, E, 'Defining Better Monopolisation Standards' (2003) 56 *Stanford Law Review* 253; Lind, RC and Muysert, P, 'Innovation and Competition Policy: Challenges for the New Millennium' (2003) 24 *European Competition Law Review* 87; Devlin, A, and Jacobs, MS, 'Microsoft's Five Fatal Flaws' (2009) *Columbia Business Law Review* 67. Some commentators also take the view that the standard SSNIP test for market definition will produce smaller product markets than they should when competition is performance- rather than price-based, as is often the case in high-technology markets. See Teece, D and Coleman, M, 'The Meaning of Monopoly' (1998) 43 *Antitrust Bulletin* 801 at 827.

between clusters of products grouped in rival systems rather than competition within a single product market.[52] Capturing the latter confers no market power. Holders of these views say path dependence can occur irrespective of any anti-competitive conduct on anyone's part. They also point out that awareness on the part of monopolists that loss of market share can be total if consumers do switch to another system in the future will act as a moderating influence on the pursuit of monopoly profits in the present.[53] Competition exists, these critics say, but it is *for* the market not *in* the market.[54]

Opponents of this way of thinking argue that high-technology markets need more regulation not less, because mistakes made now will not easily be undone later. These technoskeptics doubt the capacity of such markets to self-correct at all, much less self-correct quickly. They would also say, if an industry is truly dynamic, short-term and anti-competitive glitches may matter more.[55] Indeed the short nature of the advantage gained may provide dominant firms with an incentive to capture the upstream market before it tips.[56] In such cases competition regulators would be wise to focus on the state of affairs before the tipping innovation is brought to the market, rather than on post-innovation competition. Whichever of these competing viewpoints eventually succeeds in imposing itself on judges or regulators, it needs to be emphasised that neither of them depends on whether the technology in question is shored up by an intellectual property right. Nor are they predicated on a need to distinguish between refusals to deal and proactive tying or bundling.

Both sides in this debate ask valid and important questions of their opponents. Those questions cannot, however, be definitely answered in the absence of empirical evidence. Lacking such evidence, neither side can convincingly make a case that in technology-saturated industries the activities of dominant firms are presumptively good or bad in competition terms. Nor, indeed, could any such

---

[52] See Newberg, n 51 above; Gilbert, RJ and Sunshine, N, 'Incorporating Dynamic Efficiency Concerns in Merger Analysis: The Use of Innovation Markets' (1995) 63 *Antitrust Law Journal* 569. Such views push the evidentiary envelope. Systems competition can be a long way over the technological horizon when a competition problem first surfaces, and it is just as dangerous to conflate the possible and the probable in this context as in others.

[53] Veljanovski, n 50 above.

[54] These viewpoints are neither new nor necessarily related to high-technology industries, see Schumpeter, JA, *Capitalism, Socialism and Democracy* (London, Unwin University Books, 1942); Devlin and Jacobs, n 51 above.

[55] An early proponent of this view seemingly was the erstwhile European Union Competition Commissioner, M Monti, 'Competition and Information Technologies' in his address *Barriers in Cyberspace* (Brussels, Kangaroo Group, 18 September 2000), as noted in Veljanovski, C, 'EC Antitrust in the New Economy: Is the European Commissioner's View of the Network Economy Right?' (2001) 22 *European Competition Law Review* 115. Similar thinking appears to have been behind the approach taken by the DC Circuit in *United States v Microsoft Corporation* 253 F 3d 34 (DC Cir 2001) at para 20, that while the specific anti-competitive behaviour by Microsoft in the operating systems market might be rendered obsolete, this did not make it harmless.

[56] See Crocioni, n 30 above, at 469.

presumption be imposed in the absence of any agreed definition of what constitutes a new or emerging market. Nothing about these markets requires the abandonment of the ordinary techniques of antitrust analysis. Uncertainty and imprecision are a necessary, if regrettable, part of the rule of reason whether applied to the 'old' or the 'new' economy.[57]

There are, however, two aspects of technology-intensive industries which do merit further discussion. These are the opportunities for gaming provided by standard-setting activities, and attempts to regulate technological interoperability via intellectual property law thereby displacing the jurisdiction of competition authorities.

3.3.5 Standard setting and standard capture

It has been suggested that when an intellectual property right is allowed to act as a gateway to implementing an industry standard (allowing interoperability and compatibility between products from different suppliers[58]), its owners have been handed irreversible market power by the mere fact of their possession of that right. In the view of some commentators,[59] this means that once a particular technology is absorbed into a standard, competition from outside the standard can no longer happen. Others contend that such assumptions are based on static, simplistic, stand-alone models of how the interlocking intellectual property rights that together commonly comprise a standard interact with each other.[60] Moreover, the counter-argument continues, to make such an assumption about standard capture is to ignore the dynamic nature of standard setting in high-technology industries, where one standard tends to follows fast on the heels of another so that different intellectual property owners compete with each other for inclusion.[61]

---

[57] Pitofsky, R, 'Antitrust and Intellectual Property: Unresolved Issues at the Heart of the New Economy' (2001) 16 *Berkeley Technology Law Journal* 535.

[58] A standard for this purpose comprises a set of specifications providing a common design for a product or process, and often incorporates one or more intellectual property rights such as a patent, copyright or layout design for an integrated circuit.

[59] See Glader, M and Larsen, S, 'Excessive Pricing—An Outline of the Legal Principles Relating to Excessive Pricing and their Future Application in the Field of IP Right and Standard Setting' (2005) *Competition Law Insight* 3. See also Teece, D and Sherry, EF, 'Standards Setting and Antitrust' (2003) 87 *Minnesota Law Review* 1913 at 1929.

[60] Gerardin, D, 'Pricing Abuses by Essential Patent Holders in a Standard Setting Context' (2009) 76 *Antitrust Law Journal* 329.

[61] *Ibid*. The Hargreaves Report *Digital Opportunity: A Review of Intellectual Property and Growth* (May 2011), available at <www.ipo.gov.uk/ipreview-finalreport.pdf>, notes, at paras 6.17–6.18, that evidence suggests that in the computer technology and (mobile) telecoms industries, inventions are nearly always sequential, with innovation building cumulatively and collaboratively on previous inventions and innovations that have become standards, as opposed

Problems relating to standard setting and standard capture are not confined to discordant economics. Excessive compartmentalisation within individual competition regimes can also cause difficulties. A standard may act as a collective monopsony.[62] The process of competitors collaborating to forge a common technological platform may provide opportunity for collusion. Anti-competitive behaviour can also take place in relation to both setting and implementing the standard. A party may refuse to make intellectual property it already owns available to the standard setters, or may act as a 'patent troll', deliberately setting out to acquire patents or copyrights that are essential to the standard's functioning. Capture may be facilitated by a captor concealing or misrepresenting the existence or extent of its intellectual property rights tied up in the standard.[63] Once captured, the captor may refuse to license, license selectively or license on non-RAND[64] terms. If too rigid a regulatory line is drawn between these activities, outcomes could be perverse and gaming encouraged. Privileging either pre- or post-standard setting refusals to license, while punishing the act of acquisition or post-capture royalty setting, will only encourage parties to steer for the artificially safe harbours created by such privileges. Privileging unilateral bad behaviour over collective misbehaviour will have a similar effect.

3.3.6 Mandated interoperability[65]

There is no dispute that the ability of various software products in a system mutually to exchange information and interoperate with each other promotes incremental innovation, as well as exposing consumers/end-users to a wider choice of products. Indeed, in all our selected jurisdictions, copyright laws foster interoperability, either by allowing it under wide fair-dealing rules (as in the United States[66]) or by providing for a specific reverse engineering exception to owners' exclusive rights.[67] As the reverse engineering exception commonly operates, firm A may design a new product compatible with an existing product controlled by software owned by B, by first copying B's program in object or

to non-sequential, where a patent generally corresponds to a single product (as is more common in the drug and medical arena).

[62] See, eg, *Sony Electronics v Soundview Technologies* 157 F Supp 2d 180 (D Conn 2001).
[63] As in *Rambus v Federal Trade Commission* 522 F 3d 456 (DC Cir 2008). As it happened, Rambus's dishonest failure to reveal to a standard-setting group its own patented technologies while advocating them as a new chip standard was held to have been pointless as the standard would have been adopted anyway.
[64] See discussion at 3.7.4 below.
[65] Curley, D, 'Interoperability and Other Issues at the IP Antitrust Interface' (2008) 11 *Journal of World Intellectual Property* 296.
[66] 17 USC, § 107. *Sega Enterprises*, n 37 above.
[67] Eg, EU Member States must comply with the Directive on the Legal Protection of Computer Programs 91/250/EEC of 14 May 1991, [1991] OJ L122 in this regard.

machine code form in order to understand how it works and what is required to allow it to interact with other software. A will then not infringe B's copyright, provided it does not use a substantial amount of B's program in its own new, compatible product.

There are, however, three reasons why the reverse engineering exception under copyright law may not go very far to promote interoperability. First, some kinds of computer programs may enjoy dual protection under both patent and copyright law in some countries.[68] (Certainly, the quid pro quo for patent protection is full public disclosure of the ideas underlying patented products or processes, but registered provisional or final patent specifications may be deficient or even misleading by not providing crucial information.) Secondly, copyright holders sometimes use technological protection measures (TPMs) to lock up their programs so that they cannot be lawfully reverse engineered without breaking the lock to access them.[69] Thirdly, would-be second-comers sometimes require access to more information than just the object code owned by the first-comer in order to design an interoperable software product. The partial and incomplete allowance for interoperability under some intellectual property statutes should not be able to displace the jurisdiction of competition authorities.[70]

3.4 EFFICIENCY AND CONSUMERS: CENTRE STAGE OR AT THE MARGINS?

Debates between competing schools of economics often centre on the place of efficiency and consumer welfare in setting competition policy. For enforcement agencies and policy makers, these intra-mural disputes within the economics profession pose practical as well as theoretical questions: How can economists' definitions of efficiency and consumer welfare be converted into legal terms of art? Are these concepts appropriate surrogates for the existence or absence of

---

[68] In contrast to the situation in the United States and Japan, the European Patent Commission restricts the extent to which computer programs may be patented. Only programs able to make a 'technical contribution', such as controlling a robot, can be patented. General applications, such as improved word processing programs, may not be.

[69] While it is true that paracopyright laws may provide that lock breaking can be done to allow for lawful fair use or dealing with a work, the procedure for would-be second-comers may be potentially complex and time-consuming. See, eg, Copyright Act 1994 (NZ), s 226D(3), allowing persons who have asked for and been denied access to a computer program or other copyrighted work protected by a TPM to engage (after a *reasonable* time has passed since the request for access was denied) a qualified person to exercise their lawful rights on their behalf using a TPM circumvention device.

[70] That said, the General Court's attitude would have been very different in Euro *Microsoft*, n 6 above, had access been sought by Sun Microsystems to the underlying source code in Microsoft's software in order to replicate Microsoft's products rather than interoperate with them (see Euro *Microsoft, ibid*, at para 206).

competition? Should they be exculpatory or inculpatory in their effect? Are they regulatory goals in their own right? Not surprisingly, different jurisdictions give different answers to these questions, when they bother to answer them at all.

3.4.1 Efficiency: goal or fall-back defence?

In none of the jurisdictions surveyed in this book do courts unequivocally embrace efficiency as the sole goal of competition policy. Sometimes this is because the relevant legislation lays down broad statutory objectives that by implication exclude efficiency. In other cases, the statute recognises the importance of efficiency as a concept but grants it only a limited ex post facto role after anti-competitive purpose or outcome has been proven by other means (the so-called 'efficiency' defence in Canadian law and administrative authorisation of otherwise unlawful practices in New Zealand). Courts have generally been more reticent than regulators in giving efficiency a role in the absence of a legislative prompt in Europe and the United States.[71]

3.4.2 The three faces of efficiency

If economic efficiency were indeed to become the core concept of competition law, it would be a remarkably elusive one both in theoretical and empirical terms. Market behaviour is efficient in the broadest sense when it allows firms to achieve more or better outputs with the same or cheaper inputs.[72] A definition so wide, while it might attract universal approbation, is unlikely to be immediately useful, especially in the cut and thrust of antitrust litigation. Economists have therefore sought to put analytical flesh on these bare definitional bones by positing three types of economic efficiency: allocative, productive and innovative.

Allocative efficiency exists where goods and services find their way to those consumers who value them most, as evidenced by a willingness to pay more or forgo other forms of consumption. *Innovative* efficiency is achieved when new products and technologies are spread throughout the economy in wealth-creating ways.[73] *Productive* efficiency is found whenever goods and services are made available using the most cost-effective inputs and processes available under

---

[71] See, eg, the European Commission's *Guidance on the Commission's Enforcement Priorities in Applying [Article 102 TFEU] to Abusive Exclusionary Conduct by Dominant Undertakings* (the '*Guidance Communication*') [2009] OJ C-45/7.

[72] Professor Brodley defines efficiency as events or decisions that increase 'the total value of economically measurable assets in society': Brodley, JF, 'The Economic Goals of Antitrust: Efficiency, Welfare and Technological Progress' (1987) 62 *New York University Law Review* 1020 at 1025.

[73] *Ibid.*

current technology. While each of the trinity has its own sect of economic believers, courts and competition regulators wisely refuse to elevate any one form of efficiency over the others. Of the three, only allocative and innovative efficiency can easily be brought to bear on refusals to license situations, and even these two do not point unerringly in a single direction.

While it might be thought that innovative efficiency should have automatic primacy when intellectual property rights enter the competition equation, this is far from being the case. Innovative efficiency is loved by all but measured by few. Indeed, it is all but unmeasurable. Thus, while one might not agree with the Chicago view that allocative efficiency is the one that matters most, it is a perspective likely to win by default in a measurement vacuum. Innovative efficiency is, on this view, a by-product rather than a catalyst. Get allocative efficiency right and innovative efficiency will follow. Innovation and technological progress are best assured by marshalling capital and encouraging it to invest in innovation.[74] Broad intellectual property rights do this by pulling investment into as many derivative niches as a particular intellectual property right will stand. They are therefore to be applauded rather than feared or decried.[75] Such an approach is far too simplistic, say others. Not all innovation can be assumed to be efficient. Change and novelty are not economic objectives in themselves. Efficiency gains cannot simply be equated with the breadth and longevity of a particular piece of intellectual property, still less with the owner's assessment of its value or the cost of developing the technology which it protects. Indeed, if investment displacement theory is to be believed, over-extended intellectual property rights are themselves allocatively inefficient if they attract investors who would otherwise put their money elsewhere. Similarly, the encouraging of investment by first-comers at the expense of investment in downstream innovation and creativity is not easy to justify on the grounds of either innovative or allocative efficiency.

3.4.3 Whose welfare matters?

'Consumer welfare' has been described as the 'most abused term in modern economic analysis',[76] and yet few would deny its centrality to the setting and implementation of an economically rational competition policy. To a non-economist, consumer welfare might seem to be useful shorthand for 'anything that makes consumers better off'. For economists, however, there are three other,

---

[74] Schumpeter, n 54 above, at 83 and 89.
[75] Allocative efficiency has a muscular clarity which makes it hugely attractive to Chicago thinkers. The clarity of the model, indeed its very ability to be quantified, conceals the usual empirical hole. Deadweight loss is enticingly easy to represent by graphs. This does not necessarily make it easier to isolate and measure in the real world.
[76] Brodley, n 72 above, at 1032.

more targeted concepts wrapped up in this somewhat anodyne phrase: consumer surplus, producer surplus and total surplus[77] (the last being usually defined as the sum of the previous two). Of the three, total surplus would seem on the face of it to be more important in setting regulatory goals than benefits adhering to consumers or producers alone. Unfortunately for the internal coherence of competition regimes, total surplus is not a banner under which economists find it easy to rally.

On this issue, economists divide into two broad camps: those who would treat gains to consumers as incidental side-effects of pursuing efficiency objectives (hoped-for outcomes but not necessary to the policy); and those for whom the fostering of consumer surpluses is the end to which competition law should work and which would thus become frankly redistributive in its effect.[78] Members of the first camp justify reference to the term 'consumer welfare' by using a mixture of inductive and deductive reasoning. The logical chain[79] unfolds as follows: All producers are also consumers of something. Benefits to producers are therefore beneficial to some consumers. End consumer A is not inherently more worthy than intermediate consumer B (or as they would put it, a dollar in the hand of a producer is no less important to the economy than a dollar in the hand of a consumer). Even if this were not the case, consumers can still benefit collaterally because they are part of the wider economy in which producer profits are spent (the 'rising tide lifts all boats' argument). Efficiencies which are captured by producers will therefore benefit end-users even if the price they pay for what the producers produce does not fall. Consumers also benefit when producers reinvest their profits in new or improved goods or services. Both productive and innovative efficiency are thus served.

Economists in the other camp would say that there is too much 'might happen' in this analysis for all the links in the chain to bear the weight applied to them without snapping.[80] Better to focus only on those productive efficiencies that translate into lower prices for end-users, since these are at least measurable.

---

[77] Even then things are not so simple. Some scholars distinguish between total welfare *before* market power is acquired and total welfare afterwards. Efficiencies lost in the race to acquire market power have to be factored into the equation. See Elhauge (2009), n 37 above, 399; and Elhauge (2010), n 12 above, at 167.

[78] Lianos, I, 'Lost in Translation? Towards a Theory of Economic Transplants' (2009) 62 *Current Legal Problems* 346 at 390.

[79] This chop logic chain comes in handy when seeking to read down statutory language which, on its face, appears to give primary importance to consumer interests.

[80] Embracing consuming surplus as the appropriate measure does not have to mean the espousal of redistributory objectives (although this occurs in some cases). Redistributive outcomes, even when desired, are notoriously difficult to predict. There is also the inconvenient fact that some consumers are well-off while others are not. (The same, of course, applies to producers, but this does not matter to supporters of producer surplus standards since they would reject redistributive objectives from the outset.)

Producer gains are thus relevant only to the extent they are passed on. Consumer surplus and consumer welfare are therefore the same thing.[81]

There is an artificial rigidity to both of the above viewpoints. Both are vague as to the time period in which gains and losses to various groups are to be accessed. A more nuanced view would balance short-term losses by consumers against longer-term expenditures by producers on research and development (while, it is hoped, at the same time, not losing sight of the fact that such expenditure neither guarantees successful innovation nor measures innovative efficiency).[82] Conversely, one could accept that there might be cases in which total welfare increased even though efficiency savings were not immediately passed on to end-users, although in such cases one should be alive to the possibility that efficiency gains that are not passed on may not endure for any length of time.

The consumer–producer tug of war is really just a backhanded way of trying to rank competing efficiencies on the basis of a priori assumptions. This personalisation of competition objectives is particularly unhelpful in the context of refusals to license intellectual property, where innovation builds on innovation in a way that makes it difficult, if not impossible, to distinguish 'producer' from 'consumer', still less to allocate even notional surpluses to either of them. Nor is it easy to measure hypothetical gains and losses to consumers where a downstream market fails to emerge at all because of the existence of an intellectual property right.

Faced with these uncertainties, it is scarcely surprising that judges and regulators would want to fudge the choices being made. One way is to play with the definition of 'consumer' so that it embraces intermediate or downstream producers.[83] Another is to downgrade the significance of harm to consumers to a mere enforcement priority, rather than treating it as proof of anti-competitive effect in its own right.[84] A third way is to distinguish between consumers within the jurisdiction and those outside it. (Legislatures are sometimes obligingly enabling here.)

---

[81] Consumers can of course capture producer gains themselves even without regulatory assistance, as in the case of a buyer cartel or monopsony.

[82] See Lévêque, n 38 above, at 116.

[83] See, eg, the expanded definition of 'consumer' in the *Guidance Communication*, n 71 above, at para 19, fn 2, encompassing 'all direct or indirect users of the products affected by the conduct, including intermediate producers that use the products as an input, as well as distributors and final consumers both of the immediate product and of products provided by intermediate producers'. Cf the decision (involving Art 81 EC/101 TFEU) of the General Court in Joined Cases T-213/01 and T-214/01 *Österreichische Postsparkasse AG and Bank für Arbeit and Wirtschaft AG v European Commission* [2006] ECR II-1601, para 115, where the emphasis was on end-users.

[84] *Österreichische Postsparkasse*, n 83 above, para 115.

3.5 PROBABILITY, INTENT AND OUTCOME

Most competition regimes give a role in competition enforcement both to anti-competitive intent (or purpose) and anti-competitive outcome (or effect). The relationship between the two is seldom straightforward, however. Sometimes the competition statute will make anti-competitive intent a head of liability in itself. More often the legislative provision is ambiguous, leaving it open for courts to find that intent and outcome are both inculpatory, or that only the latter is. Another response is to simply run the two together so that proof of malign intent also establishes probable anti-competitive outcome.[85] Something similar happens (albeit in reverse) when anti-competitive intent is not established by direct evidence of a party's state of mind but inferred from 'objective' external circumstances.[86]

Neither 'intent' nor 'effect' defines itself. Effect on whom (consumers, producers, or both)?[87] Intent to do what? How is one to treat an anti-competitive purpose that turns out with hindsight to have been unachievable? Even when the legislature descends to some level of detail in proscribing particular anti-competitive purposes, as is the case in the Australian and New Zealand statutes, misuse of market power provisions can allow effects in by the back door by requiring a causal link between possession of market power and its use for those proscribed purposes.[88] 'Effect' will generally embrace both actual outcomes and foreseen ones. The degree of likelihood will be left to the court to establish in particular cases.

Thus far, we have been dealing with the situation where intent is a substantive liability trigger in its own right. Another way of feeding intent into judicial decision making is to give it an evidentiary role in rebutting objective justifications and legitimate business explanations put forward by the party whose conduct is under investigation. Something similar happens when anti-competitive intent is used to negate a presumption of legality.

The notion that intent can be a guide to outcome is far from commanding universal acceptance. Several commentators[89] have warned of the danger that generalist judges, unaccustomed to dealing with sophisticated economic evidence used to demonstrate the likely economic effect of a practice under investigation,

---

[85] See, eg, the decision of the General Court in Case T-203/01 *Michelin v European Commission* [2003] ECR II-4071. For a European perspective on intent see Akman, n 16 above, at 76.

[86] *Port Nelson Ltd v Commerce Commission* [1996] 3 NZLR 554.

[87] Attempts to depersonalise the problem by talking about the 'effect' on the 'market' are really a way of describing the effect on total welfare. Either that, or such attempts embrace a structural analysis of competitive conditions that many economists would now reject.

[88] See discussion at 7.2.3 below.

[89] See, eg, Manne, GA and Wright, JD, 'Innovation and the Limits of Antitrust' (2010) 6 *Journal of Competition Law and Economics* 153 at 200.

may be lured into relying on 'superficially intuitive intent evidence'[90] as a proxy. The issue has been explored in some depth by Professor Areeda,[91] who advocated that courts 'refuse to consider intent, unless the party relying upon it gives the tribunal reason to believe that his evidence is unusually probative'.[92] The problem is, of course, that evidence of effect (especially effect *in futuro*) is equally unlikely to be probative. The conflation of the possible and the probable that economic modelling encourages can be enticing to economically unformed judicial minds. Without case-specific empirical backing, such modelling is not obviously more reliable than a leap from intent to outcome.

3.6 THE UNCERTAIN ROLE OF BARRIERS TO ENTRY IN COMPETITION ANALYSIS

As competition law moves away from structural analysis towards a more conduct-based approach, the concept of a barrier to entry or exit assumes an increasing importance. There is little agreement, however, on what such a barrier might be and how it might work.[93] In a perfectly contestable market none of this would matter, because both entry and exit would be equally costless. Firms could enter the market easily and stay there for long enough to moderate the incumbent's behaviour. Entry costs would be recoverable on exit (that is, no costs would be sunk). Inefficient behaviour by the incumbent would precipitate entry by more efficient rivals. That entry is difficult to achieve, and a foothold difficult to sustain post-entry, simply proves that the entrant is less efficient than the incumbent. Markets are inert and entrants will be able to establish themselves before incumbents can respond. That none of these conditions exists in the real world most economists would now concede. Perfect contestability is just as much a mirage as perfect competition. This still leaves plenty of room for disagreement as to just how far real-life conditions can fall short of this unreal perfection before regulatory intervention is required. That disagreement may be presented schematically thus:

---

[90] Ibid.
[91] See Areeda, P and Turner, DF, 'Predatory Pricing and Practices under Section 2 of the Sherman Act' (1975) 88 *Harvard Law Review* 697; Areeda, P, 'Predatory Pricing' (1981) 49 *Antitrust Law Journal* 897.
[92] Areeda (1981), n 91 above, at 899–90.
[93] For an overview of the various theories, see Mialon, HM and Williams, M, 'What is a Barrier to Entry?' (2004) 94 *American Economic Review* 461. The underlying reasons for these disputes are admirably set out in Lianos, n 78 above, at 395.

3.6.1 Measurement or categorisation

Broadly speaking, economists tend to approach the problem of barriers to entry in one of two ways. There are those who see their task as simple measurement in which all costs count. We can call them *quantifiers*. Others would exclude certain types of costs from the equation before any measurement takes place. They might therefore be described (although they do not so describe themselves) as *categorisers*. The grounds on which particular costs are excluded from the analysis vary, however. Some seek to argue that lawfully-obtained economic advantages gained in the course of legitimate competition cannot be barriers at all.[94] Quantifiers, on the other hand, would say that competitive past virtue does not rule out present anti-competitive vice. The nature of this dispute is perhaps best encapsulated in the arguments over the role of Microsoft's Windows Operating System in the United States *Microsoft* litigation.[95] Microsoft sought to argue that what might seem at first blush to be a barrier to entry was no such thing but merely a reflection of consumer preference for a better product. The DC Circuit dismissed such arguments as irrelevant, saying[96]:

> It is certainly true that Windows may have gained its initial dominance in the operating systems market competitively—through superior foresight or quality. But this case is not about Microsoft's initial acquisition of monopoly power. It is about Microsoft's effort to maintain this position through means other than competition on the merits. Because the applications barrier to entry protects a dominant operating system irrespective of quality, it gives Microsoft power to stave off even superior new rivals. The barrier is thus a characteristic of the operating systems market, not of Microsoft's popularity, or as asserted by a Microsoft witness, the company's efficiency.

Other groups of economists take up the cudgel on what might be termed 'cost equality' arguments, that costs of a kind faced by anyone entering a given market can never be barriers. Only costs which are unique to new entrants count. Hurdles already faced and successfully surmounted by the now dominant incumbent do not.[97] For quantifiers, this distinction is neither theoretically sound nor workable.[98] Here again, the US *Microsoft* litigation is a case in point. Microsoft

---

[94] Evans, DS, Nichols, AL and Schmalensee, R, 'An Analysis of the Government's Case in *Microsoft*' (2001) 46 *Antitrust Bulletin* 163.
[95] *US v Microsoft* (2001), n 55 above, at 56.
[96] Ibid.
[97] Demsetz, H, 'Barriers to Entry' (1982) 72 *American Economic Review* 47; Stigler, G, *The Organisation of Industry* (Chicago, University of Chicago Press, 1968) at 67; Schmalensee, R, 'Ease of Entry: Has the Concept Been Applied Too Readily?' (1987) 56 *Antitrust Law Journal* 41; von Weizsacker, C, 'A Welfare Analysis of Barriers to Entry' (1980) 11 *Bell Journal of Economics* 399 at 400; Evans *et al*, n 94 above, at 196. This perspective also has its judicial supporters: see *LA Land Co v Brunswick Corp* 6 F 3d 1422 (9th Cir 1993) at 1427–28.
[98] Areeda, P and Hovencamp, H, *Antitrust Law: An Analysis of Antitrust Principles and Their Application* (Boston MA, Aspen Publishers, 1995) at para 420c; Weiss, LW, 'The Structure-Conduct Performance Paradigm and Antitrust' (1969) 127 *University of Pennsylvania* Law

had sought to enlist the aid of the 'cost equality' school by pointing to the large amounts it had to spend to convince software developers to write applications for the first version of Windows, and its continuing need to promote this and later versions. These are things any entrant would have to do, it said, and argued it should not be penalised for doing them. The court, however, impliedly endorsed the quantifiers, explaining[99] that when Microsoft entered the operating system market with MS-DOS and the first version of Windows[100]:

> [I]t did not confront a dominant rival operating system with as massive an installed base and as vast an existing array of applications as the Windows operating systems have since enjoyed.

The court went on to point out that because of this first-mover advantage, upgrading each new version of Windows was much less costly than for other entrants who could not freely include APIs from the incumbent Windows with their own.[101]

3.6.2 Structural versus strategic barriers

A rather more knotty dispute between economists revolves around the difference between structural and strategic barriers. Can the incumbent's own actions constitute a barrier? Courts in several jurisdictions have answered 'Yes'.[102] This puts them at odds with those law and economics scholars who would deny that market players can themselves ever construct barriers to entry. Such barriers, the latter say, can only be found in legal or economic facts beyond the incumbent's control.[103] There is, after all, a certain circularity about the idea of a strategic barrier. If the presence of a barrier is one of the tests for market power, what is one to make of a barrier that requires market power to erect it?

Review 1104 at 1119 ff; Bain, J, *Barriers to New Competition: Their Character and Consequences in Manufacturing Incentives* (Boston MA, Harvard University Press, 1956).

[99] *US v Microsoft* (2001), n 55 above, at 56.
[100] *United States v Microsoft Corporation*, 84 F Supp 2d 9 (DDC 1999) at 21 and *US v Microsoft* (2001), n 55 above at 56.
[101] *Ibid.*
[102] *US v Microsoft* (2001), n 55 above; *Queensland Wire Industries Pty Ltd v Broken Hill Pty Co Ltd* ('*Star Picket Fence Post* case') [1989] HCA 6, (1989) 167 CLR 177; Case 27/76 *United Brands v European Commission* [1978] ECR 207; and Case T-203/01 *Michelin v European Commission* [2003] ECR II-4071.
[103] Bork, n 27 above, at 240 and 259. Other commentators, while accepting the theoretical possibility of defendant-built (or heightened) barriers, would rule out certain forms of conduct (eg, tying with the intent to face would-be entrants with the prospect of entering more than one market) as barriers altogether: see Landis, RC and Rolfe, RS, 'Market Conduct Under Section 2: When Is It Anti-Competitive?' in FM Fisher (ed), *Antitrust and Regulation: Essays in Memory of John T McGowan* (Cambridge MA, MIT Press, 1985) at 135. Despite accusations of circularity, the concept of a 'behavioural barrier' seems to have taken root in European competition law: *United Brands*, n 102 above; *Michelin*, n 102 above.

3.7 THE EVER-RECEDING PERFECT REMEDY

In competition cases remedial issues not uncommonly overshadow issues of substantive liability, and nowhere is this phenomenon more evident than when courts and regulators are dealing with a refusal to license. Matching remedy to wrong is never easy in this context, and regulators are wise to proceed with caution when mandating access to complex technology backed by interlocking intellectual property rights. Caution is one thing, however, timidity another. Once liability is established, some kind of remedy has to follow. Doing nothing is not an option. Neither is reasoning backwards from remedy to breach. The two stages are distinct and should remain so. Since a remedy has to happen, predictions of the inevitability of remedial failure to be found in some of the commentary are less than helpful. Certainly, remedies have to be carefully crafted and their efficacy judiciously tested against past application and likely future outcomes, but this can all too easily slide over into a defeatist mindset in which nothing ever works and where every available remedy except the most ineffectual is endlessly weighed and found wanting. In this remedial dystopia behavioural remedies are self-defeating and unworkable, and structural remedies are unthinkable ultimate deterrents whose off-stage existence is thought sufficient to induce good behaviour without the need actually to apply them even as last resorts. Given that the economics of innovation is both disputed and empirically under-investigated, we should not be surprised that coerced licensing of intellectual property should provide particularly fertile ground for this kind of remedial Jeremiad. This is not to deny that there may sometimes be real obstacles to effective remedial action in a specific case, and these should not be downplayed where they can be shown to exist. Equally, though, it needs to be recognised that remedies cannot be endlessly fine-tuned and that the search for absolute remedial perfection is, in the end, illusory.

Even when a more considered approach to these problems is attempted, it will often be brought down by rigid categorisation of the roles played by particular remedies or the presence of gaps in a jurisdiction's remedial armoury and lack of flexibility in the remedy devised. Courts and regulators must do their best with whatever remedies are available to them.[104] That best, however, should be judged by the ability of those remedies to deter future bad behaviour rather than artificial assessments of their efficacy once past bad behaviour has permanently diverted competitors' energies elsewhere. This is turn necessitates recognition of

---

[104] A point long recognised in other areas of law and well demonstrated by the case of *Chaplin v Hicks* [1911] 2 KB 786, in which the tribunal of fact (in those days a jury) could not avoid the difficult task of quantifying as best it could the loss flowing from the loss of a chance to compete effectively for a limited number of acting positions. The court's reasoning is also interesting for the clear distinction it makes between quantification and breach: *ibid*, at 792 and 795.

the relationship between structural and behavioural remedies as being symbiotic rather than oppositional.

3.7.1 Remedial objectives in competition cases

Remedies in competition proceedings have a dual role. The first is to repair damage to competitive markets caused by the defendant's behaviour. The second is to deter future bad behaviour by the defendant or those who might be inclined to act in a similarly anti-competitive way.[105] Both objectives are equally important as competition law goals. Market repair is not to be automatically elevated over deterrence or vice versa; and while the weight given to each may not always be the same, both factors will often be present in a given case. It also needs to be remembered that the legal *form* of a remedy is not determinative of *function*. The same remedy may have both a deterrent and a market repair role to play. Thus while individual legal systems may classify a particular monetary remedy as compensatory, restitutionary or exemplary, these are classifications forged in a private law context to serve a private law purpose and should not be allowed to detract from specific regulatory objectives in what is after all a public law arena.[106] Similarly, the visible pain that attends compliance with behavioural remedies or forced restructuring can have a deterrent as well as a restorative effect.

3.7.2 Structural remedies: nuclear deterrent or conventional weapon?

There is a brutal simplicity about structural solutions to the remedial dilemma that both attracts and alarms. At first blush, divestiture of assets and corporate restructuring brings with it (or at least appears to bring with it) none of the supervisory problems attached to the behavioural remedies explored below. The surgery may be complex, but once done the surgeon is unlikely to be called upon again (or so it is thought). However, restructuring any major corporate entity in a market economy carries with it an emotional charge akin to that experienced when a major industry or firm is nationalised. More prosaically, the effect of splitting up an undertaking and hiving off parts of it is thought to have a

---

[105] Both market repair and deterrence may be further subdivided. See Melamed, AD, '*Afterword: The Purposes of Antitrust Remedies*' (2009) 76 *Antitrust Law Journal* 359.

[106] This is perhaps more easily seen in jurisdictions such as Australia that relax standing requirements for injunctive relief, see Competition and Consumer Act 2010 (Cth), s 80; and *R v Federal Court of Australia; ex p Pilkington ACI (Operations) Pty Ltd* [1978] HCA 60, (1978) 142 CLR 113 at 131.

thoroughly inimical effect on investors and the stability of capital markets in general, all the more so if restructuring does not work as planned.

Attitudes to structural remedies vary considerably across jurisdictions. They have been applied often enough in the United States to provide an empirical base for testing their efficacy. American law and economics scholars are nevertheless divided on the subject. For some, structural remedies have been shown to work, if not always and seldom perfectly. For others, the self-same historical record demonstrates that structural remedies are seldom effective in increasing competition or reducing prices to consumers.[107] Judicial responses have also been mixed. Certainly courts are more likely to order restructuring and divestiture in cases where the dominant firm acquired its dominance through merger, but examples can be found of structural relief being ordered or agreed to even where the offending firm obtained its current market position entirely through internal growth.[108] What does seem clear, however, is that the enthusiasm for structural remedies on the part of judges in the United States has dwindled over time. Whether this is because of the supposed logistical difficulties attached to splitting a corporate which has always been united in its structure (a matter of some concern to the United States District Court Circuit of Appeals in *Microsoft*,[109] for example), or whether this reflects the anti-competitive manner in which market power was acquired in the first place (a separate head of liability under section 2 of the Sherman Act) is not always made clear.

Doubts have also been expressed by some economists as to the long-term effectiveness of some of the structural remedies awarded in an earlier era in the United States, either because the anti-competitive behaviour thought to have been corrected by divestiture has resurfaced in another form or because the improvement in competitive conditions attributed to the court order would have happened anyway[110] due to changed market conditions unknown to (and probably unknowable by) the restructuring court at the time the restructuring order was made. Other critics, while conceding that restructuring is appropriate, think

---

[107] Crandall, RW, 'The Failure of Remedies in Sherman Act Monopolisation Cases' (2001) 80 *Oregon Law Review* 109.

[108] See Crandall, *ibid*, for a discussion of several early cases, including *United States v Kansas City Star Co* 240 F 2d 643 (8th Cir 1957).

[109] *US v Microsoft* (2001), n 55 above, at 65. The Court's observations on this subject lose some force by being couched in terms of heavy (but still formally hands-off) hints to a retrial court rather than propositions of law. If the observations were allowed to harden into rules, they hold out the prospect to potentially dominant firms of restructuring themselves in an outwardly unitary form to limit any antitrust fallout, thereby provoking on a much wider scale those very organisational distortions which led the DC Circuit to counsel against divestiture in the first place.

[110] Crandall, n 107 above, at 115. The same criticisms can of course be levelled at behavioural orders.

that the court has done its slicing the wrong way (or if the right way, incompletely).[111] A further off-putting aspect of structural remedies is that they offer few opportunities for second thoughts. If slicing up a corporate is calculated to alarm investors, re-slicing it at some future date in a different way will frighten them even more, and of course reconstituting it is simply unthinkable. Thus, while there are in the United States cases of conduct remedies being replaced by structural ones if the former prove unworkable, the reverse process is unknown.

All of this is calculated to induce judges and enforcement agencies to view structural remedies as a poor second best to their behavioural cousins. In the United States this tends to be a matter of obliquely expressed judicial preference. In Europe, however, the preference is legislatively mandated so that structural remedies can only be imposed[112]

> where there is no equally effective behavioural remedy or where any equally effective behavioural remedy would be more burdensome for the undertaking concerned than the structural remedy.

While this limitation may be construed to make it less restrictive than its bald words might suggest,[113] this has to be balanced against additional requirements of a positive showing that the remedy would be effective in bringing the breach to an end[114] and that there is a risk of a lasting or ongoing infringement deriving from the way in which the undertaking is structured.[115]

In the other jurisdictions studied in this book, the availability of structural remedies is even more restricted. In Australia and New Zealand, while divestiture can be a condition of allowing a merger, it is inferentially excluded in other cases.[116]

---

[111] See Comanor, WS, 'The Problem of Remedy in Monopolisation Cases: The *Microsoft* Case as an Example' (2001) 46 *Antitrust Bulletin* 115 at 119–20; and Levinson, J, Romaine RC and Salop, SC, 'The Flawed Fragmentation Critique of Structural Remedies in the *Microsoft* Case' (2001) 46 *Antitrust Bulletin* 135 at 136. Cf Evans *et al*, n 94 above.

[112] See Council Regulation (EC) No 1/2003, [2003] OJ L1, Art 7(1).

[113] See Adam, M and Maier-Rigaud, F, 'The Law and Economics of Article 82 EC and the Commission's Guidance Paper on Exclusion' (2009) 1 *Journal of Competition Law* 131.

[114] This requirement applies to both structural and behavioural remedies. It thus represents a threshold, not a choice. The remedy may be forward- as well as backward-looking, directed at not only halting the infringing behaviour of the dominant firm but also at undoing any ongoing effects of that behaviour.

[115] This derives from the general requirement in European law that remedies shall be proportionate to breach. See Council Regulation (EC) No 1/2003 (OJ L1) Recital 12.

[116] While there exists in both Australia and New Zealand a seemingly open-ended power to make 'other orders' than those listed in the statute, this has never been used to craft a structural remedy: see ch 7. In Canada, structural remedies (such as divestitures) are the preferred form of remedy (especially in merger situations), largely because they require little or no ongoing monitoring. See Canadian Competition Bureau, *Information Bulletin on Merger Remedies in Canada* (22 September 2006), at <www.competitionbureau.gc.ca/eic/site/cb-bc.nsf/eng/02170.html>.

As with the idea of a hierarchy of rights,[117] or even a hierarchy of wrongs,[118] the notion of a hierarchy of remedies brings with it an immediate definitional problem. Coerced licensing is not usually seen as a structural remedy, but if what is to be licensed represents a major part of a dominant firm's assets then the ensuing licence is more akin to divestiture than anything else, or so it has been argued.[119]

If, for example, Microsoft had been required to license its source code either in the United States or the European Union litigation, this would be a structural remedy by any definition.[120] Parsing the degree of disclosure or the size of the royalty awarded to characterise the remedy as structural or behavioural seems more than usually unproductive, and yet some such effort cannot be avoided where, as in the European Union, the need to make the distinction is legislatively mandated. Even in those jurisdictions in which this is not the case, the line between conduct and structure needs constant patrolling. Examine many structural remedies and it will quickly be found that they need a great deal of behavioural propping up to make them work, if only to prevent the newly-restructured entities from rearranging their interactions in inventive ways to minimise the effect of the court's order.[121] Conversely, the ongoing failure of a conduct remedy may give courts misgivings as to its efficacy and prompt them to order divestiture several years down the track.[122] Either way, any conceptual barrier between the structural and the behavioural would appear to be distinctly permeable. The taxonomy is also arbitrary, especially where two markets are involved, as is often the case with refusals to license. Thus while a dominant firm could be restructured so that it no longer competed in the downstream market at all, this would make sense only where it operated directly (whether by itself or through subsidiaries) in that market. A series of discriminatory licences, on the other hand, would give a structural remedy nothing obvious on which to bite.

---

[117] See 1.5.5 above, and 4.5.2 and 4.3.4 below.
[118] Such as the notion that vertical dealings are less malign in competition terms than horizontal ones, or that single firm behaviour is less problematic than bilateral or multilateral arrangements.
[119] Werden, GJ, 'Remedies for Exclusionary Conduct Should Preserve the Competitive Process' (2009) 76 *Antitrust Law Journal* 65.
[120] Waller, SW, 'The Past, Present and Future of Monopolisation Remedies' (2009) 76 *Antitrust Law Journal* 11.
[121] See Crandall, n 107 above, at 158. Crandall points out, eg, that the US Supreme Court's preference for a structural over a behavioural remedy in *United States v Paramount Pictures* 334 US 131 (1942), because the latter would necessitate ongoing detailed supervision, quickly spawned a raft of new methods of distributing films, all of which ended up in frequent returns to the courtroom to match them against the order made. See also Eagles and Longdin, n 47 above, at 324.
[122] As occurred in *United States v United Shoe Machinery Corp* 391 US 244 (1968). Germane to the present discussion was the large number of patents for shoe machinery held by the defendant in that case, that taken together made entry by competitors difficult.

3.7.3 Judicial recoil from the role of quasi regulator

A consistent theme in judicial decisions concerning refusals to deal generally is a deeply-felt reluctance to being forced into the role of quasi regulator in industries where the technology is complex, pricing is opaque, and transfers between parent company and subsidiary the norm. Behavioural remedies requiring ongoing and detailed judicial supervision over extended periods of time (and lacking the pre-emptive disclosure powers and the array of employed experts that industry-specific regulators have at their disposal) are seen as particularly antithetical to the judicial role as commonly understood, not least by the judges themselves. Judicial distaste for ongoing supervisory roles is even more apparent when there is a 'real' industry regulator waiting in the wings who possesses precisely these attributes. In such cases, judges (particularly American judges,[123] but not only them[124]), while formally forced to concede that the general competition law has not been pre-empted de jure by the presence of an industry regulator, are happy enough to accept that result de facto by falling back on the discretionary nature of injunctive relief.[125]

Two questions arise here. How real are judicial fears of being sucked unwillingly into the role of quasi regulators, and how relevant are those fears to refusals to license intellectual property?[126] As to the first, it is often forgotten that judges are not flying solo in these cases. Enforcement agencies and private plaintiffs will be doing much of the heavy lifting once a broad scheme of injunctive relief is laid down. Seeing that the scheme is adhered to need not then involve departure from the court's adjudicative role. The process may also involve (jurisdictional limitations on sub-delegation permitting) court-appointed or court-approved entities to carry out the detailed task of monitoring compliance or costing access. Over-enthusiastic recourse to the court for guidance may also be curbed by a proper system of costs operating both pre- and post-judgment.[127] In many cases too, the court will be enforcing not its own decree but an agreed settlement in which the parties can adjust the supervisory regime subject to the court's overall control. In such cases the court can operate with a lighter touch.

---

[123] *Trinko*, n 5 above.
[124] *Telecom Corporation of NZ v Clear Communications* [1994] UKPC 36, [1995] 1 NZLR 385. See discussion of case at 7.2.3 below.
[125] In some jurisdictions the boundaries between the two parallel regulatory systems are adjusted by law to exclude the general competition regime in whole or in part.
[126] Interestingly, where alternatives across regimes exist they sometimes exclude intellectual property from their purview unless integral to the functioning of the infrastructure being directly regulated, eg, the Competition and Consumer Act 2010 (Aust), s 44B (see definition of 'service').
[127] In civil cases, persons injured by an antitrust infringement under the Sherman Act may recover trebled damages and litigation costs, including reasonable attorneys' fees; see 15 USC § 15.

Does any of this change when intellectual property enters the picture? Of course, as pointed out in chapter one, not all coerced licensing requires complex ongoing supervision, but that may also be true of coerced access to tangible infrastructure. Of much greater significance is the fact that there are no alternative regulators with wide supervisory powers waiting off-stage to be used, as an explanation for judicial non-intervention. Arguments that the system of permitted uses contained within each discrete intellectual property right can provide such a system of shadow regulation in themselves are really arguments that the limits of the intellectual property right should define the parameters of competition law's intervention and would, if accepted, be applicable to any form of property. Quite apart from the question of whether the shrinking internal limitations on the exercise of particular intellectual property rights are capable of acting as a counterweight to anti-competitive uses of the right in question, it is misleading to suggest that judges in ordinary infringement proceedings can conjure detailed supervisory mechanisms out of the courts' inherent discretionary powers (or, to look at it another way, if they can do such things, they can do them in competition cases as well).

Judges confronted with the issue of whether or not to coerce behaviour are faced with two conflicting counsels of perfection. The first is the principle that the party on whom the order is imposed should know exactly what it is that it is required to do,[128] a constraint that is usually interpreted as requiring that the order be detailed, lengthy and precise. The second widely-accepted desideratum is that the order be versatile enough to cope with attempts to evade it through any loophole in its wording, yet be flexible enough to respond to changed market conditions while it is in force.[129] What needs to be recognised is that there will always be a trade-off needing to be made between these two perfectly worthy objectives that represent both ends of a rather long spectrum. It is not a justification for abandoning the remedy entirely because both cannot be met in full.

3.7.4 Pricing coerced access

Of all the self-confessed supervisory inadequacies referred to in the preceding section, the one most keenly felt by judges relates to the problem of pricing access should they decide to order it. While most would agree that any licence should be on 'reasonable, and non-discriminatory terms' (RAND) or on 'fair, reasonable,

---

[128] See, eg, Case C-308/04 P *SGL Carbon AG v European Commission* [2006] ECR I-5977; *Hartford Empire Co v US* 323 US 386 (1945) at 410; and Joined Cases 92 & 93/87 *European Commission v French Republic* [1989] ECR 405 at para 22.

[129] The longer the duration of the order, the more acute this problem is thought to be: see Barnett, TO, 'Section 2 Remedies: What to do after Catching the Tiger by the Tail?' (2009) 76 *Antitrust Law Journal* 31.

and non-discriminatory terms' (FRAND),[130] formulae used in other legal contexts,[131] simply incorporating the chosen formula in the order does not set the access price, and the order will therefore usually contain a mechanism whereby the parties in effect bargain about the price to be set, with a fall-back process requiring a return to the court where such agreement is not forthcoming.[132] Only in the event that fall-back is activated will the court be confronted with the need to set the price directly.

Pricing difficulties are compounded when economists put forward by the parties offer the court competing methodologies[133] for determining 'competitive price' (that is, the price that would prevail absent the defendant's anti-competitive behaviour).[134] To avoid taking sides in this war of the experts, courts will often prefer to benchmark against real-world prices. But where to find those prices in the absence of market precedents?[135] The intellectual property denied may never have been previously licensed at all, or may have been licensed only to

---

[130] The two terms are generally interchangeable, with FRAND seemingly preferred more in Europe than in the United States. See Working Paper, Layne-Farrar, A, Padilla, AJ and Schmalensee, R, 'Pricing Patents for Licensing in Standard Setting Organisations: Making Sense of FRAND Commitments' (October 2006), at <http://econpapers.repec.org/paper/cprceprdp/6025.htm>.

[131] Standard-setting organisations invariably use the RAND or the FRAND formula. It is usually also the basis on which statutory schemes for collective licensing of copyright and performers' rights initially proceed. These schemes may be legislatively mandated in the copyright statute (as in the United Kingdom, Australia, New Zealand and Canada), or be judicially construed as in the United States, see *US v ASCAP* 981 F Supp 199 (SDNY 1997). Courts have also faced and resolved royalty pricing problems in patent cases (eg, *ebay v MercExchange* 547 US 388 (2006)).

[132] As occurred, eg, in the *Merck case* (Decision of 15 June 2005, Case A364, *Merck-Principi Attivi*, IAA Bulletin n 23/2005, p 7), in which the Italian Antitrust Authority *(Autorità Garante della Concorrenza e del Mercato)* ordered, by way of an interim measure, that the refusing party Merck must grant the refused party Dobfar a licence within seven days of a request from Dobfar, and in the absence of an agreement between the parties, the authority itself would determine the terms of the licence with the assistance of an independent expert.

[133] See, eg, the Working Paper by Layne-Farrar *et al*, n 130 above, in which the authors compare two potential economic models: the efficient component-pricing rule (ECPR) predicated on the economic concept of market competition; and the Shapley value method reliant on cooperative game theory models and social concepts for a fair division of rents. The authors suggest that while the two different methods suggest a similar benchmark for evaluating FRAND licences, they do so in ways that might appeal differently to courts and competition authorities in the US as opposed to Europe. In any event, they conclude that under any price-setting methodology, patents covering 'essential' technologies that make a greater contribution to the value of the standard and are without close substitutes before the standard gets adopted should receive higher royalty payments after the standard has been adopted.

[134] On point here is the *cri de coeur* of Mummery J in the appellate decision *Attheraces Ltd v British Horseracing Board Ltd* [2007] EWCA 38, acknowledging that the proceedings presented the trial judge (Etherton J) and his own court with a 'range of factual and legal problems of a kind which even specialist lawyers and economists regard as very difficult'. He pointed out (at [4]) that the law on abusive pricing practices is controversial, and that it is also immensely complex in practice to determine what is the appropriate price for access to an essential facility.

[135] Heiner, D, 'Single Conduct Remedies: Perspectives from the Defence' (2009) 75 *Antitrust Law Journal* 871 at 877, 879.

a subsidiary at a transfer price with one eye on the tax regime(s) applying to the transaction. Previous licensing arrangements with third parties may have been arrived at in the absence of competition, and thus run the risk of courts being led astray by a remedial variant of the Cellophane fallacy.[136] If the protected product or process has no substitute then there will simply be no 'competitive' price to refer to.[137]

That price setting will be imprecise in these circumstances is undeniable. But it is necessary to put this in context. Having the court set the price is something that only occurs where the RAND/FRAND formula produces no agreed licence fee. When this happens, uncertainty as to what the court might do has the attraction of concentrating the parties' minds wonderfully on the need to reach an agreement. In such circumstances, imprecision becomes a virtue not a vice.[138] The point could also be made that a simple but brutal solution to the difficulty of pricing access might be to make that access royalty-free, if not in the first instance then as a fall-back position where the parties fail to agree.[139] One should not assume either that courts will always be dealing with a clean slate when mandating access to a dominant firm's technology. In many cases there will be a history or pattern of abandoned past access which can provide a map to technological pathways and act as a guide to pricing.

3.7.5 Court-created supervisory structures: assisting whom—court or regulator?

Success in straddling the flexibility/certainty divide will depend in large part on how inventive judges and regulators are permitted (or permit themselves) to be in devising intermediate structures to supervise detailed compliance with their orders or with court-facilitated settlements. This in turn would enable these orders to be expressed in terms of outcomes rather than conduct. American practise is highly flexible in this regard. It is less so elsewhere. Contrast the use of compliance officers in implementing the agreed orders in the Unites States *Microsoft* litigation with the European Commission's abortive resort to monitoring trustees in its proceedings against Microsoft, the only aspect of the Commission's order struck down by the General Court. (Whether such inhibitions are

---

[136] *United States v E I du Pont de Nemours & Co* 351 US 377 (1956).

[137] Which is why third-party prices tend not to be taken into consideration in collective licensing regimes. See *ASCAP v Showtime/The Movie Channel* 912 F 2d 563 (2nd Cir 1990).

[138] A point perceptively made by Crane, DA, 'Bargaining in the Shadow of Rate Setting Courts' (2010) 76 *Antitrust Law Journal* 307.

[139] The option of royalty-free access cannot be ruled out, at least in the United States. See *United States v General Electric* 115 F Supp 835 (DNJ 1953) 843–44; *Hartford Empire*, n 128 above, and *United States v National Lead Co* 332 US 319 (1947), in which the Supreme Court held that the issue remained undecided. Ironically, entertainment licensing agencies sometimes use pricing uncertainties to argue for zero royalties.

due to a judicial concern with improper sub-delegation by an agency with limited powers, or to an unwillingness to stretch injunctive relief beyond its traditional equitable bounds, usually the case in Australia and New Zealand, need not concern us here.) The end result of jurisdictional limitations of this sort, by forcing courts and regulators to lace their orders with a mass of imperfectly predictive detail, will encourage defendants to hunt for loopholes in response. An effective regulatory regime would do neither.

3.7.6 Retrospective assessment of efficacy

One of the criticisms frequently made of courts' or regulators' remedial efforts after the *Microsoft* litigation had concluded in both the United States and Europe, is that their efforts to correct the effect of the defendant's behaviour do not seem to have attracted significant numbers of players into the now, it is hoped, competitive market. The fact that supply-side alternatives do not immediately spring into existence is assumed by critics of the remedy to reflect a lack of demand for the now unbundled product, or an inability on the part of the competitors to do anything with the know-how previously held back by the defendant but now freely available on payment[140] of a reasonable royalty. This just goes to show, they say, how pointless a mandated contractual remedy is in the first place, and how easily the judge's or regulator's solution can be bypassed by new technology unthinkable at the time proceedings were first instigated.[141]

Once again this all rather misses the point. Focusing only on curative aspects of an order, while ignoring its prophylactic effect, results in seeing only part of the picture. Heading off future problems is also a perfectly legitimate objective for what the conduct order is trying to achieve, and may sometimes have to be an overriding one. In pursuit of this objective, courts and enforcement agencies are entitled to restrain behaviour which is similar in kind to that proven against the defendant, or which can be fairly predicted from past conduct.[142] They are also entitled to view the dominant firm's behaviour globally and prohibit combinations of acts which, while perfectly lawful looked at individually, will prevent the market from being restored to competitive health if allowed to continue *en bloc*.[143] Indeed it is irrelevant (or should be) whether the future behaviour

---

[140] Page, WH, 'Mandatory Contracting Remedies in the American and European *Microsoft* Cases' (2009) 75 *Antitrust Law Journal* 787 at 792, 799 and 801.

[141] Hesse, RB, 'Section 2 Remedies and *US v Microsoft*: What is to be Learned?' (2009) 75 *Antitrust Law Journal* 847 at 868.

[142] *Zenith Radio Corp v Hazeltine Research Inc* 395 US 100 (1969) at 132.

[143] Eg, where a single firm engages in the deliberate aggregation of a 'killer patent portfolio', a group of patents assembled either through acquisition or pooling that becomes a greater obstacle to market entry than any single patent; see Kobak, JB, 'Antitrust Treatment of Refusals to License Intellectual Property' (2002) 22 *The Licensing Journal* 1 at 11.

enjoined is unlawful at all. These are arguments against conduct remedies in general. The aim of the remedial exercise is not just to open a path blocked by the defendant's anti-competitive behaviour but also to discourage the closing-off of similar paths in the future,[144] whether by the defendant or anyone else. Remedies must be able to look forward as well as backwards[145]; but the more they do the former, the more they will test the court's or enforcement agency's predictive powers. Painting with too broad a remedial brush will bring cries of oppression. Use too narrow a one and a retrospective charge of ineffectuality will follow, with all the smug certainty that hindsight brings.

A very real problem here is the sometimes very lengthy time lag in competition litigation, which can leave enforcement agencies, as Professor Elhauge puts it, 'in the position of trying to remedy a problem that once was real but now has become moot and perhaps replaced by a new one'.[146] The solution to this, however, surely lies in a less restrictive attitude to interlocutory relief than is currently the case in most jurisdictions.[147] If fairness to the defendant requires painstaking and hence time- and resource-consuming inquiries into what has occurred, fairness to plaintiffs and the public requires that they not be unnecessarily put at a disadvantage by the length of those same inquiries. It should also be borne in mind that too great an emphasis on the retrospective efficacy of conduct remedies will inevitably shift the focus of the decision maker towards disgorgement,[148] damages and fines or pecuniary penalties (where available), and it is desirable that this should be so.

3.7.7 Reasoning backward from remedy to breach

Thus far our discussion of unilateral abuses of market power has assumed that wrong and remedy are discrete constructs in which the former precedes the latter and is distinct from it.[149] Viewed in this way the task of the judge or regulator is

---

[144] *International Salt Co v United States* 332 US 392 (1947) at 400. See also *United States v Grinnell Corp* 384 US 563 (1966) at 579.

[145] Forward-looking remedies need to be matched with procedures that will allow the presentation and contesting of evidence as to the likelihood of collateral bad behaviour (ie conduct not directly reflecting the proven breach). Under the Antitrust Procedures and Penalties Act, 15 USC §16 (the so-called Tunney Act), a procedure is laid down that must be followed whenever the United States proposes to settle a civil antitrust suit by a consent decree. Members of the public have an opportunity to comment on the proposed settlement before it is accepted by the court. See also Page, n 140 above, at 803.

[146] Elhauge, E, 'Disgorgement as an Antitrust Remedy' (2009) 76 *Antitrust Law Journal* 79 on point citing *US v Microsoft* (2001), n 55 above, at 49.

[147] Prohibitive orders may be easier to obtain than mandatory ones at the interlocutory stage. See *Shepherd Homes Ltd v Sandham* [1971] 1 Ch 340 at 341.

[148] A point made by Elhauge, n 37 above.

[149] This neat ordering is of course irrelevant when a dominant firm's abuse of market power is used defensively against it in an action it brings for infringement against a party to whom the

first to find that a refusal to license is unlawful according to some pre-existing norm, and then to reach into the remedial tool kit to select the appropriate regulatory response from a similarly predetermined range of options. The contents of the tool kit will vary across jurisdictions but the mental sequencing is the same. This thoroughly Aristotelian world view[150] is the way in which most judges and competition agencies conceive their role in most jurisdictions most of the time.[151]

Sometimes, however, judges (and more often commentators) will turn this process on its head and seek to reason backwards from remedy to breach. Rallying under the rhetorical banner of 'if it can't be fixed, it ain't broke', defenders of this approach argue that the effectiveness or otherwise of the remedy sought is an appropriate guide to the strength or weakness of arguments (whether factual or legal is not made clear) put forward at the liability stage.[152] Negativity (or as they would say scepticism) about the remedy becomes negativity about the way in which substantive tests of liability are framed or applied.[153] The fundamental flaw at the heart of such arguments is perhaps best exposed by upending them so that the simpler and more easily applied the remedy, the greater the likelihood of an inculpatory finding on liability, a way of going about things that has yet to be taken up by any court in any jurisdiction and which appears to have no adherents anywhere in academia. The Legal Realists who are the (seldom acknowledged) progenitors of the reasoning-backwards perspective, would be indifferent as to whether the remedy was liability-enhancing or liability-restricting. A liability-enhancing outcome would of course sit uneasily

---

dominant firm has refused a licence. A finding of no infringement, while not a remedy in the technical sense, has the same result.

[150] In tracing the philosophical antecedents of this binary view of rights and remedies we have unashamedly drawn on the work of Professor Weinrib; see Weinrib, EJ, 'Two Conceptions of Remedies' in CER Rickett (ed), *Justifying Private Law Remedies* (Oxford, Hart Publishing, 2008) 3.

[151] This is not to deny that in the historical evolution of judge-made private law in common law systems the remedy sometimes emerged before the 'right' was clearly articulated, but this has no relevance where the 'right' is legislatively mandated as it is in all modern competition law regimes. The fact that the legislature may have painted with a very broad brush in defining the right, or that the court may use independently evolved equitable remedies to back up those laid down in the statute, does not mean the remedy can conjure the right into existence.

[152] The reasoning-backwards methodology seems to have been first articulated by Posner J in *Brunswick Corp v Riegel Textile Corp* 752 F 2d 261 (7th Cir 1985) at 267. Posner J, however, was using it in a very limited and idiosyncratic way. The case involved an attack under § 2 of the Sherman Act on a patent allegedly fraudulently obtained (and defended groundlessly in a patent-interference proceeding), in which the plaintiff sought to have the patent transferred to it. As Posner J pointed out, this would have produced no benefit to consumers as the patent would still be extant and the remedy, in the limited antitrust sense, pointless. Nothing in the case turned on the complexity of the remedy sought or the difficulty of administering it (indeed, in this case, the remedy sought could not have been more clear-cut).

[153] See Barnett, n 129 above. To be fair, this view falls some way short of the extreme Realist position: that legal rules are simply empty shells waiting to be filled by the appropriate remedy. See Posner, RA, *Antitrust Law*, 2nd edn (Chicago, University of Chicago Press, 2001) at 273.

with the preference for false negatives over false positives often espoused by the very commentators seeking to reason backwards from remedy to right. Again, reasoning backwards makes sense, if it makes sense at all, only in relation to conduct remedies aimed at changing the defendant's behaviour. Fines, penalties and treble damages may not be able to fix what is broken but they can reduce the likelihood of future breakages. Does this tell us anything useful about substantive liability where they are the only remedies sought? Should liability outcomes vary with the remedy asked for? The effect on future compliance should not be ignored either. If, as is clearly the case in all jurisdictions, tests for monopolisation or abuse of market power are inherently imprecise, factoring in the remedy is likely to make them more imprecise still. Reasoning backwards has to have some regard for life outside the courtroom. Law-abiding firms cannot realistically be expected to adjust their behaviour to fit the contours of a remedy not yet asked for. Conversely, dominant firms bent on gaming the system will only be further encouraged by this way of doing things to ignore liability and frame their behaviour entirely according to the effectiveness or otherwise of the remedy as they imagine it may be awarded.

None of this is to suggest that breach and remedy exist on separate planets. The two are interdependent in the weak sense that the remedy sought to be applied must serve either deterrence or market repair. Thus fines and penalties need to bear some relationship to the harm done[154] or the profit gained.[155] Similarly, market repair should focus on removing obstacles to efficient competition caused by the defendant's actual or threatened unlawful behaviour.[156] Constructing 'better' markets in the abstract is not what competition law is supposed to do. But while it is no doubt true, as the United States District Court of Appeals put it in *Microsoft*,[157] that the remedy 'should be tailored to fit the wrong creating the occasion for the remedy', this does not work in reverse.[158] The shape of the remedy does not determine the existence of the wrong. In competition cases, no wrong is entirely without a remedy, even if that remedy cannot achieve all that

---

[154] H First, 'Netscape is Dead: Lessons from the Microsoft Litigation' (2008) *New York Law and Economics Working Paper* No 166 at 18.

[155] The European requirement that the fine levied should not exceed 10% of the offending firm's turnover recognises the link between gain and penalty, albeit in a rough and ready way.

[156] Here too the European insistence that judicial remedies in general be 'proportionate', 'effective' and dissuasive' to the infringement committed makes explicit what in other jurisdictions is implicit. Thus in *Magill*, n 22 above, where the coerced licensing was the only way of putting an end to the unlawful refusal, it was not considered disproportionate, or so the Court of Justice held (paras 93–94).

[157] *US v Microsoft* (2001), n 55 above, para 70.

[158] The DC Circuit made this clear in *Microsoft* where they rejected Microsoft's arguments that the Government had failed to demonstrate sufficient causal connection between Microsoft's conduct and the maintenance of its market power while at the same time accepting that the strength or weakness of the causal link could be relevant when it came to selecting or designing the appropriate remedy. *Ibid*, at para 80.

plaintiffs and enforcement agencies might want it to. Remedies may be discretionary, but that does not mean that the discretion should never be exercised.

3.7.8 Multi-purpose monetary remedies

The range of monetary remedies available to private parties, courts and enforcement agencies varies widely across jurisdictions. Treble damages are a staple of United States antitrust law but scarcely figure in the remedial armoury available to private litigants elsewhere. Conversely, the civil pecuniary penalties standing behind public enforcement in Europe, Canada, Australia and New Zealand have no counterpart in the United States.[159] Not only does the legal form of the remedy vary, so does the frequency with which it is used. Restitutionary money remedies may be available without being much used. Damages may seem an unattractive remedy in jurisdictions that do not provide for their trebling.

Behind this variety in legal form and fluctuations in usage lies an important cross-jurisdictional truth. Individual monetary remedies can both deter and repair. This is true even of those remedies, such as damages and disgorgement, which have as their starting point some real-world loss or improper gain. In both cases the money extracted from the defendant does more than simply compensate plaintiffs or transfer to them profits made possible by abuse of market power. Neither compensation nor disgorgement is an end in itself. Both have a public as well as a private purpose. By incentivising private enforcement they can relieve the pressure on public funds.[160] They can inject more confidence into discouraged competitors to re-enter or stay in a market until competition is restored, thus speeding up the pace of market repair.[161] The amount of the disgorgement or the size of the damages award also has a deterrent effect however it is calculated, and can act as a substitute for civil penalties in jurisdictions without such sanctions (clearly the main role of treble damages in the United States).[162]

---

[159] First, H, 'The Case for Antitrust Civil Penalties' (2009) 76 *Antitrust Law Journal* 127; Hellström, P, Maier-Rigaud, F and Bulst, FW, 'Remedies in European Antitrust Law' (2009) 76 *Antitrust Law Journal* 43 at 44 and 50.

[160] They can also act as a corrective to visible differences in an enforcement policy that comes with a change in administration.

[161] Gavill, A, 'Thinking Outside the Illinois Brick Box: A Proposal for Reform' (2009) 76 *Antitrust Law Journal* 167.

[162] Paradoxically, judicial concerns about whether treble damages may lead to over-deterrence sometimes result in courts shying away from finding liability in the first place. Something like this appears to have happened in *Trinko*, n 5 above, and thus it stands as a particularly egregious example of the process of reasoning backwards from remedy to breach discussed earlier. See also *Berkey Photo Inc v Eastman Kodak* 603 F 2d 263 (2nd Cir 1979) at 298, which reveals the fundamental flaw in the reasoning-backwards approach. By conceding, as the Second Circuit appears to have done, that the outcome might have been different had there been publicly-enforced action for injunctive relief, the court raises the nonsensical possibility that liability findings will vary with the nature of the relief sort.

Conversely, a fine or pecuniary penalty cannot be disconnected entirely from the harm done to the market. It is precisely because money is fungible that its transfer can serve a variety of regulatory objectives.

4

Intellectual Property and Competition Policy: Constructing the Interface

4.1 PRIVILEGE, PUNISHMENT AND NEUTRALITY

The relationship between intellectual property and competition policy has gone through different cycles at different times in different jurisdictions. At some periods the mere ownership of an intellectual property right has been equated with market power, and its actual or threatened exercise or non-exercise with abuse. At other times courts and regulators insist that intellectual property be treated no differently from other assets or business advantages. (Regulatory neutrality, when espoused, has generally been seen as a corrective to earlier periods of hostility to intellectual property rather than actively pursued as an objective in its own right.) The last phase in the cycle comes when intellectual property is privileged in various ways over other potential sources of market power whenever the activities of right holders come under regulatory scrutiny. Each of the five jurisdictions we have selected for analysis is currently at a different stage in this last cycle, with some edging back towards neutrality and others swinging definitively away from it.

Contemporaneously with these fluctuations in competition policy, but in no sense shadowing them, are developments taking place within intellectual property law itself. This time the movement is largely in one direction. Here there are no cycles of under- or over-protection to match the cycles of under- or over-regulation seen on the competition enforcement side of the fence. The history of intellectual property during most of the period under discussion is one of continuing and accelerating expansion both within and across jurisdictions. Courts and legislators leapfrog over each other to create new rights, or to extend the duration or protective reach of those that already exist. New technologies lock up information and ideas which previously formed part of the public domain. Technological locks then require to be backed by legislative measures that seek to prevent their unpicking. Multilateral and bilateral trade agreements ensure that expansionist intellectual property regimes are negotiated outwards, almost always permanently. Economic input into these expansionist jumps in protection has been minimal before the event and largely futile afterwards. Absent such input, intellectual property owners and their advocates have by and large been able to present lack of protection for new products and processes against various forms of imitation and free-riding as a problem needing to be solved. Often they have been able to persuade judges and legislators to agree with them, usually without any deep or detailed consideration of the economic arguments for or against extension in a particular case.[1] (To be fair, infringement proceedings in most jurisdictions provide few opportunities for detailed expositions by economists. Legislators have no such excuse, however.) If we see intellectual property as a form of intervention in the market and non-intervention as the baseline, we confront (a touch ironically) a repeat of the type one versus type two error tug-of-war, but this time with a silent preference for type two in the form of rights extended far beyond any possible economic rationale for protection. When the property rhetoric is peeled away, the problem could be (but seldom is) seen as one of excess of regulatory zeal rather than its opposite.

4.2 WINNERS AND LOSERS IN THE INTELLECTUAL PROPERTY GAME

An economic analysis of the effect of intellectual property rights on competitive markets would need to be able to explain and predict the likely reactions of particular market players to the actual and hypothetical expansion or contraction of legal protections for innovation and creativity in particular markets. Care must be taken, however, that in identifying potential market participants and describing and predicting their behaviour, one does not also identify with their interests. Competition policy is about protecting the process of competition itself, not persons.

4.2.1 Innovators, creators and owners

When the process of artificial simplification called modelling is applied to intellectual property rights, it tends to focus on lone inventors or creators rather than on the team of which they are nowadays so often a part or the organisation that funds or employs them. No harm is done provided that, as with all models, it is clearly understood that the aim of the exercise is clearly to present that which it is sought to predict rather than make a prediction. Individual reactions to changes in the content of a right are after all easier to model than group or corporate reactions. This necessary stripping out of complexity should not be

---

[1] A change, however, has recently been signalled in this regard in the UK, with the Hargreaves Report, *Digital Opportunity: A Review of Intellectual Property and Growth* (May 2011), expressly stating that the author had sought both to base his own judgments on economic evidence and to advise the Government to frame its policy decisions on that basis. The report is available at <www.ipo.gov.uk/ipreview-finalreport.pdf>.

allowed, however, to slide over into the rhetorical privileging of the interests of actual or supposed first-movers in the process of innovation or creation just because they are first-movers. After all, authors and inventors usually remain owners for only the shortest of times, if indeed they become owners at all.

4.2.2 Competitors as innovators

To intellectual property owners, competitors are potential infringers. That competitors may themselves be downstream innovators or creators should not be forgotten. Building on what has gone before is how market economies develop. Innovation is both sequential and cumulative. Extending intellectual property owners' rights to control adaptive or derivative use can get in the way of this process. The tactical use of blocking patents can have a similar effect.[2] Looking only at the interests of current right owners obscures a very important truth. If downstream innovation or creativity is blocked by the existence of an upstream intellectual property right, any resulting loss of innovative efficiency will have to offset whatever gains in innovative efficiency it is sought to attribute to the existence of the intellectual property right in the first place. Such netting out will not be easy given the relative 'softness' of innovative efficiency as a concept.[3] Tackling one half of the problem does not make the other half go away.

4.2.3 Users and consumers

Innovative and creative products need consumers just as much as any other goods and services. Consumers tend to get short shrift from both competition law and intellectual property. As we saw in chapter three, many economists would deny their interests any part in shaping competition policy. Their voice is not directly heard in infringement proceedings either. Even when their interests can be factored indirectly into judicial decision making (as they are occasionally in the course of legal argument made on behalf of others), consumers and users tend to be disadvantaged by the unequal status that comes from posing adverse consumer outcomes as defences rather than incorporating them in liability establishing rules. This matters greatly when it is only the defence that picks up competition values.[4]

---

[2] Patent pooling, the remedy suggested to ameliorate the effect of such blocking patents, brings with it competition problems of its own by providing a possible cover for cartelisation and market splitting.

[3] See 3.4.2 above.

[4] Van den Bergh, RJ and Camesasca, PD, *European Competition Law and Economics: A Comparative Perspective*, 2nd edn (London, Sweet & Maxwell, 2006) at 29.

4.2.4 Dispersed contributors to innovative efficiency

One of the adverse consequences of personalising contributions to innovation and creativity in the form of a property right granted to a first owner is that it ignores the effect of more widely dispersed but nonetheless important stakeholders. It cannot always be assumed, for example, that it is only right owners or derivative users who are responsible for creating the net increase in social value attributable to the right. A properly inclusive economic analysis would recognise the contributions of:

a) the owners of the technology through which the protected work or product is disseminated;
b) the creative predecessors on whose effort the inventor or author builds (not all such predecessors will themselves be protected by intellectual property rights);
c) wealth creators in society as a whole, ie anyone who contributes to the consumer surplus which makes possible the purchase of the protected work or process.[5]

The obvious difficulty with this way of thinking is that the more widely the economic net is cast, the more fuzzily imprecise the analysis. On the other hand, if policy makers ignore these dispersed stakeholders entirely, they run the risk of unfairly tipping the balance of argument in the direction of right holders by leaving qualitatively important (if not always easily quantified) factors out of the equation.

4.3 THE MAGIC OF NAMES: 'PROPERTY', 'REGULATION' AND 'MONOPOLY'

One of the difficulties inherent in constructing or deconstructing the interface between competition policy and intellectual property is the use of emotionally-charged words and concepts. While terms such as 'property', 'regulation' and 'monopoly' have become terms of art in legal discourse, all too often their technical meaning is allowed to fall away so that the war of words is conducted at a purely rhetorical level. When this happens the words come freighted with approval or disapproval. 'Property' is often viewed as good, while the terms 'regulation' and 'monopoly,' if not seen as downright bad, certainly carry negative connotations. If the good can be captured by theorists and the bad or negative fended off, the battle is half won. It is therefore useful to try to penetrate some way into this linguistic thicket before embarking on an analysis of the law and economics of intellectual property. This necessary act of deconstruction is made

---

[5] Lunney, GS, 'Re-examining Copyright's Incentives Access Paradigm' (1996) 49 *Vanderbilt Law Review* 483.

easier by the fact that some of the rhetoric is contradictory. Thus the proposition that 'property is sacred and intellectual property shares that sanctity', and the proposition that 'property is not special in competition terms but intellectual property is'[6] are both arguments invoked against regulatory intervention but with radically different starting points. What they have in common, however, is that they both assume that property and regulation are inevitably and irredeemably antithetical concepts.

4.3.1 Property's necessary ambiguities

Property is a much-debated construct in all legal systems, and it is not our intention to traverse that debate in detail here. For the necessarily limited purposes of this book, we make the following assumptions and reservations about the nature and role of property rights:

a) That 'property' is a bundle of rights, not an object or a thing.[7]
b) That 'property' can have different meanings in different legal contexts, and may be used for different legal purposes. Thus while trade secrets may be granted property status when instituting a system of registrable personal property securities,[8] this usually has little or no impact on judges' propensity to act as though they were mere liability rules or obligations on other occasions.[9]

---

[6] Or, if not special, at least different. Pitofsky, R, 'Antitrust and Intellectual Property: Unresolved Issues at the Heart of the New Economy' (2001) 16 *Berkeley Technology Law Journal* 535.

[7] We accept there are problems with this purely Hohfeldian way of looking at things, but it so widely informs property theory, particularly in relation to intangibles, that it provides a useful working model (as economists might say). We recognise, however, the identification of 'object' and property is very nearly total in some jurisdictions (as it was in German law, for example, in the scheme of the *Bürgerliches Gesetzbuch* (BGB), a situation only partially intruded upon by later constitutional overrides). For a comparative analysis of these distinctions, see Mincke, W, 'Property: Assets or Power? Objects or Relations as a Substrata of Property Rights' in JW Harris (ed), *Property Problems: From Genes to Pension Funds* (London, Kluwer, 1997) 78. Although Hohfeldian analysis has the occasional judicial fan (see *R v Morris* [1984] UKHL 1, AC 320, 331, per Lord Roskill) it also has its trenchant academic critics, such as Penner, J, 'Hohfeldian Use Rights in Property' in Harris, *ibid*, at 164.

[8] See on point, the Alberta case of *Re Gauntlet Energy Corp Ltd* [2003] ABQB 718, [2004] WWR 373, at 376, holding that confidential information was a registrable security and distinguishing criminal cases in which it was held information could not be property. See also the Personal Property Securities Act 1999 (NZ), s 16.

[9] The pattern varies across jurisdictions. In the US, trade secrets have sometimes been treated as property rights, as in *Ruckelhaus v Monsanto* 467 US 986 (1984), a compulsory taking case. This is less plausible in the case of an action for breach of confidence in English law. (All the more so now that privacy and commercial value are yoked together in the same cause of action.)

c) That all forms of 'property' require legal action for their recognition or creation,[10] and that this reality is in no way diminished by the form, visibility or antiquity of that act of recognition or creation.
d) That while economists can tell us a great deal about the consequences of allocating property rights, both the act of allocation and the subsequent categorisation of property rights are tasks for lawyers. Distinctions that are important to one group may be irrelevant or distracting to the other. 'Property' does not equal 'asset', still less 'competitive advantage'.[11]
e) That while the triad of assignability, exclusivity and severability may be taken as indicia of property, the absence of one or more of them is not necessarily fatal to the existence of a property right in a particular case.

What is the significance of these overlapping ambiguities for competition enforcement? Simply this: even if using property as a shield against regulatory intervention could be justified on economic grounds, property is too unstable a concept to provide a workable dividing line between immunity (actual or presumptive) and intervention.

---

[10] We accept, but do not choose to explore, that there is an enormous jurisprudential gulf between recognition of a natural right and property creation for purely utilitarian purposes. That jurisprudential gulf does not mean, however, that justifications for intellectual property that are based on utilitarian or natural rights cannot sometimes end up in the same place, or that the latter right makes for 'stronger' intellectual property rights than the former. See Breaky, H, 'Natural Intellectual Property Rights and the Public Domain' (2010) 73 *Modern Law Review* 208. As Breaky points out, some natural rights supporters would deny freedom of expression an independent existence as a basic right and would probably prefer to see it within a pre-existing property right; Breaky, *ibid*, at 235. We also recognise that there may be non-utilitarian values that a system of property chooses to internalise. In the case of intellectual property, the most important of these is freedom of expression. Like more utilitarian analyses, this also points in two directions: an author's natural rights to appropriate her own words (Gordon, WJ, 'A Property Right in Self-Expression: Equality and Individualism in the Natural Law of Intellectual Property' (1993) 102 *Yale Law Journal* 1533); and a potential infringer's equally natural right to adapt and modify those words in the name of artistic or political freedom (Burr, SL, 'Artistic Parody: A Theoretical Construct' (1996) 14 *Cardozo Arts & Entertainment Law Journal* 65). Commentators and courts sometimes *segue* from economics to natural rights whenever arguments based on the former falter. See Waldron, J, 'From Authors to Copiers: Individual Rights and Social Values in Intellectual Property' (1993) 68 *Chicago Kent Law Review* 841 at 851, 855. See also Rose, C, 'The Comedy of the Commons: Custom, Commerce and Inherently Public Property' (1986) 53 *University of Chicago Law Review* 771 at 778. While non-economic values are greatly obscured in most competition regimes, they nevertheless continue to exist. Of course, freedom of expression itself can (and has been) justified on purely utilitarian grounds.

[11] When economists have to talk about property rights they tend to lump them together with an economically conferred advantage designed, as Posner puts it, to reduce the gap between individual and social costs and/or benefits. Posner, RA, *Economic Analysis of Law*, 6th edn (New York, Aspen, 2003) at 47.

4.3.2 Is intellectual property really the same as other property and does it matter?

Amalgamating all forms of property for regulatory purposes[12] obscures some distinctions that do actually matter. The first is that while natural rights arguments are frequently mounted for tangible property, the case for intellectual property is usually made on more pragmatic or utilitarian grounds, in common law legal systems at least.[13] Intellectual property is explicitly designed to bring about a particular result. Older forms of property do so only by accident and indirection. Secondly, justifications for property, whether they be Lockean or utilitarian, usually speak in terms of the need to conserve scarce resources. As one eminent writer on the subject has succinctly put it, property rights manage scarcity while intellectual property creates it.[14] Thirdly, the boundaries of tangible property are usually easily recognisable (this being the true function of the physical object or parcel of land[15]), whereas the boundaries of a particular intellectual property right are by definition invisible to the external eye.[16] Fourthly, while no property right is entirely inviolable, in the sense of being free from social constraints, those constraints are generally more overt and more onerous in the case of intellectual property. Thus the originality threshold and rules about fair dealing in copyright law, the independent discovery defence in trade secret law and public interest restrictions on patent acquisition all make greater inroads into the owner's domain than is the case with the much more restricted social controls accompanying ownership of a parcel of land.[17] Lastly, the subject matter of an intellectual property right is not diminished by being consumed and may be simultaneously enjoyed by more than one consumer (a

---

[12] A strong driver for 'all property is equal' arguments in the US is the assumption made by some judges (and applauded by some commentators) that injunctive relief should be automatic rather than discretionary in the cases of intellectual property infringement; see Epstein, R, 'Intellectual Property: Old Boundaries and New Frontiers' (2001) 76 *Indiana Law Journal* 803. This assumption was decisively rejected by the Supreme Court in *eBay Inc v MercExchange LLC* 547 US 388 (2006), 126 S Ct 1837. (Interestingly, the remedy preferred in that case was a compulsory licence with the royalty fixed by the court, rather than the permanent injunction sought by the patent owner.) In other common law jurisdictions the line between property and obligation has never been dependent on the availability or otherwise of injunctive relief.

[13] And not only there. Outside the area of copyright, civilian regimes of industrial property protection can be equally pragmatic.

[14] Plant, A, 'The Economic Aspects of Copyright in Books' in A Plant (ed), *Selected Economic Essays and Addresses* (London, Routledge & Kegan Paul, 1974).

[15] This is the so-called rule of recognition. Its acceptance does not require the abandonment of the Hohfeldian perspective. Recognition is simply easier when there is some physical *res*. Calabresi, G and Melamed, AD, 'Property Rules, Liability Rules and Inalienability: One View of the Cathedral' (1972) 85 *Harvard Law Review* 1089.

[16] Calabresi and Melamed, *ibid*.

[17] In the case of land, of course, social controls tend to drive the law of nuisance or public law planning rules rather than directly limit the right.

characteristic which has a profound effect on the economic analysis of intellectual property, as we shall see).

For all of the above reasons, even a purely juristic analysis of the nature of intellectual property would have to concede important differences between it and other forms of property. Juristic differences, however, do not and should not bind the regulator. The point we are seeking to make here is not that intellectual property can never be a fully credentialed member of the property club (in some jurisdictions this would be to fly in the face of statutory affirmation that copyright, designs and patents are indeed 'property'[18]), nor that intellectual property can never share ownership features with other forms of property, but rather that neither similarity nor difference should be allowed to impede competition authorities. Perhaps the final word on this vexed subject can be left to a Canadian judge who (speaking of copyright, but the logic could be applied equally to patents or designs) pointed out that copyright law is neither tort law nor property law in classification but is statutory in origin, and it follows accordingly that copyright legislation simply creates rights and obligations upon the terms and under the circumstances set out in the statute.[19]

4.3.3 Property versus regulation: a false polarity

Property and regulation are generally treated as antithetical constructs. The first is a creature of private law. The second is as a regrettable public law intrusion into that otherwise inviolate private law world. This is something of an historical accident. Prior to the Statute of Monopolies 1623 and the Statute of Anne 1709, patents and copyright were badly- and barely-regulated monopolies, and visibly so. The passage of those particular pieces of legislation[20] could be said to have privatised those monopolies in the pursuit of mainly utilitarian goals. Viewed in this way, the clash between intellectual property and competition law is a head-on collision between two systems of regulation with divergent processes but overlapping goals.[21] In both cases there is a tension between private rights and public law objectives. This is no mere 'path not taken' whimsy. Courts and

---

[18] See, eg, 35 USC §261 (patents); Copyright Act 1994 (NZ), s 14(1). Trade Marks Act 2002 (NZ), s 9; Layout Designs Act 1994 (NZ), s 39(1); Copyright, Designs and Patents Act 1988 (UK), s 1(1). Where this leaves rights not thus legislatively labelled is an interesting question.

[19] Per Estley J in *Compo Co v Blue Crest Music Inc* [1980] 1 SCR 357 at 372.

[20] This is not only a common law historical trajectory. A similar transition may be traced in Europe, first in France and later in Germany, an historical reality that the language of authors' rights sometimes obscures. Eagles, I, 'New Zealand Moral Rights Law: Did Something Get Lost in Translation?' (2002) 8 *New Zealand Business Law Quarterly* 26.

[21] Meurer, MJ, 'Commentary: The Social Costs of Rent Seeking by Intellectual Property Owners' in M Boyer, M Trebilcock and D Vaver (eds), *Competition Policy and Intellectual Property* (Toronto, Irwin Law, 2009) 156.

commentators in Australia[22] and the United States[23] not uncommonly compare a discussion of real or apparent conflicts between general competition principles and industry-specific utilities regulation with similar real (or sometimes in the court's eyes apparent[24]) conflicts between the enforcement of intellectual property rights and competition law intervention. What these cases demonstrate is the futility of setting up a false polarity between 'property' ('unqualified good') and regulation ('necessary evil'). Stripped of its rhetorical embellishments, intellectual property is a way of regulating innovation.[25] What is at stake here is the clash of two regulatory regimes in no way more remarkable or different than the interface between competition law and the regulation of electricity transmission, telecommunications, capital markets[26] or fishing rights. Just as one cannot ignore the adequacy of direct regulation in these cases, neither should one ignore the reach or depth of an intellectual property right when assessing the degree of market power wielded by the right holder and its potential for misuse.[27]

4.3.4 Legal versus economic monopolies

Intellectual property confers upon owners the legal right to do or authorise the doing of particular acts.[28] These acts define the right, and by long usage are commonly referred to as monopolies. This, however, has nothing to do with

---

[22] See discussion of *NT Power Generation Pty Ltd v Power & Water Authority* [2004] HCA 48 in ch 7 below.

[23] First, H, '*Microsoft* and the Evolution of the Intellectual Property Concept' [2006] *Wisconsin Law Review* 1369.

[24] As it is in the most recent US cases, see ch 5 below.

[25] Donoghue, RO and Padilla, AJ, *The Law and Economics of Article 82 EC* (Oxford, Hart Publishing, 2006) at 407, 413; Eagles, I, 'Intellectual Property and Competition Policy: The Case for Neutrality' in CER Rickett and GW Austin (eds), *International Intellectual Property Law and the Common Law World* (Oxford, Hart Publishing, 2000) 285 at 322; Waldron, n 10 above, at 841; Lianos, I, 'Competition Law and Intellectual Property: Is the Property Rights Approach Right?' (2005–2006) *Cambridge Year Book of European Legal Studies* 153 at 179. The same argument may be extended to all property, although its utility is thereby correspondingly diminished, see Krier, JE, 'The (Unlikely) Death of Property' (1990) 13 *Harvard Journal of Law and Public Policy* 75 at 78.

[26] See, eg, *Credit Suisse v Billing* 551 US 264 (2007). See also *Telecom Corporation of New Zealand v Clear Communications Ltd* [1994] UKPC 36, [1995] 1 NZLR 385, in which the Judicial Committee of the Privy Council declined to find that Telecom had abused its dominant market position by charging its competitor Clear monopoly rents for access to its nationwide fixed copper wire network, because the then government, under Part IV of the Commerce Act 1996 (NZ), could have stepped in to regulate the access price but opted not to. See discussion of case at 7.2.3 below.

[27] The artificiality of property versus regulation may be seen at its clearest when the intellectual property statute itself provides for compulsory licensing.

[28] This has led one commentator to describe them as 'liberty inhibiting privileges' for just that reason. See Drahos, P, *A Philosophy of Intellectual Property* (Dartmouth, Brookfield Vermont, 1996) at 213, 223.

monopolies as economists understand the term. The key to the distinction is, once again, substitutability.[29] A patented product or process may have rivals that can compete with it without infringing. Copyright material can be out-competed by products that serve the same function or appeal to similar tastes, provided they do not cross the infringement line by appropriating form or expression. Trade secrets may be bypassed by information lawfully in the public domain.

The distinction between legal and economic monopolies pulls in two directions. The first (and most frequently invoked) is as a corrective to the wrongheaded notion once widely accepted by courts and regulators in the United States that intellectual property rights confer market power in themselves. The second and equally important (but less often referred to) iteration of the distinction is to reject the equally baseless assumption that any act done (or not done) in pursuance of a legal monopoly can never adversely affect the competitive process.

4.4 SLICING THE INTELLECTUAL PROPERTY PIE

Thus far we have assumed a common set of justifications across all manifestations of intellectual property. This is not, however, how the law and economics debate about intellectual property rights has by and large proceeded. Courts, competition regulators and commentators have approached different rights differently. Sometimes this is a matter of the legal form in which the right is cast. On other occasions it reflects the different rationales underpinning each right. While both factors are relevant to the refusals to license debate, they can distort the analysis if they suggest either that particular rights are intrinsically more virtuous or more vicious in competition terms, or that some rights are inherently more vulnerable to over-regulation than others.

4.4.1 The juristic form of the right

The intellectual property pie may be sliced in various ways, using different legal devices to separate the pieces. The most obvious (and in competition terms, the least significant) is to distinguish between statutory and judge-made rules.[30] Statutory rights may be further subdivided into those which depend on prior

---

[29] Some commentators would view this as overly simplistic. For them, low value (because easily substitutable) patents serve an important market-signalling function by acting (when accumulated) as a test of research and development virility for investors in the firms that acquire them. See Long, C, 'Patent Signals' (2002) 69 *University of Chicago Law Review* 625; Thambissett, S, 'Property as Credence Goods' (2007) 27 *Oxford Journal of Legal Studies* 707.

[30] Sometimes this is not so easy to do. Eg, UK trade secrets law largely remains an offshoot of the equitable obligation of confidence. Of course, the distinction becomes utterly meaningless once one crosses over the common law/civil law divide.

disclosure through a system of State registration and/or grant (for example, patents, registered trade marks and designs), and those (such as copyright and layout designs) which are self-constituting, coming into existence at the moment of creation or fixation. It is more useful (and arguably more principled) to try to draw a line between obligation and property.[31] On one side lies the classic trinity of patent, copyright and registered trade marks, and their more recent *sui generis* attendants, plant variety protection and some forms of design right. On the other is that penumbra of liability rules which surrounds, sustains and extends these property rights: fair trading, passing off, unfair competition and breach of confidence. While this line largely corresponds with the statutory/common law divide, the fit is not perfect.[32] Neither is the barrier impermeable. Commentators constantly urge that a particular right be pushed across the property/obligation line.[33] Very occasionally some judge will oblige.[34] Judicial resistance is as common, however.[35]

How relevant is juristic form to warding off (or encouraging) competition scrutiny? On the face of it such matters should be no more germane to the issue than any of the other subdivisions of private law. Their invocation in the refusals to license debate is usually for the rhetorical purposes as described in chapter one. Copyright, patents and trade marks being creatures of statute are not to be undone by a side blow from another statutory regime, in this case competition law. Trade

---

[31] We concede that it is possible to argue that this line too is meaningless, and that property rights are simply Hohfeldian bundles of obligations of greater or lesser magnitude and that intellectual property rights, precisely because they deal with intangibles, provide more than usually appropriate *rostra* from which to shout that this particular jurisprudential emperor has no clothes. Nevertheless, the label 'property' does have consequences for any 'bundle' so described, especially in the competition/intellectual property debate. Its theoretical dissection we are content to leave to others more skilled in the art. 'Property' possesses considerable rhetorical advantages when waved at judges and legislators in the expansionist cause, and it is on these that we wish to focus.

[32] Some liability rules, such as those relating to fair trading, are statutory. Neither is it conceptually impossible for judge-made liability rules to become fully-fledged property rights, or so Chicago thinkers like to tell judges. (Few are yet to be convinced in any jurisdiction.) While a judge-created intellectual property right might seem odd, it is no odder than judge-created property in general. (Most property rights in common law systems are precisely that.) Sometimes a statute will pick up and embellish a property right first adumbrated in the courts, witness the right of publicity under state and federal law in the United States; see *Haelan Laboratories v Topps Chewing Gum Inc* 202 F 2d 866 (2nd Cir 1953) at 868. See also Restatement (Third) Unfair Competition § 46 (1995).

[33] Usually the flow is from obligation to property; however, occasionally writers urge judicial and legislative traffic in the opposite direction. See Gordon, WJ, 'On Owning Information: Intellectual Property and the Restitutionary Impulse' (1992) 78 *Virginia Law Review* 149 at 214 and 262. Statutes do get in the way here, as even Professor Gordon concedes. Only judge-made rules can effectively be depropertised, absent a shift in legislators' perceptions and priorities.

[34] *Rolls Royce Ltd v Jeffrey* [1962] 1 ALL ER 801, at 805; and *Herbert Morris Ltd v Saxelby* [1916] 1 AC 688.

[35] *Federal Commissioner of Taxation v United Aircraft Corporation* [1943] HCA 50, (1943) 68 CLR 525 at 535; *Kellog Co v National Biscuit Co* 303 US 111 (1938).

secrets and business reputations not buttressed by a trade mark will fail this test. Conversely, if it is 'property' and 'obligation' that is to be the dividing line then commercially valuable information might make it to the protected zone, but only if one accepts the highly contentious notion that there can be property in closely-held facts.[36] Put those same facts in a database for access to which a fee is charged, and any attempt to use the term 'property' to describe the various legal protections against unauthorised access is even more contentious.[37] Given these uncertainties, 'property' seems a singularly inappropriate case breaker.

Again, while arguments can be (and have been)[38] made for privileging rights that are registration based over self-constituting rights, it is not clear what the act of registration has to tell us in competition terms, unless it is perhaps that the right, since it has been 'paid for' by prior disclosure (in the case of patents), should be more immune from 'confiscation' or 'suppression' than one (as in the case of copyright or layout designs for integrated circuits) where no such 'price' is demanded. Whether this embellishment adds anything of substance to the 'regulation equals confiscation' argument is doubtful, unless perhaps it could be argued that by extracting disclosure while reneging on the promise of protection, the State stands convicted of double dealing and duplicity. Such attempts to introduce an ethical dimension into the debate are drawing a very long bow. Rights to extract minerals or petroleum also involve disclosure (sometimes public) but carry with them no corresponding immunity from regulatory oversight. No doubt all property owners would wish to hold their rights free of interference by competition authorities, but this is a hope not a right, and any push on their part against full exposure to regulatory oversight would in no way be strengthened because their right is guaranteed by a State agency in return for payment.

Another variation on the self-constituting theme, if this time telling against immunity or privilege for right holders, is the argument that where firms are able to adjust the content of the right by limiting or expanding the circulation of information inside or outside their own organisation (as is the case under most countries' trade secret laws) then such 'adjustable' rights should be treated in the same way for competition purposes as contractual extensions of State-granted rights to activities not within the grantee's exclusive rights under the statute. As an attempt to see beyond legal form to potential anti-competitive substance, this is to be welcomed, provided always that it is understood that not all manipulations of disclosure are anti-competitive any more than is every attempt to extend a right beyond the term of a statutory grant by contract.[39] Market power and

---

[36] See Kohler, P and Palmer, N, 'Information as Property' in N Palmer and E McKendrick (eds), *Interests in Goods*, 2nd edn (London, Lloyd's of London Press, 1988) 3 at 22.

[37] See Derclaye, E, *The Legal Protection of Databases: A Comparative Analysis* (Cheltenham, Edward Elgar, 2008); Lim, D, 'Redefining the Rights and Responsibilities of Database Owners under Comparative Law' (2006) 18 *Singapore Academy of Law Journal* 418.

[38] Derclaye, n 37 above.

[39] This seems to have been a factor in the General Court's decision in Case T-201/04 *Microsoft Corporation v European Commission* ('Euro *Microsoft*') [2007] ECR II-3601, 5 CMLR 11.

anti-competitive intent or outcome on the part of the right holder must be demonstrated. In other words, the argument must be firmly grounded in the rule of reason. No presumption for or against liability attaches to the mechanisms through which secrecy and non-disclosure are maintained.[40]

4.4.2 Matching rule to rationale

A better way of looking at the interaction of intellectual property rights and competition policy would be to ignore juristic form and focus on the activity that a particular rule seeks to encourage or enhance. This would make economic dissection of the intellectual property *corpus* considerably easier. Legal rules would then be split into the following families:

(a) Rules directly fostering innovation and creativity

It is these rules on which economists have lavished most attention. Copyright and patent are the two traditional prototypes. To them may now be added *sui generis* rights protecting layout designs for integrated circuits, plant varieties and novel but non-functional designs. While these rules have the common objective of encouraging various forms of innovative and creative endeavour, they proceed towards that end by two quite distinct means. Some (patents, plant varieties and registrable designs) create true legal (but not necessarily economic) monopolies which outlaw parallel creativity or invention. Potentially infringing processes, shapes or products do not cease to become so because they have been arrived at independently. By contrast, copyright and layout designs law forbid only imitative uses of the protected work, not independent creativity as such.[41] While this tells us something about the permeability of the barriers to entry in each case, the reluctance of the courts to give much credence to claims of independent creation means that would-be entrants are unlikely to find it markedly easier to create around a copyright than to invent around a patent.

(b) Reputational rules

These are rules which restrict attempts by the right holder's rivals to confuse or mislead consumers as to the origin of goods or suggest a commercial connection with the right holder which does not exist. Trade mark law, the most developed of these rules, has never rested on an incentive justification.[42] Its objective has

---

[40] It also illustrates the futility of seeking to distinguish between action and inaction in this context.
[41] The force of the distinction is somewhat weakened by copyright's evidentiary equation that access plus substantial similarity equals a presumption of copying.
[42] Pickering, CDG, *Trade Marks in Theory and Practice* (Oxford, Hart Publishing, 1998) at 97.

always been the preservation of the mark owner's goodwill by restricting rival traders' ability to attach themselves to the business reputation represented by the mark. Similar objectives are served (if somewhat more loosely) by the tort of passing off and its legislative counterparts in various jurisdictions.[43] Unlike patent and copyright law, reputational rules do not place restrictions on the *kinds* of goods or services a competitor may supply, but only on the ways in which these goods and services might be presented to the world. It is sometimes therefore suggested that such rules pose no threats to competition, or that they actively assist competition by facilitating the product recognition[44] and differentiation on which competition often depends.[45] This is in a limited sense true, if we confine our attention to traders *inside* a given market. It underestimates, however, the potential for reputation-based rules to inhibit entry to existing markets or the creation of new ones. (Such inhibitions may be economic or, in the case of parallel importing restrictions, legal.[46])

(c) Fair dealing rules

This seemingly disparate group includes rules designed to protect information because it is secret[47] and/or valuable.[48] While they seem to lack any coherent

---

[43] Eg, the Fair Trading Act 1986 (NZ), s 9, and the Competition and Consumer Act 2010 (Aust), sch 2. The United States Trademark Act 1946 (the Lanham Act, 15 USC Chapter 22), while it casts a much wider net, also serves this function, at least in part. The various torts relating to misappropriation of commercially valuable personality in the US and Canada can probably be counted as reputational rules even though their pedigree owes as much to privacy as to the more traditional economic torts. See Kahn, J, 'The Origins of the Tort of Appropriation of Identity Reconsidered' [1996] *Legal Theory* 301. Moral rights, although yoked by statute to copyright in many jurisdictions, are best understood as directed at the preservation of artistic and authorial reputations. See Eagles, I, 'Copyright and the Sequel: What Happens Next?' in F Macmillan (ed), *New Directions in Copyright Law*, vol 6 (Cheltenham, Edward Elgar Publishing, 2007) 35 at 50.

[44] The distinction becomes blurred when trade marks are used to protect product shape and appearance.

[45] Posner, n 11 above, at 5.

[46] Petrucci, C, 'Parallel Trade of Pharmaceutical Products: The ECJ Finally Speaks. Comment on *Glaxo Smith Kline*' (2010) 35 *European Law Review* 275.

[47] In most American states trade secrets law protects information which is secret and likely to disadvantage the holder if disclosed or used without authority. Such laws usually require that the information relates to some kind of business context, even if it does not have a tradeable value in itself. In the majority of Commonwealth jurisdictions, however, such information is protected by the ordinary equitable action for breach of confidence, irrespective of commercial content or context. Whatever its original foundation, the breach of confidence action has now come to rest on notions of the legitimate expectations of the creator, imparter or subject of the information, and the actual or ascribed knowledge of the recipient or unauthorised user.

[48] Where, eg, information is protected because of the money and effort which has gone into collecting, arranging or storing it. In the US such rules are represented by the various 'non-sowing reaper' torts tracing their ancestry to the Supreme Court decision in *International News Service v Associated Press* 248 US 215 (1918). In the EU's common law jurisdictions (the

unifying principle across jurisdictions,[49] they could be said broadly to embody notions of fair dealing or commercial morality,[50] principles too vague and formless to provide even the most indirect of links with innovative efficiency. If their application does, however, turn out to be innovatively efficient in particular cases, this is by accident not design. Equating them with patent law for competition law purposes absent tests of novelty and non-obviousness is too glib an elision. This would not matter if the exercise of all three types of right were subject to case-by-case competition scrutiny. It matters very much indeed when protection against that scrutiny is sought to be conferred on whole classes of right.

4.4.3 Different jurisdictions slice the pie differently

There are two aspects to this. Some jurisdictions may recognise intellectual property rights unknown in other jurisdictions (database rights in Europe, publicity rights in the United States[51]). Alternatively, different jurisdictions may draw the boundaries between rights in different ways (the lines between design and copyright, for example). One of two things will then happen. Competition rules that do manage to operate in similar ways across jurisdictions may have the unintended effect of evening out the economic effects of these differences between intellectual property regimes. Conversely, where competition principles themselves vary from jurisdiction to jurisdiction, they will magnify any problem caused by misaligned intellectual property rights.[52]

UK and Ireland) there are *sui generis* rights protecting databases in which there has been substantial investment, see Copyright and Rights in Databases Regulations 1997 (UK), SI 1997/3022.

[49] One possible candidate for unifying trans-jurisdictional principle is restitutionary analysis based on concepts of unjust enrichment. See Gronow, A, 'Restitution for Breach of Confidence' (1996) 10 *Intellectual Property Journal* 222; Fitzgerald, BF and Gamertsfelder, L, 'Protecting Informational Products Including Databases Through Unjust Enrichment Law: An Australian Perspective' (1998) 20 *European Intellectual Property Review* 244. While academic comment abounds on matters restitutionary, it is seldom overtly referred to in judicial decisions protecting valuable or sensitive information. This is perhaps understandable. Restitution theorists divide themselves into a variety of fiercely antagonistic sects. It is also a pity. As Professor Gordon has shown, restitutionary theory can be made to mesh more readily with competition analysis than more generalised explanations based on fairness or commercial morality. (Indeed she would subsume all of these rules into a single tort which significantly enough she calls 'malcompetitive copying'.) See Gordon (1992), n 33 above. For a critique of Professor Gordon's approach, see Sterk, SE, 'Rhetoric and Reality in Copyright Law' (1996) 94 *Michigan Law Review* 1205.

[50] TRIPS Art 39(2), eg, refers to unauthorised disclosure or use 'contrary to honest commercial practices'.

[51] Semeraro, S, 'Property's End: Why Competition Law Should Limit the Right of Publicity' (2001) 43 *Connecticut Law Review* 753.

[52] A case in point here is the differential treatment of trade secrets. US antitrust law equates them with patents and copyright. European competition law is much less favourable towards

4.4.4 Paracopyright and privatised regulation

Signatories to the World Intellectual Property Organisation Copyright Treaty 1996 (WCT) are required to provide 'paracopyright' laws enabling copyright owners to block access to, and the copying of, their works in electronic form using technological protection measures (TPMs). In some jurisdictions (most notably the United States and the European Union) paracopyright protection extends copyright owners' control over their works significantly beyond that which has traditionally obtained under copyright legislation,[53] going well beyond the metaphor of a locked house[54] that would simply see someone stopped from circumventing a TPM to access a work. United States paracopyright rules[55] blithely state that they do not affect the normal fair use defence to copyright infringement, but this is little comfort to users prevented by a TPM from gaining access to a locked-up work to make fair use of it. Europe's paracopyright provisions are more draconian, lacking this broad (if often useless) fair use exemption. They make no allowance for the common copyright exemptions for research or private study, criticism or news reporting, rendering European users liable for infringement unless they can come within one of a raft of 20 or so very narrow exemptions, all bar one of them only voluntary for Member States to implement into their national legislation.[56] Paracopyright thus poses two dangers for the evolution of a coherent competition policy. The first is that courts and regulators allow the automatic extension of copyright's already over-privileged status in many competition regimes to this new area. The second is that by allowing copyright owners to thwart or bypass fair dealing and fair use rules, paracopyright severely limits copyright's ability to control anti-competitive behaviour through its own internal mechanisms.[57]

---

them, arguably because of the wide fluctuations in Member States' laws and the absence of any Directive on the subject. See Czapracka, KA, 'Antitrust and Trade Secrets: The US and EU Approaches' (2008) 24 *Santa Clara Computer and High Technology Law Journal* 207.

[53] Netanel, NW, 'Copyright and the First Amendment: What Eldred Misses and Portends' in J Griffiths and U Suthersanen (eds), *Copyright and Free Speech: Comparative and International Analyses* (Oxford, Oxford University Press, 2005) 151.

[54] Dusollier, S, 'Electrifying the Fence: Legal Protection of Technological Measures for Protecting Copyright' (1999) 3 *European Intellectual Property Review* 285; and Forsyth, M, 'The Digital Agenda Anti-circumvention Provisions: A Threat to Fair Use in Cyberspace' (2001) 82 *Australian Intellectual Property Journal* 12.

[55] Digital Millennium Copyright Act 1998 (US) (DMCA), § 1201(c)(1). The DMCA prevents persons publishing information or making available devices designed to circumvent a TPM. While it does allow reverse engineering for the purpose of achieving interoperability, again, this is of not much use if access to software object code is thwarted by a TPM.

[56] Directive on the Harmonisation of Certain Aspects of Copyright and Related Rights in the Information Society (2001/29/EC).

[57] For a discussion of these mechanisms, see 4.5.1, 4.6.2 and 4.7 below.

4.5 INTELLECTUAL PROPERTY'S LOPSIDED RELATIONSHIP WITH COMPETITION POLICY

Competition lawyers are now used to asking whether and how competition rules should be adjusted to take account of the actual or supposed idiosyncrasies of intellectual property. The question after all has practical outcomes. Intellectual property lawyers seldom have occasion to put the question in reverse and ask whether the content of an intellectual property right should be adjusted to reflect the needs of competition policy.

4.5.1 Intellectual property's internal competition controls

One of the more unfortunate consequences of treating property and regulation as polar opposites is that this way of thinking obscures the extent to which individual intellectual property regimes themselves reflect (or can be made to reflect) competition values. Very occasionally this is explicit, as in the recent enactment in Australia of provisions in the patent statute enabling the Federal Court to issue a compulsory licence[58] and revoke a patent after that grant if the patentee is acting in contravention of that jurisdiction's competition statute.[59] More commonly, competition values lie silent within other provisions until teased out by courts during infringement proceedings.

(a) Compulsory licensing provisions in patent and design law

Despite a worldwide trend against compulsory licences,[60] these can still be obtained under the patent[61] and design[62] laws of various countries where the right owner refuses to license at all, or will license only on unreasonable terms. Usually the applicant has to show that the design or patent is not being worked within the jurisdiction, and in some cases that the development of downstream

---

[58] The Patents Act 1990 (Cth), s 133(2)(b), as inserted by the Trade Practices Amendment (Australian Consumer Law) Act (No 2) 2010.

[59] *Ibid*, s 134(2)(b). This is additional to the existing ground for revocation which applies in cases where, two years after the grant of a compulsory licence, the reasonable requirements of the public have still not been met and the patentee has not satisfactorily explained its failure to exploit the patent. The new ground for revoking a compulsory licence is available in relation to anti-competitive conduct occurring after the commencement date in relation to a patent granted before, on or after that date.

[60] TRIPS Art 31 restricts the granting of compulsory licences in various ways. Applications for such licences must be considered individually and be preceded by attempts to negotiate a voluntary licence. Licences must also be reviewable when market circumstances change and be granted subject to appropriate remuneration for the licensor.

[61] Eg, Patents Act (UK) 1977, s 48A(1); Patent Act RSC c P-4, s 65(2); Patents Act 1953 (NZ), s 46; and Plant Variety Rights Act 1987 (NZ), s 21.

[62] Eg, Designs Act (NZ) 1953, s 14.

markets is unfairly prejudiced by the market being supplied from outside the country on unreasonable terms. The licences are generally subject to an array of onerous conditions and qualifications to ensure compliance with TRIPS. The tests of reasonableness and abuse in these provisions tend to be restrictively interpreted.[63]

(b) Collective copyright licensing

Copyright licences and licences of performers' rights are not uncommonly administered by collecting agencies on behalf of dispersed groups of right holders. In jurisdictions such as the United Kingdom and New Zealand such schemes are subject to confirmation and variation by a specialist tribunal at the behest of actual or would-be licensees.[64] The tests applied by such bodies are those of reasonableness and non-discrimination, and they tend to focus on the interests of stakeholders represented before them rather than on the impact of those stakeholders' actions on the competitive process itself. Whether and to what extent this form of mini-regulation is subject to competition principles is seldom made clear.

(c) Abuse of rights doctrines

In the United States the courts have extracted from intellectual property statutes an unarticulated first premise that these statutes not be interpreted in ways at odds with the statutes' underlying objectives. At the forefront of these objectives, some courts have ruled, are competitive markets. None of this, it must be stressed, hangs on the words used in the individual intellectual property statutes and appears to have had purely remedial origins. Loosely gathered together under the 'abuse of rights' label, these principles of construction (for that is what they are) have drawn heavily on the forbiddingly named and now abandoned 'Nine No-Nos'[65] under which United States regulators sought to outlaw particular licensing practices outright. The fit with antitrust law is less than perfect, however, even after further legislative tinkering in the case of patents. The doctrine of patent abuse which we explore in the next chapter[66] has been much

---

[63] Eg, *Torpharm Inc v Canada (Commissioner of Patents)* [2004] FC 673.
[64] Copyright Designs and Patents Act 1988, Pt I, Ch 8 (UK), Copyright Act (NZ) 1994, ss 205–224.
[65] The official position of the US Department of Justice and Federal Trade Commission regarding licensing practices is now set out in their *Antitrust Guidelines for the Licensing of Intellectual Property*, April 1995.
[66] See 5.8 below.

criticised[67] and likened to a court-run scheme of royalty-free licences for infringers.[68] Copyright misuse tends to blend into wider copyright doctrines such as fair dealing[69] or the idea–expression dichotomy. Defendants seem less likely to be successful in copyright abuse cases than in patent cases.

Commonwealth courts have been much slower to invoke abuse of rights theories, at least in cases involving intellectual property. In these jurisdictions their use appears to have been confined to two limited situations. The first involves mostly unsuccessful attempts to invoke the so-called 'spare parts' rule enunciated by the House of Lords in *British Leyland v Armstrong, Patents Ltd*.[70] The second concerns isolated refusal to protect business confidences where potential breaches of competition law are said to be involved. The former has been outflanked, at least on its United Kingdom home ground, by the construction of a statutory bypass.[71] Even in its heyday the Law Lords' decision found few emulators among other Commonwealth judges,[72] or indeed any application outside the narrow field of indirect copyright protection for mass-produced articles.[73]

The general public interest defence to breach of confidence might seem at first sight a more promising form of competition control. Certainly it has been applied in cases where the confidence sought to be protected involved alleged breaches of competition statutes,[74] but its limits are otherwise unclear. It may

---

[67] Lemley, MA, 'The Economic Irrationality of the Patent Misuse Doctrine' (1990) 78 *California Law Review* 1599.

[68] *Ibid*, at 1618.

[69] On the interaction of fair use and competition policy generally, see Ghosh, S, 'When Exclusionary Conduct Meets the Exclusive Rights of Intellectual Property: *Morris v PGA* and the Limits of Free Riding as an Antitrust Business Justification' (2006) 37 *Loyola University of Chicago Law Journal* 723 at 747; Ramello, GB, 'Copyright and Antitrust Issues' in W Gordon and R Watt (eds), *The Economics of Copyright* (Cheltenham, Edward Elgar, 2003) 118 at 139; Longdin, L, 'Fair Dealing and Markets for News: Copyright Law Tiptoes Towards Market Definition' (2001) 7 *New Zealand Business Law Quarterly* 10. See also Bauer, J, 'Refusals to Deal with Competitors or Owners of Patents and Copyrights: Reflections on the *Image Technical Services* and *Xerox* Decisions' (2006) 55 *De Paul Law Review* 1211.

[70] *British Leyland v Armstrong, Patents Ltd* [1986] AC 577. In essence the rule held that retail purchasers of copyright articles could not be denied access to spare parts for the purpose of effecting adequate repairs. Purchasers also had a right to adequate, competitively priced repair services. Prior authority for the rule was meagre, the Law Lords relying heavily on a perceived analogy with the 'derogation of grant' principle in real property law.

[71] The intricate provision for unregistered design rights in the Copyright Designs and Patents Act 1988 (UK) and the removal of copyright protection for most industrial designs leave little room for the application of the spare parts rule.

[72] See *Mono Pumps (New Zealand) Ltd v Karinya Industries* (1986) 7 IPR 25 and *Dennison Manufacturing Co v Alfred Holt and Co Ltd* (1987) 10 IPR 612.

[73] The spare parts rule never applied to 'true' monopolies such as patents and registered designs. In such cases buyers had to fall back on attempts to persuade the court that there was an implied licence to effect repairs; see *Solar Thomson Engineering Co v Barton* [1997] RPC 537. Such attempts were easily rebuffed by exclusionary notices.

[74] *Initial Services Ltd v Putteril* [1968] 1QB 396; *Allied Mills Industrial v TPC* (1981) FCA 11, 34 ALR 105.

apply only to intentional breaches, for example, and in some cases appears to operate as an element of the cause of action rather than a defence.

Whatever their future in particular jurisdictions, abuse of right doctrines are an undesirable development. The benefits they confer on one group of stakeholders (potential infringers) seem out of proportion to any proven harm to the competitive process. The existence of two sets of related, but on key issues divergent, rules on the American pattern is not reassuring. Judges who are called on to deal with this particular side wind in the course of ordinary infringement proceedings will be doing so without the procedural and evidentiary aids more usual in full-blown competition litigation. In particular, the opportunity for input from economists would appear to be limited, at least in jurisdictions outside the United States. Adjectival issues apart, the chief difficulty with the abuse of rights approach is conceptual. It is nothing more than the 'right equals market' fallacy writ large.

(d)   Core concepts as competition enhancers

Every intellectual property right has a set of inbuilt constraints intended to limit its scope and potential application. Some are limited in time. Others, while potentially immortal, may be lost through disclosure, inaction or inappropriate use. In addition to temporal limitations, each set of rights has a core concept which restricts the subject matter to which the right may be applied. Patents and copyright were not originally designed to protect ideas as such. Reputational rights were not intended to be cut loose from the reputations they were created to defend. In this prelapsarian world, facts were thought to be free, and mere information was protected only in the service of some notion of fair dealing (however inarticulate) or because of the original form in which it was expressed. It was also thought important that the boundaries between the various forms of intellectual property be preserved so that core concepts did not bleed into each other in ways which defeated each right's distinctive purpose. Copyright was not to be used to confer patent-like protection on functional aspects of works without the patent penalties of disclosure and registration. Know-how had to be kept secret, or be constrained by patent claims and specifications. Courts and legislators were content to leave the shape and get-up of goods to be protected by copyright or registered design law rather than have those things become reputational indicators in themselves. Judges were generally at pains to preserve these distinctions whenever it was obvious they were under threat (this was not always the case). And legislators generally did not disturb this happy state of affairs. Intellectual property statutes remained discrete and internally self-referencing.

None of the internal controls described above has any avowedly procompetitive purpose. Indeed most of them long pre-date the existence of competition law in its modern form. They may, however, be given an economic rationale after the event, and most have been. Ideas are not protected, it is said, because in many cases no particular incentive is needed to produce them,[75] or because of the massive deadweight loss which occurs when ideas are withdrawn from the public domain.[76] Investment and effort are not protected as such, since this will often reward careless business decisions, discourage proper assessment of risk[77] and pointlessly redistribute income from users to owners.[78] Whatever the validity of these ex post facto justifications, there is no doubt that the internal controls described above do limit, however crudely and blindly, right owners' ability to act in anti-competitive ways.

Absent an express statutory power to intervene in infringement proceedings or suspend the competition inquiry until the conclusion of these proceedings, enforcement agencies could be forgiven for ignoring intellectual property's own self-correcting mechanisms. To do so, however, could distort the competition analysis by overstating the market power attributable to a particular intellectual property right. Equally, though, any erosion of intellectual property's internal controls should give competition regulators, legislators and policy makers pause for thought. Elsewhere in this book we have argued strongly that intellectual property law cannot simply be assumed always to get it right in competition terms, but neither should we assume that it always gets it wrong. Intellectual property's internal self-limiting mechanisms have to be part of the analysis.[79]

4.5.2 Ranking rights in terms of utility and vulnerability

As seen in chapter one,[80] the appropriateness or otherwise of coerced licensing is sometimes sought to be assessed in terms of a hierarchy of rights, with 'strong' rights being more entitled to protection against competition scrutiny than 'weak' rights. While we argue that this distinction, even if viable, is a rhetorical distraction in competition terms, the question also needs to be asked whether any such hierarchy exists in the first place. What do people mean when they classify

---

[75] Landes, WM and Posner, RA, 'An Economic Analysis of Copyright Law' (1989) 18 *Journal of Legal Studies* 325.
[76] *Ibid*, at 347. See also Lunney, n 5 above, at 517.
[77] Gordon, n 33 above, at 170.
[78] *Ibid*.
[79] The notion that regulators should wait until remedies or defences under the intellectual property statute have been exhausted has had no visible traction in any of our five jurisdictions. In Euro *Microsoft*, n 39 above, eg, the argument that the competitor had a right to reverse-engineer the interface codes (under Art 6 of the Directive on the Legal Protection of Computer Programs 91/250/EEC of 14 May 1991, [1991] OJ L122) had no effect on the General Court's finding of abuse of market power. See Anderman, S, 'The IP and Competition Law Interface: New developments' in S Anderman and A Ezrachi (eds), *Intellectual Property and Competition Law: New Frontiers* (Oxford, Oxford University Press, 2011). The construction of an economically defensible competition/intellectual property policy would, however, require that both questions be asked and answered.
[80] See 1.6.8 above.

rights as 'strong' or 'weak', and does the distinction make any sense in economic terms? In fact two quite different hierarchies are being put forward here. The first is predicated on the assumption that some types of intellectual property are not only 'stronger' but desirably so.[81] This entirely normative polarity is said to operate not only between intellectual property regimes (trade secrets versus patents[82]), but also within them ('basic' versus 'applied' innovation).[83] This is a matter of social policy and thus susceptible to economic analysis.[84] The second hierarchy is predicated on being able to draw a distinction between claims for intellectual property protection which are clear-cut in terms of the applicable law and others where the application of that law to the activity or output under investigation is uncertain. Here the economists have to make sense of a construct that is not of their making and of no obvious social utility (unless it is sought to argue that the unclear right should never have existed in the first place). Since all intellectual property rights have their fuzzy edges somewhere, it is not quite clear where this argument is intended to lead, nor why competition policy should be the lever by which clarity is brought to a particular intellectual property regime.

4.5.3 One size fits all

In a perfect world the breadth and duration of intellectual property protection would exactly match the underlying justification. This is not, however, the way in which intellectual property works. Nor could it work that way. The amount of protection delivered cannot be adjusted on a case-by-case basis. Uniformly applicable rules will over-protect in some cases, under-protect in others. Pharmaceuticals may need 20 years of protection, fashion design five or fewer. Copyright in fictional works may need to last for 70 years plus the life of author to be effective. This is less obviously so in the case of copyright protection for computer programs which may need less. The resulting mismatch between protection and justification is said to be counterbalanced by the consequent

---

[81] In the US this assumption receives some reinforcement from the fact that copyright and patent law are constitutionally mandated while trade secrets law is not. The impact of this on antitrust enforcement to date would, however, seem to be minimal.

[82] Patents are sometimes ranked 'higher' in the hierarchy than trade secrets because they force disclosure and dissemination of the underlying idea whereas trade secrets law does precisely the opposite. On this view, patent protection has a higher social value because disclosure enables others to 'invent around' the patent'; see Landes, WN and Posner, RA, *The Economic Structure of Intellectual Property Law* (Boston MA, Harvard University Press, 2003) at 355; Peritz, RJR, 'Competition *Within* Intellectual Property Regimes' in Anderman and Ezrachi (eds), n 79 above, 36 ff.

[83] See, eg, Ghidini, G, *Intellectual Property and Competition Law: The Innovation Nexus* (Cheltenham, Edward Elgar, 2006) at 21 ff.

[84] That is not to say that a distinction between 'strong' and 'weak' rights cannot be made on natural law grounds. However as Breaky, n 10 above, convincingly demonstrates, there is no necessary convergence between natural rights theory and 'strong' intellectual property rights.

savings in transaction costs. This unfortunately leaves two questions unanswered. The first is this: If some forms of intellectual property (notably copyright) do recognise different levels of protection for different kinds of activity, why could not similar multilevels be provided in the case of patents? There would still be a mismatch, but a much smaller one.

The second unanswered question is more significant: If over-protection is a regrettable necessity in competition terms, is that necessity justified only to the extent that intellectual property rights stay within their traditional bounds and their internal competition controls remain intact? If existing rules are a less than perfect fit with underlying economic rationales, it is not obvious where any further lowering of transaction costs or gains in innovative efficiencies are to come from if the area of protection is increased.

4.5.4 Intellectual property and barriers to entry

The debate between quantifiers and categorisers outlined in chapter three has particular resonance when an intellectual property right is introduced into the mix. Categorisers, for example, would say that if the right was lawfully acquired, it cannot be a barrier to entry because anyone could have acquired it. Nor can the right be a strategic barrier. Even accepting the categorisers' logic, rights such as trade secrets are arguably self-constituting, or so the General Court accepted in its *Microsoft* decision.[85]

(a) The weak case for intellectual property as a barrier to entry

Attempts are sometimes made to argue that the costs of defeating or bypassing an intellectual property right are deterrents to entry by competitors. Such costs include litigation expenses, research and development of alternative products or processes, and the money expended to fight the branding implications of a trade mark or other reputational right.[86] These are barriers to entry only in so far as they:

---

[85] See the discussion of Euro *Microsoft* at 6.7 below.
[86] Chamberlin, EH, *The Theory of Monopolistic Competition*, 8th edn (Cambridge MA, Harvard University Press, 1962) at 62; McClure, DM, summarises these viewpoints in 'Trademarks and Unfair Competition: A Critical History of Legal Thought' (1979) 69 *Trademark Reporter* 309 at 331. Arguments treating trade marks as barriers to entry too easily slide into arguments that *all* non-factual advertising is anti-competitive. See Parr, N and Hughes, M, 'The Relevance of Consumer Brands and Advertising in Competition Inquiries' [1993] *European Competition Law Review* 157 at 158; Economides, NS, 'The Economics of Trade Marks' (1988) 18 *Trademark Reporter* 523 at 535.

a) represent sunk costs, that is, they cannot be recovered on exit from the market[87];
b) bring no collateral advantage beyond bypassing the intellectual property right; and
c) are quantifiably high enough to deter entry,[88] or qualitatively different from the costs already borne by the incumbent.[89]

Only rarely will the costs of bypassing or contesting the right qualify on all three grounds. Most would-be entrants would spend something on product differentiation or research and development even if the incumbent held no intellectual property rights, and some such expenditure would be recoverable on exit from the market. Even litigation costs are a problematic barrier, since it cannot be assumed that competition with the incumbent necessarily means contesting the right. Potential competitors may be able to compete using non-infringing products or processes.[90] The structural uncertainties associated with vague rules are perhaps more plausibly described as entry barriers. They certainly increase the right holder's opportunities for gaming,[91] but the cure cannot lie in clarifying the content of the right by over-extending it. The gaming would then be over, but only because the right holder had won the game.

(b) The strong case for intellectual property as a barrier to entry

Intellectual property is much more convincingly described as a barrier to entry not when it raises the costs of potential infringers *per se*, but when it raises them to levels which are quantitatively high enough (for the 'quantifiers') or qualitatively different enough (according to the 'categorisers') to cause real problems in real cases. This is most likely to occur when the right in question is used in such a way as to:

a) inhibit the creation of new markets by limiting derivative or developmental use of protected products or processes;
b) facilitate market segmentation by erecting geographic obstacles to product movement. Parallel importing restrictions, because they are built into intellectual property regimes themselves, can have the same effect as a purely contractual territorial restriction (the line between action and inaction is wobblier than usual here);
c) permit right holders to use the power conferred by the right to deter entry

---

[87] Costs which can be recovered in full pose no threat to would-be entrants.
[88] As quantifiers require, see 3.6.1 above.
[89] As the categorisers would prefer, *ibid*.
[90] To assume otherwise in every case is to embrace the twin fallacies that rights define markets and legal monopolies confer market power. See 3.3.1 above.
[91] As when litigation is settled by so-called reverse payments, ie when putative infringers are in effect paid not to contest rights further that may themselves be shaky in terms of intellectual property law.

into markets not covered by the right, or requiring would-be entrants to enter all markets simultaneously or not at all.

In all of these cases, both the existence of the intellectual property right and its actual or threatened exercise have the potential to deter entry. Both are therefore fit subjects for competition scrutiny. Whether the barrier is structural or behavioural is also of little moment. Its effect is the same.[92] Equally, the height of the barrier cannot be disconnected from the issue of over-protection. An intellectual property right that delivers to right holders more protection than innovative efficiency requires will by definition discourage more efficient competitors. The right holder's motive in acquiring or enforcing the right is irrelevant, as is the fact that the right was acquired or exercised perfectly legally.[93] Again, where a patent is obtained by fraud, it is not the fraud that constitutes the barrier to entry but the fact that the patent generates no efficiency gains of its own to offset any efficiency losses caused when competitors are tricked into staying out of the market. To focus on the fraud, as judges in the United States currently do,[94] is to miss the point. Any patent found to be invalid post-grant will generate the same problems, no matter how pure the motive of the patentee may have been in taking out the patent. The same logic applies when patentees seek to see off or thwart competing technologies by threatening to bring patent infringement proceedings in relation to activities that are perfectly lawful in terms of the patent

---

[92] This can perhaps be seen most clearly in the case of 'patent thickets' or 'patent clusters'. While on one hand they may have been set up purely defensively. without any anti-competitive outcome in mind, on the other hand they may well have been be solely or mainly aimed at limiting other originator companies' freedom of operation in areas of possible overlapping products or research and development poles. See Nordlander, K and Spinks, S, 'The Interplay of Patenting Strategies and Competition Law in the Pharmaceutical Sector Inquiry', *Global Competition Policy* (February 2009), available at <www.competitionpolicyinternational.com/file/view/5840>. European policy is that all patent applications do, however, need to be evaluated on the basis of the statutory patentability criteria by the patent offices, not on the basis of underlying intentions of the applicant. Thus it is not relevant to search for malign intent in applicants applying for patent rights, or consider how patents are addressed in the applicant's internal strategy documents. See the *Executive Summary* of the European Commission's *Final Report: Pharmaceutical Sector Inquiry* (adopted 8 July 2009) dealing with Patent Filing Strategies, section 3.2.1, fn 25 and the *Final Report* itself, Chapter A, at note 20 clarifying the industries' terminology and concepts to describe certain types of patents, products and related strategies such as 'defensive patents' where these terms and concepts are not defined in patent legislation. Both the Executive Summary and Final Report (in two parts) are available at <http://ec.europa.eu/competition/sectors/pharmaceuticals/inquiry/>.

[93] Interestingly, but not surprisingly, patent-conferring agencies draw the opposite conclusion, pointing out that a patent is required precisely to see off 'free-riding' competitors. See, eg, the view of the European Patent Office (EPO) in its 18 March 2009 comments on the *Preliminary Report: Pharmaceutical Sector Inquiry*, n 92 above. The comments of the EPO are available at <http://ec.europa.eu/competition/consultations/2009_pharma/european_patent_office.pdf>. We would accept the diagnosis (but not the suggested cure) of forbidding the regulator to look inside the right.

[94] See discussion of *Re Independent Service Organisations Antitrust Litigation* ('*CSU v Xerox*') 203 F 3d 1322 (Fed Cir 2000) at 5.7 below.

as granted. Competition law should be invoked not to punish the bluffer but to encourage an entry that might not otherwise have occurred. A mistaken but honest belief on the patentee's part as to the true scope of the patent will still frighten off would-be entrants. The existence of anti-bluffing provisions in some jurisdictions' patent law does not alter this dynamic.[95]

4.6 THE CONTESTED ECONOMICS OF INTELLECTUAL PROPERTY

Economic explanations as to why something like an intellectual property regime had to exist were for a long time stable if never quite unanimous.[96] In more recent years the expansion of intellectual property protection has led to a divergence of views among economists.

4.6.1 The economics of rights justification

All economists agree that intellectual property rights increase price and reduce consumer choice, at least in the short term.[97] They are tolerated because they are thought to produce long-term efficiencies which are supposed to cancel out their short-term adverse effects. Economic analysis of the role of creativity and innovation in the marketplace usually starts with the following propositions:

a) Where copying and imitation are cheap and/or hard to detect, it is usually difficult and sometimes impossible to prevent this from happening.

---

[95] See, eg, Patents Act 1953 (NZ), ss 74, 85(2); Patents Act 1990 (Aust), s 128.

[96] For a detailed analysis of the warring viewpoints on the economics of justification and expansion as applied to copyright, see Netanel, NW, 'Copyright in a Democratic Civil Society' (1996) 106 *Yale Law Journal* 283.

[97] Landes and Posner (1989), n 75 above, at 333. For a more recent empirical analysis, see the (UK) *Gowers Review of Intellectual Property* (December 2006), available at <www.hm-treasury.gov.uk/media/583/91/pbr06_gowers_report_755.pdf>, which includes a commissioned review of the *Economic Evidence Relating to an Extension of the Term of Copyright in Sound Recordings* (2006), Centre for Intellectual Property and Information Law (CIPIL), University of Cambridge, available at <www.hm-treasury.gov.uk/d/gowers_cipilreport.pdf>. See also the (2009) *Independent Studies of Copyright Term Extension*, a summary of relevant empirical research reports noted by the Centre for Intellectual Property Policy and Management (CIPPM), Bournemouth University, available at <www.cippm.org.uk/downloads/Studies_and_Signatories.pdf>. That research summary underpins the statement (by 50 attached academic signatories) sent to the European Commission on 16 June 2008 and reported as Opinion, 'Creativity stifled? A Joint Academic Statement on the Proposed Copyright Term Extension for Sound Recordings' [2008] 30 *European Intellectual Property Review* 341. The CIPPM website also contains a set of links to other empirical research (see <www.cippm.org.uk/downloads/>). The Gowers Review entered a second stage of consultation and reporting in 2008, closing March 2010. See *Taking forward the Gowers Review of IP: 2nd stage consultation on Copyright Exceptions*, available at <www.ipo.gov.uk/consult-gowers2.pdf>.

b) This may lead to an under-production of innovative or creative goods or services, since innovators or creators are likely to choose not to produce them in the first place if the fruits of their intellectual endeavours are easily appropriated by others.
c) Attempts to avoid such misappropriation by holding back disclosure so that profit can be made in one upfront hit on first sale may have an adverse effect on the dissemination of innovation and ideas.[98]
d) Creativity and innovation are, in the great majority of instances, positive contributors to net social wealth, and the few instances in which they are not can be safely ignored because of the transaction costs associated with isolating them case by case.
e) Appropriate rewards must therefore be devised for innovators and creators.
f) These rewards must be protected against third-party capture or destruction by enforceable rules. Each legal rule requires independent economic verification.[99]

None of these propositions presupposes the existence of a general property right in intangibles. Neither, as a matter of legal fact, do all legal protections for innovation or creativity take this form. Property is one answer. Case-by-case regulated privilege might be another.[100] Liability rules are a third. Property is, however, the incentive system to which most economists will instinctively turn first, if only because its context-blind rules greatly assist the process of model building. This is not to say that intellectual property rights do not have their detractors amongst economists. They exist, but are vastly outnumbered by defenders. The nature of both attack and defence has varied over time. There has been a subtle shift from justifying (or deploring) the existence of particular rights to an approach which applauds (or condemns) their expansion. It is important to separate the two processes historically, if only to contest the all-too-easy assumption that all increases in innovation and creativity are matched by increases in efficiency.

4.6.2 The economics of rights expansion

Intellectual property is now such a long-established and durable part of the legal landscape that it is easy to forget the considerable weight of serious economic commentary which once sought to demonstrate that it was or was not a good

---

[98] This would of course suggest that protecting trade secrets against competition scrutiny might not always be a good idea.
[99] The legal rule need not apply ex post facto. It could operate ex ante in the form of bounties, salaries or research funds, in which case it would be protected by the ordinary law of theft and fraud.
[100] See Drahos, n 28 above.

thing.[101] This was usually done by constructing empirically undernourished models of what the world would look like without it, and inviting us to cheer or boo the resulting almost wholly hypothetical construct.[102]

That these learned contests have faded from sight does not mean that the defenders of intellectual property always had the best of the argument. Their opponents sometimes made telling points: inventors and innovators, they said, may be driven to invest and innovate without any direct economic spur; and that if any incentives are indeed needed, they might be more effectively provided by grants to individuals or tax policies designed to direct corporate funding towards research and development and away from other forms of expenditure.[103] While these arguments may now seem both dated and intuitively wrong, this owes more to ideological fashion than rational demolition.[104] Intellectual property rights won the war because they were too firmly entrenched to be dislodged, not because the economic case for them was watertight. The reality was that both sides spent most of their time tilting at windmills because neither could convincingly isolate a control group of consumers deprived of products or processes, because these products or processes were protected (or unprotected) by intellectual property in a world where such protection has become the norm. This is not to say that such empirical studies are not sometimes attempted[105]; and such studies do not always point unequivocally in the direction of more and stronger intellectual property protection. Comparative studies using countries with under-developed or under-enforced intellectual property rights as a control group occasionally conclude that there is a negative correlation between the robustness of an economy's intellectual property regime and early economic

---

[101] Some commentators took the agnostic stance that intellectual property rights do neither observable good, nor observable harm. See, eg, Pigou, AC, *The Economics of Welfare*, 4th edn (London, MacMillan, 1960).

[102] For one of the few economists prepared to own up to the empirical underfeeding, see Priest, GL, 'What Economists Can Tell Lawyers About Intellectual Property: Comment on Cheung' (1986) 8 *Research in Law and Economics* 19.

[103] Some went further by raising the intriguing possibility that patents, for example, might actively divert research into what is patentable and away from other areas. See Plant, A, 'An Economic Theory of Patents' (1934) 1 *Economica* 30. On the general issue of over-production of information in response to legal protection, see Fame, EF and Laffer, AB, 'Information and Capital Markets' (1971) 44 *Journal of Business* 289.

[104] That elusive phenomenon in the economic analysis of legal institutions and structures known as 'path dependence'. See Roe, MJ, 'Chaos and Evolution in Law and Economics' (1996) 109 *Harvard Law Review* 641. On this view, a world of limited (or no) intellectual property represents yet another 'path not taken'.

[105] See, eg, Taylor, CT and Silberston, ZA, *The Economic Impact of the Patent System: A Study of the British Experience* (London, Cambridge University Press, 1973); and Ku, RSR, Sun, J and Fan, Y, 'Does Copyright Law Promote Creativity?' (2009) 62 *Vanderbilt Law Review* 1669. The latter study, while useful, is methodologically flawed by its use of the number of copyright works produced in a given period as a proxy for creativity. Its findings suggest that net social gains are more likely to be overstated than understated.

take-off.[106] Empirical studies which avoid the big question 'Are IP rights justified?' in pursuit of smaller objectives, such as the appropriate duration or subject matter of particular rights, seem to produce more immediately usable results.[107] Another potentially fruitful area for empirical investigation seems to lie in cross-border studies of the economic effect of variations in substantive intellectual property law across jurisdictions.[108] To be effective such studies would have to focus on clear points of difference (duration, categories of protected subject matter). They can thus easily be outflanked by the global push to harmonise the content and duration of intellectual property across jurisdictions.[109] That the debate continues to be of more than historical interest is due not to the conflicting, but largely unverifiable, positive arguments advanced by each side but to the emergence of a set of negatives on which they largely agreed. These were:

a) Intellectual property rights are not always the only, or even the most effective, way of fostering innovation and creativity.[110]
b) Rules which encourage innovation and creativity also inhibit, at least temporarily, their dissemination and use.[111]
c) The match between incentive and right is never perfect. Fixed rules about what is protected and the nature and duration of protection means that some innovative or creative activities will be over rewarded while others will be undervalued. Property-based rules are more likely to produce this result than liability rules.[112]

---

[106] See Oddi, AS, 'The International Patent System and Third World Development: Reality or Myth?' [1987] *Duke Law Journal* 831.
[107] See *Report on Vehicle and Recreational Marine Craft Repair and Insurance Industries* (Industry Commission, Australia, 1994) at 123.
[108] See Erickson, S, 'Patent Law and New Product Development: Does Priority Claim Basis Make a Difference' (1999) 36 *American Business Law Journal* 327.
[109] One area that might repay empirical study is the world of cooking and cuisine (high and low), where dishes can easily be reverse-engineered and there is no patent or copyright protection for recipes as such, and yet where innovation and creativity appear not to be in short supply.
[110] Even writers who are, on balance, supportive of intellectual property as a prime driver of research and development, acknowledge that in the case of basic scientific research, State or charitable funding may be more effective. See, eg, Arrow, K, 'Economic Welfare and the Allocation of Resources for Inventors' in *The Rate and Direction of Inventive Activity: Economic and Social Factors* (A Report of the National Bureau of Economic Research, Princeton, 1962) at 609; Nelson, RR, 'The Simple Economics of Basic Scientific Research' (1959) 67 *Journal of Political Economy* 297. Other commentators see intellectual property in general, and patents in particular, as a driver of innovation only in certain atypical industries (such as pharmaceuticals and chemicals), while in the rest of the economy they are largely irrelevant; Scherer, FM, 'Antitrust Efficiency and Progress' (1987) 62 *New York University Law Review* 998 at 1013.
[111] Easterbrook, FH, 'Insider Trading, Secret Agents, Evidentiary Privileges and the Production of Information' (1981) *Supreme Court Review* 309.
[112] Liability rules are more easily adjusted to fit extraneous social factors. See Rowley, FA, 'Dynamic Copyright Law Its Problems and a Possible Solution' (1998) 12 *Harvard Journal of Law and Technology* 481.

d) Intellectual property should be minimalist in its aspirations. Even if it is not always possible to deliver the precise quantity of protection required to trigger the optimal amount of innovation or creativity, gross mismatches between the two are to be avoided. Such an objective is better served by rights which are deliberately limited in scope to achieve the social aims in pursuit of which the rights were instituted in the first place. On this analysis more is not better, even if sometimes unavoidable within the context of a uniformly applicable system of rules.[113]

This essentially negative consensus concerning what was seen at the time as a fairly stable set of rights serving limited social ends was destined to have a very short life, undone both by the massive expansion in the set of legal constructs we call intellectual property and a direct shift in the thinking of some economists which saw them give those constructs a much more central and dynamic role in the economy.[114] Other economists continued to resist the expansionist wave, or even sought to push it back within what they saw as economically defensible borders.

Intellectual property, precisely because it is disconnected from any *res*, will have fuzzier boundaries than interests in land or physical objects. This fuzziness is what leads infringers to chance their arm. It is also what gives intellectual property rights a rubber-like expandability in the race to head off those self-same infringers. If pushed too far, such expansion will drive otherwise substitutable products or processes out of the market. But how far is too far? Can economics set rational and defensible limits to this process? Unfortunately, it is on precisely these issues that the implicit economic consensus breaks down into a cacophony of competing voices.

4.6.3 Cheering on the expansion

The expansion of intellectual property protection over the last two decades has not been without its law and economics acolytes. Let us call them the X Expansionists and the Y Expansionists.[115] While each group[116] has its own

---

[113] Breyer, S, 'The Uneasy Case for Copyright: A Study of Copyright in Books, Photocopies and Computer Programs' (1970) 84 *Harvard Law Review* 281 at 322. Breyer's views expressed here are all the more interesting because they are based on some rare (if in this case, necessarily limited) empirical fact findings.
[114] Repeating the earlier experience, it is the former which seems to have driven the latter in most instances.
[115] See Rutherford, M, *Institutions in Economics: The Old and the New Institutionalism* (New York, Cambridge University Press, 1994).
[116] We accept that affixing labels to various schools of economic thought can, on occasion, distort the viewpoints of individual writers by exaggerating differences between, and minimising the sometimes subtle distinctions within, the 'schools' so described. (For a judicial chiding

conceptual slant on the role of intellectual property in the economy, points of agreement between them far outweigh their differences. Both dismiss the 'incentive to create' approach as primitive reductionism,[117] based on 'highly dubious and decidedly non empirical assumptions about real life bargains'.[118] What they share is a belief that intellectual property is best viewed as a pricing mechanism designed to ensure that creative or innovative products and services end up in the hands of those who value them most (this being both groups' optimal measure of social gain[119]). To this end they support, wherever possible, broad property-based rights with strictly limited defences,[120] rights which are designed to capture the full value of every potential market niche for as many uses of the creative output as possible.

If the abiding fear of traditional incentive theorists is the uncreated work or invention, what keeps X Expansionists awake at night is the spectre of the undervalued output. For them, intellectual property is no more than a metering device for measuring the worth of all of the potential uses a work or invention might have. Their focus is not so much on the activities of the creator or innovator but on those who invest in getting the fruits of creativity and innovation to market, or who distribute, develop and promote those fruits once there.[121] The monopoly rents which attend any intellectual property right are not there primarily as a creativity carrot, but rather as a channel of communication through which consumers can signal their preferences in advance, thus enabling

---

on this score see *Fisher and Paykel Ltd v Commerce Commission* [1990] 2 NZLR 730 at 761.) It is also unfair to those such as Professor Gordon who have moved on from the sometimes dogmatic stances taken in their earlier writing to a more nuanced explanation of market phenomena (cf Gordon, WJ, 'An Inquiry Into the Merits of Copyright: The Challenges of Consistency, Consent and Encouragement Theory' (1989) 41 *Stanford Law Review* 1343 at 1435; and Gordon, WJ, 'On Owning Information: Intellectual Property and the Restitutionary Impulse' (1992) 78 *Virginia Law Review* 149 at 184). A general survey of the kind embarked on here, however, has to paint with a broad brush if it is to paint at all.

[117] Gordon (1989), n 116 above, at 1435; Merges, RP and Nelson, RR, 'On the Complex Economics of Patent Scope' (1990) 90 *Columbia Law Review* 839 at 842.

[118] Gordon (1992), n 116 above, at 184. As was stated earlier, building large theories on a small empirical base is a vice shared by most of the law and economics writers, neo-classicists included. Postulating likely consumer responses to hypothetically 'broad' or 'narrow' intellectual property rights as Professor Gordon does is not, to our (admittedly untrained) eyes, noticeably more scientific.

[119] Goldstein, P, *Copyright's Highway: From Gutenberg to the Celestial Jukebox* (New York, Hill and Wang, 1994) at 236. Digital technology greatly assists this process, first, by identifying all potential users and tracking their use and, secondly, by subdividing these uses into separately chargeable preferences. See Froomkin, AM, 'Flood Control on the Information Ocean: Living with Anonymity, Digital Cash and Distributed Data Bases' (1996) 15 *Journal of Law and Commerce* 395 at 450 ff.

[120] For commentators such as Goldstein, n 119 above, at 224, infringement rules which allow copying for socially-worthy causes are a deplorable distribution of wealth from owners to users. The same hostility to distributive outcomes also surfaces in competition law, as we saw in ch 3.

[121] Kitch, EW, 'The Nature and Function of the Patent System' (1977) 20 *Journal of Law and Economics* 265.

creators, innovators and their financial backers to bend their efforts to producing the kind of product or service that consumers most want.[122] Crucial to this thesis is the notion that all the potential threads by which a work or invention may be exploited should start off in a single pair of hands (not necessarily, or even desirably, those of the author or inventor). For X Expansionists, the virtue of concentrated ownership is that it requires those who wish to build on or embellish the protected invention or work to deal with its first owner, rather than utilising their own freestanding rights to capture the full value of the improvement or embellishment. This belief is in no way diminished by the need for subsequent subdivision and dispersal of that ownership, something which X Expansionists fully accept (and indeed praise). For them it is the starting point rather than the final destination that is important. In this world the first owner is to be regarded as being as much a manager of the intellectual resource as its creator.[123] None of this is contested by the Y Expansionists. While they may differ from their colleagues on some fundamental conceptual issues,[124] these differences surface in the intellectual property debate at one point only: the importance and effect of transaction costs in organising markets. X Expansionists treat transaction costs as occasional, easily avoided and essentially minor bumps on the high road to economic efficiency. Y Expansionists regard those same costs as major potholes, with the urge to avoid them as a central factor in business decision making. Where an X Expansionist would reluctantly admit that there will be cases in which transaction costs might be high enough to require the abandonment of property in favour of liability rules,[125] Y Expansionists urge that, even in these circumstances, a judicial and legislative preference for property

---

[122] One beneficial side-effect of this in the copyright arena is thought to be the conscious production of works which are particularly well-suited to the development of derivative spin-offs, eg books which are easily turned into films, or cartoon characters particularly suited to becoming toys. See Goldstein, n 119 above.

[123] Kitch, n 121 above, describes patentees as 'co-ordinators of the investment of others' whose job it is to dissuade those others from duplicating research or hoarding information. Professor Gordon initially applied the same logic to copyright, describing the owner's role as being to 'facilitate or organise post-creation dissemination of the work'; see Gordon, WJ, 'Asymmetric Market Failure and the Prisoner's Dilemma in Intellectual Property' (1992) 17 *University of Dayton Law Review* 853 at 855. She was later to resile somewhat from this view. See Gordon (1992), n 116 above. See also Edward, K, 'The Nature and Function of the Patent System' [1977] *Journal of Law and Economics* 265.

[124] Y Expansionists tend to eschew the formal model building of their X brethren, having little faith in the latter's emphasis on price rather than structure and process. The former are also more prepared to concede that markets do not always behave rationally, at least in the short term. See North, DC, *Institutions, Institutional Change and Economic Performance* (New York, Cambridge University Press, 1990). For a good, non-technical summary of the differences between these two schools, see Netanel (1996), n 96 above.

[125] Posner, n 11 above, at 51; Calabresi and Melamed, n 15 above, at 1106.

over obligation forces market players to devise new and creative ways of minimising or even eliminating transaction costs.[126] Businesses, they say, must learn to negotiate their way around market failure rather than rely on the courts to repair that failure by inventing new torts or extending old ones. It is this viewpoint which makes Y Expansionists particularly receptive to attempts to extend intellectual property through restrictive licensing arrangements[127] or technology 'lock-ins', and to applaud the horizontal aggregation of copyright through collection agencies.

None of this should be allowed to obscure the broad commonalities between these two schools of thought. If X Expansionists and Y Expansionists were each asked to paint a picture of their ideal intellectual property right, there would be a clear familial resemblance in the resulting portraits: minimal prohibitions on protectable subject matter; limited public interest defences and clear first-comer priority over developmental or derivative users. Both portraits would be framed by clear property rights, rather than the indeterminate case-by-case balancing which characterises liability rules, and both would treat the right to refuse to license as a near absolute.

4.6.4 Worried bystanders and prophets of doom

Not all economic theory points in an expansionist direction. Rational arguments may be, and are, advanced for the contrary viewpoint. Beyond their shared doubts, however, these groups have little in common. Some arguments are, in essence, restatements of incentive theory,[128] holding that any protection over and above that required to induce new works and inventions creates a deadweight loss to society as a whole, and that the aim is not to maximise the amount of innovation produced but to determine the point at which such gains are marginal. The only limitation which these reborn incentivists will accept is the administrative savings conferred by the need for uniform rules. Pragmatism drives them regretfully to agree that case-by-case fine-tuning (which pure theory seems to require in order to give each author or inventor only that precise dose of

---

[126] Krier, JE and Schwab, SJ, 'Property Rules and Liability Rules: The Cathedral in Another Light' (1995) 70 *New York University Law Review* 440 at 464.
[127] The enthusiasm of Y Expansionists for contractual extension of intellectual property rights should not be read as a general preference for contract over property. They remain zealous supporters of broadly-based property rights as an initial launching pad for later contractual enhancement.
[128] More often than not these restatements are judicial rather than academic. See, eg, *Sony Corp v Universal City Studios* 464 US 417 (1984) at 429; *Harper and Row v Nation Enterprises* 471 US 539 (1985) at 546. Restatements of the incentive theory tend to be tinged with regret that both legislative enhancement and judicial exegesis have escaped its bounds, without describing any clear way back such as might be provided by competition policy; see Sterk, n 49 above. This is perhaps just as well. Their competition analysis tends to be an over-simplified and one-dimensional, all too easily equating statutory monopoly with market power.

protection which will propel them to the word processor or laboratory bench) would in practice lead to astronomical transaction costs both for the legal system and individual litigants.[129] Some of their number are concerned that favouring 'facilitators' over creators or inventors undermines the purpose for which intellectual property was created in the first place and may lead to an undesirable concentration of market power.[130]

At the other end of the conceptual spectrum are those digital anarchists who believe that the Internet and the blogosphere are their own instigators of authorship and innovation, needing little or no legislative or judicial boost in the form of enhanced intellectual property rights.[131] In this property-less cybertopia everyone will, in the words of one of their number, 'be free to play in the fields of the word'.[132] Ironically perhaps, the digital anarchists share one thing with expansionists, the notion that all content is equal. In their case, however, it leads not to an equality of over-protection but to a conviction that the proliferation of unstructured communication made possible by social networks needs no legal protection at all to conjure it into existence. This is no doubt true, but the digital anarchists' failure to distinguish between ephemeral cyber chat and works requiring sustained intellectual effort or large financial investment, diminishes their case. Electronic dissemination tells us nothing new about authorial or investor incentives for the latter type of work.[133] More interesting than these increasingly marginalised groups (at least from a competition policy viewpoint) are the perspectives offered by three other strains of law and economics thinking: public choice analysis; game theory; and investment displacement.

Public choice theory (or at least its law and economics manifestation) seeks to demonstrate that legal rules and structures are more likely to reflect the interests of small and well-organised lobby groups than those of wider but less cohesive economic interests.[134] Translated into an intellectual property context, this means that large diffuse groups of users and consumers seldom have their interests reflected in the content of intellectual property statutes. It also means that where

---

[129] Sterk, n 49 above. The same point is sometimes made in relation to the 'rule of reason' analysis in competition cases, although in a properly working competition regime such cases would be rare exceptions to a competitively functioning market rather than a ubiquitous norm.

[130] Worthington, S, 'Art, Law and Creativity' (2009) 68 *Current Legal Problems* 168 at 193.

[131] The more exuberant of these anarchists sometimes follow their own internal logic to its ultimate destination: the abolition of copyright. See Palmer, TG, 'Intellectual Property: A Non Posnerian Law and Economics Approach' (1989) 12 *Hamline Law Review* 261.

[132] Lange, DL, 'At Play in the Fields of the Word: Copyright and the Construction of Authorship in the Post Literate Millennium' (1992) 55 *Law and Contemporary Problems* 139 at 151. Digital anarchism concentrates its attention on copyright. It has little to say about other forms of intellectual property.

[133] This is not to say that copyright can or should operate in exactly the same way in the digital and hard-copy worlds.

[134] This follows from the more general public choice principle that all collective activity confers benefits on those outside the collectivity, and the larger and more diffuse the collectivity the greater the external benefits conferred. See Olsen, M, *The Logic of Collective Action* (Boston MA, Harvard University Press, 1971).

it is necessary to reconcile the interests of well-organised groups such as authors, inventors and investors, the easiest way is to expand the scope of the intellectual property right in question so that everyone gets something, even if the slices of that something are anything but equal.[135] Whatever its empirical foundation, public choice theory certainly has an intuitive question-raising resonance when applied to efforts at intellectual property law reform in particular jurisdictions.

It is, however, *investment displacement analysis* which offers the most sustained and directly applicable critique of expanded intellectual property regimes. Looked at in this way, the costs of over-protection lie not so much in the increased cost to consumers and users but in the resources sucked out of the rest of the economy into the ring-fenced safety of the protected work or invention.[136] Some of the diverted resources might otherwise have gone into (although this is not necessary to the theory) alternative forms of creativity and innovation. (This last is particularly true of derivative or developmental uses of the over-protected work or innovation.) A competition policy that ignores the effect of over-protection would be flying blind, and wilfully blind at that. Further privileging an already over-extended intellectual property regime will simply misdirect more investment. First-comers are not presumptively more virtuous than second-comer innovators.

4.7 THE EROSION OF INTELLECTUAL PROPERTY'S OWN LIMITING MECHANISMS

As we have seen, all forms of intellectual property have a core concept which confines potentially protectable subject matter within socially (and more latterly, economically) defensible bounds. These concepts are becoming increasingly anorexic. While this has happened in different ways to different degrees in different jurisdictions, some broad trends are discernible beneath the mass of parochial detail. The erosion has been made all the easier by a tendency to scramble together the formerly discrete policies underlying each right.[137]

---

[135] Litman describes this process at work during the legislative gestation of the 1976 Copyright Act in the US, in Litman, JD, 'Copyright Legislation and Technological Change' (1989) 68 *Oregon Law Review* 275 at 317. As she puts it, 'the Bill that emerged ... enlarged the copyright pie and divided its pieces ... so that no leftovers remained.'

[136] Baxter, WF, 'Legal Restrictions on the Exploitation of the Patent Monopoly: An Economic Analysis' (1966) 76 *Yale Law Journal* 267; Hurt, RM and Schuhman, RM, 'The Economic Rationale of Copyright' (1966) 56 *American Economic Review* 421 at 430; Lunney, n 5 above.

[137] Scassa, T, 'Extension of Intellectual Property Rights' in M Boyer, M Trebilcock and D Vaver (eds), *Competition Policy and Intellectual Property* (Toronto, Irwin Law, 2009) 17 at 23 and 27.

4.7.1 Towards the fully protectable idea

Patent and copyright are gradually edging ever closer to protecting ideas as such.[138] Thus we have in patent law a conceptual drift which has seen process patents in the United States become almost entirely disconnected from any anchor in the physical world,[139] a development that has allowed such patents to be extended to business methods both in that jurisdiction[140] and elsewhere.[141]

The idea/expression dichotomy, one of copyright's core doctrines, has been similarly undermined in today's increasingly digitalised world.[142] In the so-called second generation of computer software copyright cases,[143] first-comer developers successfully claimed protection for a whole range of procedures, processes, systems, methods of operation and effects embodied in, or associated with, the operation of their electronic products in the teeth of copyright doctrine's traditional refusal to protect functions, facts, methods or anything already in the public domain.[144] While it is possible to discern in more recent software copyright infringement cases[145] a cross-jurisdictional judicial determination to

---

[138] A protection that at least one commentator regards as long overdue. See Miller, R, 'Common Law Protection for Products of the Mind: An Idea Whose Time Has Come' (2006) 119 *Harvard Law Review* 703.

[139] For a prescient comment as to where this trend might lead, see Thomas, JR, 'New Challenges for the Law of Patents' in CER Rickett and GW Austin (eds), *Intellectual Property in the Common Law World* (Oxford, Hart Publishing, 1999) 165. See also Thomas, JR, 'Of Proprietary Rights and Personal Liberties: Constitutional Responses to Post Industrial Patenting' in P Drahos (ed), *Death of Patents* (Witney, QMC and Lawtext, 2005) 110.

[140] *State Street Bank & Trust v Signature Financial Group* 149 F 3d 1368 (Fed Cir 1998); *AT&T v Excel Communications* 172 F 3d 1352 (Fed Cir 1999).

[141] For an Australian example, see *Welcome Real-Time SA v Catuity Inc* [2001] FCA 445, 51 IPR 327. Attempts to rein in these trends legislatively in the EU have been marred by loose drafting (the 'as such' limitation in Art 54 of the European Patent Convention) and have succeeded only in introducing a raft of ever finer distinctions to an already vexed subject. See Cornish, W, Llewelyn, D and Aplin, T, *Intellectual Property: Patents. Copyright, Trade Marks and Allied Rights*, 7th edn (London, Sweet & Maxwell, 2010) at 232 and 872.

[142] See generally Ghidini, n 83 above, at 17.

[143] The first generation of software copyright cases had dealt with the more tractable issue whether computer programs in source code could be protected by copyright as literary works as well as programs in source code form.

[144] *Whelan Associates Inc v Jaslow Dental Laboratory* 797 F 2d 1222 (3rd Cir 1986) and *Autodesk v Dyason* [1993] HCA 6 represent the high water-mark of judicial validation of such claims in the US and Australia respectively. In *Whelan*, the defendant was found to have infringed the first-comer's program because its structure, sequence and organisation (its 'look and feel' elements), as reflected in the screen display, had been copied; and in *Autodesk*, copyright subsistence in a computer program as a set of instructions was also extended to the information or data upon which it operated.

[145] See decisions of the Australian Federal Court in *Dais Studio Pty Ltd v Bullet Creative Pty Ltd* [2007] FCA 2054; the UK Court of Appeal in *Nova Productions Ltd v Mazooma Games Ltd* [2007] EWCA Civ 219 and the US Court of Appeals for the Federal Circuit in *Hutchins v Zoll Medical Corporation* 492 F 3d 1377 (Fed Cir 2007).

reassert the importance of maintaining a distinction[146] between an idea and its expression, that trend is far from uniform. In cases of this kind it is fatally easy for judges to lose their way in a technological fog and drift in the direction of protecting information as such, or allowing function to trump form.[147]

Even if we grant that the idea/expression dichotomy has not always been evenly applied across all forms of creative activity, and has sometimes operated at too high a level of abstraction to be immediately useful in hard cases,[148] its abandonment without any obvious replacement in sight[149] (or indeed any sign that such a replacement is being sought) is worrying from a competition perspective.

4.7.2 Cutting the link between signifier and reputation

An increasing trend in the area of reputational rights is to loosen, and in some cases cut, the connection between particular types of commercial activity and the mark, name or character (real or fictional) through which those activities impinge on the consuming public. If taken far enough, this process can result in the signifier becoming a protected (and hence commodifiable) interest in its own right. The process most commonly occurs when a worst case scenario is converted into a prophylactic rule. Courts deem a business connection to exist in the minds of consumers by attributing to them a familiarity with licensing practices which is inherently unlikely and empirically unsupported in the case before them.[150] Consumer reactions are judged not by across-the-board tests of reasonableness, but by concentrating on the likely reactions of the numerically

---

[146] Such rescue was explicit in *Nova*, n 145 above, in which Jacob LJ asserted (at [31]) that the idea/expression distinction 'is intended to apply and does apply to copyright in software'.

[147] Lim, PH and Longdin, L, 'Fresh Lessons for First Movers in Software Copyright Disputes—A Cross Jurisdictional Convergence' (2009) 4 *International Review of Intellectual Property and Competition Law* 374.

[148] It has always been more of a desired outcome than a workable, bright-line rule. See comments of Learned Hand J in *Peter Pan Fabrics Inc v Martin Weiner Corp* 274 F 2d 487 (2nd Cir 1960) at 489; and those of Pritchard J in *Plix Products Ltd v Frank M Winstone Ltd* (1984) 3 IPR 390 at 419.

[149] One interesting substitute suggested by Lunney, n 5 above, at 561 and 601 is a test expressly reliant on market power analysis, one which would overtly distinguish between pro- and anti-competitive copying. However compelling this test might be to competition lawyers, there is no sign of any move towards its adoption in any jurisdiction. A similar approach was also put forward by Abrahamson, S, 'Making Sense of the Copyright Merger Doctrine' (1998) 45 *University of California Law Review* 1125.

[150] See *Children's Television Workshop Inc v Woolworths (NSW) Ltd* [1981] RPC 187, [1981] NSWLR 273; *Hogan v Koala Dundee Pty Ltd* [1988] FCA 333, 83 ALR 187; *Pacific Dunlop Ltd v Hogan* [1989] FCA 185, 87 ALR 14.

insignificant, the marginally afflicted and the congenitally unperceptive.[151] Honest traders lose their rights to use their own names on the remote chance that potential customers of same-name rivals might be deceived or misled.[152] Trade marks (at least those ones deemed to be famous) have to be protected against feared dilution and tarnishment, even when the defendant's use in trade is related to products or services completely unconnected to those of the mark owner.[153] All of these developments can harm competition by limiting not only what competitors may say about their own product, but also what they may say about the right owner's product. Competition is thus conducted with one hand behind the competitor's back.[154] A counter-trend is yet to emerge.[155]

4.7.3 Effort and investment protected *per se*

All legal systems have some difficulty devising principled rules to protect information which is not secret but on the collection, retrieval or storage of which money or effort has been expended. Fair dealing and commercial morality are such vague and unsatisfactory principles that they can easily slip out of sight altogether, leaving courts and legislators to be seduced by three attractive but dangerous fallacies that:

---

[151] This is a seemingly inevitable consequence when broadly-drafted consumer protection statutes are captured by intellectual property lawyers; see Eagles, I, 'Of Firms, Families and Fair Trading' [1998] *New Zealand Law Journal* 241.

[152] *Neumegen v Neumegen* [1998] 3 NZLR 310.

[153] See the European Trade Mark Directive to approximate the laws of the Member States relating to trade marks, 89/104/EEC, [1989] OJ L40, 11/02/1989, Arts 4(4)(a) and 5(2), and the Trade Mark Dilution Act 1996, 15 USC § 1125 (c). For a study of developments under the latter legislation, see Oswald, LJ, 'Tarnishment and Blurring under the Federal Trade Mark Dilution Act 1995' (1999) 36 *American Business Law Journal* 255; and, for a comparison of both legislative initiatives, see McCarthy, JT, 'Dilution of a Trademark: European and United States Law Compared' (2004) 94 *Trademark Reporter* 1193. After amendment by Congress in 2006, the US Trade Mark Dilution Act 1996 Act still protects only famous marks, but now there is also express protection against a use of a mark that is 'likely' to cause dilution, obviating any need to prove actual dilution. For trade mark owners, blurring through association has become more a threat with the advent of non-commercial use of marks on the Internet, Facebook and other social media.

[154] Restrictions on comparative advertising are a case in point here, see *Villa Maria Wines v Montana Wines Ltd* [1984] 2 NZLR 422; cf *PC Direct Ltd v Best Buy Ltd* [1997] 2 NZLR 723. Attitudes of US courts are far less restrictive; see *Smith v Chanel* 402 F 2d 562, 159 USPQ 338 (1968). The Trade Marks Act 1994 (UK), s 10(6) attempts to strike a balance between these two positions. As to the European position on comparative advertising generally, see McCormick, J, 'The Future of Comparative Advertising' [1998] *European Intellectual Property Review* 241.

[155] A tiny step backwards perhaps can be seen in the United States Trademark Technical and Conforming Amendment Act (2010), amending 15 USC, in that it requires the Secretary of Commerce to study and report to Congress on 'the extent to which small businesses may be harmed by litigation tactics attempting to enforce trademark rights beyond a reasonable interpretation of the scope of the rights granted to the trademark owner'.

a) Mere possession of information entitles the possessor to protection.[156]
b) Investment in information creates rights in the investor.[157]
c) Value equals property, or in other words, because information is valuable, the possessor must in some sense 'own' it.

These conceptual slippages are aided by two of the law's more runaway metaphors: that one should not reap where one has not sown, and that attempts to do so must be prevented as 'free-riding' on the efforts of the sower. Like other examples of sound-bite law, these propositions have a glib facility which conceals their intellectual impoverishment.[158] The further one moves towards protecting investment, the closer one comes to protecting collections of facts or purely functional aspects of informational products.[159] Expenditure and effort are not proxies for innovative efficiency.

Different jurisdictions have taken different roads to this principle-less limbo. In the United States, it is via misappropriation torts based on notions of 'quasi-property'[160] or vulgarisations of unjust enrichment theory.[161] In the

---

[156] Sometimes called the 'what I have, I hold' theory; see Gordon (1992), n 33 above, at 170 and 194.

[157] For a succinct demolition of the 'investment equals legally guaranteed reward' formula, see Waldron, n 10 above, at 854.

[158] Such metaphors can lead even economists astray. See, eg, the use of research and development costs to establish the baseline for intellectual property protection in Lichtman, DG, 'The Economics of Innovation: Protecting Unpatentable Goods' (1997) 81 *Minnesota Law Review* 693.

[159] For a particularly naked form of investment protection, see the Directive on the Legal Protection of Databases (96/9/EC), 11 March 1996, [1996] OJ L77. The same result may be achieved without a legislative nudge; see the decisions of the New Zealand Court of Appeal in *Land Transport Safety Authority of New Zealand v Glogau* [1999] 1 NZLR 261 (involving a vehicle logbook) and *The University of Waikato v Benchmarking Services Ltd* (2004) 8 NZBLC 101 at 561 (involving a benchmarking survey incorporating ratios and mundane descriptive headings such as 'average', 'median' and '25th percentile'). In both cases the full panoply of exclusive economic rights attaching to 'literary works' were granted to the owners of informational products that were either functional, or factual or both.

[160] This was the original conceptual umbrella under which the US Supreme Court sought to bring its decision in *International News Service v Associated Press*, n 48 above. For a discussion of the hollowness of 'quasi-property' used in this way, see Balganesh, S, 'Hot News: The Enduring Myth of Property in News' (2011) 419 *Columbia Law Review* 422.

[161] This seems to be part of a trans-jurisdictional trend towards a greater willingness to explore the 'enrichment' side of the restitution question while neglecting the much harder 'unjust' issue, at least in those cases where the enrichment occurs via the acquisition or use of information. A principled restitutionary analysis balances the interests of plaintiff and defendant according to some pre-existing calculus depending on the defendant's state of mind and the vulnerability of the plaintiff. That calculus should also, as Professor Gordon points out, make room for the wider public interest, one factor in which should be the preservation of competitive markets, see n 33 above, at 215, 220 and 227. It should also take into account that creating a cause of action can involve greater transaction and enforcement costs than denying one, *ibid*. Restitutionary theory also poses another problem in this context. To the extent that it is dependent on corrective justice 'restoring' already recognised legal interests, it has an obvious

United Kingdom something similar occurs when so-called 'sweat of the brow' tests in copyright law drive originality thresholds to new depths.[162] From here it is but a short step to *sui generis* protection for databases, a step already taken in the European Union.[163] If one steps back and views this development from a competition perspective, what we have is the extraordinary spectacle of governments which loudly proclaim their opposition to picking winners doing precisely that when it comes to information-intensive industries. In economic terms this is State-directed investment, no more, no less.

4.7.4 Widening the copyright infringement net

In its infancy copyright law was concerned with near literal copying. The infringement net has now been cast vastly more widely, and expansive tests based on 'substantial similarity' are now the norm in most jurisdictions. Such tests are not necessarily inherently anti-competitive. They can, however, raise barriers to entry through the uncertainty they create. The problem is compounded when they are supplemented by evidentiary presumptions favouring right holders,[164] or combined with allegations of subconscious[165] or indirect copying.[166] One should not underestimate the deterrent effect of these developments on the forensically under-funded but potentially innovative competitor. At the very least they increase the right owner's opportunity for gaming.[167]

---

circularity when used to determine whether such rules or interests should exist in the first place. See Sterk, n 49 above.

[162] Eg, *Waterlow Directories v Reed Information* (1990) 20 IPR 493, [1992] FSR 409.

[163] The final step was arguably unnecessary in the UK given the general prevalence there of the 'sweat of the brow' test; *ibid*. This posed a dilemma for the UK when enacting database protection, a dilemma solved by the conceptual legerdemain of importing the higher civilian creativity threshold when protection is sought for these works under copyright law (a move resisted for other works) and removing it entirely under the *sui generis* limb.

[164] There has been a certain logical slippage in these presumptions. Thus, 'substantial similarity' plus proof of access equals presumed copying (*LB Plastics Ltd v Swish Products Ltd* [1979] RPC 551 at 619) can become the faintly circular 'substantial similarity presumes access and therefore copying' (*Francis Day and Hunter Ltd v Bron* [1963] Ch 587 at 612). The probative goalposts can be shifted even further if the court accepts possible, rather than actual, access as its starting point: *Francis Day, ibid*, at 614. For a similar process at work in the US jurisprudence, see *Nelson v PRN Productions Ltd* 873 F 2d 1141 (8th Cir 1989) at 1142; *Gaste v Kaiserman* 863 F 2d 1061 (2nd Cir 1988) at 1067.

[165] See *Abkco Music Inc v Harrison's Music Ltd* 722 F 2d 988 (2nd Cir 1983) at 997; *EMI Music Publishing Ltd v Papathanassiou* [1993] EMLR 306.

[166] The furthest extension of the concept of indirect copying is perhaps represented by those cases where the link between the plaintiff's work and the infringing copy is provided by a mere description. See *Plix Products*, n 148 above, and *House of Spring Garden Ltd v Point Blank Ltd* [1984] IR 611.

[167] Copyright statutes lack the 'bluffing' liability provisions of their patent counterparts; see, eg, Patents Act 1953 (NZ), s 24.

4.7.5 Restricting follow-on innovation and creativity

Innovation and creativity do not exist in a vacuum.[168] Not only do most innovators and creators build on the work of others, the pursuit of efficiency goals requires that they continue to be able to do so. The law must therefore configure the right balance between protecting first-comers and encouraging transformative or improving uses of their work by others. While the problem is not confined to copyright,[169] it is there that it is at its most acute. In part this is due to the extension of tests for infringement. A more important factor, however, is the concept of the derivative work or adaptation. Never very easy to square with the idea/expression dichotomy, it now seems to have broken out of square entirely. Originally introduced to deal with the problem of simple translations, the test for derivative work is now wide enough in some jurisdictions, most notably the United States, to confer on copyright owners something approaching a veto on the use of particular characters (or even the fictional world they inhabit).[170] Again, while courts have generally been vigilant to prevent authors from capturing whole *genre* in the case of traditional literary works, they have been much less charitable to the derivative user in the case of popular music.[171] Similarly, the existence in some jurisdictions of 'a voraciously open jawed definition of "compilation" in the copyright statute capable of swallowing whole other categories of work, demolishing half a century of carefully crafted case law as it feeds'[172] can inhibit follow-on innovation in some parts of the software industry. While economists differ as to the likely anti-competitive effects of these

---

[168] Ironically, the closer the creator or innovator comes to that vacuum, the less likely she is to have legal protection because what she does is more likely to be characterised as an unprotectable idea.

[169] The softening of the obligation for patentees properly to describe the patented product or process has arguably had a similar effect in the United States. See *Northern Telecom v Datapoint* 908 F 2d 931 (Fed Cir 1990) at 942. The ability to invent around blocking patents in general has been further restricted by the absence of an experimental use defence in some jurisdictions and its sidelining in others, see eg, *Roche Products v Bolar Pharmaceutical Co* 733 F 2d 858 (Fed Cir 1984). In patent law the problem is sometimes reversed, so that it is the second-comer who is unfairly advantaged. The purer the research, the less likely it is to be patentable. See Hart, MS, 'Getting Back to Basics: Reinventing Patent Law for Economic Efficiency' (1994) 8 *Intellectual Property Journal* 217 at 231.

[170] The so-called prequel or sequel problem. See Eagles, n 43 above.

[171] For an excellent transnational analysis of the phenomenon, see van Melle, B, 'Facing the Music: Liability for Musical Plagiarism in Contemporary Popular Music' [1997] *New Zealand Intellectual Property Law Journal* 160. The problem may have been compounded by the recent reception of moral rights in common law jurisdictions. See Tackaberry, P, 'Look What They Have Done to My Song Ma: The Songwriter's Moral Right of Integrity in Canada and the United States' (1989) 11 *European Intellectual Property Review* 356.

[172] See Longdin, L, 'Computerised Compilations: A Cautionary Tale from New Zealand' (1997) 5 *International Journal of Information Technology Law* 249 at 264–68.

developments,[173] anything that inhibits the emergence of whole new markets or products is worrying, from both an allocative and an innovative efficiency perspective, whatever one's views as to the rationality of leveraging across markets.[174]

Once again, it is the absence of empirical evidence that makes the problem of follow-on innovation so intractable. Are right holders more or less likely to continue innovating themselves if protected against attempts by second-comers to do the same? In what sense is the later work or product substitutable for the earlier one in the eyes of consumers in a market as yet untested and which the existence of the intellectual property right itself ensures will remain so? Might not there be more rather than less follow-on innovation or creativity if both first- and second-comers are pushed into leapfrogging over each other's creations and innovations? Until answers can be provided to such questions, it would be unwise to tilt the balance of protection further towards first-comers.

4.8 PUSHING AT THE TIME/SPACE ENVELOPE

For reasons which come as no surprise to public choice theorists, intellectual property owners have been highly effective at the lobbying game. Among their more notable victories has been ability of copyright owners to secure the extension not only of the life of the right but also its geographical reach.

4.8.1 Extending the term of the right

The temporal boundaries of intellectual property rights tend to remain fixed for long periods of time. (This is why more than the usual limited amount of empirical research can be done on them.) When they move, however, they move in large leaps. The patent term is now 20 years in most jurisdictions. The

---

[173] Some economists are relatively relaxed about restrictions on transformative use of prior works. See Gordon, WJ, 'On the Economics of Fair Use: Systemic Versus Case by Case Responses to Market Failure' (1997) 8 *Journal of Law and Information Science* 1620 at 1628; Goldstein, P, *Copyright*, 2nd edn (Cornell, Legal Information Institute, 1996) at § 5–79; Landes and Posner, n 75 above, at 328 and 354. Others for a variety of reasons advocate either cutting back on the adaptation right, or eliminating it altogether; Lunney, n 5 above, at 650; Sterk, n 49 above.

[174] It was precisely such 'whole market' pre-emption which prompted the Court of Justice to prohibit it in Joined Cases C-241/91 P and C-242/91 P *Radio Telefis Eireann and Independent Television Publications v European Commission* ('*Magill*') [1995] ECR I-743, discussed below in ch 6. Much will depend on how the markets in question are defined. See Teyerman, BW, 'The Economic Rationale for Copyright Protection for Published Books: A Reply to Professor Beyer' (1971) 18 *University of California Law Review* 1100 at 1110.

duration of copyright has also been extended by an extra 20 years in Europe and the United States, and this without having to make any concessions on the continued use of the author's life as the other boundary peg, a usage which is beginning to look exceedingly quaint in economic terms given that the great majority of authors retain copyright for only the briefest of periods.[175] It looks even quainter when one remembers that much copyrightable output is now the result of team or group efforts in which the ascription of individual authorship is either impossible or confessedly artificial and arbitrary.

The existence of fixed terms of protection across large and differentiated classes of economic activity has always been the Achilles heel of intellectual property's claims to promote innovative efficiency.[176] The likelihood of a single, arbitrarily selected term delivering optimal protection in all circumstances is seldom seriously advanced.[177] Equally arbitrary extensions to such terms are no easier to justify.[178]

In the absence of any empirical benchmark, disputes about duration are likely to be won by the best-funded and most assertive lobby groups.[179] Extended terms of protection being highly specific can easily be exported through bilateral and multilateral trade agreements. The effect on incentives to innovate and (not the same thing, as we have seen) innovative efficiency in downstream markets for

---

[175] This strange form of family protection has long passed its economic 'use by' date. It is retained largely out of legislative habit, or perhaps a wish to conciliate those civil law jurisdictions which are accustomed to regarding an author's non-economic (ie 'moral') rights as immortal.

[176] Trade secrets are, of course, potentially immortal, with a lifespan bounded only by the right holder's willingness or ability to keep the sensitive information secret. When a right is effectively open-ended in duration then scope of grant restrictions on extending the life of a right by contract have no application; see *Warner-Lambert Pharmaceutical Co v John J Reynolds Inc* 178 F Supp 655 (SDNY 1959), aff'd 280 F 2d 197 (2nd Cir 1960).

[177] Some economists seek to solve the 'one term can't fit all situations' conundrum by suggesting (in an unlikely convergence with the civilians) that fixed terms should in principle be abolished so that intellectual property becomes as open-ended in duration as any other form of property: see Landes and Posner, n 82 above, at 361; Meiners, RE and Staaf, RJ, 'Patents, Copyrights and Trademarks: Property or Monopoly?' (1990) 13 *Harvard Journal of Law and Public Policy* 911 at 924. Chicago thinkers in general tend to favour longer terms because this fits best with their overall preference for encouraging the production of works with as many potential valued uses as possible. The longer the period, the more time the owner has to explore what those uses might be and find customers for them.

[178] Writers such as Professor Gordon, while acknowledging that the term of protection properly varies across the three traditional intellectual property families (trade marks, copyright and patents) so that the duration of the protection is inversely proportional to the potential market power conferred by each type of right, do not apply this insight *within* each family. For an attempt to do so in patent law, see Hart, n 169 above, at 225.

[179] This may be seen most clearly in the process whereby the copyright term in the US was extended from life of author plus 50 years to life of author plus 70 years by the so-called the 'Sonny Bono' Copyright Extension Act 1998, amending 17 USC. Neither during Congressional debates, nor as part of the later constitutional challenge (culminating in the US Supreme Court decision in *Eldred v Ashcroft* 537 US 186 (2003)), was any serious attempt made to justify the extension in empirical terms.

derivative works and adaptations can then quietly be ignored. Once extended, the period of protection is unlikely to be reduced,[180] even if economic benefits from such a reduction could be demonstrated.

4.8.2 Towards the inexhaustible right

The subject matter of intellectual property law may be intangible but that law itself has always been heavily dependent on dealings in tangibles to set the parameters of infringement. For most of its history it was the *sale* of pirated copies which right owners sought to stamp out. With this, however, went a recognition that purchasers too had rights, and that in general they should be free to sell on copies which had been legitimately acquired. In some jurisdictions this was explicitly stated as an 'exhaustion of rights' rule. In others it had to be inferred from the manner in which infringement was defined in the statute in question. Whatever their name and provenance, such rules operated as real constraints on the power of right holders to subdivide markets horizontally or segment them vertically.[181] Increasingly, however, these constraints are being bypassed.

(a) Parallel importing restrictions

The freeing-up of international trade has given new force to parallel importing restrictions long dormant within individual countries' intellectual property regimes. In a protectionist world such restrictions were only of marginal significance in competition terms, because of the existence of much higher and more effective barriers to entry in the form of tariffs and import controls. Once the latter fell, however, the former took on a much more prominent role. Private regulation could now replace State action, with anti-competitive possibilities which right owners and their licensees were quick to recognise and sometimes act upon. The trend was only marginally dented by isolated examples of legislative reversal in jurisdictions such as New Zealand (where it was sudden and drastic),

---

[180] The legislative and political cold-shoulder awaiting the interesting (and empirically-based) arguments advanced by Boldrin, M and Levine, D in 'Growth and Intellectual Property', *NBER Working Paper No 12769* (2007), and in *Against Intellectual Property* (New York, Cambridge University Press, 2008), that patent protection for computer programs could be reduced from 20 to 10 years and the copyright term to two years, can only be imagined. See *NBER WP 12769*, available at <www.nber.org/papers/w12769.pdf>.

[181] Neither horizontal nor vertical constraints need be anti-competitive in themselves. They may become so if they: (i) fall foul of the *per se* prohibitions in particular competition regimes; or (ii) are used as a mechanism for furthering anti-competitive dealings; or (iii) enable those with power in one market to leverage that power into other markets.

Singapore and Australia.[182] Even then right owners and licensees did not remain passive in the face of repeal. Not only was much legal ingenuity expended on replacing statutory barriers with contractual ones (although competition authorities still remained free to challenge these last), but cross-border passage of electronic products such as video games became increasingly controlled by technological means. In the negotiations for the new multilateral Anti-Counterfeiting Trade Agreement, jurisdictions that ventured to repeal parallel importing restrictions are now facing pressure to recant in return for collateral trade advantages (real or supposed) from countries such as the United States, which consider themselves advantaged by the existence of such restrictions and against whom the WTO would be powerless to provide a remedy.[183]

(b) From sale to access

Exhaustion of rights makes sense only when the intellectual property right in question is embodied in a physical object, property in which at some stage passes out of the hands of the right holder.[184] As the focus of copyright and database protection moves away from hard-copy sales to rights to view, display or further transmit, exhaustion of rights becomes less and less relevant. While this trend is not new, the digitalisation and technological barricading of much that was formally held only in hard-copy form has greatly speeded up the process. All of this greatly enhances the ability of copyright owners to impose potentially anti-competitive conditions on both initial access to, and subsequent use of, the protected material. A parallel development may be seen at work in patent law as applicants recast their claims from product to process, thus side-stepping the exhaustion rules which have always applied to the former.[185]

---

[182] To date such reversals apply only to copyright law. The restrictive possibilities of trade mark law, although less generous to licensees, continue to be able to be exploited. It can also be argued that such reversals are the antithesis of a coherent competition policy because they focus on consequences not causes and price rather than efficiency. Not every exercise of a power to restrict imports has anti-competitive results. Neither should we assume that there can never be legitimate business reasons for resisting parallel imports, where, eg, identical trade marks mask a difference in quality or function, or the entry barrier acts as a surrogate for effective cross-border checks on piracy (assuming that the ineffectiveness of border controls in a particular jurisdiction can be demonstrated as a matter of fact).

[183] Exhaustion of rights issues are placed outside the scope of TRIPS by Art 6 of that document.

[184] The intellectual property need not, and usually will not, pass with the title to the physical object. We are dealing with two property rights here, not one: *Pacific Film Laboratories Pty Ltd v FCT* [1970] HCA 36, 121 CLR 151; *Barson Computers (NZ) Ltd v John Gilbert and Co Ltd* (1984) 4 IPR 533; *WGN Continental Broadcasting Co v United Video Inc* 693 F 2d 662 (7th Cir 1982); *United States v Goss* 803 F 2d 638 (11th Cir 1986); *Rockford Map Publishers Inc v Directory Service Co of Colorado* 768 F 2d 145 (7th Cir 1985).

[185] See Thomas, n 139 above.

4.8.3 Exporting over-protection

The globalisation of markets in general, and intellectual property markets in particular, has exacerbated the growing imbalance between intellectual property protection and competition values. Jurisdictions which view themselves as important exporters of intellectual property, or of intellectual property-protected products or services, not unnaturally wish to see their own strong (and expanding) intellectual property regimes as the model to which all jurisdictions should move as quickly as possible.[186] Equally natural is the wish of right holders to structure their activities in ways which attract the protection of these stronger regimes. That both are increasingly able to have their wish is due to two factors. The first stems from the expansionist bias built into the process of negotiating international conventions. When the negotiating parties come up against a fundamental conceptual clash, the easiest exit from deadlock is to ensure that no jurisdiction loses a protection to which its right owners have become accustomed.[187] Harmonisation in this scheme of things almost always means harmonisation up, not harmonisation down, thus projecting onto the international stage the distortions endemic in domestic intellectual property law reform. The second factor, facilitating the export of overly-protectionist intellectual property regimes, is the emergence of choice of law rules which erode the territoriality principle which had hitherto prevailed in transnational intellectual property litigation.[188]

---

[186] This can sometimes be accompanied by a strong whiff of hypocrisy when the intellectual property-exporting country seeks to impose strong tests for infringement while depriving a target jurisdiction of the relaxed fair use rules that it applies internally. The same could be said of supranational free trade areas which relax or abolish parallel importing restrictions between members while maintaining them against the rest of the world.

[187] A process aptly described by one commentator as the 'global intellectual property ratchet'. See Drahos, P, 'BITS and BIPS: Bilateralism in Intellectual Property' (2001) 4 *Journal of World Intellectual Property* 791 at 798.

[188] Austin, GW, 'Copyright Across (and Within) Borders: Jurisdictional Issues and Choice of Law' in CER Rickett and GW Austin (eds), *Intellectual Property in the Common Law World* (Oxford, Hart Publishing, 1999) 105.

5

Refusals to License in the United States

5.1 THE FRAGMENTATION OF UNITED STATES MONOPOLISATION LAW

United States anti-monopolisation law has few unifying features. Looked at in the round, jurisprudence under section 2 of the Sherman Act[1] (employing few words and language old-fashioned enough to enable the courts to paint with a broad interpretive brush) presents as a series of discrete, highly-contextualised sub-rules, each built around a particular type of anti-competitive conduct: tying, predatory pricing and raising rivals' costs, to list some examples. Unilateral refusals to deal, on this view, are part of the same phenomenon. The reasons for this contextual fragmentation are too complex to trace in detail here. Neither are we concerned with the wider consequences for United States antitrust law.[2] What can be said, however, is that the separate evolution of these sub-rules over time, and the relative infrequency of their consideration (and reconsideration) by the Supreme Court, ensure that they embody very different attitudes to the efficacy of regulatory intervention (sometimes even falling on opposite sides of the rule of reason/*per se* divide at particular stages of their separate histories). This in turn has made it very difficult for the law to adopt or maintain an approach of regulatory neutrality between different manifestations of market power or different modes of exploiting it. In this fragmented environment the only unifying factors tend to be the rhetorical negatives outlined in chapter two, in which judicial *aperçus* have to do the conceptual heavy lifting for which they are

---

[1] 15 USC §2 reads: 'Every person who shall monopolize, or attempt to monopolize, or combine or conspire with any other person or persons, to monopolize any part of the trade or commerce among the several States, or with foreign nations, shall be deemed guilty of a felony ... '

[2] For an in-depth explanation of both phenomena, see Elhauge, E, 'Tying, Bundled Discounts and the Death of the Single Monopoly Theory' (2009) 123 *Harvard Law Review* 397. Historically, one of the reasons for fragmentation was the enthusiasm of an earlier generation of American judges for constructing *per se* prohibitions focused on particular business practices. Often, however, the characteristic fragmentation has survived abandonment of the *per se* position for a rule of reason approach, and continues to be both conduct-based and contextual.

particularly unsuited.[3] Refusals to license intellectual property raise all of these issues in a very acute way.

5.2 THE PUSH-ME-PULL-YOU INTELLECTUAL PROPERTY–ANTITRUST RELATIONSHIP

The history of the intersection of antitrust and intellectual property law in the United States has been largely characterised by alternating cycles of over- and under-enforcement in which first antitrust and then intellectual property prevails.[4] This recurring pattern, in which one regulatory regime moves into the front seat for a time, leaving the other relegated to the back, has prevented the two systems from interacting coherently or consistently. When cases have arisen, they have tended to involve patents rather than copyright or trade secrets. In periods of antitrust over-enforcement, this has had the effect of magnifying perceptions of the market power able to be wielded by patent owners. In times of under-enforcement, the emphasis has tended to be on the careful social bargain inherent in the patent system, under which ex ante disclosure and dissemination are supposedly traded off against relatively strong and unassailable protection. There has thus emerged a notion of a hierarchy of rights, but a reversible one in which the stronger or weaker intellectual property rights are balanced commensurately by more or less forensic antitrust scrutiny.[5]

This jostling for supremacy between the intellectual property and antitrust laws was first evident during the early twentieth century, when patent holders, attempting to expand their traditional rights beyond the first sale of their products, ended by provoking a strong antitrust reaction, resulting in amongst other things judicial recognition of the doctrine of patent misuse.[6] This period of

---

[3] Although some commentators have been searching for a unifying theory for monopolisation cases (see the arguments by leading proponents in Elhauge, E, 'Defining Better Monopolization Standards' (2003) 56 *Stanford Law Review* 253 and Hovenkamp, H, 'The Harvard and Chicago Schools and the Dominant Firm' in R Pitofsky (ed), *How the Chicago School Overshot the Mark: The Effect of Conservative Economic Analysis on US Antitrust* (New York, Oxford University Press, 2008) 109. Others are vociferously critical and dismissive of the search. Eg, Crane, DA, 'Chicago, Post-Chicago, and Neo-Chicago' (2009) 76 *University of Chicago Law Review* 1911 at 1921 describes it as bordering on the 'obsessive'. The US Department of Justice Antitrust Division, in its Discussion Paper *Competition and Monopoly: Single-Firm Conduct under Section 2 of the Sherman Act* (2008), para 41, has also rejected a general test for monopolisation. (See nn 12–14 below re the September 2008 Report that followed this consultation, and the subsequent withdrawal of the Report in May 2009.)

[4] Lemley, MA, 'A New Balance Between IP and Antitrust' (2007) 13 *Southwestern Journal of Law and Trade in the Americas* 1.

[5] *Ibid*, at 16.

[6] See *Motion Picture Patents Co v Universal Film Manufacturing Co* 243 US 502 (1917), in which the Supreme Court held that a patent owner had misused its patent by seeking to impose conditions on the licence outside the scope of the patent right. See 5.3 below.

ascendancy of antitrust law (or more properly antitrust concepts, since abuse of patent law existed in a formal sense outside the Sherman Act but drew heavily on jurisprudence under that statute) over patent rights came to an end in the 1950s, after patent rights were strengthened following the passage of the Patent Act 1952.[7] Antitrust, however, regained the upper hand during the 1960s and 1970s, when the validity of many patents was successfully contested and patent owners were susceptible to a finding of antitrust liability if they attempted to enforce invalid patents or engaged in certain kinds of licensing practices.[8] Antitrust lost ascendancy once again in the 1980s,[9] when patents became increasingly easier to obtain and defend, and the Patent Misuse Reform Act 1988 narrowed the circumstances under which a defendant could claim patent misuse by way of defence.

Another factor at play during this era was the Reagan Administration's express spurning of the regulatory authorities' restrictive rules regarding intellectual property licensing practices. Fresh guidelines concerning such practices were issued in 1995 by the Department of Justice and the Federal Trade Commission during the Clinton Administration, and the late 1990s witnessed a flurry of regulator-initiated antitrust claims and cases, including *United States v Microsoft Corporation*.[10] This resurgence of activity then dropped away dramatically with the advent of the George W Bush Administration in 2001,[11] in which the Department of Justice issued a report on the issue of single-firm conduct under section 2.[12] That report, issued not long before the incoming Obama Administration, was formally withdrawn soon afterwards,[13] avowedly, in part, because of its 'overly lenient approach to enforcement'.[14]

---

[7] The Act inserted a new provision, s 271(d), that certain specified activities did not constitute patent misuse. See 35 USC §271 (d).

[8] Lemley, n 4 above, at 16.

[9] The Federal Circuit (established in 1982 to hear all patent cases) went on to validate and enforce an increasing percentage of patents. *Ibid*, at 16–17.

[10] *United States v Microsoft Corporation* 253 F 3d 34 (DC Cir 2001).

[11] The Antitrust Division brought only three, relatively insignificant, s 2 cases (involving single-firm conduct) during that eight-year period.

[12] US Department of Justice, *Competition and Monopoly: Single-Firm Conduct Under Section 2 of the Sherman Act* (2008), available at <www.usdoj.gov/atr/public/reports/236681.pdf>.

[13] Department of Justice Press Release, 'Justice Department Withdraws Report on Antitrust Monopoly Law' (11 May 2009), see <www.usdoj.gov/atr/public/press_releases/2009/245710.pdf>.

[14] According to Christine Varney, Assistant Attorney General, US Department of Justice, 'Vigorous Antitrust Enforcement in This Challenging Era, Remarks as Prepared for the Center for American Progress' 8 (11 May 2009), see <www.usdoj.gov/atr/public/speeches/245711.pdf>.

5.3 THE INTERRUPTED JOURNEY TOWARDS REGULATORY NEUTRALITY

The current case law and regulatory practice on the appropriate interface between competition law and intellectual property in the United States, is best understood as a reaction against earlier unreflective assumptions by both courts and regulators equating legal with economic monopolies, and treating the former as an automatic source of market power to be approached with suspicion and sometimes outright hostility. While these views lasted (and the period of their ascendancy was lengthy[15]), a presumption of illegality hovered over all sorts of actions by intellectual property owners that would nowadays be seen as harmless or even pro-competitive. *Per se* liability was imposed on some licensing practices and the onus of proof reversed where others were present. The high water-mark of the presumed illegality approach was the formulation of a black list of putatively unlawful intellectual property licensing practices issued in 1971 by the Antitrust Division of the Department of Justice and its sister regulator, the Federal Trade Commission, a list referred to at the time as the 'Nine No-Nos'.[16]

Fortunately for the intellectual coherence of United States antitrust law, this prescriptive approach was first eroded by the courts[17] then abandoned by the regulators.[18] New guidelines were issued proclaiming the principle of regulatory neutrality, under which intellectual property would be treated no differently from other forms of property for antitrust purposes. Unfortunately, however, the dominance of the former way of thinking persisted long enough, and generated sufficient controversy, to provoke its own over-reaction. Under-analysed presumptions of vice were replaced by equally under-analysed presumptions of virtue or claims for absolute immunity.[19] Even where such extreme stances were not taken, neutrality proved in practice to be distinctly one-sided. There was an

---

[15] Running from the time of the early 20th-century case of *Motion Picture Patents*, n 6 above.

[16] The practices known as the 'Nine No-Nos' substantially mirror licensing practices held to constitute patent misuse. In 1977 the Department of Justice set out its official position regarding these practices in its *Antitrust Guide for International Operations*, see [Jan–June] *Antitrust & Trade Regulation Report* (BNA) No 799, at E-1 (1 February 1977). The list of purportedly deviant practices covered: (i) royalties not reasonably related to sales of the protected products or service; (ii) restraints on licensees' activities outside the scope of the right (tie-outs); (iii) requiring the licensee to purchase unpatented materials from the licensor (tie-ins); (iv) mandatory package licensing; (v) requiring the licensee to assign to the patentee other patents that might be issued to the licensee after the licensing arrangement was in place; (vi) licensee veto power over grants of further licences; (vii) restraints on sales of unpatented products made with a patented process; (viii) post-sale restraint on resale; and (ix) setting minimum prices on resale of the patent products. Not all of the Nine No-Nos were accurate reflections of prior case law.

[17] *Continental TV Inc v GTE Sylvania* 433 US 36 (1977); *Broadcast Music Inc v Columbia Broadcasting System* 441 US 1 (1979).

[18] *Antitrust Guidelines for the Licensing of Intellectual Property* (6 April 1995), issued by the US Department of Justice and the Federal Trade Commission.

[19] As discussed above, see 1.5 and 2.7.

emphasis in both cases and commentary on the need to remove disabilities previously suffered by intellectual property owners. The possibility that there might be a downside in regulatory neutrality for these same owners was seldom adverted to, much less discussed. In this climate it was scarcely surprising that acts or omissions previously penalised might now be regarded as positively privileged. Logically this did not have to follow, as a few judges recognised. If there was an economic case for exempting or limiting the antitrust liability of intellectual property owners, it had to be made separately. It did not ineluctably flow from the goal of regulatory neutrality.[20] Such responses became increasingly rare, however.

The way in which this lopsided notion of neutrality gradually took hold is perhaps most clearly seen in the different approaches adopted over time by judges and regulators to the boundaries of intellectual property rights. In the era of the Nine No-Nos, any step by intellectual property owners beyond what the intellectual property statute allowed was apt to be seen as liability creating in itself.[21] This was of course an economic nonsense, and was ultimately rejected as such. It was only a short step, however, from treating what happened *outside* the right as presumptively anti-competitive (or worse deeming it to be such) to regarding what happened *within* the parameters of a particular intellectual property right as actually or presumptively immune from antitrust attack (the scope of grant principle discussed above at 1.6.2). As we shall see, that step was increasingly taken.

5.4 THE RIGHT TO REFUSE AND ESSENTIAL FACILITIES IN UNITED STATES ANTITRUST LAW

The essential facilities doctrine had its origins in the early years of the twentieth century, and thus long pre-dated the explicit reception of economic theory in United States antitrust law. Its beginnings (if not its name) are usually traced back to *United States v Terminal Railroad Association*,[22] a classic bottleneck dispute in which it was claimed that the Terminal Railroad Association (TRA), a group of railroad owners, was in breach of section 2 of the Sherman Act by denying non-cartel competing railroad services access to and from the city of St Louis via a terminal and rail bridges built over the Mississippi River, facilities

---

[20] Eg, the District of Columbia Court of Appeal's famous baseball bat aphorism in *Microsoft*, n 10 above, at para 82. Microsoft had made the bold claim that possessing intellectual property in its software gave it overarching power to use that property howsoever it wished, and legally justified the entire raft of anti-competitive provisions contained in its licensing arrangements with original equipment makers. The Court brushed off this broad (and, in its view, frivolous) argument as 'no more correct than the proposition that use of one's personal property, such as a baseball bat, cannot give rise to tort liability'.
[21] *Siegel v Chicken Delight* 448 F 2d 43 (9th Cir 1971) at 56.
[22] *United States v Terminal Railroad Association* ('*Terminal Railroad*') 224 US 383 (1912).

controlled by the cartel. Because of the peculiar topography of the region and the narrowness of the valley through which all rail lines had to pass, the Supreme Court found the TRA's refusal oppressive, and held that the TRA was required to act impartially in allowing access to competitors on reasonable terms or break up the association.[23] In coming to its decision, the Court introduced a concept plucked somewhat uncritically from the common law doctrine of prime necessities,[24] a doctrine which even at its most fully developed did not require the sharing of resources which were merely useful.

5.4.1 Expansion and refinement of the essential facilities doctrine

If matters had been left where they lay in *Terminal Railroad*, the impact on United States antitrust law would have been minimal. *Terminal Railroad* was, after all, no more than a collective boycott, one not much different from others of its kind. The Supreme Court in *Associated Press v United States*[25] went on to apply similar logic to a news cartel that was, in the words of the court,[26]

> a vast, intricately reticulated organisation, the largest of its kind, gathering news from all over the world, the chief single source of news for the American press [and] universally agreed to be of great consequence.

In the result, the Court determined that by-laws allowing the cartel to prevent its members from selling its news reports to non-members were in breach of the Sherman Act because, while those news reports might be attributable to the association members' own 'enterprise and sagacity', they were clothed 'in the robes of indispensability'. Since the press association controlled 96 per cent of news circulation in the United States, it was, in the view of Frankfurter J, akin to a public utility. The finding, at first instance, went unchallenged that it was 'a business infused with the public interest, required to serve all', and that a need existed for the maximum flow of information and opinion.[27]

---

[23] *Ibid*, at 405 ff.
[24] The concept appears to have been first articulated by Lord Hale (Lord Chief Justice on the Kings Bench in the 1670s). In *Allnutt v Inglis* (1810) 12 East 527, at 530, the Court noted Lord Hale had observed in his *Treatise de Portibus Maris* that a wharf owner should not be able to charge 'arbitrary and excessive duties' for use of his wharf and crane because those facilities were affected by the public interest, an interest which meant that access disputes would fall outside the realm of matters merely *juris privati*.
[25] *Associated Press v United States* 326 US 1 (1945).
[26] *Ibid*, at 18.
[27] *Ibid*, at 29. An illuminating contrast is provided here by *Paddock Publications Inc v Chicago Tribune Co* 103 F 3d 42 (7th Cir 1996) at 44, in which a refusal to license intellectual property in the form of *New York Times* articles and crossword puzzles led the Seventh Circuit to find that the New York Times News Service (the only service supplying them) was not an essential facility (although its puzzles were the 'best known') on the grounds there were at least three other major competing news services.

It was not until *Otter Tail Power Co v United States*[28] that the essential facilities doctrine can be said to have assumed its modern form. In that case, the Supreme Court was for the first time faced with applying the doctrine in the context of a purely unilateral refusal. On the facts, the Otter Tail company not only enjoyed a monopoly over the transmission of electricity in its local area but the company was also vertically integrated. Upstream it generated the power that it supplied to its own grid, while downstream it distributed electricity at retail rates to customers in the local area by way of selling off monopoly franchises. Otter Tail refused to supply the power that it generated itself at cheaper wholesale rates to several municipalities who sought to set up their own retail distribution systems. It also denied transmission of electricity over its grid to municipalities who could have acquired power that had been independently generated. Since the Court considered the refusal went further than merely imposing a handicap on potential new competitors in the downstream market for retail electricity and precluded all possibility of competition in that market, it ordered Otter Tail both to sell its own electricity to municipalities at wholesale rates and to transmit other independently-generated wholesale electricity to those municipalities who wanted it for their own retail distribution systems.[29]

Otter Tail paved the way for a later generation of American judges to take hold of the essential facilities doctrine and extend it to refusals to deal by a single dominant firm, often comparable to a public utility of some kind but not necessarily also vertically integrated. The first case in which the concept of 'essential facility' was judicially aired as a term of art was *Hecht v Pro-Football Inc*.[30] The claimed essential facility to which access had been denied was a sizeable stadium used for professional football matches. In finding the facility essential and the denial anticompetitive, the Court expounded on the circumstances under which the doctrine could successfully be invoked[31]:

> [If] facilities cannot practically be duplicated by would-be competitors, those in possession of them must allow them to be used on fair terms. It is [anticompetitive] to foreclose the scarce facility ... To be 'essential', a facility need not be indispensable; it is sufficient if duplication of the facility would be economically infeasible and if denial of its use inflicts a severe handicap on potential market entrants.

A later, much-cited decision in which the parameters of the essential facilities doctrine were more clearly articulated was *MCI Communications Corporation v AT&T*.[32] MCI had challenged AT&T's refusal to interconnect its telephone lines

---

[28] *Otter Tail Power Co v United States* ('*Otter Tail*') 410 US 366 (1973).
[29] *Ibid*, at 381–82.
[30] *Hecht v Pro-Football Inc* 570 F 2d 982 (DC Cir 1977).
[31] *Ibid*, at 992.
[32] *MCI Communications Corporation v AT&T* ('*MCI*') 708 F 2d 1081 (7th Cir 1983).

with AT&T's then nationwide telephone network on the grounds that interconnection *was essential if MCI were to compete in the long-distance telecommuni*cations market. It was held that it had been 'technically and economically feasible for AT&T to have provided the requested interconnection, and that AT&T's attempt to thwart MCI constituted an act of monopolization'. In finding AT&T's refusal governed by the doctrine, the Court stated in general terms[33]:

> [A] monopolist's control of an essential facility (sometimes called a 'bottleneck') can extend monopoly power from one stage of production to another, and from one market into another. Thus the antitrust laws have imposed on firms controlling an essential facility the obligation to make the facility available on non-discriminatory terms.

There is no hint here of any doubt as to the existence, rationality or durability of cross-market leveraging, something that previously could only be teased out of the facts of cases like *Otter Tail*.[34] Indeed the two-market factor was clearly of pivotal importance in *MCI* itself, in which the Seventh Circuit found that AT&T had complete control over the local distribution network to which MCI required interconnection in order to offer long-distance services. What was not clear, alas, for precedential purposes (because on the facts it did not have to be clarified) was whether cross-market leveraging was the only situation in which the essential facilities doctrine could operate; or to put the question another way, whether the need to identify two markets was a necessary or merely a sufficient test of liability.[35]

The Seventh Circuit did, however, proceed to lay down a four-point, conjunctive checklist to be satisfied before the essential facilities doctrine could apply. There had to be established[36]:

a) control of the essential facility by a monopolist;
b) a competitor's inability practically or reasonably to duplicate the essential facility;
c) the denial of the use of the (essential) facility to a competitor; and
d) the feasibility of providing (access to) the (essential) facility (to a competitor).

---

[33] *Ibid*, at 1132 (para 191). This statement of the law was said by the Court to be in line with *Terminal Railroad*, n 22 above, at 410–11, and *Byars v Bluff City News Co* 609 F 2d 843, 856 (6th Cir 1979).

[34] *Otter Tail*, n 28 above, at 377–79.

[35] The Federal Circuit in *Intergraph Corporation v Intel Corporation* ('*Intel*') 195 F 3d 1346 (Fed Cir 1999) at para 53, expressly suggested the doctrine may apply irrespective of whether the situation involves one market or two. However, that suggestion came only by way of *obiter* since that case did not itself involve a single-market situation. It appears, however, that no essential facility has failed merely for want of the plaintiff's failure to identify to the court two vertically-related markets: Pitofsky, R, 'The Essential Facilities Doctrine under United States Antitrust Law', a paper submitted to the European Commission in support of National Data Corporation in its essential facilities case against IMS, p 23, fn 25. See <www.ftc.gov/os/comments/intelpropertycomments/pitofskyrobert.pdf>.

[36] *MCI*, n 32 above, at 1132–33 (para 192). List form added.

That the first two factors are closely interrelated (ie that the second factor has a great deal to do with determining what amounts to an essential facility in the first place) was a point made by the Ninth Circuit in *City of Anaheim v Southern California Edison Co*.[37] It sensibly solved the chicken-and-egg conundrum by addressing the first two factors concurrently,[38] here building on what it had said in its own earlier decision in *Ferguson v Greater Pocatello Chamber of Commerce Inc*[39]:

> [The essential facilities doctrine imposes] on the owner of a facility that cannot reasonably be duplicated and that is essential to competition in a given market a duty to make that facility available to its competitors on a non discriminatory basis.

This succinct restatement can perhaps lay claim to being the broadest summation of the essential facilities doctrine at its zenith. Two aspects of that summation are worth emphasising:

a) the reference to non-discriminatory access necessarily carries with it the seeds out of which a notion of constructive refusal could grow; and
b) the fact that the *Ferguson* court's paraphrasing of the doctrine contained no allusion to the need for the existence of two markets.

Later decisions progressively parsed and qualified the criteria in the *MCI* checklist. Thus, the Ninth Circuit in *Metronet Services Corporation v US West Communications*[40] explicitly recognised that a constructive refusal could be inferred from situations in which access is not refused outright but where the imposition of unreasonable terms and conditions results in practical denial of access.[41] An important gloss was also put on the fourth criterion relating to the feasibility of granting access to an alleged essential facility when the Ninth Circuit upheld on appeal a District Court's finding in *Paladin Associates Inc v Montana Power Co*[42] that no legitimate business justification could be found on the facts for refusing access, a question that the District Court had expressly factored into its analysis, thereby recognising, if only in a backhanded way, what was to become an exculpatory exit from the application of the doctrine.

Unfortunately perhaps for our purposes, it is only first instance courts that have had to address directly the issue of whether intellectual property may be thought of as an 'essential facility'. For example, in *Bellsouth Advertising v*

---

[37] *City of Anaheim v Southern California Edison Co* 955 F 2d 1373 (9th Cir 1992).
[38] Ibid, at para 44.
[39] *Ferguson v Greater Pocatello Chamber of Commerce Inc* 848 F 2d 976 (9th Cir 1988) at 983.
[40] *MetroNet Services Corporation v US West Communications* ('*MetroNet*') 329 F 3d 986 (9th Cir 2003) at 1012.
[41] See *Pacific Bell Telephone Co v Linkline Communications Inc* ('*Linkline*') 555 US 07–512 (2008), 129 S Ct 1109 (2009).
[42] *Paladin Associates Inc v Montana Power Co* 97 F Supp 2d 1013, 1038 (D Mont 2000), 328 F 3d 1145 (9th Cir 2003).

Donnelley,[43] the defendant, who had copied the organisation and headings of the plaintiff's yellow pages directory and was sued for copyright infringement, raised an antitrust objection to denial of access by way of counterclaim. While the District Court found that the defendant had infringed Bellsouth's copyright, it proceeded to hold that there was a genuine issue for trial as to whether Bellsouth's copyrighted yellow pages directory was an essential facility to which it should grant access. The Court was unfazed by the fact that the doctrine of essential facilities had been applied only to tangibles in the past, and saw no reason why it could not also apply to information wrongfully withheld. In the Court's view, the result in both situations is the same: a person is denied something essential to compete.[44] The intellectual property issue was later side-stepped by the Federal Circuit in *Intergraph Corporation v Intel*,[45] when it was faced with a claim by Intergraph seeking not a licence under Intel's patents and copyrights, but a reinstatement of its preferred position as the recipient of:

(i) Products that embodied that intellectual property before these products were made commercially available to the public; and

(ii) Access to trade secrets … [ie] technical information that is not generally known, samples of new products before they are available to the public, and individualized technical assistance.

In its review of the essential facilities doctrine (invoked by Intergraph), the Court commented on the absence of competition between the two parties and lack of any flow-on consequences for a downstream market. It noted that although the protected products and trade secrets were considered essential by Intergraph to maintain its 'strategic customer' position, it was not the role of courts to 'transform cases involving business behavior that is improper for various reasons … into treble-damages antitrust cases'. It was, it went on, to say 'inappropriate to place the judicial thumb on the scale of business disputes in order to rebalance the risk from that assumed by the parties'. Simply because Intergraph had previously been supplied with the withheld products and information could not in itself be determinative of a valid antitrust claim, however relevant it might be in a claim for breach of contract, it said.

5.4.2 The *Colgate* principle

One possible reason why the essential facilities doctrine evolved in the way in which it did was that it was seen as a way for courts in the United States to extract

---

[43] *Bellsouth Advertising v Donnelley* 719 F Supp 1551 (S D Fla 1988), reversed on other grounds, 999 F 2d 1436 (11th Cir 1993).
[44] *Ibid.*
[45] *Intel*, n 35 above, at para 70.

themselves from the corner into which they had previously painted themselves on refusals to deal. Instead of focusing on the remedial problems associated with pricing and monitoring access in technologically complex situations,[46] they preferred to express themselves in terms of what sounded like an absolute right not to deal even for dominant players. This approach was dubbed the '*Colgate* principle' after the decision in *United States v Colgate & Co*,[47] in which the Supreme Court delivered itself of the view that:

> In the absence of any purpose to create or maintain a monopoly, the [Sherman Act] does not restrict the long recognized right of a trader or manufacturer engaged in an entirely private business freely to exercise his own independent discretion as to parties with whom he will deal ...

Instead of questioning this over-extended and seemingly unqualified statement of principle (after all, a refusal to deal is just one of many ways of exerting market power where it exists), a later generation of American judges simply tacked the essential facilities doctrine on to *Colgate* in order to soften any anti-competitive outcomes that might flow from it in 'hard' cases. The ad hoc rolling-back of the *Colgate* principle in an attempt to achieve an intuitively fair result was the sort of thing courts tended to do before they became economically literate.

5.4.3 The significance of fair dealing

Another qualification of the *Colgate* principle is to be found in the decision of the Supreme Court in *Aspen Skiing Co v Aspen Highlands*.[48] There the issue was how to respond to the situation where the monopolist/gatekeeper, by refusing, had ceased participation in a previously cooperative venture. In the result, the Court found that a unilateral termination of a voluntary (and presumably profitable) course of dealing was dispositive, suggesting a willingness in the monopolist to forgo short-term profits to achieve an anti-competitive end.

In *Aspen Skiing*, the defendant owned three of the four mountains in the Aspen, Colorado ski area, while the plaintiff owned the fourth mountain. For many years they had jointly offered a 'joint ticket' in the form of a multiple-day, multiple-area pass, providing skiers with admission to all four mountains. Purchasing this ticket tended to be a cheaper option for skiers than purchasing multiple single-day tickets. Under the joint ticket system, profits were split between the two parties commensurate with the percentage of use of each of the four mountains made by buyers of the joint ticket. The defendant effectively discontinued the joint ticket arrangement by making the plaintiff an offer to

---

[46] See 3.7.4 above. Indeed, the Privy Council expressed precisely such remedial reservations in *Telecom Corporation of NZ v Clear Communications* [1994] CLC 1312, [1995] 1 NZLR 385.
[47] *United States v Colgate & Co* ('*Colgate*') 250 US 300 (1919) at 307.
[48] *Aspen Skiing Co v Aspen Highlands* ('*Aspen Skiing*') 472 US 585 (1985).

continue it only on the basis that the plaintiff accepted a fixed percentage of joint ticket revenues considerably lower than the historical average based on actual usage of the plaintiff's mountain. When the plaintiff rejected the offer, the defendant proceeded to sell a joint ticket admitting skiers to its three mountains only. The plaintiff then attempted to market its own multiple-day, multiple-area package, by offering ski passes to the fourth mountain along with vouchers, each equal to the retail price of a single-day ticket to one of the defendant's mountains. The defendant, however, refused to accept these vouchers and to sell any lift tickets to the plaintiff at retail price. In upholding a jury verdict in favour of the plaintiff on its claim that the defendant had monopolised the market for downhill skiing services,[49] the Court, while avoiding the language of 'essential facility', imposed what could be (and subsequently was) read as an obligation upon monopolists to continue dealing with those with whom they had dealt in the past[50]:

> [T]he monopolist did not merely reject a novel offer to participate in a cooperative venture that had been proposed by a competitor. Rather, the monopolist elected to make an important change in a pattern of distribution that had originated in a competitive market and had persisted for several years.

Although subsequently interpreted as an essential facilities case by lower courts, *Aspen Skiing* always sat rather uneasily within that paradigm. Nevertheless, evidence of anti-competitive animus of the kind punished in *Aspen Skiing* persuaded some courts in refusal to deal cases subsequently to find antitrust liability. Thus, at first instance in *Intergraph Corporation v Intel Corporation*,[51] the District Court (before being overruled on appeal) concluded that Intel, the owner of patent rights and other intellectual property rights in the microprocessors and sophisticated technical information with which it had ceased supplying Intergraph, had

> no legitimate basis [to] refuse to supply ... since Intel has been doing so for the last four years on a mutually beneficial basis.

It was no justification for severance of the long-standing licensing arrangement in the view of the Court that Intel had immediately ceased supply after learning that Intergraph was suing it for infringement of patents owned by Intergraph.[52] This fits in with the earlier finding of the Supreme Court in *Eastman Kodak v*

---

[49] Ibid, at paras 7 and 8.
[50] *Aspen Skiing*, n 48 above, at 603.
[51] *Intel*, 3 F Supp 2d 1255 (N D Ala 1998). (The finding of anticompetitive animus was not disturbed even though the decision which ordered Intel to supply Intergraph with microprocessors and product information was reversed by the Federal Circuit largely on the basis that Intel did not compete with Intergraph in any downstream market; there was no leveraging of market power by Intel and nor was harm established to competition in any downstream market. See *Intel*, n 35 above, at 1357–60.
[52] *Intel*, n 35 above, at 1278.

Image Technical Services[53] that the right to refuse 'exists only where there are legitimate competitive reasons for the refusal'.

5.4.4 The *Trinko* retreat: squeezing the life out of essential facilities

The expansion of the doctrine provoked Professors Areeda, Hovenkamp and other eminent commentators[54] into arguing strongly for its abolition, and it has now been heavily downplayed (if not quite extinguished) by the Supreme Court in *Verizon Communications Inc v Law Offices of Curtis V Trinko LLP*),[55] in which the Court somewhat coyly neither confirmed nor denied whether the doctrine was still part of United States law, pointing out only that they themselves had never expressly endorsed it.[56] The Court reaffirmed that there was no general obligation on single firms (as opposed to a consortium) possessed of market power to deal with others unless they had previously dealt or co-operated with them. Neither would the monopolist be under an obligation to offer any explanation for its refusal where there had been no prior dealing between the parties. By so holding, the Court made plain that its earlier decision in *Aspen Skiing*[57] now stood simply for the principle that terminating an existing and voluntary business relationship without a legitimate efficiency reason might (not, be it noted, must) be unlawful in some unstated circumstances.

The *Trinko* Court also emphasised that there was no room for whatever was left of the essential facilities doctrine to apply where a parallel regulatory structure had been set up by statute to mandate and control terms and conditions of access.[58] It recoiled from any notion that antitrust courts could be involved in

---

[53] *Eastman Kodak v Image Technical Services* ('*Kodak I*') 504 US 451 (1992), at 483, fn 32. See also in similar vein *Image Technical Services Inc v Eastman Kodak Co* ('*Kodak II*') 125 F 3d 1195 (9th Cir 1997), at 1210–11. Both *Kodak I* and *Kodak II* are discussed below at 5.6.

[54] Areeda, P, 'Essential Facilities: An Epithet in Need of Limiting Principles' (1990) 8 *Antitrust Law Journal* 841. As Professor Areeda said: 'You will not find any case that provides a consistent rationale for the doctrine or that explores the social costs and benefits ... It is less a doctrine than an epithet.' See also Hovenkamp, H, *Hornbook on Federal Antitrust Policy: The Law of Competition and Its Practice*, 2nd edn (Minnesota, West Publishing, 1999) at 305. Both authors later were to become more emphatic in their views, see Areeda, P and Hovencamp, H, *Antitrust Law*, 2nd edn (New York, Aspen, 2002) at 771, and again in *Antitrust Law* (2004 Supp) urging that the doctrine should be abandoned.

[55] *Verizon Communications Inc v Law Offices of Curtis V Trinko, LLP* ('*Trinko*') 540 US 398 (2004).

[56] This was technically true. The words 'essential facility' were never used in *Terminal Railroad*, n 22 above, nor in *Aspen*, n 48 above.

[57] *Aspen*, n 48 above.

[58] See *Trinko*, n 55 above, at 407. This they held to be so even though the statute in question expressly preserved ordinary antitrust remedies and there was no jurisdictional pre-emption. See also *MetroNet Services Corporation v Qwest Corporation* 383 F 3d 1124 (9th Cir 2004), at 1128–30. This case was retried by the Ninth Circuit after its original decision was vacated by the Supreme Court, see 5.5 below. See also *Covad Communications Co v Bellsouth Corp* 374 F 3d

enforcing sharing, a task that the Court said would require them 'to act as central planners, identifying the proper price and quantity, and other terms of dealing, a role for which they are ill suited'.[59] (As far as the Court was concerned, the Telecommunications Act 1996 had already provided the machinery for access to local telephone services[60] and, furthermore, a regulatory provision compelling nearly global interconnection as well as the very connection to independent local telephone service providers that was at issue in the case.) The *Trinko* Court also poured cold water on earlier Supreme Court authority[61] suggesting that leveraging could be anti-competitive if done by a monopolist. There had to be something over and above the leveraging, it said, and that something could not be a refusal to deal.[62]

Whatever its views on essential facilities, the *Trinko* Court was at pains to affirm *Colgate*, finding an added reason for doing so in the possibility that forced negotiation might 'facilitate the supreme evil of antitrust collusion'.[63] This, if taken literally, would greatly inhibit the ability of first instance courts to nudge parties towards agreements on the price of access to technology protected by intellectual property rights.[64]

Just where *Trinko* leaves the supposed 'obligation' to continue dealing remains unclear.[65] Some commentators have read the case as continuing *Aspen Skiing* for this limited purpose.[66] Others refuse to concede it even this narrow role, pointing to the existence of cases such as *Intel*[67] where discontinued relationships triggered

---

1044 (11th Cir 2004) at 1050; and *New York Mercantile Exchange Inc v Intercontinental Exchange Inc* 323 F Supp 2d 559 (SDNY 2004) at 568–70. All three courts used *Trinko* as authority for the point that the doctrine is inapplicable where access is publicly regulated.

[59] See *Trinko*, n 55 above, at 879. As discussed in ch 7 below, the Privy Council in *Telecom Corporation of New Zealand v Clear Communications Ltd*, n 46 above, had a similarly negative reaction to the notion that courts could be left to regulate access to telecommunication networks and adjudicate on access costs when the Government had set up an alternative, specialist regulatory system (although in New Zealand, the regulatory system was more apparent than real).

[60] A local telephone service customer claimed that the dominant incumbent Verizon Communications had breached § 2 of the Sherman Act by failing to fulfil orders for interconnection from rival service providers on a reasonably timely and non-discriminatory basis. The Court's riposte was that regulated access was not access withheld, and indeed Scalia J described the telecommunications regulators as 'effective steward [s] of the antitrust function'. See *Trinko*, n 55 above, at 413.

[61] *Spectrum Sports Inc v McQuillan* 506 US 447 (1993) at 459.
[62] *Trinko*, n 55 above, at 415.
[63] *Ibid*, at 408.
[64] See 3.8.4 above.
[65] Absence of a prior relationship is now a negative factor: see *New York Mercantile Exchange*, n 58 above.
[66] Schoen, FX, 'Exclusionary Conduct After *Trinko*' (2005) 80 *New York University Law Review* 1625 at 1640.
[67] *Intel*, n 35 above.

no liability.[68] A small minority continue to offer a spirited defence of the doctrine's ongoing relevance and usefulness.[69] More pragmatically, and as demonstrated in *Bell Atlantic Corp v Twomby*,[70] some antitrust lawyers sought to sidestep the problems posed by *Trinko* by venturing to convert what would otherwise have been a section 2 monopoly case into a section 1 agreement case. In that case, several incumbent local telephone exchange owners had refused to share their facilities with smaller competitors or new entrants. *Trinko* was intended to be bypassed by the allegation that the incumbents had agreed among themselves that each could resist applications for sharing in their respective local geographic area and that each would refrain from entering adjacent zones where their neighbours were the incumbent monopoly.[71]

In sum, whatever life is left in the essential facilities doctrine post-*Trinko*, (a subject that has generated much commentary[72]), its impact is likely to be further eroded by two important limitations placed on it by lower courts applying the *MCI* checklist. One occurs where a facility or infrastructure owned or controlled by a monopolist or cartel is not considered 'essential' because its denial merely leads to reduced profits for the plaintiff or keeps it at a competitive disadvantage.[73] The other relates to lack of anti-competitive animus. The motive for

---

[68] Hovencamp, H, Janis, MD and Lemley, MA, 'Unilateral Refusals to Licence' (2006) 2 *Journal of Comparative Law and Economics* 1 at 18. The authors point out that the level of past access cannot indefinitely be projected into the future as some kind of customer right. Nor are past prices determinative as to current prices for competitive access by the rest of the world; *ibid*, 13.

[69] Frischmann, B and Waller, SW, 'Revitalising Essential Facilities' (2008) 75 *Antitrust Law Journal* 1. The authors offer an apologia for the doctrine's apparent open-endedness on the supply substitutability side by pointing up the importance of demand-side considerations that, in their view, have only been fitfully brought into the legal analysis; *ibid* at 10. As to the positive externalities flowing from regulated access to infrastructure, in this context Frischmann and Waller would define that term widely enough to include technology, whether or not that technology is protected by intellectual property. See also Rose, CM, 'The Comedy of the Commons: Custom, Commerce, and Inherently Public Property' (1986) 53 *University of Chicago Law Review* 711, arguing that open access can result in high social gains because of the more intensive use of the resource.

[70] *Bell Atlantic Corp v Twomby* 550 US 544 (2007).

[71] In the result, however, the Supreme Court (by a 7:2 margin) dismissed the complaint (reversing the Court of Appeals) and found mere parallel conduct is not enough to support a conspiracy claim, either because parallel conduct can be independent (and a competitive response to common cost drivers) or because parallel conduct can be the result of oligopolistic interdependence without the need for any prior agreement. See discussion of the case in Hay, G, 'The Quiet Revolution in US Antitrust Law' (2007) 26 *University of Queens Law Journal* 27.

[72] See, eg, Frischmann, and Waller, n 69 above, at 43; Troy, DE, 'Unclogging the Bottleneck: A New Essential Facilities Doctrine' (1983) 83 *Columbia Law Review* 441 at 485; Cavanagh, ED, '*Trinko*: A Kinder, Gentler Approach to Dominant Firms Under the Antitrust Laws?' *St John's University Legal Studies Research Paper Series 06–0058*, October 2006, available at SSRN <http://ssrn.com/abstract=940398>.

[73] *Robinson v Magovern* 688 F 2d 824 (3rd Cir 1982); *Morris Communications Corporation v Professional Golf Association* 364 F 3d 1288 (11th Cir 2004) and *Alaska Airlines v United Airlines* 948 F 2d 536 (9th Cir 1991) at 544.

denying access must be exclusionary. If the monopolist can point to a legitimate business explanation for its conduct, it can avoid liability.[74] Thus the prevention of free-riding may be a bona fide business justification in itself.[75] As to the application of the doctrine to intellectual property, it was never consistently applied, as the pre-*Trinko* cases show.[76] Courts either denied that intellectual property could be an essential facility, or ignored the intellectual property angle entirely.[77]

5.5 THE CONTINUING PROBLEM OF CONSTRUCTIVE REFUSAL AND MARGIN SQUEEZE

As explained above (at 5.4.1), the Ninth Circuit in *MetroNet*[78] was prepared to recognise the notion of a constructive refusal in situations where access is not refused outright but the imposition of unreasonable terms and conditions results in practical denial of access. Not surprisingly, the Supreme Court shortly thereafter vacated the *MetroNet* decision[79] in the light of its decision in *Trinko*,[80] on the grounds that MetroNet was unable to prove the existence of an essential facility in the form of a local exchange network because the Telecommunications Act 1996 had already provided the means (as it had in *Trinko*) for the company to obtain access by setting up a regulatory structure designed to deter and remedy anti-competitive harm. Admittedly, the Supreme Court in *Trinko* (even had it been minded to apply the essential facilities doctrine) had some difficulty with the notion of constructive refusal, but the point that it forcefully made, that 'Verizon's alleged *insufficient assistance* in the provision of service is not a recognised antitrust claim under [the Supreme Court's] existing refusal to deal precedents',[81] can be taken as requiring actual denial or something very close to it.

As in Europe and our other jurisdictions, another practice with debatable antitrust implications is the 'price squeeze' or 'margin squeeze', which may occur when a vertically-integrated monopolist sells its upstream bottleneck input to firms that compete with the monopolist's production of a downstream product

---

[74] See *Morris Communications*, n 73 above.
[75] *Ibid.*
[76] *Data General Corporation v Grumman Systems Support Corporation* 36 F 3d 1147 (1st Cir 1994); *Sun Dun Inc v Coca-Cola Co* 740 F Supp 381 (D Md 1990) at 394; *Hudson's Bay Co v American Legend Co-op* 651 F Supp 819 (DNJ 1986) at 843, fn 14.
[77] See n 53 above re *Kodak I* and *Kodak II*.
[78] See *MetroNet*, n 40 above.
[79] *Qwest Corporation v MetroNet Services Corporation* (formerly *US West Communications*) 540 US 1147 (2004), 124 S Ct 1144.
[80] See *Trinko*, n 55 above.
[81] *Ibid*, at 410 (original emphasis). The Court's observations need to be read in the light of the fact that even on the facts alleged by the plaintiff, there probably would have been no constructive denial of access even on the earlier, more generous test.

138 REFUSALS TO LICENSE IN THE UNITED STATES

sold to end-users. Typically, margin squeeze claims involve a competitor finding that the margin between the wholesale price and retail price it is being charged by a monopolist is too small to enable it to achieve its desired level of profit. Sometimes the margin is even negative. The pricing policy is susceptible to attack under section 2 of the Sherman Act on the grounds that the monopolist is monopolising the downstream market, or sometimes because the monopolist is using unlawful means to maintain its existing monopoly over the bottleneck input.[82] At issue for pinning antitrust liability on the monopolist is the size of the margin between its input price and its retail price.

The question of whether expensive or hiked-up costs of access and margin squeezes may be tantamount to an anti-competitive refusal to license arguably remains an open one in the United States, despite the unanimous decision of the Supreme Court in *Linkline*[83] that has continued to make it very difficult (as in *Trinko*) for an antitrust plaintiff to prove that a defendant contravenes section 2 when it unilaterally refuses to deal with a rival. The Court reversed the Ninth Circuit,[84] by holding that a 'price squeeze' or 'margin squeeze' claim cannot be brought under section 2 of the Sherman Act if a defendant is under no duty to sell inputs to the plaintiff in the first place. Although *Trinko* involved denial of services, and *Linkline* pricing issues, the Supreme Court ruled in the latter case that *Trinko's* reasoning 'applied with equal force to price squeeze claims'. Thus, it reasoned, if *Trinko* meant that a party has no antitrust duty to deal with its competitors at wholesale, that party has no duty to deal under terms and conditions that its competitors find favourable. That said, the Supreme Court did note that 'there are ... limited circumstances in which a firm's unilateral refusal to deal with its rivals can give rise to antitrust liability'. In so saying, the Supreme Court may have had in mind earlier lower-court decisions[85] establishing that offering unfavourable terms or unduly high prices to a rival could amount to an illegal refusal to deal, where the terms or price were not as generous as the defendant had voluntarily offered previously or was willing to offer or charge those who were not its rivals. What this means is that margin squeeze cases can probably succeed, post-*Linkline* and *Trinko*, only where there has been an *Aspen* type of prior dealing, and possibly not even then.

5.6 SPARE PARTS AND AFTER MARKETS: A DEAD END?

One line of American authority giving rise to particular difficulty comprises those cases involving denial of spare parts, consumables or services necessary for

---

[82] See Sidak, JG, 'Abolishing the Price Squeeze as a Theory of Antitrust Liability' (2008) 4 *Journal of Competition Law & Economics* 279.
[83] See *Linkline* 555 US 07–512, n 41 above, at 1118.
[84] *LinkLine Communications Inc v SBC California Inc* 503 F 3d 876 (9th Cir 2007) at 887.
[85] *United States v Aluminium Co of America* 148 F 2d 416 (2nd Cir 1945).

servicing previously purchased products (generally dubbed 'after markets'). While the parts and services in question may have been backed by intellectual property rights, the presence or absence of such rights was seldom the deciding factor. Certainly this was the case in *Kodak I*,[86] the first Supreme Court case to confront the after markets issue. The case arose out of Kodak's attempts to prevent independent service organisations from servicing its photocopiers post-sale by refusing to supply them with the parts they needed to carry out their activities. While there was vigorous competition in the 'primary' photocopying market, only Kodak and independent (that is non-Kodak) service organisations competed in the after or secondary market for supplying parts and services for Kodak equipment, and Kodak was the only source for most of the parts. Kodak argued (and obtained an order for summary judgment based on that argument) that the presence of competition in the primary market rendered inquiry into competition into the after market otiose. When the case reached the Supreme Court it set aside the summary judgment, holding that the possibility that Kodak both possessed market power in the after market and used it anti-competitively in that market could not entirely be ruled out because buyers of photocopiers may have been locked in by the high switching costs of dumping their defunct machines in favour of other equipment. Again, while the majority (in the face of a strong dissenting opinion delivered by Scalia J) was prepared to accept the possibility that Kodak's government and business customers would already have factored the higher cost of Kodak parts and service into their decision to purchase, the same could not be assumed for all customers who were exposed to information asymmetries. The majority was also influenced by Kodak's 'installed base opportunism', that is, the fact that it had initiated its challenged policy of denying parts to independent service organisations only after many customers had already purchased Kodak equipment. The presence of all these contested facts made summary judgment entirely inappropriate, the Court held. Indeed, once the case was remitted for full trial in *Kodak II*,[87] the Ninth Circuit found that although protection of intellectual property rights could possibly amount to a valid justification for denying supply to a competitor,[88] antitrust liability arose because Kodak could offer no legitimate business justification for its refusal to license patents over its parts and copyrights over its service manuals. Significantly, the Ninth Circuit found Kodak somewhat tardy in raising its intellectual property flag, claiming patent rights and copyright by way of defence many years after the litigation had commenced. This blow against the interests of right holders provoked considerable academic controversy but now appears, in retrospect, to have been merely a glancing one. It was not long before *Kodak I* was qualified into near impotence in the lower courts, a process it is not proposed to

---

[86] See *Kodak I*, n 53 above.
[87] See *Kodak II*, n 53 above.
[88] *Ibid.*

trace in detail here.[89] The so-called spare parts and consumables cases revolve around highly technical discussions of what constitutes the before and the after market, the timing and effectiveness of attempted lock-ins by manufacturers, the role of information asymmetries affecting consumers' 'life cycle' pricing decisions (that is those that take after-market prices into account whether or not to purchase the primary product or service), and the corresponding ability of manufacturers to price-discriminate between the wise and the ignorant.

The continued relevance of these decisions ironically depends on the Supreme Court's willingness to adhere to its reasoning in *Kodak I*. (Indeed one of the smaller mysteries of *Trinko* is that Court's complete silence on the subject of its earlier decision in *Kodak I*, and this despite Scalia J having written the majority decision in the former and a vigorous dissent in the latter.) Indeed a direct assault on *Kodak I* seems only a matter of time post-*Trinko*.[90] *Kodak I* also sits rather uneasily with *Illinois Tool Works v Independent Ink Inc*,[91] in which the Supreme Court rejected the hitherto prevalent idea that there was a (admittedly rebuttable) presumption that patent possession *per se* conferred market power in antitrust proceedings.[92] It is worth pointing out, however, what *Illinois Tool* does *not* decide. It is not authority for the proposition that patents never confer or sustain market power. It establishes only that whether a particular patent confers monopoly power in economic terms is a question of fact (and by inference susceptible to empirical analysis) not an issue of law. Any other finding would render most of the jurisprudence in the spare parts and consumables cases irrelevant. If those cases are to continue to have resonance in the refusals to license debate, it is as a reminder that it does not really matter whether the market power alleged to exist is derived from an intellectual property right, technological compatibilities or even economies of scale. The legal answer should be the same in each case. Unfortunately, as the next section shows, it is not.

---

[89] This has been admirably done by Goldfine, D and Vorassi, K, 'The Fall of the *Kodak* After Market Doctrine: Dying a Slow Death in the Lower Courts' (2004) 72 *Antitrust Law Journal* 209.
[90] See *Trinko*, n 55 above.
[91] *Illinois Tool Works v Independent Ink Inc* ('*Illinois Tool*') 547 US 28 (2006), 126 S Ct 1281 (2006) at 1292.
[92] In so finding, the Court pointed out that antitrust guidelines issued jointly by the Department of Justice and the Federal Trade Commission in 1995 stated that the enforcement agencies, in the exer-cise of their prosecutorial discretion, 'will not pre-sume that a patent, copyright, or trade secret necessarily confers market power upon its owner'. See *Antitrust Guidelines for the Licensing of Intellectual Property* (6 April 1995), §2.2. The Court also pointed out that while it was not bound by that choice, 'it would be unusual for the Judiciary to replace the normal rule of lenity that is applied in criminal cases with a rule of severity for a special category of antitrust cases' (*ibid*, at 16). (While not mentioned by the Court, in Canada, its close neighbour, the regulator also took a similar approach to applying the Competition Act to conduct involving intellectual property rights in its 2000 *Intellectual Property Enforcement Guidelines*; see 8.7.1 below.)

5.7 VARIATION ACROSS THE INTELLECTUAL PROPERTY SPECTRUM: UNEVEN TREATMENT OF PATENTS AND COPYRIGHT

To compound the confusion in the spare parts cases, the Federal Circuit in *Re Independent Service Organisations Antitrust Litigation*[93] expressly declined to follow the decision of its sister Ninth Circuit in *Kodak II*,[94] despite highly convergent facts.[95] The Federal Circuit treated Xerox's refusal to license products protected by intellectual property according to the nature of the intellectual property right involved, a somewhat perverse approach since software products nowadays in the United States and many other jurisdictions can have concurrent patent and copyright protection for at least as long as the patent is valid.[96] The court thus expressly laid down two rules, one for patents and another for copyright.[97]

In considering Xerox's refusal to license its patented parts, the Federal Circuit (here anticipating *Illinois Tool*[98]) first pointed to its earlier ruling in *Abbott Laboratories v Brennan*[99] that possession of a patent alone does not demonstrate market power. The Federal Circuit also noted that there was 'no reported case in which a court had imposed antitrust liability [under section 2 of the Sherman Act] for refusal to sell or license a patent'.[100] That said, it went on to add that a patentee's right to exclude was not without limits,[101] and posited what was intended to be for all intents and purposes a *per se* rule of legality, rebuttable only under two disjunctive circumstances: where a patent owner has obtained the denied patent by fraud; or where a lawsuit brought to enforce a patent was a

---

[93] *Re Independent Service Organisations Antitrust Litigation* ('*CSU v Xerox*') 203 F 3d 1322 (Fed Cir 2000).

[94] See *Kodak II*, n 53 above.

[95] The intellectual property issue was raised as a defence in *Kodak* II (1997), *ibid*, but constituted part of the cause of action in *CSU v Xerox* (2000), n 93 above.

[96] See 3.3.6 above.

[97] Antitrust law as applied to patents is a question of Federal Circuit not regional circuit law, and thus the Federal Circuit applied its own law to the patent claims over the component parts for Xerox's copiers; but as far as the copyright claims over expression in technical manuals were concerned, the Court applied the law of the Tenth Circuit since the case originated in the District of Kansas.

[98] See *Illinois Tool*, n 91 above.

[99] *Abbott Laboratories v Brennan* 952 F 2d 1346 (Fed Cir 1991) at 1354. They were much influenced here by the view expressed in the Department of Justice and Federal Trade Commission *Antitrust Guidelines for the Licensing of Intellectual Property* (1995), that even if the patent did confer market power, this would not automatically impose on the intellectual property owner an obligation to license the use of that property to others.

[100] *CSU v Xerox*, n 93 above, at 1326.

[101] This aspect of the case is best thought of as an examination of the scope of grant principle. It is important to note, however, that while bluffing and sham litigation may fall outside the grant, it does not therefore follow that they are heads of antitrust liability in themselves. Only if the firm doing the bluffing has market power is there a problem.

sham.[102] The Federal Circuit also pressed home the point that it saw no more reason to inquire into the subjective motivation of Xerox for exercising its statutory rights by refusing to sell or license its patented works than it found in evaluating the subjective motivation of a patentee in bringing suit to enforce those same rights, a stance the Court reiterated it would still maintain in the face of a patentee's refusal to sell or license its patented invention having an anti-competitive effect, provided, however, that the anti-competitive effect was not illegally extended beyond the statutory patent grant.[103] Thus, it seems a defendant with market power who refuses to supply a product on the basis of an invalid or shaky, but not blatantly fraudulent patent may fall painlessly through the cracks in these bright-line rules. Some empirical evidence exists to suggest that a significant number of patents should never have been granted at all in the United States[104] as elsewhere, and that most of these invalid patents result not from fraud but procedural flaws that make it difficult for the current patent-granting regime to differentiate between strong and weak applications.[105] Again, a lack of investigative resources means that patent examiners are challenged for time in the conduct of their examination of patent specifications.[106] The Federal Circuit also did not foresee the advent of patent 'trolls', organisations often set up by lawyers and funded by venture capitalists, that buy up patent portfolios they have no intention of exploiting themselves. Rather their only activity is to extract licences generating royalty streams from companies wanting to use the processes or products ostensibly patented, and to threaten costly and time-consuming litigation should the companies baulk at paying up.

Turning to the antitrust claims arising from Xerox's refusal to license its copyrighted parts,[107] the Federal Circuit in *CSU v Xerox* was mindful that although the Supreme Court had at one stage expressed the view that the proprietary right granted by copyright cannot be used with impunity to extend power in the market beyond what Congress intended,[108] the Court had not

---

[102] *CSU v Xerox*, n 93 above, at 1326.
[103] *Ibid*, at 1327.
[104] See Allison, JR and Lemley, MA, 'Empirical Evidence on the Validity of Litigated Patents' (1998) 26 *American Intellectual Property Law Association (AIPLA) Quarterly Journal* 185 at 295. Indeed one large-scale study of patents issued in the US between 1989 and 1996 found 46% of them invalid; *ibid*, at 205, fn 60.
[105] Shelanski, HA, 'Unilateral Refusals to Deal in Intellectual and Other Property' (2009) 76 *Antitrust Law Journal* 369 at 387, fn 62.
[106] *Ibid*. See also Hovencamp, H, 'Patent Deception in Standard Setting: The Case for Antitrust Policy' (July 2010) *University of Iowa Legal Studies Research Paper*, at <http://ssrn.com/abstract=1138002>; and Cotter, T, 'Patent Holdup, Patent Remedies, and Antitrust Responses' (December, 2008) *Minnesota Legal Studies Research Paper No 08–39*, at <http://ssrn.com/abstract=1273293>.
[107] Claims determined under regional circuit law as opposed to the antitrust claims arising out of the refused patented parts that were determined under the exclusive jurisdiction of the Federal Circuit.
[108] This is laid down as the exclusive right to distribute the protected work by 'transfer of ownership, or by rental, lease, or lending' in 17 USC § 106(3). See *United States v Loew's Inc* 371

directly addressed the antitrust implications of a unilateral refusal to sell or license copyrighted expression. In search of precedent from other circuits, the Federal Circuit fastened on the strict legal standard laid down by the First Circuit in *Data General Corporation v Grumman Systems Support Corporation*.[109] That case involved a copyright infringement claim by Data General over its diagnostic software, against the defendant who required to use it in order to participate independently in an after market for the repair of computer hardware. In addressing the defendant's antitrust counterclaim that Data General's denial of a copyright licence excluded it and other third-party maintainers from that after market, the First Circuit laid down that[110]

> while exclusionary conduct can include a monopolist's unilateral refusal to license a copyright, an author's desire to exclude others from use of its copyrighted work is a presumptively valid business justification for any immediate harm to consumers.

The First Circuit did, however, proceed to soften this presumption of validity ever so slightly, by stating that it could be rebutted by evidence in those rare cases in which imposing antitrust liability would not frustrate the objectives of the Copyright Act. As to what those rare cases might involve, the Court did not proceed to speculate.[111]

It is true that the Federal Circuit in *CSU v Xerox* did at one point toy with the idea of declining to adopt the *Data General* hard line and preferring its subsequent modification at the hands of the Ninth Circuit in *Kodak II*.[112] The Ninth Circuit, it will be remembered, had in that case held that proffering the defense that exploitation of the copyright grant as a legitimate business explanation in its own right might be no more than a pretextual justification masking anti-competitive conduct. What dissuaded the Federal Circuit from applying the Ninth Circuit's softer (and admittedly woollier) standard, however, were the 'hazards' it found inherent in this approach, which it said were evident from the outcome reached. The Federal Circuit had considerable difficulty with the fact that the jury in *Kodak II* had been instructed to examine each and every proffered business justification for pretext, and that no weight had been given to the different intellectual property rights in the instructions to the jury. This, it said, meant that the jury had been set free to second-guess the subjective motivation of the copyright holder in asserting its statutory rights to exclude under copyright law without properly weighing what it called the presumption of legitimacy in asserting its rights under that law. (While not alluded to in the case, one wonders whether the spectre of a large award of damages, such as the $71.8 million treble

---

US 38 (1962) at 47–48, in which the Supreme Court found that the practice of block-booking copyrighted motion pictures contravened the Sherman Act.

[109] See *Data General*, n 76 above.
[110] *Ibid*, at 1187.
[111] *Ibid*, at 1187, fn 64, and 1188.
[112] See *Kodak II*, n 53 above.

damages award by the jury in *Kodak II*, may also have exerted a restraining influence on the Federal Circuit in *CSU v Xerox*.)

In treating the First Circuit's strict approach in *Data General* as more consistent with both antitrust and copyright law, and in the absence of any evidence that Xerox's copyrights were obtained by unlawful means or were used to gain monopoly power beyond the statutory copyright grant, the Federal Circuit set its face against the need to conduct any examination of Xerox's subjective motivation in asserting its right to exclude under copyright law.[113]

5.8 PARALLEL JURISPRUDENCE ON ABUSE OF RIGHTS

As foreshadowed in chapter four, in the United States a separate, but nevertheless in some senses parallel, body of jurisprudence has flowered alongside the antitrust laws.[114] This is the doctrine known as copyright or patent misuse, a principle of wide application, uncertain provenance[115] and equally uncertain future. In its fully-developed form the doctrine prevented intellectual property owners from enforcing their statutory rights if the effect of such enforcement would undermine the policy underlying the patent[116] or copyright statute under which they were claiming to act.

The abuse of rights approach used in patent cases can generally be mapped against that adopted in antitrust proceedings,[117] but with something of a time lag. Indeed the misuse of patent doctrine is said by some to be yesterday's antitrust law.[118] Courts sometimes allowed claims of patent misuse to succeed whether or not there was any proof that the patent conferred market power.[119]

---

[113] See *CSU v Xerox*, n 93 above, at para 8.
[114] See 4.5.1(a) above.
[115] It seems to have originated as a remedial 'clean hands' bar to injunctive relief and only later to have become a principle of statutory interpretation. The distinction would matter were it ever sought to extend the principle to non-statutory forms of intellectual property.
[116] See *Morton Salt Co v Suppiger Co* 314 US 488 (1942), in which the Supreme Court refused to allow a patent holder to prevent competition in products not protected by the patent; and *Brulotte v Thys Co* 379 US 29 (1964), in which it held that a patent holder's attempt to collect royalties beyond the term of the patent constituted misuse of the patent.
[117] *Senza Gel Corp v Seiffhart* 803 F 2d 661 (1986) at 670 (para 69), fn 14.
[118] Lemley, MA, 'The Economic Irrationality of the Patent Misuse Doctrine' (1990) 78 *California Law Review* 1599. See *Mercoid Corporation v Mid-Continent Investment Co* 320 US 661 (1944), in which the Supreme Court found misuse of a patent prima facie anti-competitive absent proof of anti-competitive effect. In that case the patent misuse arose when a patent holder tied a patented device to a product with no commercial use other than in connection with the patented device.
[119] *Mercoid*, n 118 above. See also later cases: *Noll v OM Scott and Sons* 467 F 2d 295 (6th Cir 1972) at 301; *Berlenbach v Anderson Thompson Ski Co* 329 F 2d 782 (9th Cir 1964) at 784; *Transition Electronics Corporation v Hughes Aircraft Corp* 487 F Supp 885 (D Mass 1980) at 892; cf *Mallinckrodt Inc v Medipart Inc* 976 F 2d 700 (Fed Cir 1992) at 708.

Nor did they always insist on a showing of harm to the competitive process.[120] More importantly, patent misuse was an all-or-nothing defence which ignored the possibility of adjusting the right owner's behaviour to ensure a competitively neutral outcome.[121] Alarmed by these developments, Congress amended the United States patent statute to require proof of market power whenever patent misuse was raised as a defence in infringement proceedings.[122]

While in theory patent misuse and antitrust law occupied different jurisdictional spaces, there had always been a considerable degree of cross-fertilisation between the two. Indeed, it was in precisely this fashion that the absence of a market power stipulation in patent misuse cases morphed into the presumption that mere possession of a patent conferred market power on the possessor.[123] Given this degree of intersection, it was thus entirely unsurprising that a retreat (albeit legislative) on one side of the jurisdictional fence would be matched by a similar retreat (this time judicial) on the other, and this duly came with the decision of the Supreme Court in *Illinois Tool*.[124]

The question whether copyright misuse is an equally robust defence is more complicated. In this case the link with antitrust is very nebulous,[125] the courts being chiefly concerned with attempts to expand copyright beyond its core function of protecting expression by converting it into a patent-like monopoly protecting ideas. For that reason, judicial discussions of copyright misuse have been largely subsumed into analyses of such pivotal copyright issues as what degree of second-comer 'borrowing' from a first-comer's work constitutes fair dealing or substantial taking (not so surprising considering that many of the leading copyright misuse cases have tended to involve allegations of infringement of copyright in computer programs by reverse engineering or abusive software-licensing practices). This is an area in which lack of judicial consensus over the precise boundaries of copyright subsistence in software and inconsistent judicial outcomes in infringement claims in relation to this highly technical subject matter have generally made the task of extracting usable precedents difficult.[126]

---

[120] See *Senza*, n 117 above. But see *Braun Medical Inc v Abbott Laboratories* 124 F 3d 1419 (Fed Cir 1997) at 1426.

[121] The doctrine has been likened to a court-run scheme of royalty-free licences for infringers. See Lemley, n 118 above, at 1618.

[122] 35 USC §271 (d) states: 'No patent owner otherwise entitled to relief for infringement or contributory infringement of a patent shall be denied relief or deemed guilty of misuse or illegal extension of the patent right by reason of his having [...] (4) refused to license or use any rights to the patent.'

[123] *International Salt Co v US* 332 US 392 (1947); *United States v Loews* 371 US 38 (1962) at 46; and *Jefferson Parish Hospital District No 2 v Hyde* 466 US 2 (1984) at 16.

[124] See *Illinois Tool*, n 91 above.

[125] Lemley, MA, 'Beyond Pre-emption: The Law and Policy of Intellectual Property Licensing' (1999) 87 *California Law Review* 113 at 153.

[126] See Lim, PH, and Longdin, L, 'Fresh Lessons for First Movers in Software Copyright Disputes: A Cross Jurisdictional Convergence' (2009) 4 *International Review of Intellectual Property and Competition Law* 374.

Thus in *Lasercomb America v Reynolds*,[127] the Court found copyright misuse where the holder of copyright in computer software imposed a term in a licence agreement preventing licensees from using not only protectable expression but also unprotectable ideas contained in its software to write their own programs. A similar situation arose in *Alcatel USA Inc v DGI Technologies Inc*,[128] a case in which DGI was sued for infringement by reverse engineering copyrighted software to create compatible replacement hardware used in Alcatel telephone switches (although Alcatel had not patented the switches themselves, they had owned copyright in the computer program that operated them). In the result, the court found Alcatel had misused its copyright in leveraging it to claim patent-like protection over its hardware.

The advent of paracopyright laws in the Digital Millennium Copyright Act 1998 introduced the potential for alleged copyright infringers to resist claims brought against them under this Act by invoking the misuse defence against right holders relying on technological protection measures (TPMs)[129] to restrict copying of and access to their works even when that use would be permitted on ordinary fair use principles.[130] Although the doctrine was not mentioned expressly in either the Federal Circuit decision in *Chamberlain Group Inc v Skylink Technologies Inc*[131] or the Sixth Circuit decision in *Lexmark International Inc v Static Control Components Inc*,[132] the outcome of the two cases and the Courts' reasoning was similar to that in *Alcatel*. In both *Skylink* and *Lexmark*, one of the parties was prevented by the court from using a TPM to leverage its copyright in computer code to create or maintain a monopoly for itself in a

---

[127] *Lasercomb America v Reynolds* 911 F 2d 970 (4th Cir 1990).
[128] *Alcatel USA Inc v DGI Technologies Inc* 166 F 3d 772 (5th Cir 1999).
[129] Probably the best-known (certainly much-litigated) example of a TPM locking up a work is the content scramble system (CSS) used by US movie studios to stagger the release of their movies on DVDs to eight regions in the world. CSS controls access to the sound and graphic files contained on DVDs via a dual-key encryption system. Encrypted files on a DVD are decrypted by an algorithm stored on both the DVD itself and the DVD player or any other authorised platform.
[130] In *Sega Enterprises Lt v Accolade Inc* 977 F 2d 1510 (9th Cir 1992), Accolade had reverse engineered several of Sega's video games in order to develop games of its own compatible with Sega's Genesis console. The Ninth Circuit established it could be fair use to engage in reverse engineering of protected computer code, even though the process technically involves copying all the protected expression of it, if the aim is to ascertain how it works in order to create code that is different in expression but carries out the same task, or to create a new product that is compatible or interoperable with a protected product (where consumers might otherwise be denied the alleged infringer's new product).
[131] *Chamberlain Group Inc v Skylink Technologies Inc* ('*Skylink*') 381 F 3d 1178 (Fed Cir 2004).
[132] *Lexmark International Inc v Static Control Components Inc* ('*Lexmark*') 387 F 3d 522 (6th Cir 2004). Lexmark sold discount toner cartridges for its printers that only Lexmark could re-fill. The printers contained a microchip designed to prevent them from functioning with toner cartridges that Lexmark had not re-filled. In an effort to generate competition in the cartridge market, Static Control Components had mimicked Lexmark's computer chip and sold it to companies interested in selling re-filled toner cartridges.

secondary market for a common everyday manufactured product (a remote garage door-opener in *Skylink*, and a refilled printer cartridge in *Lexmark*).

While copyright misuse may be successfully invoked as a defence,[133] it cannot be used as the basis of an affirmative claim.[134] But whatever the precise scope of the doctrine, it may not survive long should the issue of its existence come before the Supreme Court[135] and should that Court seek to apply the same kind of reasoning used in *Illinois Tool* to a copyright case. There never, in any event, existed the same clear-cut and judicially-articulated presumption of copyright-derived market power for copyright holders as once was supposed to exist for patent holders, and thus there was no felt need to erase it legislatively. There also remains the inconvenient fact that the 1995 *Antitrust Guidelines*, on which the *Illinois Tool* court placed considerable weight, are expressed to apply to copyright and trade secrets as well as patents. Until the Supreme Court pronounces unequivocally on the subject, the possibility exists that copyright misuse will be treated more onerously than patent misuse in the lower courts, thereby reinforcing the notion of a hierarchy of rights.

5.9 THE UNCERTAIN LINE BETWEEN ACTION AND INACTION IN US LAW

One of the side-effects of the lack of any unifying principle in United States anti-monopolisation law is the emergence of a distinction between action and inaction that, while now embedded in the cases, has seldom been put under the economic microscope. We refer here to the separate evolution of the rules on tying and refusals to deal. What is odd (at least to those outside the jurisdiction) about all this is that the same set of facts will often throw up both forms of behaviour (necessarily so when one considers that the almost automatic outcome of a rebuffed tie-in will be a refusal to deal). The result is that while there is a clear conceptual distinction between tying (action) and refusals to deal (inaction), with intervention more likely in the case of the first than the second,[136] the distinction is not itself based on clearly expressed economic rationale. Proponents of a rule of reason approach to tying do not usually suggest that there is a 'right to tie' paralleling the 'right' to refuse to deal. Even under a rule of reason approach, liability may still attach to tying. Tying is inculpatory in its effect, a

---

[133] Whether or not the copyright holder must actually have market power in order to invoke the defence, or whether lack of market power merely makes misuse more difficult to prove on the part of the defendant, is another unresolved issue; see *Data General*, n 76 above.

[134] *Novell Inc v CPU Dist Inc* US Dist Lexis 9952 (SD Texas, May 12 2000); *Warner/Chappel Disc Inc v Pilz Compact Disc Inc* 52 USPQ 2d (BNA) 1942 (ED Pa 1999) at 1947, fn 5.

[135] Certainly this was the view expressed in the Antitrust Modernization Commission, *Report and Recommendations* (April 2007) at p 105 (see pt 19).

[136] Once again, it is not necessary to this distinction that tying remain a *per se* breach as, post-*Illinois Tool*, it clearly is not.

refusal to deal exculpatory.[137] There is thus clear motivation for dominant firms to seek to characterise their behaviour as a refusal to deal, while their opponents just as understandably will try to present it as an example of an actual or an attempted tie-in. This is not simply a matter of advocacy in the courtroom. There is a real risk that pre-trial business behaviour will be adjusted via appropriate compliance programmes with a particular legal box to tick in mind. Gaming the system is thereby not merely enabled, it is positively encouraged.

5.10 A SUMMARY OF JUDICIAL RESPONSES TO REFUSALS TO LICENSE IN UNITED STATES COURTS

Whether courts in the United States approach refusals to license cases from an essential facilities or a spare parts/consumables perspective, there is a fragile and narrow consensus across both approaches that may be summarised thus:

a) First, right owners are free to license or not as they see fit. This may be presented either as a substantive right, or as a principle of regulatory caution in the face of remedial inadequacy[138] and evidentiary uncertainty, or sometimes both. (The distinction is never treated as in any way determinative.)
b) Secondly, departures from this freedom to choose are either non-existent or rare (the emphasis varies).

Beyond this point consensus dwindles drastically, and three distinct judicial responses to coerced licensing may be discerned at work:

a) Absolute immunity from antitrust scrutiny for dealings or refusals to deal within the scope of the intellectual property grant.[139] Proponents of this viewpoint usually concede, if they mention the subject at all, that sham litigation and invalid patents take the right owner's actions outside the grant, as would attempts to project statutory powers into markets not covered by the grant.[140]

---

[137] Hovencamp et al, n 68 above, at 37 ff.
[138] Unlike remedies applicable to aggregated anti-competitive conduct (which might involve returning parties to their former competitive positions), those given to address a unilateral refusal to supply are likely to embroil courts and regulatory bodies in compliance and monitoring activities as well as price and/or capacity settings, tasks that might be outside not only their capabilities but also their remits. See Alese, F, *Federal Antitrust and EC Competition Law Analysis* (London, Ashgate, 2008) at 300.
[139] Typical of this absolutist approach is the decision of the Federal Circuit in *CSU v Xerox*, n 93 above.
[140] Even this is not much of a deterrent nowadays; see *Rambus Inc v Federal Trade Commission* 552 F 3d 456 (2008) at 466, in which the DC Circuit held that a patentee did not infringe antitrust laws when it failed to disclose to a standard-setting organisation that it held patents over the technology that the organisation was considering setting as the standard.

b) An evidentiary presumption of virtue under which a right owner's wish to prevent others from free-riding on the innovation or creation by enforcing its intellectual property would be treated as a legitimate business reason in its own right without inquiry into the motive of the refuser.[141] Some other kind of evidence would have to be found to rebut the presumption.
c) Turning the previous approach on its head by allowing the presumption of virtue to be negated by evidence of anti-competitive intent,[142] evidence that even post-*Trinko* is more easily found when there have been prior dealings between the parties.[143]

Tugging at all three approaches is the potential for distinctions to be made between patents, copyright and trade secrets, and the blurred line between active and constructive refusal.

---

[141] The viewpoint adopted by the First Circuit in *Data General*, n 76 above. This case dealt with a refusal to license diagnostic software which resulted in exclusion from an after market (the repair of computer hardware). See also *Morris Communications*, n 74 above.

[142] As in *Kodak I*, n 53 above. Also *Lorain Journal v United States* 342 US 143 (1951), in which a monopolist publisher had blatantly refused to accept local Lorain advertising from parties who had also used a local radio station for advertising, in an attempt to drive the radio station (with which it was competing for local advertising) out of the market.

[143] See, eg, *Covad Communications*, n 58 above, at 1049; *Nobody in Particular Presents v Clear Channel Communications* 311 F Supp 2d 1048 (D Colo 2004) at 1113.

6

Europe's Exceptional Circumstances Test

6.1 SOFT AND HARD LAW IN EUROPE

In the European Union unilateral refusals to license fall to be considered under the open-ended prohibition against abuse of market dominance in Article 102 TFEU[1] (ex Article 82 EC).[2] Although fleshier than its skeletal United States counterpart (section 2 of the Sherman Act), it nowhere alludes in its non-exhaustive list of examples of anti-competitive conduct to unilateral refusals to deal in general, let alone to refusals to license intellectual property in particular.[3] Exactly when refusals to license are unlawful under Article 102 remains an intractable question, despite decades of intensive judicial, regulatory and academic analysis. The European Commission has recently attempted to make it less so by issuing the communication *Guidance on the Commission's Enforcement Priorities in Applying [Article 102 TFEU] to Abusive Exclusionary Conduct by Dominant Undertakings* (the '*Guidance*').[4] That initiative, like all such regulatory

---

[1] Treaty for the Functioning of the European Union (TFEU), also known as the Treaty of Lisbon 2007, signed by 27 countries, which became effective as of 1 December 2009, [2008] OJ C-115/47.

[2] In previous incarnations, Art 102 TFEU was known as Art 82 EC (Maastricht 1992) and Art 86 EC. The substance of the provision has remained the same despite the renumbering.

[3] Art 102 TFEU provides that: 'Any abuse by one or more undertakings of a dominant position within the common market or in a substantial part of it shall be prohibited as incompatible with the common market insofar as it may affect trade between Member States. Such abuse may, in particular, consist in: (a) directly or indirectly imposing unfair purchase or selling prices or other unfair trading conditions; (b) limiting production, markets or technical development to the prejudice of consumers; (c) applying dissimilar conditions to equivalent transactions with other trading parties, thereby placing them at a competitive disadvantage; (d) making the conclusion of contracts subject to acceptance by the other parties of supplementary obligations which, by their nature or according to commercial usage, have no connection with the subject of such contracts.'

[4] The Commission's 2009 *Guidance* communication was issued 3 December 2008 and formally adopted by the European Commission on 9 February 2009: [2009] OJ C-45/7. It eventuated after a lengthy consultation process in which the Commission reviewed its methodology and approach to dominance and abuse of dominance under Art 102 TFEU (ex Art 82 EC). The aim of the review was 'to evaluate policy, to assess how it could be made more effective and to define ways in which [the Commission] might make it more transparent'. The *Guidance* addresses the specific abuses of exclusive dealing, tying and bundling, predation, refusal to supply and margin squeeze.

guidelines, is a 'soft law' instrument.[5] The Commission cannot usurp the role of the General Court and the Court of Justice as definitive interpreter and synthesiser of the substantive law. The *Guidance* articulates the circumstances in which the Commission is, or is not, likely to intervene, and provides details of the economic methodology it proposes to introduce into future cases in which it does opt to intervene to enforce the TFEU's abuse of dominance provision. Indeed the phenomenon of some regulatory guidelines, while never binding on courts, ending up institutionalised and framing anti-competitive discourse[6] has not escaped the notice of commentators,[7] and there is an intermittently applied tradition of deference to the regulator by European judicial bodies, the decision in *Microsoft*[8] being the most recent example. At least one commentator has pointed out that the Commission considers its initiative to be the basis for a future substantive reinterpretation of Article 102 TFEU,[9] while another has ventured that describing the *Guidance* as merely setting out 'enforcement priorities' creates a false dichotomy, because it is in reality offering an interpretation of the law.[10] Of course, the *Guidance* remains, like any form of soft law, susceptible to challenge[11] if its interpretations of substantive law are clearly at variance with those laid down by the European courts.[12]

In this chapter, therefore, we have at least to entertain the possibility that the *Guidance* could be instrumental, if only in a roundabout way, in engineering a shift in the European Union's abusive unilateral conduct *grundnorm*. Were such a shift to occur, future refusals to license cases would be treated by the Commission in a more hands-off fashion; but in the event regulators did intervene in a

---

[5] Indeed the *Guidance* includes the caveat that it is not intended to be a statement of law; *ibid*, at para 3.

[6] The phenomenon, strictly speaking, has been analysed more in the US than Europe, and also more in relation to merger guidelines than other kinds of soft law. See Greene, H, 'Guideline Institutionalisation: The Role of Merger Guidelines in Antitrust Discourse' (2006) 48 *William and Mary Law Review* 771; and Professor Eleanor Fox's famous aphorism that 'economists are kings' when it comes to the influence of regulators' guidelines on courts where those guidelines incorporate economic methodology, in Fox, E, 'The 1982 Merger Guidelines: When Economists are Kings' (1983) 71 *California Law Review* 281.

[7] Lianos, I, 'Judging Economists' in I Lianos and I Kokkoris (eds), *The Reform of EC Competition Law* (The Netherlands, Kluwer, 2010) 185 at 187.

[8] Case T-201/04 *Microsoft Corporation v European Commission* [2007] ECR II-3601, 5 CMLR 11.

[9] Witt, AC, 'The Commission's Guidance Paper On Abusive Exclusionary Conduct: More Radical Than It Appears?' (2010) 35 *European Law Review* 214 at 235.

[10] Gormsen, LL, 'Why the European Commission's Enforcement Priorities on Article 82 EC Should be Withdrawn' (2010) 31 *European Competition Law Review* 45 at 51.

[11] See, eg, the warning shot delivered in the opinion of AG Kokkott in Case C-8/08 *T-Mobile Netherlands BV & Others* [2009] ECR I-4529 at para 29.

[12] Deference to the regulator by European judges, while never guaranteed, will play its part here depending on whether the economic issues are presented to them as issues of fact (as they largely were in *Microsoft*, see n 8 above) or policy justifications for a legal rule (as in Case C-7/97 *Oscar Bronner v Mediaprint Zeitung und Zeitschriftenverlag GmbH* ('*Oscar Bronner*') [1998] ECR I-7791).

particular case, parties can expect a more energetic deployment of economic methodology and analysis by the Commission in its assessment of the effects of the practice under scrutiny. While taking these developments into account where appropriate, this chapter will focus for the most part on the current substantive law on unilateral refusals to license which have led to their special treatment by the courts and the evolution of a body of European jurisprudence built up around what has become Europe's signature 'special circumstances' test.

6.2 HALLMARKS OF EUROPEAN REFUSALS JURISPRUDENCE

While European Union case law relating to refusals to deal shares several traits with that of the other jurisdictions analysed in this book, it nevertheless bears its own idiosyncratic stamp. The jurisprudence has tended to develop silo-style, with much depending on whether that which is denied is tangible or intangible but also on other factors, such as lack of an objective or competitively neutral justification for the refusal and a history of previous supply. Reconciling these different strands of authority is not something which either the General Court or the Court of Justice has so far felt the need to take on in the absence of a more malleable set of facts. (Indeed to date the only serious attempts at synthesis have been by way of academic commentary[13] and soft law in the form of the *Guidance*.)

6.2.1 The nexus between market power and ownership of intellectual property right

There has never been in European law any legislative or regulatory presumption that possession *per se* of an intellectual property right necessarily confers a dominant position on the holder.[14] Neither, on the other hand, is there any explicit disavowal of that proposition in the manner of *Illinois Tool*.[15] Indeed the Court of Justice adroitly bypassed any real dissection of this issue when asked by

---

[13] Some serious and insightful attempts by academic commentators to reconcile the different lines of authority have been made. See, eg, Derclaye, E, 'Abuses of Dominant Position and Intellectual Property Rights: A Suggestion to Reconcile the Community Courts' Case Law' in C Graham and F Smith (eds), *Competition, Regulation and the New Economy* (Oxford, Hart Publishing, 2004) 55; and Ritter, C, 'Refusal to Deal and Essential Facilities: Does Intellectual Property Require Special Deference to Tangible Property?' (2005) 28 *World Competition* 281.

[14] This also has resonance in para 75 of the *Guidance* (n 4 above), where it is is explicitly assumed, as an overarching rule, that any undertaking, dominant or not, should have the right to choose its trading partners and to dispose freely of its property.

[15] *Illinois Tool Works v Independent Ink Inc* ('*Illinois Tool*') 547 US 28 (2006). See 5.6 above.

the United Kingdom High Court in *Volvo v Veng*[16] whether mere ownership of an exclusive registered design right over a Volvo car front-wing panel was enough in itself to give the owner a dominant position in the market for manufacturing and importing such a product. The establishment of the existence of a dominant position remains one for factual confirmation for owners and non-owners of intellectual property alike, said the Court, applying the now well-established test for dominance that it laid down in *United Brands v Commission*[17] and *Hoffmann-La Roche & Co v Commission*.[18] Absent any definition in the Treaty itself as to what constitutes a 'dominant position', the Court held in the former case that it is a position of:[19]

> economic strength enjoyed by an undertaking which enables it to prevent effective competition being maintained on the relevant market by affording it the power to behave to an appreciable extent independently of its competitors, its customers and ultimately ... consumers.

What seems clear, however, from *Volvo v Veng*[20] (and later endorsed by the Court of Justice in *IMS Health GmbH v NDC Health GmbH*[21]) is that a refusal to grant a licence by an undertaking in a dominant position cannot in itself be abusive without proof of something more. It is in the description of that something more that the uniqueness and difficulty of the exceptional circumstances approach lies.

6.2.2 Close and enduring embrace of the essential facilities doctrine

One key feature of European refusals jurisprudence relates to the extent to which the essential facilities doctrine has both taken hold and continued to thrive in contrast to its post-*Trinko*[22] decline in the United States. The concept (dubbed a 'powerful tool to pry open markets' by one commentator[23]) was first formally recognised by name in *Sealink/B&I–Holyhead*,[24] in which the Commission

---

[16] Case 238/87 *Volvo v Erik Veng (UK) Ltd* [1988] ECR 6211.
[17] Case 27/76 *United Brands v Commission* [1978] ECR 207.
[18] Case 85/76 *Hoffmann-La Roche & Co v European Commission* [1979] ECR 461.
[19] *United Brands*, see n 17 above, at para 65.
[20] *Volvo v Veng*, see n 16 above.
[21] Case C-418/01 *IMS Health GmbH v NDC Health GmbH* ('*IMS*') [2004] ECR I-5039, 4 CMLR 28, paras 34 and 35.
[22] *Verizon Communications Inc v Law Offices of Curtis V Trinko, LLP* ('*Trinko*') 540 US 398 (2004).
[23] Furse, M, 'The Essential Facilities Doctrine in Community Law' (1996) 16 *European Competition Law Review* 469 at 473.
[24] *Sealink/B&I–Holyhead* [1992] 5 CMLR 255. The doctrine was developed in two later port-related cases: *Port of Rødby* [1994] OJ L55/52, in which the doctrine was extended to refusals to new, as well as existing customers; and *Morlaix (Port of Roscoff)* [1995] CMLR 177, in which it extended to a situation where the dominant undertaking was not competing downstream. It was also applied in relation to air transportation regarding routes of vital importance:

referred to an essential facility as 'a facility or infrastructure without access to which *competitors* cannot provide services to their customers' (emphasis added).[25] It was not, however, until *Tiercé Ladbroke SA v European Commission*[26] that the parameters of the essential facilities doctrine were explored in express terms by the General Court. The case involved two French copyright owners' refusal to license the right to transmit televised pictures and sound commentaries relating to horse races in France to Tiercé Ladbroke which ran betting shops in Belgium. The General Court held that Pari Mutuel Urbain Français (PMU) and Pari Mutuel International (PMI) (collectively *les sociétés de courses*) were not competing in the Belgian betting market at all, and that since Tiercé Ladbroke already had the largest share in that market, the refusal did not result in any restriction of competition in it. As the Court noted[27]:

> The refusal to supply the applicant could not fall within the prohibition laid down by [Article 102 TFEU] unless it concerned a product or service which was either essential for the exercise of the activity in question, in that there was no real or potential substitute, or was a new product whose introduction might be prevented, despite specific, constant and regular potential demand on the part of consumers.

Precisely why the doctrine found such great favour with both courts and regulators[28] (albeit in a heavily contextualised way) is not altogether clear, since there never was, after all, any early European embrace of the *Colgate* principle[29] to be beaten back into its box. Indeed in Europe, the conduct of dominant undertakings has always tended to be subject to more searching scrutiny than

---

see, eg, *British Midlands/Aer Lingus* [1992] OJ L96, [1993] 4 CMLR 596, in which Aer Lingus, the dominant undertaking in the market for the Dublin–London air route, was ordered to enter an interlining arrangement with a new entrant, British Midland; and *Flughafen Frankfurt/Main AG* [1998] OJ L72/30, 4 CMLR 779. In *Aer Lingus*, the Commission concluded (at para 30) that Aer Lingus had 'not been able to point to efficiencies created by its refusal to interline nor to advance any other persuasive and legitimate business justification for its conduct'. The Commission was not impressed by Aer Lingus's excuse that it was concerned to avoid loss of market share and not put its operating margin under pressure (*ibid*). See generally: Temple Lang, J, 'Defining Legitimate Competition: Companies' Duties to Supply Competitors and Access to Essential Facilities' (1994) 18 *Fordham International Law Journal* 437; Ridyard, D, 'Essential Facilities and the Obligation to Supply Competitors under UK and EC Competition Law' [1996] *European Competition Law Review* 438; Overd, A and Bishop, B, 'Essential Facilities: The Rising Tide' [1998] *European Competition Law Review* 183.

[25] *Sealink*, n 24 above, at 265.
[26] Case T-504/93 *Tiercé Ladbroke SA v European Commission* [1997] ECR II-923.
[27] *Ibid*, at para 131.
[28] Indeed some EU Member States, such as Ireland, also recognise by statute that denial of an essential facility may be an abuse of dominant position; see Competition Act 2002 (Ir), s 5. Germany too expressly provides that networks or infrastructure controlled by dominant undertakings can be essential facilities to which they cannot deny access to prevent a rival competing concurrently with them on an upstream or downstream market; see *Gesetz gegen Wettbewerbsbeschränkungen* [GWB] [Act Against Restraints of Competition] 1958 (as amended 2005), § 19(4), para 4.
[29] *United States v Colgate & Co* 250 US 300 (1919). See 5.4.2 above.

that of non-dominant undertakings.[30] In addition, European notions of what constitutes an essential facility have been allowed to expand beyond physical infrastructure, so that it now can easily accommodate all features of today's broadband- and satellite-based economy, and recognise the role of economic factors such as network[31] and lock-in effects as well as sophisticated technological standards.

Whatever the reasons for its overall acceptance,[32] the essential facilities doctrine has taken on a distinctly European cast, splitting off into several other discrete but interwoven lines of authority. One of these seemingly stand-alone lines (seen at its less-tangled and most-developed in cases such as *Radio Telefis Eireann and Independent Television Publications v European Commission*[33] and *IMS*[34]) applies a version of the doctrine where intellectual property rights are involved. The so-called 'exceptionality' test that has emerged from this body of precedent, while in some ways heavily reliant on essential facility-type reasoning, moves beyond that reasoning in ways that are potentially more restrictive than in other contexts.

Notwithstanding Europe's regulatory and judicial love affair with the essential facilities doctrine (not always under that name), it should not be thought that the highly contextual resort to its concepts evident in the cases ever resulted in the doctrine being erected into the sort of rule of general application that it became in the United States during its heyday. Nor, unfortunately, has it become intellectually coherent enough to offer an easy exit from the problem of how a competition regime should approach refusals to license intangibles. One reason for this is obvious. European judges have in the main been content to employ methodology applying the doctrine that merely asks a series of questions derived

---

[30] Case T-111/96 *ITT Promedia NV v European Commission* [1998] ECR II-2937; Joined Cases C-395/96 P and C-396/96 P *Compagnie Maritime Belge Transport SA v European Commission* [2000] ECR I-1365.

[31] See *Software Cellular Network Limited v T-Mobile (UK) Ltd* [2007] EWHC 1790 (Ch), in which the High Court allowed network effects to offset relatively low market share effectively to find an essential facility. See also the *Guidance*, n 4 above (at para 83, fn 3), in which the Commission notes that a refused input is generally likely to be considered impossible to replicate when it involves a natural monopoly due to scale or scope economies, where there are strong network effects or when it concerns so-called 'single source' information. However, it suggests in all cases, account should be taken of the dynamic nature of the industry and, in particular, whether or not market power can rapidly dissipate.

[32] Perhaps one reason lies in the late arrival on the European scene of direct European-wide mechanisms for regulating telecommunications, energy and transportation; see Mestmäcker EJ and Schweitzer, H, *Europäisches Wettbewerbsrecht* (Munich, CH Beck, 2004). Art 102 TFEU has had to take up the slack (and still does for some unregulated utilities). See also *Sealink/B&I–Holyhead*, n 24 above, and *Sea Containers/Stena Sealink* 94/19/EC [1994] OJ L15/8. The European Commission's attitude to these utilities has become less punitive in the wake of *Oscar Bronner*, n 12 above.

[33] Joined Cases C-241/91 P and C-242/91 P *Radio Telefis Eireann and Independent Television Publications v European Commission* ('Magill') [1995] ECR I-743, 4 CMLR 718.

[34] See *IMS*, n 21 above.

from common ground between the leading essential facilities cases, without troubling unduly as to whether these are in essence emanations of a single unitary principle or discrete situation-dependent rules. A good example here is Etherton J's methodology, seen at work at first instance in the United Kingdom High Court decision in *Attheraces Ltd v The British Horseracing Board Ltd*,[35] in which he found information in the form of race data (unprotected by any form of intellectual property) to be an essential facility. Although the case was subsequently overturned by the United Kingdom Court of Appeal,[36] this particular finding was not disturbed. Indeed Mummery J, delivering the judgment of the court, observed[37]:

> Abuse of a dominant position by refusal to supply may occur ... as a result of the cutting off of an existing customer, or refusing to grant access to an essential facility, unless the act or refusal is objectively justified. It may also consist of the refusal to grant a licence of an IP right.

6.2.3 Leveraging theory and the multiple markets debate in Europe

Article 102 TFEU contains no stipulation that the use of a dominant position be restricted to the dominated market. This has allowed leveraging theory to flourish. The concept of cross-market leveraging was clearly articulated (if not by name) by the Court of Justice in *Télémarketing*,[38] where it was said liability for breach of Article 102 TFEU could arise

> Where without any objective necessity, an undertaking holding a dominant position in a particular market reserves for itself [or maybe a subsidiary] an ancillary activity which might be carried out by another undertaking as part of its activities in a neighbouring market with the possibility of eliminating all competition from such an undertaking.

Subsequently, as discussed later in this chapter, the Court of Justice, in deciding the outcome of the long-running nine-year litigation in *Magill*,[39] famously fleshed out the concept of leveraging as part of the a three-step test for abuse of market power.[40] Not only did the *Magill* Court recognise that leveraging was a viable commercial strategy (after finding in the case that the refused party's

---

[35] *Attheraces Ltd v The British Horseracing Board Ltd* [2005] EWHC 3015 (Ch).
[36] *Attheraces Ltd v The British Horseracing Board Ltd* [2007] EWCA Civ 38. The appellate court reversed the finding at first instance that there had been abuse of market power, on the grounds that the trial judge had failed to apply the correct test in determining whether the price charged for the essential facility was so excessive as to amount to a constructive refusal.
[37] *Ibid*, at [108].
[38] Case 311/84 *Centre Belge d'Etudes du Marché-Télémarketing SA (CBEM) v Compagnie Luxembourgeoise de Télédiffusion (CLT)* [1985] ECR 3261, at para 27; [1986] 2 CMLR 558.
[39] See *Magill*, n 33 above.
[40] See 6.5.2 below.

comprehensive weekly TV guide, would have competed with the three stand-alone weekly guides for individual television channels to which access had been denied), it also expressed itself in a way that strongly suggested that in future refusals to license cases, it was the effect on the downstream market that counted. This has led some commentators to suggest that the effects on competition in the upstream market covered by the intellectual property right must be ignored unless there are also effects in the downstream market. This may be reading too much into *Magill*'s highly constraining facts.

Post-*Magill*, however, dedicated judicial adherence to the actuality of leverage and determination by the Court of Justice that the conditions in *Magill* were cumulative[41] have led to a ready acceptance (especially in relation to refusal to license intangibles) of even the faintest spectre of a secondary market.[42] This is an approach that opens up more questions than it can answer. The literature remains deeply divided as to whether the refusing party has to reserve the secondary market (whether hypothetical or real) for its own exploitation or must leverage its advantage onto a secondary market, or whether it will merely suffice that a secondary market is foreclosed to competition. One thing remains clear, however, European courts remain wedded to the view that market power can be leveraged from one market to another, a clear rejection of the notion popular in Chicago circles[43] and endorsed by the United States Supreme Court in *Trinko*[44] that leveraging power across markets is so economically irrational as to be unsustainable.

6.2.4 Entrenchment of the need for objective justification

In a line of cases during the 1970s and 1980s, the Court of Justice at first strongly suggested and then bluntly insisted in *United Brands*[45] that there was a duty on dominant firms to continue to supply a claimant if it is 'a long standing customer who abides by regular commercial practice if the orders placed by the customer are in no way out of the ordinary'.[46] This was softened somewhat by other

---

[41] See *IMS*, n 21 above, at para 35.
[42] See Court of Justice decisions in *Oscar Bronner*, n 12 above, and in *IMS*, n 21 above.
[43] See discussion at 3.3.3(a) above.
[44] See *Trinko*, n 22 above, at para 415.
[45] See *United Brands*, n 17 above.
[46] *Ibid*, at para 182. The Guidance (see n 4 above, at para 84) segregates refusals cases into those that involve disruption of previous supply by a dominant company and those in which the firm has not previously supplied to others. It indicates that termination of an existing supply arrangement is more likely to be found abusive than a *de novo* refusal to supply. It gives the example that if the dominant firm had previously been supplying the requesting undertaking, and the latter had made relationship-specific investments in order to use the subsequently refused input, the Commission may be more likely to regard the input in question as indispensable. Similarly, it proceeds to state, the fact that the owner of the essential input in the

decisions establishing that a dominant undertaking may be justified in refusing to supply a previous customer if its own reputation or commercial interests are at stake. In such cases, however, the dominant firm's response must be fair and proportionate to the threatened or actual commercial harm done, and not motivated by any anti-competitive purpose.[47]

The Commission (upheld by the General Court) developed this line of authority even further in *Liptons Cash Registers v Hugin*,[48] holding that an undertaking (not dominant in the market for cash registers but dominant in the much narrower market for its own spare parts) acted anti-competitively when it refused without objective justification to supply spare parts to a firm in the business of repairing its machines.[49] Lack of objective justification was also a pivotal factor in *Boosey v Hawkes*,[50] in which the General Court was not dissuaded from finding abuse where a dominant party refused to supply products by way of reprisal against a customer who had had the temerity to associate itself with a potential competitor of the dominant party.

One tantalising question raised (albeit much later) by the Greek competition regulator (*Epitropi Antagonismou*) in *Synetairismos Farmakopoion Aitolias & Akarnanias (Syfait) and others v Glaxosmithkline AEVE (Syfait)*,[51] but not addressed for want of jurisdiction by the Court of Justice,[52] was whether the refusal by Glaxosmithkline's Greek subsidiary to satisfy in full orders it had received from wholesalers could be seen to be objectively justified if the dominant company had intended by that mechanism to limit parallel trade in its pharmaceuticals in the European Union. In his opinion Advocate General Jacobs considered the refusal could be deemed reasonable if done in order to defend the

past has found it in its interest to supply is an indication that supplying the input does not imply any risk that the owner receives inadequate compensation for the original investment. It would therefore be up to the dominant company to demonstrate why circumstances have actually changed in such a way that the continuation of its existing supply relationship would put in danger its adequate compensation.

[47] See, eg, the analysis based on objective justification and proportionality in Case 395/87 *Ministère Public v Tournier* [1989] ECR 2521 at paras 38–46, and the finding that a refusal to deal may be objectively justified where there is a shortage of a product in Case 77/77 *British Petroleum v European Commission* [1978] ECR 1513 at para 34.

[48] *Liptons Cash Registers v Hugin* [1978] OJ L22/23, [1978] 1 CMLR D19.

[49] The *Guidance*, para 29, goes even further, stating it would not be objectively justified for a dominant undertaking to take steps on its own initiative to exclude products which it regards, rightly or wrongly, as dangerous or inferior to its own product.

[50] *Boosey v Hawkes* [1987] OJ L286/36, [1988] 4 CMLR 67.

[51] Case C-53/03 *Synetairismos Farmakopoion Aitolias & Akarnanias (Syfait) and others v GlaxoSmithKline AEVE* [2005] ECR I-4609.

[52] The Court of Justice declined to address the question referred to it by the Greek Competition Authority on the grounds that the latter body was not a court or tribunal of a Member State from whom it had jurisdiction to accept a reference.

dominant undertaking's commercial interests. He went on to narrow this, however, by saying that[53]

> conduct by a dominant pharmaceutical undertaking which more clearly and directly partitioned the common market would not be open to a similar line of defence [thus clarifying that] a restriction of supply by a dominant pharmaceutical undertaking might fall foul of ... established case-law on refusal to supply if it had negative consequences for competition arising other than as a consequence of its restriction of parallel trade.

With these cases, the shift seems to have been made from outcomes based on found facts to a definitive legal duty to supply in the absence of any objective justification for the refusal.[54] It is at this point, however, that other lines of authority surface to confuse matters.

6.3 REFUSALS TO SUPPLY TANGIBLES

As early as 1974 an undertaking was held liable by the Court of Justice under Article 102 TFEU (then Article 82 EC) for refusing to continue to supply a raw chemical substance to a former customer, Zoja. This was in *Istituto Chemioterapico Italiano SpA & Commercial Solvents Corp v European Commission*,[55] and the chemical in question (aminobutanol) was necessary for the downstream production of an anti-tubercular drug (ethambutol). Not only was Zoja a former customer but it was also a competitor of the firm, since both parties were active in that derivative market. As the Court found in a much-quoted passage:

> [A]n undertaking which has a dominant position in the market in raw materials and which, with the object of reserving such raw material for manufacturing its own derivatives, refuses to supply a customer, which is itself a manufacturer of these derivatives, and therefore risks eliminating all competition on the part of this customer, is abusing its dominant position.

Typically for the time, neither efficiency considerations nor consumer benefit or harm[56] (as those terms are variously defined) figure at all in the judgment. Pivotal to that first finding of an anti-competitive refusal were three factors:

---

[53] Opinion of AG Jacobs, handed down 28 October 2004, in *GlaxoSmithKline*, n 51 above, at paras 103–04.

[54] Indeed in the German competition statute the legal duty is made explicit. An undertaking may not hinder another undertaking without an objective justification, if it possesses superior market power in relation to other undertakings.

[55] Joined Cases 6/73 and 7/73 *ICI and Commercial Solvents v European Commission* [1974] ECR 223, [1974] 1 CMLR 309.

[56] Cf the *Guidance*, n 4 above, which states (in para 5) that the Commission will now concentrate on pursuing those types of conduct that are most harmful to consumers.

a) the goods in question were crucial to the claimant entering and remaining in an adjacent market;
b) the defendant had the upstream market completely sewn up; and
c) there was no apparent objective justification for the refusal on the part of the defendant.

6.4 REFUSALS TO SUPPLY INTANGIBLES

Relatively early on, European competition authorities seemed as willing to find refusals anti-competitive in relation to intangibles as they did in relation to tangible property. Thus, the Commission had little hesitation finding in *London-European Airways v Sabena*,[57] for example, that Sabena had breached Article 102 TFEU by denying London-European access to its computer reservation system 'Saphir' by means of which the undertaking had been able to dominate the market in Belgium for computerised air travel reservations.[58] In another case, also in the 1980s, it intervened when International Business Machines (IBM), once dominant in the computer industry, refused to provide interface information (it regarded as involving trade secrets) to other firms to allow development of interoperable components and systems, and made frequent changes to its interfaces, causing licensees' previously compatible technologies to be less compatible or wholly incompatible. IBM settled the lawsuit by agreeing to pre-disclose changes to its interfaces to aid other firms in adapting their products in a timely manner.

The General Court did not feel any need to articulate or explore the tangible versus intangible theme in *Clearstream Banking AG v Clearstream International SA*[59] (a case involving denial of access to an intangible in the form of primary banking clearing and settlement services as well as delays in service provision). It simply came to the conclusion that a refusal would be judged anti-competitive if it was 'likely to eliminate *all* competition on the market on the part of the person requesting the service' and that 'such refusal must not be capable of being objectively justified, and the service must in itself be indispensable to carrying on that person's business.'[60]

---

[57] *London-European Airways v Sabena* [1988] OJ L317/47, [1989] 4 CMLR 662.
[58] *Ibid*. It may be inferred from the case that the Commission considered access to Saphir essential for London-European to compete on the Brussels–Luton route.
[59] Case T-301/04 *Clearstream Banking AG v Clearstream International SA* [2009] ECR II-3155, [2009] 5 CMLR 24.
[60] *Ibid*, at para 147 (emphasis added). National courts in Europe have been also willing to find refusals to supply intangibles anti-competitive on very similar grounds. Eg, in *Software Cellular v T-Mobile*, n 31 above, which involved the denial of interconnection between a mobile phone company T-Mobile and Truphone, a company seeking to provide a new Skype-like service using voice over the Internet protocol technology to enable cheaper call charges for

What is noteworthy about these cases is that they appear to make no distinction between different forms of property right, or even between property and non-property (the computer reservation system in *Sabena*, or the bank clearing services in *Clearstream*). Nor did anyone think that the trade secret aspect of the IBM settlement merited a different approach, even though trade secrets are generally, if not entirely accurately, subsumed under the intellectual property label. Neither the General Court nor the Commission showed any desire to classify technological or organisational advantages according to any private law categories.

6.5 REFUSALS TO LICENSE INTELLECTUAL PROPERTY

Court of Justice jurisprudence on the intersection of competition law and intellectual property under Article 102 TFEU, while prepared to allow that even dominant intellectual property-owning firms should be free to choose their licensees, also concedes that 'exceptional circumstances' might nevertheless exist in which a refusal to license intellectual property rights might constitute an abuse of dominant position. The case law has evolved in such a way, however, that while the presence of certain factors may be said with some (if not complete) certainty to meet the test of exceptionality, it is less clear is whether it is *only* these factors that can satisfy that test or whether there exist any other, as yet unstated sets of exceptional circumstances. The position is further confused by the fact that the Court of Justice has also yet definitively to bless (or reject) some interpretations of its decisions by the General Court and the Commission.

6.5.1 The emergence of the concept of exceptional circumstances

It will be recalled that the Court of Justice in *Volvo v Veng*[61] baulked at finding any duty on the part of a registered design right owner to license the design right in car parts to manufacturers desirous of making and selling such parts. The Court held the right to deny third parties 'constitutes the very subject matter [or scope of the grant] of that exclusive [design] right'. The Court, however, went on to qualify the exercise of this right by postulating three hypothetical situations in which a refusal to supply might constitute abusive conduct, ie:[62]

---

users. The UK High Court ordered T-Mobile to activate Truphone's mobile telephone numbers (already allocated by that country's Office of Communications) under domestic abuse of dominance provisions in s 18(1) of the Competition Act 1998 (UK).

[61] See *Volvo*, n 16 above. See also Case 53/87 *CICCRA & Maxicar v Renault* [1988] ECR 6039, [1990] 4 CMLR 265, decided at the same time.
[62] *Volvo*, n 16 above, at paras 8 and 9.

the arbitrary refusal to supply spare parts to independent repairers, the fixing of prices for spare parts at an unfair level or a decision no longer to produce spare parts for a particular model even though many cars of that model are still in circulation provided that such conduct is liable to affect trade between Member States.

In the result, the Court of Justice found that none of the circumstances thus described were present on the facts before it. Nevertheless the so-called 'spare parts cases' provoked an outpouring of academic commentary. While many commentators readily identified a dichotomy between the *existence* of intellectual property rights (not anti-competitive in themselves) and the *exercise* of such rights (that could be), their general explanations remained largely inconclusive and unsupported by authority.[63]

Further stoking of the *existence/exercise* debate was to follow when the Court of Justice handed down its decision in *Magill*.[64] This appeared to open a wider window of opportunity for those on the receiving end of a refusal to license who might wish to attack that refusal by owners of copyright (and arguably of other kinds of intellectual property too) under Article 102 TFEU. The outcome in *Magill* was an expansion of the concept of 'exceptional circumstances' by the Court of Justice, which treated copyrighted material as something like an essential facility and imposed liability for refusal to supply it. On the facts of the case, Magill had published a comprehensive weekly guide to three television channels received in Ireland and Northern Ireland, but had been successfully sued for copyright infringement by the three television stations which had for some time been publishing stand-alone guides to their own programmes. On appeal, both the General Court and the Court of Justice upheld the decision of the European Commission against the three television stations for abusing their dominant position in relation to the information contained in their separate guides. Both Courts found that a refusal to license copyrighted material, but nothing more, established neither dominance nor abuse, but if the former was proven by other means, the latter might be present under exceptional circumstances. For the *Magill* Court, exceptionality lay in[65]

> The [television channels'] refusal to provide basic information by relying on national copyright provisions which thus *prevented the appearance of a new product*, a comprehensive weekly guide to television programmes, which the appellants did not offer and *for which there was potential consumer demand.*

---

[63] While the Commission's investigation into IBM in relation to refusal to disclose computer interface information ended in IBM providing an undertaking to supply and disclose the information in *European Commission v International Business Machines* [1984] 3 CMLR 147, the Commission's analysis added little to the debate. The suspension of proceedings against IBM is discussed in the *Fourteenth Report on Competition Policy* of the European Commission, at paras 94–95, and the text of the undertaking is available at <http://openmainframe.org/legal/1984-ibm-european-commission-undertaking.html>.
[64] *Magill*, n 33 above.
[65] *Ibid*, at para 54.

In the view of the Court of Justice, the requirements of a 'new product' and 'potential consumer demand' for it, in conjunction with the television channels' failure to offer the new product themselves, had clear resonance in the actual text of Article 102(b) TFEU (ex Article 82(b) EC) which stipulates that abuse may arise by 'limiting production, markets or technical development to the prejudice of consumers'. However, it should in no way be inferred from this that the Court of Justice intended to lay down that all future cases involving refusal to license copyrighted material necessarily had to be brought within the terms of Article 102(b); that, after all, is only one of four non-exhaustive illustrations of the ways in which dominance may be abused.

6.5.2 Judicial refinement of the concept of exceptionality

The scope of the 'exceptional circumstances' exception in *Magill* was subsequently parsed and construed in two other refusals cases: first by the General Court in *Tiercé Ladbroke*,[66] and then by the Court of Justice in *Oscar Bronner*.[67] Judicial, regulatory[68] and academic[69] uncertainty lingered for some time both as to whether the criteria were to be read cumulatively (did 'and' really mean 'and'?) or disjunctively (could 'and' be construed as meaning 'or'?), and as to whether the list of circumstances was exhaustive or merely illustrative. The Court of Justice addressed and attempted to clarify these issues in *IMS*.[70]

IMS Health GmbH was a company that for some time had been providing pharmaceutical manufacturers with a detailed analysis of retail sales of pharmaceutical products in Germany. In order to produce these regular breakdowns, it used a sales-tracking map it had designed in cooperation with customers and adapted to many of their internal marketing and data retrieval systems. This 'brick structure' (as it came to be dubbed) divided the country into 1,860 segments based on political boundaries, postcodes and retail distribution systems. Use of the brick structure extended well beyond IMS's immediate customers to doctors, retail pharmacies and health insurers, whose use of it IMS neither charged for nor objected to. For any potential competitor of IMS, the brick

---

[66] *Tiercé Ladbroke*, n 26 above. In this case, denial of access to Ladbroke of French horse-racing broadcasts by the *sociétés de courses* was not held to prevent Ladbroke conducting its principal business of bookmaking. Furthermore, Ladbroke was unable to rely upon *Commercial Solvents* (n 55 above) as Ladbroke and the *sociétés de courses* were not competing in the same market.
[67] *Oscar Bronner*, n 12 above. Unlike *Magill*, n 33 above, and *Tiercé Ladbroke*, n 66 above, *Oscar Bronner* was not a case involving intellectual property.
[68] See, eg, the decision of the UK Office of Fair Trading, involving a refusal to supply unprocessed holographic photopolymer film: Case CP/1761/02 *EI du Pont de Nemours & Co and Op Graphics (Holography) Ltd* (2003) OFT CA98/07/2003.
[69] See Derclaye, E, 'The *IMS Health* Decision: A Triple Victory' (2004) 27 *World Competition* 397.
[70] *IMS*, see n 21 above.

structure posed a formidable barrier to entry, given the evident and unsurprising reluctance of IMS's customers to accept anything other than reports based on it. In effect the brick structure had become the industry standard. When a competitor devised a look-alike reporting methodology to shield users from the cost of switching to its system, IMS claimed copyright ownership in the brick structure and sued its rival for infringement in the German courts, which, after granting IMS interim relief and finding it dominant in the market for pharmaceutical sales data in Germany, asked the Court of Justice for a preliminary ruling as to whether IMS's refusal to license its brick structure amounted to abuse in terms of Article 102 TFEU (ex Article 82 EC).

In *IMS* the Court of Justice treated the exceptional circumstances as laid down in *Magill* as cumulative, in the limited sense that if all factors were present there was a breach of Article 102 TFEU. It then laid down its conditions of its own (conditions alternatively described as 'sufficient' or 'determinative') to formulate its own five-point test under which a refusal to license copyright by its dominant owner would be anti-competitive if:

a) a copyright license was essential for carrying on the would-be licensee's business;
b) that business was in a separate (secondary) market from the (primary) market in which the copyrighted material might be sold, although one or both markets might remain purely hypothetical until the license issue was resolved;
c) the refusal prevented the emergence of a new product that the copyright owner does not offer and for which there is a potential consumer demand;
d) there was no 'objective' justification for the refusal;
e) the refusal foreclosed all competition in the secondary market.

What was not clarified, and indeed still awaits clarification, was whether the cumulative five-point test was intended to be exhaustive.[71] The *IMS* decision is also silent as to whether refusals could be constructive.[72] Another key issue left to be probed and resolved by future courts and regulators was the newness of a product or process, and whether the question whether it was 'new' should be judged objectively, subjectively or subjectively through an objective lens. Although it seems clear that the Court of Justice was not mandating that the 'new' product or process had to meet patent law's high standard of novelty and non-obviousness, it is far from clear whether a product that looks and feels much

---

[71] For detailed discussion of the debate as it was conducted at the time, see Ahlborn, C, Evans, DS and Padilla, AJ, 'The Logic & Limits of the "Exceptional Circumstances Test" in *Magill* and *IMS Health*' (2005) 28 *Fordham International Law Journal* 1109. As discussed below, the General Court subsequently treated the *IMS* limbs as cumulative but not necessarily exhaustive in its decision in *Microsoft*, see n 8 above.

[72] Cf *Deutsche Post AG* Case COMP/C-1/36.915, [2001] OJ L331, in which the interception, surcharging and delaying of incoming international mail by the dominant German postal authority was found to amount to a constructive refusal to supply.

the same as an existing product but is more technically advanced or cheaper would meet the 'newness' test. Also left up in the air was whether a product is to be considered 'new' merely because it competes directly with one offered by the intellectual property right owner, or whether 'new' in this context can simply mean non-substitutable.

The Court of Justice was not much more forthcoming on how one should decide when it can be said that a withheld licence was *essential* for carrying on the would-be licensee's business in the secondary market. Does 'essential' mean technically irreplaceable or merely unaffordable; and if the latter, what, if anything, should turn on whether the denied party is a large or small player, or what its chances might be of surviving in the market even with a licence? Another pivotal issue left under-explored was how newness and essentialness were to be accurately assessed in markets that had yet to materialise and that might remain forever hypothetical. The Court's only thoughts on this subject were to flirt inconclusively with the idea of a notional market for the copyright itself, even though the putative copyright subsisting in the sales data itself[73] was not 'sold' to any user, nor indeed was it ever intended to be. For future cases, the approach adopted by the Court appears to render the two-market requirement irrelevant. If the secondary market identified can be, as the Court of Justice accepted, potential or even hypothetical,[74] to what extent will it matter that the second-comer's intentions to produce something not offered by the intellectual property owner is insincere, or if sincere, impossible for it to achieve or improbable even if possible?

Again, how pivotal was it in *IMS* that it was a competitor who had sought the access denied? If it was so, subsequent litigation in at least one national court has pointed up that this can be a hard distinction to make, and an artificial one if made.[75]

---

[73] Intellectual property in the sales data at the operative time of the refusal could have potentially existed under copyright proper under German law (although this was by no means certain as the originality threshold for protection in that Member State is much higher than in the UK which uses the 'sweat of the brow' test) and/or under the Directive of the European Parliament and of the Council of 11 March 1996 on the Legal Protection of Databases (96/9/EC) [1996] OJ L77, where a database is protected *qua* database where there has been a 'substantial investment' in quantitative or qualitative terms in obtaining, verifying or presenting its contents.

[74] The General Court agreed with the view of the Advocate General that it is sufficient that a potential or hypothetical market be identified and had ventured further that 'products or services are indispensable in order to carry out a particular business and where there is an actual demand for them on the part of undertakings which seek to carry on the business for which they are indispensable.' See *IMS Health GmbH v IMS Health GmbH* Case C-418/01 (2004), para 44.

[75] Eg, *Attheraces v The British Horse Racing Board Ltd*, n 36 above.

6.5.3 National treatment of refusals to license intellectual property

Even before the finding by the General Court in *Microsoft*,[76] some judges and national competition regulators in European Union Member States[77] were not entirely reluctant to apply the essential facilities doctrine to refusals to license intellectual property, or to acknowledge the emergence of a so-called 'competition law defence' or 'euro defence' to a patent infringement claim brought by a market-dominating patentee, a defence that enables the defendant to claim that the dominant owner of an essential patent was obliged to license its patents under FRAND terms, and that the owner's refusal amounted to abuse under Article 102 TFEU or its national law equivalent. Thus, in *Standard-Spundfass*,[78] the *Bundesgerichtshof* found the owner of a patent that controlled access to a technological standard had owed a duty to license it on non-discriminatory terms and had abused its dominant position by not doing so. The *Bundesgerichtshof* was subsequently more specific in *Orange-Book-Standard*,[79] pointing out that a patent proprietor is liable for abusive behaviour only if it rejects an unconditional offer by the defendant to enter into a binding licence agreement and acts discriminatingly or anti-competitively in doing do. In return the defendant (since it is already using the subject matter of the patent) must comply retrospectively with the obligations that the licence agreement yet to be concluded imposes for the use of the licensed subject matter.[80]

The precedential value outside Germany of these decisions may be diminished by the fact that German competition legislation[81] adopts an approach to unilateral refusals to deal by dominant undertakings that is somewhat stricter than Article 102 TFEU. That said, in Italy in *Merck*,[82] the Italian Antitrust Authority ordered as an interim measure, and relying ultimately on Article 102 TFEU, that Merck, the refusing party, must license a pharmaceutical patent within seven

---

[76] *Microsoft*, n 8 above.
[77] In Member States, national competition authorities have been able since 1 May 2004 to apply Art 102 TFEU directly in parallel with their domestic competition provisions.
[78] *Standard-Spundfass* Case KZR 40/02 (2004) BGH (German Federal Supreme Court).
[79] *Orange-Book-Standard* Case KZR 39/06 (2009) BGH (German Federal Supreme Court).
[80] Adapted from a translation of the judgment available at <www.ipeg.eu/blog/wp-content/uploads/EN-Translation-BGH-Orange-Book-Standard-eng.pdf>.
[81] *Gesetz gegen Wettbewerbsbeschränkungen* (GWB) [Act Against Restraints of Competition] ARC 2005 § 19(4). This provides that: '[A]n abuse of a dominant position exists if a dominant undertaking as a supplier or purchaser of certain kinds of goods or commercial services ... refuses to allow another undertaking access to its own networks or other infrastructure facilities against adequate remuneration, provided that without such concurrent use, the other undertaking is unable for legal or factual reasons to operate as a competitor of the dominant undertaking on the upstream or downstream market; this shall not apply if the dominant undertaking demonstrates that for operational or other reasons such concurrent use is impossible or cannot reasonably be expected.'
[82] Decision of 15 June 2005, Case A364, *Merck-Principi Attivi*, IAA Bulletin n 23/2005, p 7.

days, and in the absence of an agreement between the parties, the regulator itself would determine with the assistance of an independent expert the terms of the licence.

In French competition law, however, the road towards acceptance of a wide test for unilateral abuse of market power when the denied intangible resource involves an intellectual property right has been somewhat rockier, as demonstrated in litigation involving an alleged software standard. The French competition authority *Conseil de la concurrence*, made an interim order requiring Nouvelles Messageries de Presse Parisienne (NMPP), the largest press distributor in France, to grant Messageries Lyonnaises de Presse (MLP) direct access to its software/database system, Presse 2000, which was used by the 200 or so wholesale press distributors operating in France to exchange information on such matters as deliveries, sales, unsold items and proceeds of sales. MLP had claimed that although it possessed the technical and financial resources to design a system like Presse 2000, Presse 2000 had become the current standard for those operating in the press distribution sector and the wholesalers would object to having to use an equivalent system (were it to create one) in parallel with Presse 2000. The *Conseil de la concurrence* thus broke new ground, because European courts had previously determined that only facilities that could not be reasonably duplicated in economic terms could be considered essential. However, while its decision was upheld by the Paris Court of Appeals,[83] it was overturned by the *Cour de cassation*[84] because, as it noted, MLP was already operating without the access it sought. Thus Press 2000 could not qualify as an 'essential facility' as it was not indispensable for MLP to carry out its activities. Interestingly, an equally restrained approach had earlier been taken by the *Conseil de la concurrence* when it was required to decide the lawfulness of the refusal by Apple Computers (dominant in the markets for portable music players and downloaded music) to license its popular iTunes standard FairPlay (protected by digital rights management software) so that its competitor VirginMega could encode its own musical services/devices to be compatible.[85] The regulator rejected the notion that Apple should grant access to FairPlay for a number of reasons, the main ones being[86]:

a) only a small segment of the market at that time actually listened to music from portable devices, most listeners prefer to listen to music on a computer or to burn songs onto a CD;
b) the market for portable music players was competitive enough because several other alternative portable players were available as well as the iPod for processing VirginMega's DRM standard;

---

[83] Judgment of 12 February 2004, *NMPP v Conseil de la Concurrence*, as noted in Bulletin Officiel de La Concurrence, de La Consommation et de La Répression des Fraudes 4 May 2004, n 5.
[84] Judgment n 1159 of 12 July 2005, *NMPP v MLP* (Appeal n Y 04–12.388).
[85] Conseil de la Concurrence, Décision n 04-D-54, 9 November 2004.
[86] *Ibid*, paras 96–103.

c) consumers had a choice because access to the FairPlay standard was not indispensable for them to access VirginMega's music; and
d) the market for online music was competitive as there were at least two major players active in that market.

The *Conseil de la concurrence* also failed to find any causal link between the refusal of access by Apple and VirginMega's comparatively smaller share of the market, observing that Apple was the market leader because it probably employed more successful business strategies and, were access to be mandated, free-riding might well result.

6.6   *OSCAR BRONNER*: ANOMALY OR PATH THROUGH THE WOODS?

The Court of Justice in *IMS* drew heavily on its own previous decision in *Oscar Bronner*.[87] The case (neatly sandwiched both conceptually and chronologically between *Commercial Solvents*[88] and *IMS*) dealt with an attempt by the owners of a small Austrian newspaper (with a national circulation of 3.6 per cent) to be included, on payment of fair remuneration, in the home delivery system run by a competitor newspaper group (Mediaprint) holding a much more substantial (46.8 per cent) share in the national market for daily newspapers. Oscar Bronner argued that Mediaprint had constructively locked it out of Mediaprint's delivery network by making access conditional on the purchase of additional services that Oscar Bronner did not want or need.

The most important feature of the case for present purposes is that the Court of Justice had to consider whether the existing jurisprudence on intellectual property rights could also be applied to the intangible distribution system. (In strictly legal terms such a system was no more than a network of interlocking contracts and not itself a form of property, intellectual or otherwise.) As the Court observed[89]:

> [E]ven if the case law on the exercise of an intellectual property right were applicable to the exercise of any property right whatever, it would still be necessary for the *Magill* judgment to be effectively relied upon … [that is in asking whether the refusal constitutes an abuse of dominant position, to prove] not only that the refusal of the service comprised in home delivery [would] be likely to eliminate all competition in the daily newspaper market on the part of the person requesting the service and that such refusal [would] be incapable of being objectively justified, but also that the service in itself [would] be indispensable to carrying on that person's business, in so much as there is no actual or potential substitute in existence for that home delivery scheme.

---

[87] See *Oscar Bronner*, n 12 above.
[88] See *Commercial Solvents*, n 55 above.
[89] See *Oscar Bronner*, n 12 above, judgment, para 41.

What is not being made clear here is whether the Court intended to recognise the existence of some kind of hybrid category or was using the intellectual property case law as a Trojan horse to allow *Magill*'s limiting principles to infiltrate into the wider law on refusals to deal in general. (If the latter was the case then it must be noted that the 'new product' requirement laid down in *Magill* failed to make the transition. Indeed it is hard to see how it could do on the facts.) Alternatively, one can read backwards from *IMS* to *Oscar Bronner*, because the Court of Justice's five-step test in *IMS* clearly builds on its earlier embellishment of the indispensability and foreclosure issues in *Oscar Bronner*.

In *Oscar Bronner* there was only one home delivery system operating in the country and the costs of duplicating it were high, at least for small players such as the disgruntled news magazine owner. Nevertheless, Advocate General Jacobs[90] considered that several other available avenues (such as shops and kiosks) existed for distributing newspapers to their readers, albeit that some were not nearly as convenient. It was not therefore the case, he said, that the dominant undertaking had a genuine stranglehold on the market, in which case a refusal *could* be abusive.[91] He was also of the view that big players were likely to be well-funded enough to be able to establish their own distribution systems should they choose to enter the market.[92] Thus the home delivery facility must have been not only crucial to Oscar Bronner's own activities (which as it happened, it was not) but also essential to larger and hence more competitive entrants (whose existence at this stage remained merely spectral). This last distinction recognises (although only impliedly) that it is not the proper role of an economically rational competition regime to foster inefficient entry, nor to assist small businesses merely because they are underfunded and needy. Advocate General Jacobs's views on all these points were endorsed, if succinctly, by the Court of Justice in its judgment[93] and led to the finding that Mediaprint's constructive refusal to grant access on Oscar Bronner's terms was not an abuse of a dominant position.

On its own facts *Oscar Bronner* was a perfectly justifiable decision, a salutary reminder that redress for refusals to supply under Article 102 TFEU is limited to those affecting the process of competition, not individual competitors.[94] It also illustrates the context-specific way in which courts should approach complex economic issues. Viewed with a cold eye, however, there was no need whatsoever to draw the highly-restrictive *Magill* principle into the analysis at all. Neither, in hindsight, did the starting point of that analysis have to be a freedom to deal. The outcome would have been no different had none of these things been mentioned.

---

[90] *Ibid*, AG Opinion, at para 67.
[91] *Ibid*, at paras 65–66.
[92] *Ibid*, para 68.
[93] *Oscar Bronner*, n 12 above, judgment, paras 43 and 46.
[94] A point also made by Bergman, M, 'The Bronner Case—A Turning Point for the Essential Facilities Doctrine?' [2000] *European Competition Law Review* 59 at 62; and Strothers, C, 'Refusal to Supply as an Abuse of Dominant Position: Essential Facilities in the European Union' [2001] *European Competition Law Review* 256 at 259.

The risk presented by a decision such as *Oscar Bronner* is that the illusory search for the holy exceptionality grail could end up becoming part of *all* unilateral refusal cases under Article 102 TFEU. Either that, or Article 102 TFEU enforcement could end up becoming atomised US-style into a whole raft of discrete conduct-based rules.

6.7 EURO *MICROSOFT*

The judgment of the 13-strong full chamber of the General Court in *Microsoft Corporation v European Commission*,[95] upholding the European Commission's finding that Microsoft had breached Article 102 TFEU (ex Article 82 EC) by refusing to disclose code, communication protocols and other necessary interoperability information to competitors seeking to develop interoperable systems, proved disappointing to anyone hoping the Court might draw together the loose ends left dangling in previous European jurisprudence on refusals to supply intellectual property by dominant firms. The General Court could not, and did not, assault head-on the *Magill/IMS* orthodoxy that while firms with a substantial degree of market power are entitled to select their business partners,[96] in exceptional circumstances competition policy may trump freedom of contract. However, if cannot be said that the Court dramatically stretched the *Magill/IMS* principles, neither did it greatly clarify their reach. That is not to say, however, that it left the *IMS* test entirely untouched. Some limbs of the test were tinkered with in ways that promise significantly to ease the investigatory burden on regulators in future refusal to licence cases. No overtly new ground was broken in *Microsoft*, however, because the General Court simply assumed (not entirely plausibly) that Microsoft's behaviour could be brought within the pre-existing exceptional circumstances test as laid down in *Magill* and *IMS*.[97] The Court studiously declared[98] it was conducting only a necessarily limited review of the technical and complex appraisals made by the Commission, an example of deference to the regulator not always evident in its own earlier decisions, or indeed those of the Court of Justice.

The General Court's methodology was in fact considerably more proactive than its avowed hands-off approach might suggest. Its strategy was first to proceed on the basis that the *Magill/IMS* factors were not exhaustive (a concession that had no influence on the decision) and then consider whether the facts

---

[95] *Microsoft*, n 8 above.
[96] *Ibid*, at para 319.
[97] For a review of the case by the present authors, see Eagles, I and Longdin, L, 'Microsoft's Refusal to Disclose Software Interoperability Information and the Court of First Instance' (2008) 5 *European Intellectual Property Law Review* 205.
[98] See *Microsoft*, n 8 above, at para 3.

fitted the *Magill/IMS* exceptionality framework, which it found they did after conducting a comprehensive analysis of the total factual background to Microsoft's refusal to license. This involved essentially what was a constructive denial of access[99] to 'interoperability information' to its competitor Sun Systems, and refusal to authorise the use of such information to allow the development and distribution of products potentially competing with Microsoft's own products in the work group server operating systems market. (A market for operating systems designed and marketed to deliver collectively basic infrastructure services to a relatively small number of client PCs connected to small or medium-sized networks.)

In applying the *IMS* test, the General Court observed it had been particularly impressed by the following factors:

a) The importance attached by the Community legislature to software compatibility and mandatory disclosure of interoperability information, as evidenced by the Directive on the Legal Protection of Computer Programs.[100]
b) The extraordinary level of Microsoft's market power in the client PC operating systems market, and its consequent ability to leverage that power onto the adjacent work group server operating market in ways that severely restricted competition in the latter.
c) The fact that Microsoft's conduct involved disruption of a previous level of supply.
d) Evidence indicating that Microsoft's refusal to supply Sun was part of a broader conduct of not disclosing interoperability information to vendors of work group server operating systems vendors.

In relation to the 'essential' limb of the *IMS* test, the issue was whether the inoperability information held by Microsoft was indispensable for rivals to be

---

[99] The following facts in *Microsoft* provide an illuminating example of a constructive refusal. On 15 September 1998, California-based Sun Microsystems wrote to Microsoft (also US based) requesting to be provided with the 'complete information' and technology necessary to allow its own work group server operating systems to communicate seamlessly with Microsoft's WPC/OS and other Windows-based software. Microsoft replied in an upbeat and chatty, but nevertheless markedly unhelpful, vein three weeks later on 6 October, advising its rival that the interface information it had requested was already published and available to it and every other software developer in the world via the Microsoft Developer Network (MSDN). Another way to obtain the technical information sought, Microsoft suggested, was for Sun to send a significant number of its programmers to Microsoft's Professional Developers Conference to be held in Denver from 11–15 October. Sun was then advised that in the event it should (*after* attending the conference and reading through *all* the public MSDN content) *still* require additional support, Microsoft would make its Lead Program manager available. Sun construed this as a 'flat' refusal by Microsoft to provide interoperability information, a claim endorsed by the Commission (and upheld by the General Court) who found that the technologies involved were so complex that Sun could not be expected to know precisely what it needed. See *Microsoft*, n 8 above, at paras 749, 751. Microsoft had argued that it had been Sun's responsibility to clarify what it needed, *ibid*, para 719.
[100] 91/250/EEC of 14 May 1991 [1991] OJ L122/42.

able to compete with the Windows work group server operating system.[101] The General Court found that competing work group server operating systems must be able to interoperate with Windows on an 'equal footing' basis.[102] The refusal strengthened the dominant position of Microsoft by inducing users to utilise its work group server operating system as opposed to those of its competitors.[103] This limb of the *Magill/IMS* test was thus tweaked by the Court's ruling that Microsoft's information could be treated as indispensable if it was necessary to keep a viable competitor in the market (or to persuade one to enter) and the dominant firm was the only economically feasible source of that information.

The General Court then sought to gauge what degree of 'elimination of competition' in the secondary market for work group server operating systems was needed to fulfil the foreclosure limb of the *IMS* test. Microsoft claimed it had to be shown that the refusal was likely to eliminate *all* competition, using a probative standard close to certainty or a 'high probability'. The General Court, however, rejected these arguments, determining that the Commission was right to tackle Microsoft's behaviour before all competition had vanished from the affected market and it was enough that there was a 'likelihood' or 'risk' of 'effective' competition being eliminated. (It would otherwise have been necessary to explain why rival forms of work group server operating systems were still clinging to toeholds in the market.) As some commentators were quick to point out,[104] the General Court's view that the Commission was not required to wait until competitors were about to be driven from the market but could act to safeguard such competition as still existed[105] may be seen as a relaxation of the standard as articulated in *Magill/IMS*.

Microsoft had also argued in relation to the new product limb of the *IMS* test that its refusal had not prevented the introduction of anything produced by a competitor for which there was consumer demand.[106] In expressly rejecting this contention, the General Court found it sufficient for there to be a possibility that a new product or a variation of an existing product might have emerged but for Microsoft's conduct. To this end, it looked behind the *Magill* and *IMS* decisions themselves to the actual words of Article 102 TFEU itself for guidance.[107] The General Court was thereby able neatly to dovetail the Commission's rather tenuous argument that the new product requirement could be met where there

---

[101] *Microsoft*, n 8 above, at para 230.
[102] *Ibid*, para 421.
[103] *Ibid*, para 422.
[104] Graham, C, 'All Hail the European Union: Implications of *Microsoft v Commission* on Global Antitrust Enforcement' (2008) 21 *Pacific McGeorge Global Business & Development Law Journal* 285 at 302; Andreangeli, A, 'Interoperability as an "essential facility" in the *Microsoft* case—encouraging competition or stifling innovation?' (2009) 34 *European Law Review* 584 at 593. See also Eagles and Longdin, n 97 above.
[105] *Microsoft*, n 8 above, para 561.
[106] *Ibid*, para 621.
[107] *Ibid*, para 647.

merely exist 'elements that result from the licensee's efforts' into its own wide interpretation of Article 102(b) TFEU to the effect that liability for a dominant firm's refusal could arise where it led to limitation of 'technical development'. Again as commentators were quick to note, this finding has lowered the threshold as regards the 'new product' requirement laid down in *Magill* and *IMS*.[108] The reformulation is certainly 'far-reaching' and has led to its being dubbed a 'new features' test rather than a 'new products' test,[109] one that allows vague claims by parties denied access to particular features of the dominant firm's technology that they could have enhanced their existing products with new or improved features of value to consumers.[110]

In order to meet the objective justification condition in *IMS*, the onus lay on Microsoft to establish that there was indeed such a justification for its refusal to supply. It argued its actions were justified by its desire to protect its intellectual property rights.[111] However, as ruled by the Commission and upheld by the General Court, mere possession of an intellectual property right does not satisfy the test for objective justification.[112] Were this not the case, the decision in *Magill* would be impossible to explain.

It is important to note that throughout its decision, the General Court was at pains to stress that what it was being presented with was a factual problem in a highly technical milieu, not an opportunity further to develop *Magill/IMS*. This can clearly be seen in the way in which it handled the conflicting claims of Microsoft and the Commission on the interoperability issue. Both, it is true, agreed that interoperability was a question of degree, not an absolute, and that various software products in a system 'interoperate' when they are able to exchange information and mutually use it once exchanged.[113] Beyond this there was little common ground. Microsoft argued that the information that Sun wanted from it would permit competitors to 'clone' features of its products, allowing non-Microsoft server operating systems to function in all respects like a Windows server operating system. The General Court rejected this winner-takes-all definition of interoperability. In its view, the Commission had rightly dismissed Microsoft's concept of interoperability information as 'inaccurate,' 'narrow' and 'one-way', in no way reflecting the way in which real-world businesses organise their computer network systems. The Court therefore had no difficulty upholding the Commission's finding that what Microsoft was being asked to hand over was only information that would enable competitors to develop products which would function differently from, but would be able to

---

[108] Batchelor, B, 'The Fallout from *Microsoft*: the Court of First Instance Leaves Critical IT Industry Issues Unanswered' (2008) 14 *Computer and Telecommunications Law Review* 17 at 18.
[109] Graham, see n 104 above, at 303.
[110] Batchelor, n 108 above, at 18.
[111] *Microsoft*, n 8 above, at para 665.
[112] *Ibid*, at para 689.
[113] *Ibid*.

understand the messages conveyed by, Microsoft's products. This fell far short of the sort of material that would enable competitors to replicate those same products; what was being taken from Microsoft was less than what it owned. Confiscation was not on the agenda. Was this concern to avoid exact duplication or cloning intended to be a legal limitation applicable in future cases, or merely a case of fine-tuning the remedy to do as little damage as possible to the ordinary operation of the market? It can be read either way. Perhaps more useful in future cases is the General Court's dismissive response to attempts by both parties to take refuge in the wording of the Computer Programs Directive. While the Court was prepared to accept that the Commission's understanding of interoperability conformed more closely to the Directive, it went on stress that Article 102 TFEU clearly outranked the Directive in the Community's legislative pecking order, and that it was the degree of interoperability necessary to achieve the former's objectives that mattered in this case.[114]

The facts by which the General Court set so much store were not always 'real' or 'found' facts. This can clearly be seen in the way in which it sidestepped one major issue left open in *Magill/IMS*: how far beyond copyright did the principle laid down in these cases extend? By simply assuming (as the Commission had also done) for the purposes of the case in front of it that all of the *Magill/IMS* factors were present on the facts, neither the Commission nor the Court had therefore to explore the issue of what *kind* of intellectual property was covered by the *Magill/IMS* principles. They simply took it as read that all of the information sought by Microsoft's rivals was protected by whatever bundle of rights the *Magill/IMS* test had been applied to in the past, or might be applied to in the future. This meant that the Court did not have to decide as a matter of law whether the *Magill/IMS* principles extended beyond copyright to patents, trade secrets or technical 'lock-outs' in which intellectual property of one kind or another may or may not have subsisted. Neither did it have to trouble itself about trans-jurisdictional variations in the content of particular intellectual property rights across Member States. Because its reasoning rested on this hypothetical assumption, the General Court had no reason to ask, much less answer, the question: Are all intellectual property rights entitled to the benefits of the exceptionality principle, or are some more equal than others in this regard? The only hint of a hierarchy of more or less privileged rights comes with the Court's concern to point up what it saw as an important difference between true property rights, such as copyright and patents, and the liability rules protecting know-how and trade secrets in most jurisdictions; the latter were self-constituting, depending not on the inherent creativity or innovation of the material sought to be protected but on a unilateral business decision by the possessor of the information in question to restrict access to it.[115] It would be

---

[114] *Ibid*, para 227.
[115] *Ibid*, para 693.

drawing a very long bow indeed to see this as some commentators have, as an endorsement of the view that *Magill/IMS* 'exception' applies only where the availability of intellectual property protection was uncertain in the first place (as it arguably was in *Magill*).[116]

In the process of upholding all the Commission's substantive findings, the General Court was able both to reassert competition first principles (stressing the role and importance of consumer choice in competition analysis) and resist a US-style slide towards a presumption of legality for refusals to deal. The Commission was, however, overruled in relation to the details of mechanisms it had prescribed for the implementation and oversight of the two remedies ordered against Microsoft. The Commission had provided that it would appoint a monitoring trustee from a list of persons nominated by Microsoft, who would issue opinions (upon application by the Commission itself, a third party, or on his or her own motion) as to Microsoft's compliance with the Commission's decision and on any other issue of interest relating to the enforcement of the decision. The trustee was to have had access to Microsoft's employees, premises, documents and information, including relevant source code. All costs incurred which related to the monitoring trustee, including remuneration, were required to be borne by Microsoft. The General Court, however, found the Commission, in setting up the mechanism of a monitoring trustee and giving it independent investigatory powers with no time limit, and allowing third parties to call upon it to act, went well beyond its regulatory powers. In short, the Court found the Commission lacked the authority to compel Microsoft to grant to a monitoring trustee powers which the Commission itself was not authorised to confer on third parties. The Commission's decision was accordingly overturned in so far as it required Microsoft to submit a proposal for the appointment of a monitoring trustee with the power to have access, independently of the Commission, to Microsoft's assistance, information, documents, premises and employees, and to the source code of the relevant Microsoft products, and in so far as it had provided that all the costs associated with that monitoring trustee be borne by Microsoft. All of this is likely to severely hobble future attempts by the Commission to devise effective supervisory structures in cases where the technology is complex. The end result of this remedial *lacuna* may turn out to be precisely that loophole-hunting gaming that we deplore in chapter three.[117]

---

[116] Czapracka, KA, 'Where Antitrust Ends and IP Begins—On the Roots of the Transatlantic Clashes' (2006–2007) *Yale Journal of Law and Technology* 44 at 80; Dolmans, A, 'Restrictions on Innovation: An EU Antitrust Approach' (1998) 88 *Antitrust Law Journal* 455 at 470; Korah, V, 'The Interface Between IP and Antitust: The European Experience' (2002) 69 *Antitrust Law Journal* 801 at 810–13; Strothers, C, 'The End of Exclusivity? Abuse of IPRs in the EU' (2002) 24 *European Intellectual Property Review* 86 at 92–93.
[117] See 3.7.5 above.

6.8 LITTLE GUIDANCE FROM THE *GUIDANCE*

Refusals to license intellectual property do not figure largely in the *Guidance*.[118] In the entire body of the document there are only two direct references. A refusal to license, in the Commission's view, is no longer to be viewed as significantly special, just as one more example of a broad range of potentially abusive practices.[119] By contrast, the *Discussion Paper* circulated by the Director General Competition in December 2005 (a preparatory paper intended to galvanise both economists and lawyers into print) not only had dedicated a whole section to refusals to licence intellectual property,[120] but also had contained a subsection on refusals to supply information needed for interoperability.[121] Indeed the *Discussion Paper* had gone so far as to suggest an intervention differential between refusals to license intellectual property in general and refusals to license interoperability information, pointing out that even if the interoperability information that had been denied could be considered intellectual property (in the form of a trade secret), it might not be appropriate to apply to the refusal the same high standards for intervention as those prescribed for refusals to license patents or copyright.[122]

The *Guidance*, however, makes no such distinction between the two situations, or indeed between the different forms of intellectual property. It simply places refusal to license intellectual property right situations (including those in which the licence in question is necessary to provide interface information) into the same box as a broad range of practices, including refusals to supply products to existing or new customers and refusals to grant access to an essential facility or a network.[123] Since the *Guidance* is silent as to whether anything turns on whether a refused licence relates to 'strong' or 'weak' rights in any of the senses outlined in chapter four, one must assume that it rejects the notion of a hierarchy of rights. All species of refusals to supply tangibles and intangibles alike are then to be exposed to the same three-pronged test intended to guide the Commission's enforcement in this area. To trigger intervention the Commission declared that all the following circumstances needed to be present[124]:

---

[118] See *Guidance*, n 4 above.

[119] The *Guidance, ibid*, para 78, states that refusals to supply may cover a broad range of practices, such as refusal to supply products to existing or new customers, refusal to license intellectual property rights, including when the licence is necessary to provide interface information, and refusal to grant access to an essential facility or a network.

[120] *Discussion Paper*, section 9.2.2.6, paras 237–40. The Commission's public consultation document, *DG Competition discussion paper on the application of Article 82 of the Treaty* [now Article 102 TFEU] *to exclusionary abuses* (Brussels, December 2005) is available at <http://ec.europa.eu/competition/antitrust/art82/discpaper2005.pdf>.

[121] *Discussion Paper, ibid*, section 9.2.3, paras 241–42.

[122] *Ibid*, section 9.2.3.

[123] *Guidance*, n 4 above, para 78.

[124] *Ibid*, para 81.

a) The refusal relates to a product or service that is objectively necessary to be able to compete effectively on a downstream market.[125]
b) The refusal is likely to lead to the elimination of effective competition on the downstream market.
c) The refusal is likely to lead to consumer harm.

The three-pronged test is stated to apply both to cases of disruption of previous supply and to refusals to supply products or services which the dominant company has not previously supplied to others. The *Guidance* indicates, however, that termination of an existing supply arrangement is more likely to be found abusive than a *de novo* refusal to supply.

The second and third limbs of the test for refusals to supply picking up on foreclosure likely to lead to consumer harm have equal resonance in the Commission's general approach to exclusionary conduct. Apropos what effects precisely might be construed as an adverse impact on consumer welfare, the Commission has signalled those effects could present in the form of higher price levels than would have otherwise prevailed, or in some other form such as limiting quality or reducing consumer choice.[126]

There are two ways of reading the Commission's three-step formula. The first is that there is indeed nothing about intellectual property requiring special treatment under Article 102 TFEU, a welcome concession. Less welcome, however, is the extension of some (but not all) of the *Magill/IMS* criteria, *Oscar Bronner* style, to refusals to deal in general. Intellectual property is thus depriviledging, but at the expense of re-privileging actions over inaction.

Perhaps of more significance than the attempt in the *Guidance* to incorporate the prior case law into its methodology, is its emphasis on the integration of more econometric analysis into abuse cases (including refusals) through the adoption of an 'effects-based' approach,[127] an approach the Commission supposes to be

---

[125] The *Guidance* also spells out that the requirement that the input should be objectively necessary does not mean that, without the refused input, no competitor could ever enter or survive on the downstream market. It means rather that there is no actual or potential substitute on which competitors in the downstream market could rely so as to counter, at least in the long term, the negative consequences of the refusal. In this regard, the Commission will normally make an assessment of whether competitors could effectively duplicate the input produced by the dominant undertaking in the foreseeable future. *Ibid*, para 84.

[126] *Ibid*, para 19.

[127] *Ibid*, para 22. It is more accurate perhaps to say that the Commission's new approach reflects (rather than implements) the approach proposed in the Economic Advisory Group for Competition Policy (EAGCP) *Report on an Economic Approach to Article 82 EC* (July 2005). That Report suggested an economics- or effects-based approach in every case (including refusals to license), by which the anti-competitive effects of conduct would be pitted against its pro-competitive effects to determine whether it was on balance anti-competitive. The Report was originally commissioned by the DG Competition's first Chief Economist in a conscious attempt to inject more economic analysis into the interpretation of Art 102 TFEU.

more in tune with that of the United States[128] and considered less prone to 'type' errors rather than the more traditional, formalist approach based on ordoliberal principles for which the regulator had shown a strong predilection for several decades. The Commission has also signalled reluctance to intervene in relation to conduct that is unlikely to result in direct consumer harm.[129] Adoption of this approach, focusing as it does on identifying net harm to consumers, balancing efficiencies and refraining from treating different categories of behaviour as abusive *per se*, means the regulator will require economic verification of harm. To this end, the *Guidance* indicates the need for a causal link between conduct and actual or potential 'anticompetitive foreclosure'.[130] Roundly criticised by lawyers and economists alike,[131] the *Guidance* provides not much more transparency than before as to what might be regarded as sound economics-based evidentiary methodology to establish that causal link. Neither is the regulator apparently expected to have to make any real economic assessment of an alleged objective justification for a refusal, and nor is it offered any clues as to the probative value of the different types of economic evidence. (The *Guidance* merely alludes to a 'sufficient' degree of probability.)

In venturing to change tack, methodologically speaking, in abuse of dominance cases, the Commission is forfeiting the security of a formulaic rules-based approach which is relatively easy to apply and predict. Implementation of the effects-based approach is intended to propel regulatory and judicial authorities out of their comfort zone and prompt them, as part of the 'verification of competitive harm' process, to assimilate complex economic concepts accompanied by empirical evidence (generally thin on the ground, as we saw in chapter two). It means, for example, in complex constructive refusals to license cases involving allegations of excessive pricing, that regulatory and judicial authorities would find themselves grappling with economic pricing principles furnished by economic expert witnesses to establish the 'competitive price' or a 'non-abusive right price' for a sought-after facility before determining the fairness of the

---

[128] And also, not surprisingly, with a number of the Commission's other guidelines in which it has placed more emphasis on consideration of consumer welfare and economic efficiency in the overall assessment of anti-competitive harm. See *Application of Article 81(3) of the Treaty* [2004] OJ C101/97, para13; *Guidelines on the Application of Article 81 of the Treaty to Technology Transfer Agreements* [2004] OJ C101/2, para 5; *Guidelines on Vertical Restraints* [2000] OJ C291/1, para 7; *Guidelines on the Assessment of Horizontal Mergers under the Council Regulation on the Control of Concentrations Between Undertakings* [2004] OJ C31/5, para 8; and *Guidelines on the Assessment of Non-Horizontal Mergers under the Council Regulation on the Control of Concentrations Between Undertakings* [2008] OJ C265/6, para 10.

[129] *Guidance*, n 4 above, paras 5 and 19.

[130] *Ibid*, para 71.

[131] See, eg, Petit, N, 'From Formalism to Effects?—The Commission's Communication on Enforcement Priorities in Applying Article 82 EC' (2009) 32 *World Competition* 485, available at <http://ssrn.com/abstract=1476082>; and Ezrachi, A, 'The European Commission Guidance on Article 82 EC—The Way in which Institutional Realities Limit the Potential for Reform', *Oxford Legal Studies Research Paper No 27/2009*, September 2009, available at <http://ssrn.com/abstract=1463854>.

alleged excessive price. This would matter less if the Commission were not at the same time denied the ability to create workable supervisory structures to assist it in this regard.

A harbinger of the difficulties future adjudicators may experience when attempting to verify anti-competitive harm by applying such cost benchmarks may be seen in the English Court of Appeal decision in *Attheraces Ltd v British Horseracing Board Ltd*[132] (an unusual case in which the essential facility at issue was access to an intangible, unique and ephemeral product in the form of racing data generated by the party in possession of it). One does not need to delve too deeply between the lines of the judgment of Mummery LJ (speaking for all members of the Court) to realise that judges could easily become confused in the face of information asymmetries that are an inevitable part and parcel of this type of case. The court is required to determine not only the appropriateness of applying a particular suggested economic pricing methodology, but also whether that methodology has been properly applied. As Mummery LJ cautioned[133]:

> The claim of abuse of dominant position in relation to the information poses this crucial question: when is the price charged by the person controlling access to the information so high as to be excessive or unfair? This question prompts other questions. Is there a pricing principle which can be applied to such a case? If so, what is a non-abusive 'right price' and how is it to be ascertained by the court? Is it, as was held in this case, the cost of production of the information plus a reasonable profit (called 'cost +')? If the possessor of the information may only lawfully charge a price calculated in this way, how does the court set about ascertaining the cost + price? In comparing the price charged and the cost incurred, what should be included in the allowable costs incurred? Is it only the costs directly involved in the secondary activity of creating, collating and compiling the information, or does it include, or reflect, all, or only some, and, if so, which, of the costs incurred in conducting the primary activity to which the information relates?

Notwithstanding the fact that the court still made a stab at ascertaining the competitive price for access to the essential facility at issue, Mummery LJ suggested *obiter* that judges perhaps might not be the most appropriate bodies to carry out such a task in all cases. As he observed[134]:

> The nature of these difficult questions suggests that the problems of gaining access to essential facilities and of legal curbs on excessive and discriminatory pricing might, when negotiations between the parties fail, be solved more satisfactorily by arbitration or by a specialist body equipped with appropriate expertise and flexible powers. The adversarial procedures of an ordinary private law action, the limited scope of expertise in the ordinary courts and the restricted scope of legal remedies available are not best suited to helping the parties out of a deadlocked negotiating position or to achieving a business-like result reflecting both their respective interests and the public interest.

---

[132] *Attheraces Ltd v The British Horseracing Board Ltd*, n 36 above.
[133] *Ibid*, at [6].
[134] *Ibid*, at [7].

It is of course precisely such expertise and flexibility with which the Commission sought to arm itself in *Microsoft* in the form of a monitoring trustee, and which was rejected for want of jurisdiction by the General Court.

As emphasised earlier, the *Guidance* is soft law, not binding on either courts or competition authorities. Indeed, at least one national regulator (the German *Bundeskartellamt*) has expressly baulked at being steered in the direction of injecting more economic analysis into its application of Article 102 TFEU to exclusionary abuses.[135] That said (and here we speculate rather than attempt to predict), future judges and regulators more predisposed and open to using economic analysis to help resolve refusal to license disputes may well turn to the effects-based approach advocated in the *Guidance*. This is not to suggest that such a move might wean them away from the current substantive law on refusals to license and application of the exceptional circumstances test, but rather since that jurisprudence has been incrementally built up, it may well continue to evolve by incorporating more economic methodology. The alternative would be to fall back on remedial counsels of despair and presumptions of legality. Nothing is gained if yesterday's rule-based prohibitions are replaced by tomorrow's equally rule-based exemptions for particular types of behaviour.

---

[135] See the statement by the *Bundeskartellamt* and German Ministry of Economics and Technology in the *DG Competition discussion paper on the Application of Article 82 EC [Article 102 TFEU] 82 to exclusionary abuses* (Bonn, 2006), available at <www.bundes kartellamt.de/ wDeutsch/download/pdf/Stellungnahmen/0703_Stellung nahme_DE_Art82_e.pdf>.

7

Refusals to License in Australia and New Zealand: Parsing the Hints and Silences

7.1 CONVERGENCE AND ITS LIMITS

The Australian and New Zealand competition regimes make an interesting case study in that they have achieved a high degree of convergence as to the content and structure of their substantive law concerning unilateral abuses of market power,[1] without having to set up anything very much in the way of joint enforcement mechanisms to keep that convergence on track.[2] This is not simply a matter of harmonised legislative structures, although these are important, but also an awareness by judges on both sides of the Tasman Sea (an awareness perhaps felt more strongly on the New Zealand side) of the need to keep each other's case law well in mind when giving meaning to what are by the standards of section 2 of the Sherman Act and Article 102 TFEU relatively detailed legislative provisions. There is a reverse side to the convergence coin, however, and that is this: where there are differences in the wording or gaps in the coverage between the two statutes, these can take on more significance than would perhaps

---

[1] The convergence is perhaps less marked in the case of multilateral arrangements lessening competition, where the New Zealand jurisprudence has taken off in directions of its own in some respects. Thus under s 27 of the Commerce Act 1986 (NZ), unrealised (and unrealisable) intent can create liability, and much conduct assailable under s 36 can also attract liability under s 27 by attributing the 'purpose' of the arrangement to the dominant party and ignoring the possibly coerced motives of the other participants in the scheme. See the Court of Appeal decision in *Port Nelson Ltd v Commerce Commission* [1996] 3 NZLR 554. A brief note about judicial hierarchies in the two jurisdictions is perhaps useful here to clarify the sometimes confusing terminology attached to them. In New Zealand the High Court is the court of first instance in competition cases, whereas in Australia that is the role of a single judge in the Federal Court. The intermediate appellate level is occupied by the Court of Appeal in New Zealand and by the Full Federal Court in Australia. The highest appellate level in Australia is the High Court, whereas in New Zealand it is now the Supreme Court (replacing the Privy Council in that role from 2004).

[2] The only significant legislative move in the direction of joint enforcement has been the inclusion in both countries' competition statutes of extended definitions of 'market' to include markets on either side of the Tasman Sea, and the creation of separate heads of liability in relation to these trans-jurisdictional markets. See Commerce Act 1986 (NZ), s 36A, and Competition and Consumer Act 2010 (Aust), s 46A. These provisions have been almost entirely unused.

be the case were the two regimes more divergent overall. Whether this holds true in relation to refusals to license remains to be seen, there being as yet no case speaking directly to the subject in either jurisdiction. Parsing the near judicial silence, a silence broken only occasionally and usually with wider objectives in mind, is what this chapter seeks to do.

7.2 TAKING ADVANTAGE OF MARKET POWER

Section 36 of New Zealand's Commerce Act 1986 and section 46 of Australia's Competition and Consumer Act 2010[3] are the key provisions in each country's competition statutes prohibiting the unilateral exercise of market power. They may be invoked by firms seeking access to a product or process dependent on an intellectual property right, although their application is far broader. In 2001 New Zealand aligned its threshold for market power with that of Australia, and now both countries prohibit a firm taking advantage of a substantial degree of power in a market for a prohibited purpose. Before this harmonisation took place, New Zealand's threshold was the higher one of dominance, as in Article 102 TFEU.[4] Cases were still being adjudicated on the basis of this higher threshold as late as 2010.

7.2.1 The statutory provisions

Section 36(2) of the Commerce Act 1986 (NZ) gives the flavour of the two provisions, and its relevant post-2001 wording is set out below:

36. Taking advantage of market power –

(2) A person that has a substantial degree of power in a market must not take advantage of that power for the purpose of –
   (a) restricting the entry of a person into that or any other market; or
   (b) preventing or deterring a person from engaging in competitive conduct in that or any other market; or
   (c) eliminating a person from that or any other market.

---

[3] Replacing the Trade Practices Act 1974 (Aust).
[4] Although not always similarly interpreted. It has to be said that while dominance is generally considered to be the higher threshold, this is yet to be demonstrated.

Its Australian counterpart, section 46 of the Competition and Consumer Act 2010 (Aust), is longer and more detailed (in keeping with Australian traditions of legislative drafting) but operates to similar effect.[5]

The New Zealand section 36B, introduced into the statute in 2001, provides that the existence of any of the purposes specified in section 36 may be inferred from the conduct of any relevant person or from any other relevant circumstances. It too has a close Australian counterpart.[6]

The statutory wording makes two things clear. First, the possibility of leveraging has been given the statutory nod by the use of the phrase 'that or any other market'. Secondly, to establish liability, regulators and private plaintiffs must be able to show that:

a) the defendant has the required degree of market power; and
b) the defendant has taken, or is taking, advantage of that market power; and
c) the defendant, in taking advantage of its market power, has carried out (or is carrying out) at least one of the three proscribed purposes.

The key to interpreting section 36 and its Australian counterpart is the presence or absence of a causal link between each of the three elements, usefully dubbed by one commentator[7] the 'threshold issue', the 'connection issue' and the 'purpose issue' respectively. Missing from these provisions is any illustrative list of forms of abuse in the manner of Article 102 TFEU. Practices such as selective margin squeezing or excessive pricing cannot therefore be erected into separate heads of liability. Nor does the legislative scheme require that a distinction be made between constructive and actual refusals to deal.

7.2.2 Australia: many roads home

In determining whether a firm has taken, or is taking, advantage of its market power for a proscribed purpose under section 46, the High Court of Australia has adopted a variety of approaches to linking the three limbs of the section. It is important to understand, however, that in Australian judicial eyes, these are merely alternative methodologies for bringing about the same result. All may be resorted to simultaneously, and sometimes are. These are not distinctive legal rules competing for supremacy.

---

[5] The differences are partly drafting curiosities (eg, the reversal of the order of the proscribed purposes). For other small variations, see Robertson, D, 'Taking Advantage of Market Power in the Modern Economy' (2004) 10 *New Zealand Business Law Quarterly* 26.

[6] Competition and Consumer Act 2010 (Aust), s 46(7).

[7] See van Roy, Y, 'Taking Advantage of Market Power: Should New Zealand Adopt the Approach of the High Court of Australia?' (2005) 11 *New Zealand Business Law Quarterly* 319.

(a) The would/could counterfactual test

The first refusal to deal case under section 46 to reach the High Court of Australia was *Queensland Wire Industries v The Broken Hill Pty Co Limited*.[8] The Broken Hill Company (BHP) enjoyed substantial market power, not only itself producing around 97 per cent of steel in Australia, but also supplying about 85 per cent of the country's steel and steel products.[9] One of its products was Y-bar, used in the construction of the rurally ubiquitous star-picket fence. The company sold Y-bar in Australia only to its retailer/subsidiary AWI. The pivotal issue of whether BHP had misused its undisputed market power for a proscribed purpose arose only after Queensland Wire Industries (QWI), an aspiring rival retailer of rural fence posts, asked BHP to supply it with Y-bar so it could make and sell its own posts and was refused, at first outright and then constructively, when BHP offered Y-bar at an excessively high price.

In finding BHP's refusal had breached section 46, the majority of the High Court did not require it to be shown that BHP had had any hostile intent before it could be said to have taken advantage of its market power.[10] Instead, it took the approach that a defendant may not be held to have taken advantage of its position if it would have acted (or not acted) in the same way if the market had been competitive.[11] This hypothetical question, a form of economic modelling that posits another parallel reality, subsequently became known as the 'counterfactual test'. It was more clearly articulated by Lockhart J in *Dowling v Dalgety Australia Ltd*[12]:

> The central determinative question to ask is: has the corporation exercised a right that it would be highly unlikely to exercise or could not afford for commercial reasons to exercise if the corporation was operating in a competitive market?

A great deal of inconclusive debate then ensued (both in the cases and the commentary[13]) as to whether the inductive reasoning that the counterfactual test appeared to mandate also required the court to establish that the firm with market power *could* engage in the same allegedly anti-competitive conduct without that market power, or whether the firm *would* do so. This debate[14] was

---

[8] *Queensland Wire Industries v The Broken Hill Pty Co Limited* ('*QWI*') [1989] HCA 6, (1989) 167 CLR 177.
[9] *Ibid*, at 183–84.
[10] *Ibid*, at 190–91, 194 and 202.
[11] *Ibid*, at 192 (per Mason C J and Wilson J); 202 (per Dawson J); and 216 (per Toohey J).
[12] *Re Dowling v Dalgety Australia Ltd* [1992] FCA 35 at para 151.
[13] Eg, Richardson, M, 'The High Court of Australia Revisits Misuse of Market Power: Implications for Intellectual Property Right Holders' (2002) 24 *European Intellectual Property Review* 81; Robertson, n 5 above; van Roy, n 7 above; Ahdar, R, 'Escaping New Zealand's Monopolisation Quagmire' (2006) 34 *Australian Business Law Review* 260.
[14] The *could* approach has been described by one commentator as involving 'analysis of the particular conduct that occurs, in terms of whether it is consistent with the firm's survival', compared to the *would* approach that requires an 'inquiry not only into whether the behaviour

prompted by the use of 'would' by two of the four majority judges[15] in *QWI*, and the taking of a 'could' approach by the other two.[16]

Later, the majority of the High Court in *Melway Publishing Pty Limited v Robert Hicks Limited*[17] also used both terms indiscriminately, but again without expressly preferring one over the other. Neither did any of the judges in *Melway* refer to the counterfactual test by name to describe what they were doing. It was not until the High Court decision in *Rural Press Ltd v Australian Competition and Consumer Commission*[18] that the majority of the High Court articulated a preference for *could*, ostensibly in line with the approach supposedly taken in *Melway*. Thereafter, whenever the counterfactual test has been applied by the High Court (again not necessarily by that name), the 'could' approach appears to have gained the upper hand.[19] Certainly *could* sits better with the way in which most economists would frame the issue, although it has to be said that any difference in outcomes does not appear to have been envisaged by judges using the alternative formulation. What is more important than this inconclusive (and possibly unintended) verbal duelling is that Australian courts have always made it plain that the counterfactual test is not the sole, nor even always the most appropriate, test to be applied in section 46 cases. As Toohey J put his concerns about the counterfactual test in *Melway*[20] (and tellingly, using both *could* and *would*):

> The four members of [the *QWI* Court] reasoned by inference from the premise that BHP *could* not have refused supply to QWI in a competitive market to the conclusion that its behaviour was made possible by the absence of competitive constraint (ie by market power). The source of the premise is not entirely clear. It seems to involve unstated assumptions about the nature and structure of the competitive market. There is nothing in s 46 that assists in that regard. An absence of a substantial degree of market power does not mean the presence of an economist's theoretical model of perfect competition. It only requires a sufficient level of competition to deny a substantial degree of power to any competitor in the market. To ask how a firm *would* behave if it lacked a substantial degree of power in a market, for the purpose of making a judgment as to whether it is taking advantage of its market power, *involves a process of economic analysis which, if it can be undertaken with sufficient cogency, is consistent with*

---

is consistent with the firm's survival but also whether it minimises the firm's opportunity cost in the long run'; see Clough, D, 'Misuse of Market Power: "Would" or "Could" in a Competitive Market' (2001) 29 *Australian Business Law Review* 311 at 315.

[15] See *QWI*, n 8 above, per Mason CJ and Wilson J.
[16] *Ibid*, per Dawson and Toohey JJ.
[17] *Melway Publishing Pty Limited v Robert Hicks Limited* ('*Melway*') [2001] HCA 13; (2001) 205 CLR 1.
[18] *Rural Press Ltd v Australian Competition and Consumer Commission* ('*Rural Press*') [2003] HCA 75, (2003) 216 CLR 53 at para 52.
[19] See the detailed analysis of *Boral Besser Masonry Ltd v Australian Competition and Consumer Commission* [2003] HCA 5 and *NT Power Generation Pty Ltd v Power and Water Authority* ('*NT Power*') [2004] HCA 48 by van Roy, n 7 above, at 338.
[20] See *Melway* (HCA), n 17 above, at para 52 (emphasis added).

the purpose of s 46. But the cogency of the analysis may depend upon the assumptions that are thought to be required by s 46.

The counterfactual test is the most widely applied of all the methodologies described in this section. This is scarcely surprising, as it is both simple to state and, on the face of it, offers the strongest causal connection between power, use and purpose. As with any hypothetical, however, the need to conjure up imagined scenarios which may never happen (and which perhaps can never happen) can make outcomes anything but predictable. It can also lead to the sterile battle of the models feared by Toohey J in *Melway*. This may explain why, when applying the test, judges faced with the same set of facts have managed to come to very different conclusions.[21]

(b) Material facilitation

An alternative test for 'taking advantage' of market power is that of material facilitation. The reasoning behind it is perhaps best described by Toohey J in *Melway*.[22] Thus:

> [I]n a given case, it may be proper to conclude that a firm is taking advantage of market power where it does something that is *materially facilitated* by the existence of the power, even though it may not have been absolutely impossible without the power.

In other words, section 46 would be contravened if a corporation's market power had made it *easier* for the corporation to act for a proscribed purpose than otherwise would be the case. The 'material facilitation' test was subsequently applied by the High Court in *Rural Press*,[23] and by the Full Federal Court in *Australian Competition and Consumer Commission v Australian Safeway Stores Pty Ltd*.[24] What the latter case demonstrates quite clearly, however, is that material facilitation is just another way of thinking about the problem, not a test vying for first place over the counterfactual test. Thus while the Full Federal Court was able to say that what the defendant Safeway had done was 'not absolutely impossible' without substantial market power, it found that Safeway would not have engaged in the impugned conduct had it not had that power, because it would not have anticipated being able to achieve its anti-competitive purpose in those imagined circumstances.[25]

---

[21] See van Roy, n 7 above, at 319.
[22] *Melway* (HCA), n 17 above, at para 51 (emphasis added).
[23] *Rural Press*, n 18 above, at para 53.
[24] *Australian Competition and Consumer Commission v Australian Safeway Stores Pty Ltd* [2003] FCAFC 149.
[25] *Safeway*, *ibid*, at para 329.

(c) Power plus purpose equals use

The so-called 'purpose test', first propounded by Deane J in *QWI*, is another option available to regulators and judges. It derives its name from the suggestion by Deane J that taking advantage for section 46 purposes could be inferred from a defendant corporation's substantial market power and purpose.[26] In essence the test asks whether the purpose of the allegedly anti-competitive conduct could have been achieved only by virtue of the defendant's substantial market power. It provides the required causal nexus between the conduct and substantial market power but approaches the issue in reverse. It is arguably a more appropriate test than the counterfactual test in cases where conduct that might be of no concern—or even pro-competitive—if engaged in in a competitive market may be anti-competitive in the market as it is.[27] The purpose test is not merely speculative. It was used as a stand-alone test by Finkelstein J in the Full Federal Court decision in *Northern Territory Power Generation Pty Ltd v Power and Water Authority*,[28] its application, separate from the counterfactual test, was subsequently approved of as 'sound' by the High Court in that case.[29]

The purpose test also comports with the High Court's observation in *Melway* that sometimes there is no need to propose a hypothetical market and carry out a counterfactual analysis because courts can sometimes find a taking of advantage from direct observation of conduct.[30]

(d) Legitimate business purpose: stand alone test or exculpatory factor?

The High Court has not directly addressed the question whether being able to offer a legitimate business reason for its conduct may absolve a firm with substantial market power from liability under section 46. Perhaps the closest it came to this was in *Melway*.[31] Melway was the owner of copyright in street directories for Melbourne and Sydney, and had (in the days before electronic global positioning systems took hold) 80–90 per cent of the Melbourne street directory market and about 10 per cent of the Sydney street directory market. It had for many years operated a selective and rigid distribution system for its street directories in both cities. This entailed subdividing the retail market into segments and allocating exclusive wholesalers to each segment. Melway believed its system was efficient and maximised sales, particularly in Melbourne where it had published 26 editions at the time of trial. Melway terminated its arrangement in

---

[26] *QWI*, n 8 above,, at 197–98.
[27] See van Roy, n 7 above, at 347.
[28] *NT Power Generation Pty Ltd v Power and Water Authority* ('*NT Power*') [2002] FCAFC 302, at para 154.
[29] *NT Power Generation Pty Ltd v Power and Water Authority* [2004] HCA 48, (2004) 219 CLR 90, at paras 149–50.
[30] *Melway* (HCA), n 17 above, at para 53.
[31] Ibid.

Melbourne with one wholesaler distributor (Robert Hicks), and refused to meet a large order from Hicks for 20–50,000 street directories because it believed Hicks intended to bypass Melway's established distribution system and sell them to any retailer it wanted. What appeared to have impressed the High Court that the refusal carried no liability under section 46 was the fact that Melway had also established the same distribution system in Sydney where it had relatively very little market power. The High Court agreed with Merkel J at first instance, who pointed out that what had been characterised, by way of convenient shorthand, as a refusal to supply might equally well have been characterised as a termination of a distributorship. The Court also had no quarrel with Merkel J's finding (here echoing *Colgate*) that Melway was entitled to maintain its distribution system without contravention of the competition statute, and that it was not the purpose of section 46 to dictate to Melway how to choose its distributors.[32]

That having a legitimate business purpose may have an exculpatory effect had already been recognised by Heerey J in his dissent in the Full Federal Court decision in *Melway*.[33] He found Melway's reasons for strict adherence to its selective distribution system to be pro-competitive and legitimate,[34] and observed that if the firm had acted to conduct its business more efficiently, there would be no taking advantage of market power. In another lower court decision, *Australian Competition and Consumer Commission v Boral Ltd*,[35] Heerey J also took pains to point out that having a legitimate business reason for a practice may play a part in the determination of misuse disputes. As he put it[36]:

> If the impugned conduct has a business rationale, that is a factor pointing against any finding that conduct constitutes a taking advantage of market power. If a firm with no substantial degree of market power *would* engage in certain conduct as a matter of commercial judgment, it would ordinarily follow that a firm with market power which engages in the same conduct is not taking advantage of its power.

That said, what still remains unclear is whether having a legitimate business reason for conduct can suffice as a defence on its own or is simply one, albeit important, factor in applying the counterfactual test.[37]

---

[32] *Ibid*, at paras 15 and 17.
[33] *Melway Publishing Pty Ltd v Robert Hicks Pty Ltd* [1999] FCA 664 (FC) at para 13. See also the Full Federal Court decision in *General Newspaper Pty Ltd v Telstra (formerly Australian & Overseas Telecommunications Corp Ltd)* [1993] FCA 473, (1993) ATPR 41–274, which was largely influenced by the existence of a legitimate reason for the impugned conduct.
[34] *Melway* (FCA), n 33 above, at para 20.
[35] *Australian Competition and Consumer Commission v Boral Ltd* [1999] FCA 1318, (1999) 166 ALR 410.
[36] *Ibid*, at para 158 (emphasis added).
[37] Indeed, the New Zealand Supreme Court took the latter view in *Commerce Commission v Telecom Corporation of New Zealand Limited ('0867')* [2010] NZSC 111 at para 26, seeing it simply as part of carrying out a comparative exercise. See 7.2.3 below.

(e) Legislative endorsement of multiple tests in Australia

In the face of the evolving smorgasbord of judicial tests, the Australian legislature sought to take matters in hand in 2008 by adding to the misuse provision a non-exhaustive range of tests that courts might legitimately use in determining whether a corporation has taken advantage of its substantial degree of power in a market. Section 46(6A) states that courts may, but need not, have regard to any or all of the following factors:

a) whether the conduct was materially facilitated by its substantial degree of power in the market;
b) whether it engaged in the conduct in reliance on its substantial degree of power in the market;
c) whether it is likely it would have engaged in the conduct if it did not have a substantial degree of power in the market;
d) whether the conduct is otherwise related to its substantial degree of power in the market.

Conspicuous by its absence is any reference to how courts may treat conduct which might be considered to have a legitimate business rationale. However, since the legislators have backed *would* over *could* as the suggested mode of inductive reasoning in any counterfactual analysis the court may choose to carry out, this preference for the narrower and less inclusive approach would arguably see courts able to take into consideration what might be a rational business practice.

While section 46(6A) tells us nothing particularly new about the content of the tests (apart from the legislative preference for *would* over *could*), it does make it clear that all the tests it propounds are part of the armoury of the courts. This is a matter of some significance when we come to the way in which the Australian section 46 jurisprudence has been understood by New Zealand judges, there being no equivalent of section 46(6A) in the latter jurisdiction.

7.2.3 New Zealand: one test to rule them all

In its recent decision *Commerce Commission v Telecom Corporation of New Zealand Limited* ('*0867*'),[38] the Supreme Court endeavoured to synthesise the principal Australian and New Zealand authorities on misuse of market power. The Court considered it important that the way in which issue is approached be broadly the same on both sides of the Tasman Sea, since under agreements between the two countries, competition law in Australia and New Zealand and associated enforcement provisions are increasingly being framed in a common way to address anti-competitive practices affecting trans-Tasman trade.

[38] *Ibid.*

In the result, the Court unanimously not only found (in upholding the decision of the Court of Appeal[39]) that the counterfactual test is the sole test for 'taking advantage', but renamed it the 'comparative exercise'[40] because it involves making a comparison between the actual market and a hypothetical, workably competitive market. Ironically, as a result of its purported drawing together of all the threads in its harmonisation exercise, the Supreme Court has now put New Zealand out of alignment with Australia which, as seen above, remains flexible, permitting a range of approaches in determining misuse.

(a) The 0867 case

Since the events occurred before the amendment to section 36 in 2001, the case was dealt with according to the language of the section at that time, which then referred to use of a dominant position rather than, as now, taking advantage of a substantial degree of market power. However, nothing in the case turned on that difference as far as the threshold of market power was concerned, since the respondent, Telecom (as the owner, after privatisation in 1989, of the nationwide copper-based wire network to which all other would-be providers of fixed or mobile telephone services required access), could easily meet both thresholds. As regards the change from 'use' to 'taking advantage', the Court from the outset treated the two expressions as essentially involving the same inquiry.

The *0867* case concerned the introduction by Telecom during 1999 of a dial-up Internet service known as '0867'. Prior to this, in 1996, Clear Communications and Telecom had entered into an agreement about interconnection and termination charges whereby when a customer of one provider called the other provider's network, the originating network paid a per minute charge to the terminating network. Clear ended up paying Telecom more, largely because most voice calls terminated on Telecom's much larger network. The balance of payments changed when the use of dial-up Internet became common, with Telecom customers making long calls to Internet Service Providers (ISPs). (It should be noted here that Telecom was bound to provide all residential customers with local calls that were free no matter how long they lasted, as part of the arrangement it had struck with the New Zealand Government upon privatisation.) Telecom then had to pay higher termination charges to Clear when its own residential customers dialled an ISP on Clear's network. In order to take advantage of this new turn of events, Clear attracted ISPs to its network by charging minimal or low fees. It also agreed with the ISPs it hosted to share termination charges received from Telecom. Telecom then introduced the 0867 service to encourage residential customers and ISPs on Clear's network to migrate to Telecom's. Those residential customers who used the 0867 prefix were not charged at all for their calls (no matter how many

[39] *Ibid.*
[40] *Ibid*, at para 32.

or how long), but if their ISP was Clear's ISP and not Telecom's, they were charged two cents per minute beyond 10 hours of Internet use per month.

The primary issue before the Supreme Court was whether Telecom had used an assumed dominant position (whether this was in the retail or wholesale market or both was not seen by the Court as requiring close analysis) for one of the proscribed purposes under section 36(2). The Court of Appeal had found that it had, by applying the counterfactual test that it considered to have been endorsed as 'legitimate and necessary' in section 36(2) cases by two decisions of the Judicial Committee of the Privy Council[41]: *Telecom Corporation of New Zealand Limited v Clear Communications Limited*[42] and *Carter Holt Harvey Building Products Group Limited v Commerce Commission.*[43] On appeal, the Commerce Commission, New Zealand's competition regulator, argued the counterfactual test did not have to be the sole test for misuse and that it was useful *only* when a court could cogently apply it. In support of its claim, it argued that Australian authorities had used other tests, such as Deane J's purpose test in *QWI* and the material facilitation test in *Melway*, and that section 36(2) was flexible enough to accommodate these.

In disallowing the appeal, the Supreme Court did several significant things: First, it affirmed both Privy Council cases, saying it was necessary to apply the counterfactual test as the sole test, which it preferred to refer to as the 'comparative exercise' because, in its words, 'the simpler idea of comparing actual with hypothetical is a more straightforward and illuminating description of the process'.[44] The Court then applied the counterfactual test itself, finding that the Commission had failed to show that in a hypothetical workably competitive market, a hypothetical company X would (for fear of losing retail customers) not have introduced an 0867 service. It pointed out that the advent of dial-up Internet had made the termination charges regime under the Clear/Telecom 1996 interconnection agreement unsustainable for a firm on the wrong side of the asymmetry, and that any firm acting competitively, whether dominant or not, would have taken steps to mitigate the loss by introducing a scheme analogous to the 0867 package rather than continue to incur substantial losses.[45] Secondly, the Supreme Court analysed all the principal Australian High Court authorities and their alternate tests, and pointed out that the differences in approach were more apparent than real.[46] All boiled down essentially to the need to conduct a

---

[41] Before 2004, when New Zealand established the Supreme Court and abolished appeals to the Privy Council, this was the country's highest appellate court.

[42] *Telecom Corporation of New Zealand Limited v Clear Communications Limited* [1994] UKPC 36, [1994] CLC 1312, [1995] 1 NZLR 385.

[43] *Carter Holt Harvey Building Products Group Limited v Commerce Commission* [2004] UKPC 37, [2006] 1 NZLR 145.

[44] The *0867* case, n 37 above, at para 13.

[45] *Ibid*, at para 49.

[46] *Ibid.* See para 16, in which the Supreme Court pointed out that in *QWI* (n 8 above), Mason CJ and Wilson J had held that 'it was only by virtue of its control of the market and the

comparative exercise. Lastly, it adopted a very cautious approach to the input of economic analysis in section 36 cases, saying[47]:

> Economic analysis may be helpful in constructing the hypothetically competitive market and to point to those factors which would influence the firm in that market. But it must always be remembered that the 'use' question is a practical one, concerned with what the firm in question would or would not have done in the hypothetically competitive market. As the question is one of rational commercial judgment, the test should be what the otherwise dominant firm would, rather than could, do in the hypothetical market.

While a degree of caution when dealing with the deductive face of economics is, as we argue in chapter two, pure prudence, the Supreme Court's dose of cold water sits oddly with its preference for the counterfactual test. Once the economics is removed from the counterfactual test, what remains is only a judicial stab in the dark as to the dominant firm's likely response in a competitive world. If a less deferential attitude to economic input was what the Supreme Court was after, almost any of the other tests used by the Australian courts would have served them better.

(b) Before 0867

Telecom Corporation of New Zealand Limited v Clear Communications Limited[48] (described by Professor Baumol, an economic expert in the case, as the 'first modern litigation on the pricing of interconnection among rival local telephone companies') was the principal authority on section 36(2) before the *0867* case and met with considerable criticism in the commentary.[49] Clear had wanted to enter and compete with the dominant incumbent Telecom in the market for the

---

absence of other suppliers that BHP could afford, in a commercial sense, to withhold supply of Y-bar from Queensland Wire. If BHP had lacked market power—in other words, if it had been operating in a competitive market—it was highly unlikely that it would have refused supply and allowed Queensland Wire to secure Y-bar from a competitor.' This, the Supreme Court said, was 'essentially the same comparison as that later adopted by the Privy Council. The comparison is between the conduct of the firm in the actual market and that of the same firm in a hypothetically competitive market.' In similar vein, see also para 17 in relation to Deane J's purpose test: the Supreme Court pointed out that 'in his judgment in *QWI* Deane J had observed that BHP's anticompetitive purpose could only be, and had only been, achieved by virtue of BHP's power in the market.' The Court then noted that the approach, 'albeit focussed on purpose, again implicitly involves a comparison between what BHP could achieve with dominance and what it could have achieved without dominance—the actual and the hypothetical.'

[47] The *0867* case, n 37 above, at para 35.
[48] *Telecom v Clear* (PC, 1994), n 42 above.
[49] Round, D and Smith, R, 'Strategic Behaviour and taking Advantage of Market Power: How to Decide if the Competitive Process is Really Damaged?' (2001) 19 *New Zealand Universities Law Review* 427; van Roy, n 7 above; Ahdar, n 13 above; Longdin, L, 'The New Zealand Communications Industry: The Worst of Two Worlds' (1995) 1 *Computer and Telecommunications Law Review* 26.

provision of telecommunications services for businesses in the three main central business districts in New Zealand. To do this it needed access to the nationwide fixed, copper wire infrastructure owned by Telecom. The fact that it was wholly impractical and uneconomic to duplicate this network, and that it therefore constituted a bottleneck facility (in the days before satellite and broadband communication technologies became commonplace), was not seriously contested.

When the State-owned enterprise Telecom Corporation of New Zealand was privatised in 1989 there were three significant omissions:

a) No provision was made for any statutory rights to interconnection.
b) No legislative guidelines were given as to the terms and conditions on which the company owning the network was to give access to another company who was not only a consumer but a potential competitor.
c) No specialist, independent, regulatory body was set up (such as the Australian AUSTEL or British OFTEL) to set the standard interconnection price and the conditions of supply by the incumbent.

Indeed, the Privy Council in *Telecom v Clear* took the opportunity to deliver a very thinly-veiled criticism of the New Zealand Government's 'light handed' regulatory regime, observing that it had left the dominant player Telecom and would-be new entrant competitors free to negotiate 'in a fog' all the terms and conditions of access to the network.

Clear alleged that the conditions imposed by Telecom for interconnection were so unfavourable as to amount to misuse of market power. The connection fees Telecom wanted to charge its would-be competitor were based on a pricing rule referred to as the 'efficient components pricing' rule[50] (or sometimes the 'Baumol-Willig' rule, after Professor Baumol, one of the US-based economists whom Telecom engaged in the case). According to the pricing mechanism arrived at by Telecom's expert witnesses, if Telecom, in a fully contestable market, sold to a competitor the facilities necessary to produce a service that Telecom could otherwise provide, Telecom would *not* be abusing its dominant market position if it demanded a price equal to the revenue it would have received had it provided those facilities itself. That is to say, Telecom was entitled to its lost 'opportunity costs' assessed on the basis of regular reviews. (Telecom had conceded that necessary periodic adjustments would have to be made in the assessment of those costs.)

It was of some concern to the High Court, at first instance, that what Clear was asked to pay could include monopoly rents. It found that it was self-evident that if there were monopoly rents included in Telecom's charges (and consequently in Telecom's opportunity cost), adoption of the Baumol-Willig rule would enable

---

[50] The rule derives its name from the fact that it is meant to promote productive efficiency in the downstream market by deterring the entry of inefficient firms.

Telecom to continue to recover such monopoly rents. Despite this last, the High Court was still able to find that competition in the contested area would be 'likely'. To the Court of Appeal, however, the fact that monopoly profits could continue to be reflected in the access charge was wholly unacceptable. Before the hearing of Telecom's appeal to the Privy Council, Professor Baumol discussed the rejection of the Baumol-Willig pricing model by the Court of Appeal in a joint article with another economist,[51] an article Clear argued contained a recantation of the Baumol-Willig rule. The Privy Council noted that Professor Baumol had qualified his views thus[52]:

> [T]he efficient component-pricing model plays its full beneficial role *only* when adopted as part of a set of complementary rules designed to promote consumer welfare. One such rule is that a monopolist should not be permitted to charge a price for a final product sold to consumers that is higher than the price that would attract an efficient entrant into the market—a price equal to the stand alone cost of producing the final product. But ... no such price exists under the present laws and regulations of New Zealand. It is therefore understandable that the Court of Appeal ordered Clear and Telecom to renew negotiations to set an access price that excluded any monopoly profit foregone by Telecom.

The Privy Council also noted that the article had addressed the possible perpetuation of monopoly rents if opportunity costs are charged to a new entrant, but that it had gone on to observe that[53]

> The villain is not the efficient pricing rule. The real problem is that [Telecom] has been permitted to charge monopoly profits for the final product in the first place. Had the ceiling upon final product prices been based on the stand alone cost, which ... it should be, [Telecom] could never have earned a monopoly profit in this regulatory scenario. The error, therefore, is the failure to impose the stand alone cost ceiling on the final-product price, not the use of the efficient component-pricing rule.

The Privy Council thus rejected any suggestion that anything in the passages above indicated that Professor Baumol had intended to recant. Throughout, it said, he had accepted that his pricing rule would initially perpetuate monopoly rents until either:

a) they were competed out by Clear's competition in the contested area; or
b) they were removed by regulatory action.

---

[51] Baumol, WJ and Sidak, JG, 'The Pricing of Inputs Sold to Competitors' (1994) 11 *Yale Journal of Regulation* 171.
[52] *Telecom v Clear* (PC), n 42 above, at 1328 (emphasis added).
[53] *Ibid.*

Their Lordships noted, however, that the economic experts had not apparently been aware that Part IV of the Commerce Act 1986 (NZ) did in fact provide for a regulatory machinery which could have been, but was not, brought into operation.[54]

By way of conclusion, the Privy Council accepted that, apart from the risk of monopoly rents, the Baumol-Willig rule was a 'closely reasoned' economic model which seeks to show how the hypothetical firm would conduct itself in a perfectly contestable market. Even so, their Lordships emphasised, the question of what constitutes 'use of a dominant position' depends ultimately on the construction of section 36, not on any economic model.[55] They then proceeded to apply the rule, positing for that purpose that the hypothetical seller was in the same position vis-à-vis its competitors as Telecom, apart from the lack of a dominant position. In its view, the question whether there had been use of a dominant position involved a comparison between the actions of the dominant firm in the actual market and what it, or its surrogate, would do in a hypothetically competitive market. As the Privy Council phrased the counterfactual test for the first time[56]:

> [I]t cannot be said that a person in a dominant market position 'uses' that position for the purposes of s 36 [if] he acts in a way which a person not in a dominant position but otherwise in the same circumstances would have acted.

In *Carter Holt*, the Privy Council, by a 3:2 majority, subsequently confirmed its previous finding in *Telecom v Clear* that it was 'legitimate and necessary' to apply the counterfactual test when assessing whether a firm had used its dominant position,[57] an observation that the Supreme Court in *0867* considered justifying the stance it took. It is important to remember, however, that nowhere in *Telecom v Clear* or *Carter Holt* did the Privy Council consider melding the case law of Australia and New Zealand into a unitary whole. In sum, the problem is not that the Supreme Court was not entitled in *0867* to opt for the counterfactual test as the only legitimate test, but that all five judges took the view that this is what they thought their Australian brethren were doing, something that close acquaintance with the Australian authorities would demonstrate was untrue.

---

[54] Interestingly, after the Privy Council decision in which their Lordships commented on the omission in Baumol's brief of any reference to the existence of the potential but not invoked machinery for price control under Part IV of the Commerce Act 1986 (*ibid*, at 1329), Baumol and Sidak subsequently published another article: Baumol, WJ and Sidak, JG, 'The Pricing of Inputs Sold to Competitors: Rejoinder and Epilogue' (1995) 12 *Yale Journal of Regulation* 177. In this, at 181, they note that Baumol should have pointed out that no such price regulation—while possible—was in effect during the litigation.

[55] See *Telecom v Clear* (PC), n 42 above, at 1327.

[56] *Ibid*.

[57] See *Carter Holt* (PC), n 43 above, at para 60.

7.3 FEEDING INTELLECTUAL PROPERTY INTO THE LEGISLATIVE MIX

In considering how the convoluted case law described above might be brought to bear on refusals to license, several factors have to be kept in mind. The first is that while there are parts of each jurisdiction's competition statute that relate to intellectual property in various ways, none of these provisions addresses refusals to license directly. The second is that there is a mismatch between these legislative interventions across the two jurisdictions.

7.3.1 The legislated line between action and inaction in relation to intellectual property in Australia and New Zealand

Both the Australian and New Zealand competition statutes contain provisions fencing off licences and assignments of most (but not all) forms of intellectual property from the operation of those sections of the statute forbidding anti-competitive agreements and arrangements (roughly comparable in scope and design to section 1 of the Sherman Act and Article 101 TFEU).[58] These protections for intellectual property dealings are very wide, without any of the internal checks and balances that characterise the Technology Transfer Block Exemption in the European Union.[59] Section 45 of the New Zealand Commerce Act 1986, for example, protects consensual arrangements authorising the doing of anything 'that would otherwise be prohibited' by the intellectual property right in question. Its Australian counterpart, section 51(3) of the Competition and Consumer Act 2010, is even more loosely expressed, protecting clauses in licensing agreements to the extent that they *relate to* the subject matter of the right.[60] Both are encapsulations of a 'scope of grant' approach described in chapter one to the extent that these involve intellectual property. Significantly, neither applies to breaches of the misuse of market power provisions of their respective statutes. An

---

[58] The most frequently invoked of these controls on multilateral behavior are s 27 of the Commerce Act 1986 (NZ) and s 45(2) of the Competition and Consumer Act 2010 (Aust).

[59] The Technology Transfer Block Exemption (Commission Regulation (EC) No 772/2004 of 27 April 2004 on the application of Article 101(3) TFEU to categories of technology transfer agreements [2004] OJ L123, automatically exempts from Art 101 (1) TFEU certain kinds of technology transfer agreements entered into between two undertakings.

[60] Both provisions contain drafting infelicities that are not explored here. For a detailed examination of their scope and interpretation, see Eagles, I, 'Regulating the Interface Between Competition Law and Intellectual Property in New Zealand' (2007) 13 *New Zealand Business Law Quarterly* 95; Eagles, I, and Longdin, L, 'Competition in Information and Computer Technology Markets: Intellectual Property Licensing and Section 51(3) of the Trade Practices Act 1974' (2003) 3 *Queensland University of Technology Law and Justice Journal* 1.

arbitrary line is thus drawn between proactive arrangements, such as tying and exclusive dealing, and unilateral exercises of market power involving those same rights.[61]

7.3.2 Judicial hints and silences in Australia

Section 46 of the Competition and Consumer Act 2010, as we have seen, is contextually silent. Australian judges have therefore had no need to approach refusals to license intellectual property as a special problem requiring a special solution. In this unitarian universe there is no particular need to separate refusals to deal from other unilateral abuses of market power. Nor do courts in that jurisdiction attach deep significance to the fact that what is being refused is access to the subject matter of an intellectual property right. This does not mean that courts have not at some times expressed views on both these things. These views, however, have tended not to occupy centre-stage in the cases in which they are expressed. Judicial attitudes to refusals to license therefore often have to be teased out of sometimes fleeting references.[62] Where the courts do venture on a more detailed analysis, that analysis is often tangential to the issues they are being asked to decide. Examples of both may be seen in what follows.

(a) Accumulated rights and not quite refusals: Ceridale

The decision of the Full Federal Court of Australia in *Australasian Performing Rights Association Ltd v Ceridale Pty Ltd*[63] is interesting for two reasons: that the source of market power came not from individual intellectual property rights but from their aggregation; and the Court's rebuff of attempts to present a disputed licence fee as a constructive refusal to license. The plaintiffs in the case, the Australian Performing Rights Association (APRA), a copyright licensing agency, owned the right to the public performance of nearly all popular music in Australia. The defendant was the owner of night clubs where recorded music was played. Licences had previously been granted in respect of the night clubs, but

---

[61] The line is made even more arbitrary by the fact that both practices can also be attacked under the unilateral abuse of market power provisions as well. See Corones, S, 'Technological Tying in the Computer Industry: When Does it Contravene S 46 of the Trade Practices Act?' (2003) 3 *Queensland University of Technology Law and Justice Journal* 47.

[62] *Melway* is perhaps illustrative here. Apart from the finding by Merkel J at first instance (*Robert Hicks v Auto Fashions (Melway Publishing)* (1999) 42 IPR 627) that Melway's copyright in the street directory of Melbourne operated as a high barrier to entry because of the low level of supply-side substitutability (hard-copy directories being time- and labour-intensive to prepare from scratch), the issue was largely ignored by both the Full Federal Court (*Melway* (FCA), n 33 above) and the High Court (*Melway* (HCA), n 17 above).

[63] *Australasian Performing Rights Association Ltd v Ceridale Pty Ltd* [1990] FCA 516; (1991) ATPR 41-074.

had not been renewed because fees were in arrears. After a somewhat murky and unresolved dispute about change of ownership, application forms for a licence were sent by APRA to Ceridale but were ignored, and APRA sued for copyright infringement. One of the defences raised by Ceridale was that it had been refused a licence in breach of section 46, a claim that the trial judge accepted. On appeal the Full Federal Court had no difficulty with the idea that APRA's accumulated copyrights gave it substantial market power or dominance, even if the other two limbs of section 46 had not been met. As to purpose, the Court ruled, APRA's aim in denying Ceridale a licence was not to prevent Ceridale from competing in the night-club market; APRA had nothing to gain from putting Ceridale out of business, the Court said[64]:

> On the contrary, it was in the interests of APRA to maximise the number of users of its material, so long as they paid licence fees. APRA's purpose was merely to prevent unauthorised use of its material and the integrity of its licensing system.

The Association was willing to grant new licences if and when Ceridale applied for a licence in the appropriate way.[65] There was therefore no 'taking advantage' in terms of section 46. The Court also made it clear that 'purpose' should not be confused with effect. No doubt an enjoined Ceridale would find it hard to compete in the night-club market without access to an APRA licence, but that was not the outcome APRA was trying to achieve. The Court did, however, add the rider that if at some future date a licence was applied for and refused, the conditions attached to that refusal could be looked at. Of particular relevance here was a possible threat to extract solicitor/client costs from Ceridale. On this subject, the Full Federal Court could only observe darkly[66]:

> We share the trial Judge's disquiet about the threat concerning costs. The threat could only have been made by a person who was in a dominant position in the market. Had the circumstances arisen whereby this threat became relevant to the parties' conduct, a real question may have arisen about contravention of s 46. But they did not. Although we express the hope that APRA will not adopt that position in any future case, the threat about costs does not affect our view that there was here no contravention of s 46.

No doubt this 'don't even think of it' warning had its effect on APRA's future behaviour. No doubt too, the owner of a copyright in a single musical work or recording could not have made good on this kind of threat, there being plenty of other music to be played in night clubs. Markets do not correspond with rights, but an accumulation of rights can, once some tipping-point is passed, constitute a market. Had the claim of breach of section 46 been initiated directly by Ceridale

---

[64] *Ibid.*
[65] *Ibid.* Ceridale had submitted a perfunctory application form that failed to disclose usage of APRA's music and was not accompanied by a licence fee, both of which things APRA was entitled to demand, the Full Federal Court said, before issuing a licence.
[66] *Ibid*, at 41–075.

or the regulator rather than invoked by way of defence to a copyright infringement claim, these things could have been said less obscurely. The Full Federal Court's minatory warning might not, however, be so easy to unpick for other intellectual property owners contemplating conditional refusals of a different kind in the future.

(b) Multiple and conflicting purposes: Pont Data

ASX Operations Pty Ltd v Pont Data Australia Pty Ltd[67] had at its core the withholding of information of the kind that elsewhere might nowadays be the subject of database rights. At the time in Australia such information was protected from unauthorised use, if it was protected at all, only by the ordinary rules of breach of confidence and/or by copyright.

ASX Operations (ASXO) was a subsidiary of ASX, a nationwide stock exchange formed out of previously independent exchanges and regulated pursuant to a joint federal/state legislative scheme.[68] Crucially, ministerial approval was necessary for other stock exchanges to operate lawfully. No such approval had been given for any Australia-wide exchange. ASXO supplied Pont Data with stock market data in electronic form. Some of this was accessible through non-ASXO sources but a significant proportion of it was not. Pont Data then used this information to compile various forms of investment advice for its clients. ASXO also competed with Pont Data in a downstream market, but not to any great effect.[69] There were thus three markets involved: the share trading market, and separate retail and wholesale share information markets. ASXO required Pont Data to commit contractually to supplying it with the names and addresses of its customers, and to promise not to sell on the information to other information wholesalers. ASXO's purpose in imposing these arrangements, as its own witnesses admitted, was to contrive as much as possible to keep the wholesale information market to itself. Tellingly, information had been previously supplied to Pont Data by ASXO without any of the contested restrictions. Pont Data initiated proceedings for, inter alia, breach of section 46, and succeeded at first instance[70] where the court found two distinct breaches:

a) an attempt to monopolise the existing wholesale market[71]; and

---

[67] *ASX Operations Pty Ltd v Pont Data Australia Pty Ltd* [1990] FCA 515, (1991) ATPR 41–069, 97 ALR 515.
[68] See Securities Industry Act 1980 (Aust). There were corresponding provisions in state legislation.
[69] This aspect of ASKO's business operated at a loss, and there was evidence that it was poorly regarded by clients. Its services were offered more cheaply than ASKO's other services.
[70] Other breaches of the competition statute were also alleged.
[71] Attacked under s 46(1)(k) of the then Trade Practices Act 1974 (Cth).

b) an attempt to prevent the establishment of rival stock markets outside Australia that might compete with ASXO's parent ASX.[72]

On appeal, the Full Federal Court similarly divided its analysis, but found against ASXO only on the first ground. The result is a degree of disconnect between the two parts of the section 46 case. The Full Federal Court held that fending off the establishment of a putatively unlawful 'shadow' stock exchange within Australia[73] could not be for the improper purpose of preventing entry, but was dismissive of arguments on behalf of ASXO that it believed itself to be heading off an equally unlawful infringement of its intellectual property rights. No doubt revelation of ASXO's subjective intent in the first case, and the absence of any such direct proof in the second, played a part here,[74] but there also seems to have been at work an assumption that the maintenance of a public law regulatory regime was virtuous in ways in which the enforcement of private rights was not. Clearly, then, the Full Federal Court did not see intellectual property as a parallel system of regulation, whatever else it might have been.

Looked at from both policy and doctrinal perspectives, however, the Full Federal Court's decision not to allow private rights to act as a shield was undoubtedly correct. Correct too was its focus not on what the law of copyright and the equitable principles relating to breach of confidence *allowed* ASXO to do,[75] but on what ASXO *thought* those rules allowed them to do and whether that belief drove ASXO to act as it did. ASXO's belief as to the content of its legal rights may or may not have been as it claimed, but those beliefs did not motivate its actions. ASXO's 'purpose' was the admitted one of preventing the wholesaling of data it supplied to Pont Data. Its legal rights (real or imagined) were merely a means to that end.

---

[72] Attacked under s 46(1)(b), *ibid.*

[73] Section 46 could not reach attempts to hinder the establishment of rival stock exchanges outside the country, it held. Oddly, no attempt was made to argue by ASXO that its actions could be brought within the provisions of s 51(1) of the competition statute providing a limited protection for acts done under statutory authority.

[74] Of relevance here is the fact that the 'statutory authority' exemption in s 51(1), does not apply to acts specifically authorised in patent, copyright, trade marks or design legislation. If this formed part of the Full Federal Court's reasoning in *Pont Data*, it did not say so.

[75] The breach of confidence claim was shaky, resting as it did on the protection of information concerning events on the trading floor (in those days, real rather than electronic) of the various exchanges. The copyright claim might have been sustainable on the low and easily-met 'sweat test' for originality that prevailed in Australia before the decision in *Telstra Corporation Limited v Phone Directories Company Pty Ltd* [2010] FCA 44 raised that country's threshold to something like that prevailing under US law; see *Feist Publications Inc v Rural Telephone Service Co* 499 US 340 (1991). What ASXO was really trying to protect was its investment in collecting and transmitting the data speedily and efficiently in a form most likely to be useful to retail subscribers. It was just a 'hole' in existing trade secrets and copyright law that led to the enactment of *sui generis* database rights in Europe.

(c) Legal and economic monopolies distinguished: Broderbund and Subaru

Australian courts have generally resisted attempts to conflate the scope of intellectual property protection and intellectual property markets.[76] In *Broderbund Software Inc v Computermate Products Australia Pty Ltd*,[77] it was sought to argue that a particular educational computer game and its underlying protected copyright software constituted a 'unique' product market in its own right ('unique' apparently because only it could develop a particular combination of geographical awareness and computing skills in the children at whom it was directed). The Court instead defined the market at its narrowest as being for educational software in general, of which market, the Court pointed out, Broderbund had a 17 per cent share at the most.

Broderbund also traversed the issue of whether the strict parallel importing restrictions then in force in Australia under its copyright statute[78] constituted a barrier to entry (section 46 had been raised in the course of infringement proceedings). Broderbund's copyright, said the Court, did not constitute a barrier to entry as there were many alternatives capable of developing the same skill sets in children readily available and able to be brought into the country.

The decision in *Regents Pty Ltd v Subaru Australia Pty Ltd*[79] is more problematical. The facts somewhat resemble those of *Volvo v Veng*[80] and the United States Supreme Court decision in *Eastman Kodak*.[81] The case arose out of attempts by a Subaru distributor to resist the termination of its distributorship. Richardson J, however, marginalised the relevance of those European and United States precedents by holding that there was a composite market for cars, parts and after-sales service.[82] He also found that there was a parallel market for vehicle distributorships. In markets so widely defined, there was little prospect of Subaru possessing or using market power because there was no brand-specific market for Subaru cars or the parts and services that went with them, only a market for cars, plus parts, plus services in general. Even if this were not the case, Richardson J

---

[76] See the discussion at 3.3.1 above.

[77] *Broderbund Software Inc v Computermate Products Australia Pty Ltd* [1991] FCA 563, (1992) ATPR 41–155.

[78] The facts of the case preceded Australia's relaxation of its parallel importing restrictions in relation to certain copyright works. For a succinct account of the pre-reform Australian position, see McKeogh, J, *Intellectual Property in Australia*, 2nd edn (Sydney, Butterworths, 1997) at 204–5. For details of the reforms themselves, see Longdin, L, 'Parallel Importing Post TRIPS: Convergence and Divergence in Australia and New Zealand' (2001) 50 *International and Comparative Law Quarterly* 54.

[79] *Regents Pty Ltd v Subaru (Australia) Pty Ltd* [1998] FCA 730, (1998) 84 FCR 218.

[80] Case 238/87 *Volvo v Erik Veng (UK Ltd)* [1988] ECR 6211. See 6.2.1 above.

[81] *Eastman Kodak v Image Technical Services* 504 US 451 (1992). See 5.6 above.

[82] In reaching this conclusion, Richardson J was very taken with the conceptually vague notion of 'submarkets' that we criticise in 3.3 above. Cf *Port Nelson*, n 1 above, in which the New Zealand Court of Appeal rejected the idea of a composite market for stevedoring, tugs and pilots. See Eagles, I, 'Of Ports, Pilots and Predation: New Zealand Courts Reassess Some Competition Fundamentals' (1996) 17 *European Competition Law Review* 462.

held, there was no anti-competitive purpose because Subaru had demonstrated that it was the distributor's failure to sell enough cars that led to the decision not to renew the distributorship, a legitimate business explanation. While this second finding is unexceptional, in the sense that this would be any head distributor's response whether it had market power or not, the first finding of a single composite market seems to have been arrived at without an analysis of consumer perceptions at the point of sale, usually an important factor in an economic analysis rejecting the existence of separate after markets, as we have seen.[83]

(d) *NT Power: demolishing the property defence*

The clearest indication of the High Court of Australia's likely response to the use of intellectual property as a shield against a finding of liability under section 46 comes as a digressive, but considered, aside in *NT Power*,[84] a case that is in some ways a replay of *Trinko*[85] but with a very different outcome and accompanied by fervent denials of *Trinko's* persuasive authority. On this occasion it was an electricity grid rather than a telecommunications network that was at the centre of the dispute.

NT Power revolved around the activities of the Power and Water Authority (PAWA), a statutory entity that not only regulated the supply of electricity in the Northern Territory but also generated and transmitted most of that electricity itself through a distribution network that it owned. PAWA's regulatory role was to issue licences to other would-be generators and transmitters. NT Power was a small operator initially producing electricity for a particular mine, and selling its small and intermittent surplus back to PAWA which fed it into its own grid for sale to end-users. Aware that the Northern Territorial government was moving towards privatisation, NT Power decided it would like to supply electricity directly to consumers in two of the Northern Territory's urban areas. Its requested access to PAWA's grid to this end was turned down. NT Power claimed to be acting under its existing licence, a claim that was upheld at first instance and all later appellate levels.[86] PAWA was therefore to be judged as a competitor rather than a regulator. When the High Court came to consider the section 46 aspect of the case,[87] it applied the standard counterfactual test to hold that

---

[83] Richardson J preferred to focus on industry practice and producer perception.
[84] *NT Power* (HCA), n 29 above.
[85] *Verizon Communications Inc v Law Offices of Curtis V Trinko LLP* 540 US 389 (2004).
[86] The High Court held that PAWA had acted as a business protecting its revenue rather than as a regulator, and there were no issues such as lack of capacity, technical difficulties or safety that would have justified resort by PAWA to its regulatory role.
[87] There were other issues, notably PAWA's claim to derivative Crown immunity for itself and a subsidiary and the true construction of a licence granting exemptions in the competition statute itself. Issues of market definition also figured largely at all levels. Interesting for our purposes was the High Court's rejection of PAWA's submission that no market existed because up to that point no buying or selling of electricity had taken place. The High Court had no

PAWA's ownership of the grid operated as a barrier to entry and was thus a source of market power of which PAWA had taken advantage with the purpose of deterring NT Power from entering the retail electricity market.[88]

How, then, does intellectual property enter the picture? By an exceedingly tortuous journey through the judgments of the first instance court and one of the members of the intermediate appellate court in *NT Power* itself. One of the arguments put forward by PAWA at the initial hearing was that, even if it possessed market power, it was not using that market power but merely exercising its rights as owner of the grid.

The first instance court was not prepared to concede that any such general 'property' defence existed.[89] Only one member of the Full Federal Court chose to engage with this issue. This was Lee J, who took the contrary view that there was indeed a general property defence to section 46 and that it applied in this case.[90] Lee J offered some examples to support this thesis, one relating to tangibles and the other to refusals to license intellectual property. Both are revealing. Thus, in the case of tangibles, he offered an *Oscar Bronner*-ish illustration of a party dominant in the wholesale market for lobsters who maintains a fleet of refrigerated vehicles to get the lobsters from isolated costal ports to its own premises. There would be no breach of section 46, he said, if that wholesaler refused to carry competitors' lobsters or hire its refrigerated vehicles to them. Things might be different, he thought, if the dominant wholesaler also carried on business as a general carrier in the refrigerated goods market; but where the property of the wholesaler is used solely for its own business, a demand for access to that property could not of itself lead to a breach of section 46 if the demand is refused. If this seems to be a back-to-front endorsement of 'there have to be two markets', this is less clear in Lee J's reference to intellectual property owners being entitled to refuse to license where that would enable the would-be licensee to compete with the owner (whether such competition is to be solely in the market covered by the right, he does not say, although as he refers to *Magill* at this point,[91] one must presume he was familiar with the phenomenon of primary and secondary markets).

---

difficulty in holding (see *NT Power* (HCA) n 29 above, at para 109) that in line with its own previous decision in *QWI* (see n 8 above), the 'market' in this context could be purely theoretical.

[88] PAWA claimed that its purpose here was the high-minded desire to put off entry only until there were enough entrants to make the market competitive.

[89] *NT Power Generation Pty Ltd v Power and Water Authority* [2001] FCA 334 at para 335.

[90] *NT Power* (FCAFC), n 28 above, at FCR 404. Such arguments were not entirely without authority, at least in the lower Federal Court. See *Dowling v Dalgety Australia Ltd*, n 12 above, a case which all three courts in *NT Power* read in entirely different ways.

[91] Lee J refers not to the case itself, but to a law journal article on the subject. See van Melle, A, 'Refusals to License Intellectual Property Rights: The Impact *of RTE v EC Commission* (*Magill*) on Australian and New Zealand Competition Law' (1997) 25 *Australian Business Law Review* 4.

When the High Court came to consider these matters it reversed the logic of Lee J and used it as a stepping-stone to a rejection of any general 'I'm just doing what any owner would be doing' defence in section 46 cases. Pointing out that the protective provisions in section 51(3) of the Act (relating to proactive licensing and assignment) were explicitly made not to apply to proceedings brought under section 46, it went on to rule that[92]

> The fact that s 46 can apply to intellectual property rights, and hence to the market power which they can give, suggests that it can apply to the use of market power derived from other property rights not specifically mentioned in the Act.

It therefore followed, the High Court said,[93] that to suggest that there is a distinction between taking advantage of market power and taking advantage of property rights is to set up an entirely false dichotomy, one which lacks any basis in the language of section 46, adding for good measure that intellectual property rights are often a very clear source of market power.

Significantly too, the High Court rejected *Trinko* as an aid either to the construction of section 46 as a whole,[94] or to decoding any of its detailed parts.[95] Unlike section 46, it said, section 2 of the Sherman Act was backed by the sanction of imprisonment. It also stressed that the Australian statute, while it provided for the direct regulation of industries like electricity generation and transmission, also expressly preserved the direct operation of section 46.[96]

Equally relevant in the refusals to license debate was the High Court's forthright reaction to the 'access equals confiscation fallacy' traversed in chapter one[97]:

> PAWA contended that it was entitled, as owner of the infrastructure assets, to decline to consent to the use of them by others. That overstates the matter: PAWA was not asked to deliver its assets into the hands of NT Power's employees but merely to receive and transmit, via its infrastructure, electricity generated by NT Power.

Whether the High Court will adhere to the views expressed in *NT Power* when an actual refusal to license case comes before it is unclear. Demolition of the property defence was only the first step in its analysis. That analysis is most emphatically not an endorsement of the view widespread amongst United States courts prior to *Illinois Tool*[98] that the mere possession of an intellectual property right conferred market power. An Australian court would still be faced with what

---

[92] See *NT Power* (HCA), n 29 above, at para 85.
[93] Ibid, at para 125.
[94] Ibid, at para 121.
[95] It thought *Trinko* distinctly unhelpful when it came to deciding whether PAWA was a 'supplier' in terms of s 46(4)(c); *ibid*.
[96] The High Court seem to have misread *Trinko* on this last point. The US Telecommunications Act 1996 also explicitly preserves the right to bring claims under the general antitrust law. The US Supreme Court did not see this as an obstacle to its use of the system of alternative direct regulation to reject what it saw as an expansion of liability under § 2 of the Sherman Act.
[97] See *NT Power* (HCA), n 29 above, at para 123.
[98] See 5.6 above.

the High Court in *NT Power* called the 'notoriously difficult task'[99] of satisfying whatever test for establishing liability under section 46 it chose to apply.

7.3.3 A New Zealand oddity: section 36(3) of the Commerce Act

New Zealand's Commerce Act contains what on the face of it appears to be a legislative helping-hand for intellectual property owners faced with an accusation that they have taken advantage of whatever market power the intellectual property right confers. This is the enigmatic section 36(3), which reads:

> For the purposes of [section 36], a person does not take advantage of a substantial degree of power in a market by reason only that the person seeks to enforce a statutory intellectual property right, within the meaning of section 45(2) in New Zealand.[100]

Section 36(3) has no Australian equivalent and has only once been directly raised by an intellectual property owner, and then only for inconclusive interlocutory purposes. The 'statutory rights' it refers to are patents, registered designs, copyright, plant variety rights, layout designs and trade marks, and extend not only to the exclusive rights conferred by the statute in question but also to those that the statute acknowledges as valid. These would include protection for right holders' technological protection measures introduced into the copyright statute by the Copyright (New Technologies) Amendment Act 2008. Excluded from the list of privileged rights are the obligations created by the law of passing off[101] and the equitable rules protecting trade secrets. As we saw in chapter four, reputational rules seldom raise competition issues, save in the context of parallel importing. The withholding of trade secrets does raise competition problems and is discussed further below.

Two issues face the would-be interpreter of section 36(3):

a) Does the subsection confer substantive immunity on right owners, or is it merely an evidentiary provision?
b) Does an intellectual property owner 'seek to enforce' a right by refusing to license it?

(a) Substantive immunity or evidentiary nudge?

If the legislature intended to create substantive immunity for right holders, it has chosen some very maladroit wording through which to achieve that objective. To

---

[99] *NT Power* (HCA), n 29 above, para 85.
[100] Section 45, it will be remembered, sets out the list of exempt rights for the purposes of that section. Section 36(3) simply picks up that definition; see discussion at 7.3.1 above.
[101] The common law rules have been statutorily extended in New Zealand and Australia. See Fair Trading Act 1986 (NZ); and Competition and Consumer Act 2010 (Aust), s 18, sch 2, replacing s 52 of the Trade Practices Act 1974 (Aust).

say that right holders are not using their market power 'by reason only' of the fact they are trying to 'enforce' their rights implies that there are other, unstated ways in which right holders can wield market power. The provision does not say that intellectual property rights cannot confer market power, or that their owners are incapable of forming one of the proscribed purposes in section 36(2).

A more plausible interpretation of section 36(3) would be as an instruction to courts not to draw adverse inferences against right holders from the mere fact of their exercising or seeking to exercise their rights. More direct evidence of anti-competitive intent is required (*Illinois Tool*,[102] *avant la lettre*). Certainly when section 36(3), or more strictly its predecessor,[103] first found its way onto the New Zealand statute book, adverse inferences of the kind described were not uncommon on the part of United States judges, and thus New Zealand legislators may have wished to head off something similar, but this is conjecture.[104]

Backhanded support for an evidentiary construction of section 36(3) (or strictly speaking its predecessor) may be found in an observation by Gault J in delivering the New Zealand Court of Appeal's judgment in *Electricity Corporation v Geotherm Energy*,[105] that the presence of this subsection in the Act was 'consistent' with Australian and United States authorities allowing anti-competitive purpose to be deduced from the exercise of a legal right. Were this not the case, suggested Gault J, there would be no need for the presence of section 36(3) to give intellectual property favoured treatment.[106] Thus far, Gault J appears to be adopting an evidential perspective on the subsection; but what, then, is one to make of his statement, a few lines later, that there had to be in such cases facts over and above the attempt to enforce the right that point to one of the three prescribed anti-competitive purposes? If this is so then section 36(3), far from being 'necessary', as he puts it, would be otiose. There would be no presumption to rebut, because in the absence of extrinsic evidence, attempted or threatened enforcement of a right but nothing more would raise no presumption. There would thus be nothing against which section 36(3) needed to protect intellectual property owners. We need to remember that Gault J was not here trying to shed light on the subsection for its own sake, but rather using its existence to demonstrate a general truth about how courts should approach allegations that a legal right has been abused for anti-competitive purposes. Precision to the meaning of section 36(3) in itself was not necessary to that end. He was merely making the same point made later by the High Court of Australia in *NT Power*[107] in similar circumstances.

---

[102] *Illinois Tool Works Inc v Independent Ink Inc* 547 US 28 (2006), 126 S Ct 1281 (2006).
[103] This was the identically worded s 36(2) of the original 1984 enactment. The subsections were renumbered.
[104] The legislative history and pre-history offer no guidance.
[105] *Electricity Corporation v Geotherm Energy* [1992] 2 NZLR 641.
[106] *Ibid*, at 657.
[107] See *NT Power* (HCA), n 29 above.

(b) 'Seeking to enforce' and refusals to license

Refusing to license an intellectual property right is not obviously the same thing as seeking to enforce it. It has to be conceded, however, that such a hair-splitting and literal construction does not sit well with modern notions of purposive interpretation. Some commentators[108] have suggested that enforcing here means 'maintaining', 'upholding' or 'compelling the observance of', but these are not the words the legislature has used. In the absence of any extrinsic guide to Parliament's intentions[109] in enacting section 36(3), a purposive interpretation is impossible to extract either from the structure of the provision itself or from its context. There is also a slippery-slope aspect to this kind of reasoning. Arguments that start with 'I am only protecting indirectly what the statute allows me to enforce directly' can easily slide into 'preserving my investment right in X' and end with 'maintaining the integrity of the statutory scheme as a whole'.[110] It has to be said, though, that drawing a line between action and inaction in the way apparently mandated by section 36(3) has little economic merit, as indeed we argue elsewhere.[111] The solution, however, lies not in extending the subsection's reach in open-ended and unpredictable ways, but in rethinking the need for it in the first place.

The only case to shed any light on this aspect of section 36(3), and then only the merest glimmer, is *Telecom New Zealand Ltd v Clear Communications Ltd*,[112] an action brought to enforce an earlier settlement in which the defendant alleged by way of counterclaim that Telecom was in breach of section 36 by threatening to bring proceedings of various kinds against it in relation to allegedly misleading and imitative advertising by Clear. One of the threatened actions was for copyright infringement. Smellie J had no hesitation striking out this aspect of the counterclaim, holding that direct enforcement of its copyright was precisely what the predecessor to section 36(3) allowed the plaintiff to do.[113] Certainly this tells us rightly, if quite unnecessarily, that enforcement that is actually threatened is

---

[108] Calhoun, D and Brown, B, 'New Zealand: Interface Between Misuse of a Dominant Position and the Exercise of Intellectual property Rights' (1990) 12 *European Intellectual Property Review* 437 at 438.

[109] A position paper prepared by the government department sponsoring the original bill merely observed cryptically that the subsection's function was to 'exempt the legitimate enforcement of legal rights' in the courts from the Commerce Act. As cited by van Melle, n 91 above. If it was an endorsement of 'private right trumps public enforcement' in the manner of some of the pre-*NT Power* cases in Australia, it seems to have been rejected by Gault J in *Geotherm*, n 105 above.

[110] Such projections are not fanciful. Similar slippery-slope arguments were urged on (and rejected by) the District of Columbia Court of Appeals by Microsoft in *United States v Microsoft* 253 F 3d 34 (DC Cir 2001) at 63. See discussion in Eagles, I, and Longdin, L, 'The Microsoft Appeal: Different Rules for Different Markets?' (2001) 7 *New Zealand Business Law Quarterly* 296 at 312.

[111] See ch 1 above.

[112] *Telecom New Zealand Ltd v Clear Communications Ltd* [1992] 3 NZLR 247 (HC).

[113] *Ibid*, at 254.

within section 36(3), but it does not say (and Smellie J did not need to say) that standing put and saying no is a form of indirect enforcement. Copyright 'infringement' was only one of Telecom's threatened actions. The others alleged passing off and breach of statutory prohibitions against unfair trading, neither of which is among the statutory rights picked up by section 36(3) but which Smellie J held were causes of action Telecom was equally entitled to pursue. The principle on which he decided the case accordingly was the much wider one that a party does not breach the Commerce Act by invoking or threatening to invoke the jurisdiction of a court or administrative agency and nothing more.[114] On this logic, even if copyright had not been one of the rights to which section 36(3) applied, Smellie J would have treated it no differently.

7.3.4 Restraint of trade and breach of confidence preserved by statute

A shared peculiarity of the Australian and New Zealand competition statutes is the presence in both of them of them of savings provisions allowing the continued operation of much, but possibly not all, of the judge-made law concerning restraint of trade and breach of confidence. Section 4M of the Competition and Consumer Act 2010 (Aust), for example, stipulates that:

This Act does not affect the operation of:

(a) the law relating to restraint of trade in so far as that law is capable of operating concurrently with [the Act] or
(b) the law relating to breaches of confidence

but nothing in the law referred to in paragraph (a) or (b) affects the interpretation of [the Act].

Section 7 of the New Zealand statute is similarly expressed.

The potential for the pre-existing law of restraint of trade to clash head-on with the competition statute is of course considerable, hence the proviso in the Australian section 4M and its New Zealand counterpart.[115] Since the preservation of breach of confidence rules is not also accompanied by a similar proviso in either jurisdiction, a refusal to provide access to trade secrets or know-how is

---

[114] The 'nothing more' echoes the views of Gault J in *Geotherm* (CA), n 105 above, and implies that 'something more' or some *'je ne sais quoi'* element could—in some cases—be found. Like Gault J in *Geotherm*, Smellie J in *Telecom v Clear* (HC), n 112 above, was prepared to concede that the pursuit of a legal right could sometimes be 'unreasonable'. Smellie J was clearly uncomfortable with much US case law on sham litigation as a device for raising the costs of rivals. See Scott, P, 'Abuse of Judicial and Administration Processes—An Antitrust Violation?' (1993) 21 *Australian Business Law Review* 389. Of course, had any of the threatened actions actually been pursued, s 36 could have been asserted by way of a defence. Section 36(3) would then be directly in issue.

[115] The proviso in s 7(1) of the Commerce Act 1986 (NZ) reads more tersely, requiring only that the common law rules relating to restraint of trade not be inconsistent with that Act.

arguably protected against *all* forms of competition scrutiny. In Australia, such a result would be particularly perverse. Information protected by breach of confidence would be legislatively walled-off from such scrutiny, but not material protected by copyright or patent law. A hierarchy of rights would be established, but an upside-down one.

The New Zealand situation is complicated by the existence of section 36(3). If this is given substantive effect, there would be no such dichotomy.[116] Conversely, whatever section 7 of the Commerce Act might mean, its operation cannot be confined to the evidentiary sphere. It either provides a substantive shield or it is powerless to ward off liability under section 36(1). If it is such a shield, it is one that makes no distinction between enforcing and refusing. While such an interpretation would preserve the section's internal logic in a strictly legal sense, it does nothing to make it defensible in economic terms.

Because these are savings provisions, the Australian section 4M and New Zealand section 7 preserve the public interest limitations on breach of confidence, including those relating to anti-competitive actions on the part of the possessor of the trade secret. As we saw in chapter four, however, these restrictions are neither particularly robust nor well articulated.[117]

---

[116] Indeed, as we have seen, no such dichotomy was perceived to exist by Smellie J in *Telecom v Clear*, see n 112 above. Nowhere in that case does the court refer to s 7(2) of the statute.

[117] See 4.5.1 above. They may apply only to those trade secret owners who knowingly act in an anti-competitive way.

8

Canada: Legislative Solutions and Regulatory Bypasses

8.1 A THREE-PRONGED LEGISLATIVE ASSAULT

The Canadian competition statute[1] provides three discrete potential points of entry to the refusals to license and essential facilities debate.[2] Their structure and interaction are determined largely by the complicated history of competition law in that country, the complex way in which enforcement powers have been allocated between the various actors in the regulatory process, and the fact that the statute distinguishes between criminal behaviour subject to fines, imprisonment and private actions for damages and behaviour that is a civil reviewable practice subject only to a remedial order (except abuses of a dominant position, which may also be subject to administrative monetary penalties).

The relevant provisions (which are analysed below) are section 75, targeting refusals to deal in particular, section 79, a general misuse of market power provision (with both these provisions being subject to the jurisdiction of the Competition Tribunal[3]) and section 32, creating special remedies for abuse of intellectual property rights (and subject only to the jurisdiction of the Federal Court).

---

[1] Competition Act 1985, RSC 1986, C-34 (consolidated as at 25 January 2011). The federal statute is administered by the Competition Bureau. There is no provincial legislation.

[2] The essential facilities debate has not had a wide airing in Canada. See, however, *Canada (Director of Investigation and Research) v Bank of Montreal* ('*Interac*') CT-1995–002 Doc 93a: Reasons for Order; [1996] 68 CPR (3d) 527, in which the Competition Tribunal (see n 3 below) considered the denial of an essential facility in relation to a claim of misuse of market power. See also the recent settled case involving denial of access to intellectual property (trade marks), *Commissioner of Competition v The Canadian Real Estate Association* CT-2010–002 Doc 75: Consent Agreement registered 25 October 2010.

[3] The Competition Tribunal, Canada's specialist adjudicative body for competition law, comprises both judges from the Federal Court and lay members (economists or persons with business expertise). It has no independent authority to consider a matter, nor any investigatory powers of its own, but decides cases referred to it by the regulators (the Commissioner of Competition and Competition Bureau). An application to the Tribunal may in the case of a refusal to deal also be initiated by an affected party. The Tribunal has wide remedial discretion to grant structural or behavioural remedies under C-34, s 104(1), but not damages.

8.2 ENFORCEMENT AND ADJUDICATION

A small irony that has not escaped the attention of Canadian commentators is that, until its amendment in 2002, the Competition Act allowed a public monopoly over the enforcement of laws intended to redress the evils of private monopoly.[4] Prior to 2003, when the amendment came into force, private parties had no right to litigate for refusals to license. Now they may seek leave[5] from the Tribunal to bring a refusal to deal claim under section 75, but they have no right to claim under the general abuse of dominance provision section 79, nor to bring an action under section 32.

8.3 SECTION 75: REFUSALS TO DEAL

Unusually, Canadian law contains a specific refusal to deal provision, section 75(1) of the Competition Act 1985[6] (as amended in 2002), that empowers the Tribunal to order one or more suppliers of a 'product' in a market to accept a person as a customer on usual trade terms,[7] within a specified time,[8] where all elements of the following five-part test are met[9]:

a) A person is substantially affected in his business or is precluded from carrying on business due to his inability to obtain adequate supplies of a product anywhere in a market[10] on usual trade terms.

b) The person referred to in paragraph a) is unable to obtain adequate supplies

---

[4] Roach, K, and Trebilcock, MJ, 'Private Enforcement of Competition Laws' in *Policy Options* (16 October 1997), available at <http://ssrn.com/abstract=1157563>.

[5] See Competition Act 1985, n 1 above, s 103.1.

[6] *Ibid*, at s 75.

[7] *Ibid*. Section 75(3) defines 'terms' in respect of payment, units of purchase, and reasonable technical and servicing requirements.

[8] Unless, within that specified time, in the case of an article, any customs duties on it are removed, reduced or remitted, and the effect of the removal, reduction or remission is to place the person on an equal footing with other persons who are able to obtain adequate supplies of the article in Canada.

[9] To get to this point, the Tribunal will have considered an application either by the regulator (Commissioner of the Competition Bureau) or a person granted leave under s 103.1 of the Act.

[10] Should a party refused a licence have already formally agreed to obtain certain products or services only from the refusing party, no other real source of supply legally exists for that person. Thus, it could be argued that the refusing party is 'the market' for the purposes of s 75(1) because the refusing party has effectively closed off other avenues of supply to the refused party. Some support for this argument can be found in the US Supreme Court decision in *Eastman Kodak v Image Technical Services* ('*Kodak I*') 504 US 451 (1992) at 482, where it was found that a single brand could constitute a market if would-be-but-denied buyers are tied up in a buy/sell arrangement with the refusing provider.

of the product because of insufficient competition among suppliers of the product in the market.
c) The person referred to in paragraph a) is willing and able to meet the usual trade terms of the supplier or suppliers of the product.
d) The product is in ample supply.
e) The refusal to deal is having or is likely to have an adverse effect on competition in a market.

Section 75 does not require that the business refusing to supply be dominant or impel the Tribunal to inquire into whether the purpose of the refusal is predatory, disciplinary or exclusionary in nature. Neither does it require proof of substantial lessening or prevention of competition. However, what it does require is that the person's inability to obtain adequate supply is the result of insufficient competition among suppliers.[11]

The first refusal to deal ruling of the Tribunal under section 75(1) occurred in the private action *B-Filer Inc v The Bank of Nova Scotia*[12] (the refusal did not involve intellectual property). The Tribunal noted that even had the five necessary conditions of section 75(1) been met (which they had not), it would still have exercised its discretion to deny relief on the basis that the defendant bank had had objectively justifiable, non competition-related business reasons for terminating a pre-existing relationship with the plaintiff.[13] It is interesting to speculate whether the Tribunal might in future just as easily accept arguments in the form of a defendant's own pro-competitive rationales.

---

[11] Canadian Competition Bureau, *Intellectual Property Enforcement Guidelines* ('IPEGs') (2000), available at <www.competitionbureau.gc.ca/eic/site/cb-bc.nsf/eng/01286.html>.

[12] *B-Filer Inc v The Bank of Nova Scotia* CT-2005–006 (2006) Comp Trib 42, at paras 161 and 172.

[13] In the case, the two applicant companies, B-Filer (operating under the name GPAY) and NPAY, with the same controlling shareholder, conducted a joint venture business with another company, UseMyBank Services. The joint venture involved processing on-line payments by Internet gaming site customers. While GPAY and NPAY interfaced with banks, UseMyBank handled the marketing. Whenever customers opted to pay via UseMyBank, they would be transferred to its website and asked for their bank account numbers and passwords. GPAY and NPAY would then use this confidential information to access customers' accounts and transfer funds to themselves, either directly as a bill payee (if granted that status by the customer's bank) or alternatively via an e-mail money transfer (EMT). GPAY and NPAY would then pay the merchants on behalf of the users. When ScotiaBank first limited, then completely terminated, GPAY and NPAT's banking arrangements, they sought to be reinstated as bank customers with bill-payee status and given unlimited EMT services. The Tribunal found ScotiaBank had objectively justifiable, non competition-related business reasons for the termination. The bank wished to avoid breach of the Canadian Payments Association Rules (that provide a payer's electronic signature is not to be shared with a payee) and UseMyBank's requirement that customers disclose their electronic banking IDs and passwords had made breach of the rules a potentiality. Furthermore, GPAY appeared unable to comply with statutory anti-money laundering and anti-terrorism safeguard requirements.

In another private action, *Sears Canada Inc v Parfums Christian Dior Canada Inc and Parfums Givenchy Canada Ltd*[14] (again involving a refusal to deal, but not of intellectual property), the well-known department store chain Sears challenged the decision of the defendant French perfume makers to cease supplying its stores. This time, the Tribunal focused not on whether the defendants' reasons were justified, but on whether Sears had been 'substantially affected' in its business under section 75(1)(a) by the refusal. It was found not be, since the $16 million value of the lost perfume sales was hardly substantial in the context of a business worth overall $6 billion. The 'public' aspect of the competition statute barely figures.

Prior to its amendment in 2002, section 75(1) had required only four conditions to be met before relief could be granted, and most of the jurisprudence relating to the interpretation and application of that provision precedes the addition of the fifth condition that a refusal to deal must cause or be likely to have an 'adverse effect' on competition in a market. One case invoking the truncated version was *Canada (Director of Investigation and Research) v Chrysler Canada Ltd*.[15] The case touched on trade mark ownership and control, and involved a refusal by the Canadian subsidiary of the United States Chrysler Corporation to continue to supply spare parts for its cars to one Brunet who was in the business of exporting such parts to markets outside North America. Brunet had been supplied with parts, prior to a policy change by Chrysler. Indeed his exporting ventures had been actively encouraged by that company. After Chrysler's rebuff, Brunet was able to obtain parts from other authorised Chrysler dealers, an avenue of supply quickly quashed by Chrysler once it found out about it. The Tribunal held, first, that the relevant 'product' (as the Act required[16]) comprised 'proprietary' Chrysler parts[17] and, secondly, that insufficient competition existed among suppliers. More troubling to the Tribunal, however, was Chrysler's explanation that its decision to cut off Brunet's access to its parts was inevitable because of its American parent's changed strategy to source most

---

[14] *Sears Canada Inc v Parfums Christian Dior Canada Inc and Parfums Givenchy Canada Ltd* CT-2007–001 Doc 30: Reasons for Order; (2007) Comp Trib 6; 2007 CACT 6 (CanLII).

[15] *Canada (Director of Investigation and Research) v Chrysler Canada Ltd* CT-1988–004 Doc 185a: Reasons and Order; [1989] 27 CPR 3d 1 (Comp Trib); 1989 CPR LEXIS 1741.

[16] Competition Act 1985. 'Products' are of course not necessarily coterminous with 'markets', a dissonance which might give rise to difficulty in the interpretation of s 75 in its post-2002 form (which requires it to be shown that the impugned refusal has an actual or potential effect in a 'market'). Section 75 as amended does, however, make it clear, in s 75(2), that a branded or proprietary product cannot be considered to be a separate product in a market simply because of its trade-marked or proprietary status. Such a product can constitute a separate product in a market only where it occupies such a dominant position in that market so as substantially to affect the ability of persons to carry on their business without it. Thus persons refused a licence to intellectual property must establish that by nature the withheld property is quite unique (apart from its proprietary status) and that a similar product cannot be acquired anywhere else in the market.

[17] This did not mean that the parts had to be protected by 'trade marks', though they may have been.

exports to the Western Hemisphere (Canada apart) from its United States plants, plants that had demanded in return that a condition be imposed on independents such as Brunet not to sell to licensed dealers outside the United States and Canada, the very condition that Brunet had allegedly breached. This Canadian version of what in the United States would be termed a legitimate business explanation, and in the European Union an objective justification, was rejected by the Tribunal on factual grounds. Chrysler was undone by its own internal memoranda that showed it had been just as much, if not more, concerned that parts sold to Brunet should not find their way onto the domestic Canadian market and there had been considerable doubt as to whether Brunet had actually accepted 'a no sales outside North America' limitation. Having placed something closely resembling the onus of persuasion on Chrysler,[18] the Tribunal held that the company had failed to discharge it.[19] The Tribunal did, however, go to some pains to point out that Chrysler could have had multiple objectives, one of them being to increase the 'efficiency'[20] of its operations worldwide, the implication being that, had that been its *sole* motivation for acting as it did, the outcome in the case could have been otherwise. The Tribunal also placed considerable weight on Chrysler's previously harmonious dealings with Brunet and its failure to warn him about the consequences of continuing to export to destinations in Europe and Latin America. While falling short of finding a European or *Aspen*-style 'duty'[21] on the part of a dominant firm to continue dealing, its practical effect was not dissimilar.

The next decision of the Tribunal to involve the application of section 75 was *Canada (Director of Investigation and Research) v Xerox Canada Inc (Xerox Canada)*.[22] The case derived, like its United States counterpart a decade later,[23] from Xerox's decision to discontinue the supply of copier parts to independent service organisations to enhance (or at least preserve) the market positioning of Xerox's own after-sales service activities. When the policy was put into effect in Canada, Xerox's Canadian subsidiary found itself on the receiving end of a claim under section 75, still unencumbered, as the section then stood, by any need to point to any adverse effect on the competitive process. The Tribunal was thus able

---

[18] The mechanism through which this inchoate onus was imposed was that, even should all of the elements of s 75 be made out, the Tribunal's powers to issue an order remained discretionary, and thus it was for those resisting the remedy to justify its exercise in their favour.
[19] *Chrysler*, n 15 above, at 26 (Comp Trib).
[20] Canadian competition law does contain an explicit 'efficiency' defence, but only in relation to merger applications: Competition Act, s 96(1).
[21] Eg, Joined Cases 6/73 and 7/73 *Istituto Chemioterapico Italiano SpA & Commercial Solvents v European Commission* [1974] ECR 223, 1 CMLR 309; and *Boosey v Hawkes* [1987] OJ L286/36, [1988] 4 CMLR 67.
[22] *Canada (Director of Investigation and Research) v Xerox Canada Inc ('Xerox Canada')* CT-1989–004 Doc 88a, [1990] 33 CPR 3d 83. The case also raised issues as to the constitutionality of s 75 and the Tribunal's role in relation to it.
[23] *Re Independent Service Organisations Antitrust Litigation ('CSU v Xerox')* 203 F 3d 1322 (Fed Cir 2000). See discussion at 5.7 above.

to focus on the effect on competitors alone, an effect it found easily proven. On the subject of inadequate supply, it rejected arguments that it should take into account those parts resuscitated from defunct machines[24] or else provided on an incomplete, unpredictable and haphazard basis by independent manufacturers.[25]

The Tribunal's attempts to pinpoint the market in which the refusal to supply operated were more than a little tentative. It is true that it ultimately found untenable Xerox's contention that the appropriate market was the one in which it saw itself competing, a single unified market for the provision of a 'package' of equipment parts and services, preferring instead the regulator's definition of a market for parts for Xerox copiers. The Tribunal also stressed that market definition depends on legislative context,[26] thus hinting at the possibility that the definition might have been different for the purpose of meeting the competition statute's other liability-creating provisions. Less helpfully perhaps, it suggested that even should it be wrong on these two points, the circle could still be squared by characterising the market for replacement parts as an 'intermediate' market.[27] This flirtation with the now discredited notion of a submarket, while harmless in this context, could have more serious implications if more widely applied in leveraging situations.

As to the link between market definition and market power, the Tribunal pointed out[28] that section 75, while it required the market in which the inadequate supply had occurred to be identified, did not stipulate that the party refusing supply had to wield any power in that market. (Indeed the section still does not so stipulate, even in its post-2002 incarnation, and while complainants may now have to prove an adverse effect[29] on competition in a market, this may, of course, be the downstream market, in this case post-sales servicing.) The Tribunal was similarly dismissive of suggestions that Xerox had acted for the legitimate purpose of changing its distribution system, holding that the switch to

---

[24] *Xerox Canada*, n 22 above, Doc 88a p32.
[25] *Ibid*. The parts available from independent manufacturers did not include all of those necessary to service the machines properly. The Tribunal also rejected as inadequate the trickle of supplies obtained on behalf of the independent service organisations for machines on display.
[26] *Ibid*, at para 71.
[27] Ibid, at para 64.
[28] *Ibid*, at para 80. The Tribunal did not rule out the existence of such 'package' markets in the abstract but held that Xerox had failed to offer a factual basis for it. The Tribunal also found untenable Xerox's contention that since s 75(1)(b) refers to 'suppliers' in the plural, the 'market' had to consist of more than one supplier, and hence the relevant market had to be one in which the photocopier manufacturers competed. This, the Tribunal said, would require them to import a logical inconsistency into the section by holding that one of three or four suppliers could be subject to attack under s 75 while a non-supplier with a monopoly position would not be. *Ibid*, at para 88.
[29] The 'adverse effect' threshold, being lower than the substantial lessening or preventing tests in s 75, could arguably be met without anyone having power in a market once the other elements are made out.

in-house servicing was taken for the very purpose of curtailing competition in the downstream market.[30]

While intellectual property considerations were merely in the wings in *Chrysler* and *Xerox Canada*, they occupied centre stage in *Canada (Director of Investigation and Research) v Warner Music Canada Ltd*.[31] The case arose out of the refusal by Warner and its Canadian subsidiary to grant a mail order firm, BMG Canada, licences to reproduce sound recordings in which Warner owned the copyright. BMG Canada wanted the licences so that it could compete effectively against Warner's own licensees in the mail order record club business in Canada, by manufacturing its own records instead of buying them at wholesale prices. The Tribunal struck out the proceedings in an application for summary judgment, holding that the requirements in section 75 for an 'ample supply' of a 'product' and usual trade terms for a product show that the 'exclusive legal rights over intellectual property cannot be a product'.[32] It went on to expand on this[33]:

> [T]here cannot be an 'ample supply' of legal rights over intellectual property which are exclusive by their very nature and there cannot be usual trade terms when licences may be withheld. The right granted by Parliament is fundamental to intellectual property rights and cannot be considered to be anti-competitive, and there is nothing in the legislative history of section 75 of the Act which would reveal an intention to have section 75 operate as a compulsory licensing provision for intellectual property.

The Tribunal thus justified its decision on two grounds. The first was a narrow one (here recast as a canon of statutory interpretation) and involved a literal reading of section 75 which would deny an intellectual property licence the status of a 'product'. The second was an endorsement of the 'what the State has granted it must expressly take away' fallacy discussed in chapter one.[34] While the case concerned copyright licences, the Tribunal's approach could be applied more widely. The first 'narrow' approach could be applied to almost anything other than a physical object, and therefore would place beyond the reach of section 75 the kind of distribution system that figured in *Oscar Bronner*[35] and the protocols for allowing product interoperability that lay at the heart of the *Microsoft* litigation in Europe.[36] The wider approach is equally open-ended but is not easily applied, as we have seen, to forms of intellectual property not created by express

---

[30] *Xerox Canada*, n 22 above, at para 91.
[31] *Canada (Director of Investigation and Research) v Warner Music Canada Ltd* ('*Warner*') CT-1997–003 Doc 22: Reasons and Order; [1997] 78 CPR 3d 321.
[32] *Ibid*, at para 333. The Tribunal was also influenced by the existence in the Competition Act of ss 32 and 79(5), which make specific provision for intellectual property rights. It saw this as militating against any easy equation of 'licence' and 'product'; *ibid*.
[33] *Ibid*.
[34] See 1.5.1 above.
[35] Case C-7/97 *Oscar Bronner v Mediaprint Zeitung und Zeitschriftenverlag GmbH* ('*Oscar Bronner*') [1998] ECR I-7791, [1999] 4 CMLR 112.
[36] Case T-201/04 *Microsoft Corporation v European Commission* [2007] ECR II-3601, 5 CMLR 11.

statutory grant. The Tribunal's thinking could be said to point in two different directions on the issue of coverage. From a policy perspective, however, the actual decision on the facts in *Warner* is unexceptionable. The record companies had no anti-competitive intent, neither was there an anti-competitive outcome. BMG Canada's claims would have been regarded as unmeritorious by most courts in most jurisdictions. Ironically, post-2002, the Tribunal could have found for Warner without artificially reading down the meaning of 'product' or postulating an unstated legislative intent not to interfere in property rights.

8.4 SECTION 79: GENERAL AND SPECIFIC PROHIBITIONS

Section 79 is Canada's general misuse of market power provision. Under it, dominant firms attract liability if they have engaged in (or are engaging in) a 'practice of anti-competitive acts' that have an intended negative effect on a competitor that is exclusionary, predatory or disciplinary, with the result that competition has been, is being or is likely to be prevented or lessened substantially. An inclusive rather than an exhaustive list of such anti-competitive acts is set out in section 78. Of the activities there listed, three are capable on their face of applying to refusals to deal. These are:

a) 'Squeezing' by a vertically-integrated supplier of the margin available to an unintegrated customer who competes with the supplier, for the purpose of impeding or preventing the customer's entry into, or expansion in, a market.[37]
b) Pre-emption of scarce facilities or resources required by a competitor for the operation of a business, with the object of withholding the facilities or resources from a market.[38]
c) Adoption of product specifications that are incompatible with products produced by any other person and are designed to prevent entry into, or elimination from, a market.[39]

It will be noted that while the general prohibition in section 79 is effects-based, all the enumerated examples, with their referencing to 'purpose' and 'object', revolve around the dominant firm's intentions. These are very mixed signals to be sending the regulator. Unsurprisingly, the resulting confusion is reflected in the regulator's enforcement policy, as will be seen.

Much more fatal to the application of section 79(1) to refusals to license is section 79(5), which stipulates:

---

[37] Competition Act, n 1 above, s 78(1)(a).
[38] *Ibid*, s 78(1)(e).
[39] *Ibid*, s 78(1)(g).

done and geographical spread of placements. Tele-Direct reserved to itself all other business (approximately 90 per cent of the total) by bundling the provision of advertising space and downstream services.[50] This, the Tribunal held, amounted to tied selling under the discrete tying provisions of the Canadian competition statute,[51] in the process observing that leveraging across markets can, and in this case did, occur.

The Tribunal's analysis of the tying claim was detailed and evidence-based, one that explored in detail rival economic approaches to the different weight to be given to functional interchangeability, past pricing policy, and practices and industry perceptions in defining the product markets. It also engaged in a complex US-style dissection of the 'is it a one or two product?' problem,[52] while at the same time rejecting the then prevalent technique of trying to soften a rigid *per se* tying rule with a series of equally rigid exceptions, an approach it thought incompatible with the rule of reason approach to tying required under the Canadian statute.[53]

None of this complex reasoning was carried over into the Tribunal's treatment of Tele-Direct's refusal to license its trade marks, a refusal the Tribunal found to be fully justified even if motivated by a desire to exclude. As it found[54]:

> [Tele-Direct's] refusal to license [its] trade-marks falls squarely within [its] prerogative. Inherent in the very nature of the right to license a trade-mark is the right for the owner of the trade-mark to determine whether or not, and to whom, to grant a licence; selectivity in licensing is fundamental to the rationale behind protecting trade-marks.

There was no discussion of whether or how the trade mark might affect substitutability, and no attempt to apply (if only to reject) the two products requirement of the tying cases to refusals to license that figured so largely in

---

[50] There was some debate as to whether the downstream market extended beyond the telephone directory advertising to advertising in other media such as newspapers. In the result, the Tribunal held it did not. *Ibid.*

[51] Competition Act, n 1 above, s 77. While tying is explicitly legislated against, s 77 is not a *per se* provision. The provision requires a showing that competition has been substantially lessened by the alleged tying and that the perpetrator is a 'major supplier' of the product or service. The tying aspect of *Tele-Direct* is analysed in detail in Trebilcock, M, Winter, RA, Collins, P and Iacobucci, EM, *The Law and Economics of Canadian Competition Policy* (Toronto, University of Toronto, 2002) at 487–93.

[52] This was a pivotal issue in *Jefferson Parish Hospital District No 2 v Hyde* 466 US 2 (1984). See *Tele-Direct*, n 49 above, at 32.

[53] The Tribunal declined, eg, to apply the exception recognised in *Jefferson Parish* (n 52 above), *Directory Sales Management Corporation v Ohio Bell* (1987) 833 F 2d 606 and *Beard v Parkview Hospital* 912 F 2d 138 (6th Cir 1990), that would exclude from the ambit of the *per se* rule situations in which the defendant derives no economic benefit from the sale of the tied product. (Tele-Direct had somewhat disingenuously argued that its 'single fee' system meant that it derived no 'extra' benefit for advertising services because it did not separately charge for them, a claim the Tribunal dismissed. A benefit, it said, could be identified without any need to pinpoint how profits were distributed across Tele-Direct's dual activities.)

[54] See *Tele-Direct*, n 49 above, at 30.

Magill[55] and *IMS*[56] and dominated tying cases prior to *Illinois Tool*[57] in the United States.[58]

This relative reticence can in part be explained by the existence of section 79(5), but that cannot be the whole answer. The Tribunal did concede that the limitation built into the subsection that the exempted act be 'engaged in pursuant *only*' (our emphasis) to the 'exercise' or 'enjoyment' of the protected right or interest, thus leaving open, even if only the merest of chinks, the door to future coerced licensing. The Tribunal made it clear, however, that such intervention would not in general be justified. Its starting (and for most purposes its finishing) point was that the trade marks statute allows trade mark owners to choose to whom they will license their trade marks,[59] however selectively the right to refuse might be exercised (for example, to exclude future competitors) and whatever the motives of the excluder.[60] This near-absolute discretion in the right holder was justified by the Tribunal on various grounds. The first was that coerced licensing would amount to a compulsory and involuntary sharing of goodwill.[61] The second was that because the trade marks legislation did not contain any provision for compulsory licensing, this silence should be taken as an instruction from the legislature that such coercion should not be applied in other statutory contexts.[62] Both these grounds manifest the kind of circular reasoning criticised in chapter four. The third ground is more idiosyncratically embedded in the intricacies of Canadian trade marks law, in this case in the requirement in the Trade-Marks Act 1985 that licences may be invalidated where the licensor has 'no direct or indirect control over the character or quality' of the goods or services protected by the mark.[63] How, the Tribunal rhetorically asks, could Tele-Direct be expected realistically to exercise such control over competitors who shared no commonality of interest with it. Also noteworthy was the clear line the Tribunal drew between refusals to license and situations where anti-competitive provisions were actively attached to a trade mark licence.[64]

---

[55] Joined Cases C-241/91 P and C-242/91 P *Radio Telefis Eireann and Independent Television Publications v European Commission* ('*Magill*') [1995] ECR I-743, 4 CMLR 718.

[56] Case C-418/01 *IMS Health GmbH v NDC Health GmbH* ('*IMS*') [2004] ECR I-5039, 4 CMLR 28.

[57] *Illinois Tool Works v Independent Ink Inc* ('*Illinois Tool*') 547 US 28 (2006), 126 S Ct 1281 (2006).

[58] The requirement may still have an attenuated afterlife despite its irrelevance to a rule of reason, as seen at 5.8 above.

[59] See *Tele-Direct*, n 49 above, at 33.

[60] *Ibid*.

[61] *Ibid*, at 32–33.

[62] *Ibid*. The Tribunal does not qualify this statement in any way, even though some such qualification would seem to be implied by its acknowledgement of regulatory intervention, however marginal and unlikely that intervention might be.

[63] Trade-Marks Act 1985, RSC, c T-13, s 50(1).

[64] See *Tele-Direct*, n 49 above, at 32.

One perhaps surprising feature of the Tribunal's analysis of the trade marks issue, in contrast to the literalist approach to statutory construction generally favoured in section 75 cases, is just how little it owes to the actual words of section 79(5). It does not, for example, pick up on the fact that Tele-Direct had explicitly threatened outside advertising agencies that any written use of the words 'Yellow Pages' would be dealt with, and thus could be said to be actively exercising or enjoying its rights, thereby precluding distinctions of the kind arguably made possible by looser words in section 79(5)'s equivalent New Zealand provision.[65]

The Tribunal's unwillingness to make any substantive link between its exploration of the tying problem and the trade mark issue had its effect on the remedies granted in the case as well. Thus, even assuming that the Tribunal was correct in its holding that no substantive liability attached to the refusal to license in its own right, nothing in such a finding limited the making of an order concerning limited use of the Yellow Pages logo and nomenclature as an adjunct to the remedial orders made in relation to the tying aspects of the case. Indeed without some such order it is difficult to see how the Tribunal's coerced unbundling would work. This is especially so when one considers the form of the order actually made, which was in effect to compel Tele-Direct to expand the range of accounts on which it would pay commission[66] and deal directly and fairly with customers who submitted their orders through outside consultants. In such circumstances, restrictions on the terminology the outside consultants could use in dealing with 'their' clients could continue to hobble their effectiveness as competitors of Tele-Direct.

Two further points remain to be made about the *Tele-Direct* litigation. The first is that the Tribunal, by conceding, however hypothetically, that circumstances might exist in which dominant owners of intellectual property rights might, in its words, be doing 'something more' than merely exercising those rights, has opened up a potential search for what that 'more' might be, a search the outcome of which might be unpredictable once embarked upon (as the European jurisprudence on 'exceptional circumstances' demonstrates). In Canada, as discussed below, it is only restraints imposed by the regulator itself that prevent this search from taking place.

The second point that needs to be made about *Tele-Direct* is that it is the absolutist rhetoric used by the Tribunal in arriving at its decision on the trade mark point that exposes it to criticism, not the decision itself. Had the Tribunal permitted itself to engage in the kind of nuanced analysis undertaken by the General Court in the European *Microsoft* litigation, the outcome might well have

---

[65] Commerce Act 1986 (NZ), s 36(3), uses the expression 'by reason only that …'. See 7.3.3 above.

[66] The Tribunal preferred this to ordering Tele-Direct to offer different prices for space and services, an option it thought too easy for Tele-Direct to manipulate given the extent of the company's dominance.

(remedies apart) been the same. (As it was, little or no evidence was offered as to the actual effect of withholding trade marks on the operation of the market for advertising services.)

8.5 SECTION 32: SPECIAL REMEDIES FOR ABUSE OF INTELLECTUAL PROPERTY RIGHTS

Unlike the other provisions considered here, section 32 of the Competition Act is specifically directed to preventing the abuse of intellectual property rights. It differs from sections 75 and 79 of the Act not only because it falls under the Federal Court's exclusive jurisdiction, but also because it requires the meeting of a competitive impact test. Section 32 allows the Federal Court to award a range of remedial orders, including directing the grant of a licence to use an intellectual property right on any terms it considers appropriate. Thus the Court may[67] void a particular licence or prohibit the carrying out of its terms; compel the granting of a licence or order the removal of a patent, trade mark or layout design from the relevant register.[68] The provision, however, has seldom been invoked, and indeed the regulator's 2000 *Intellectual Property Enforcement Guidelines*[69] suggest it will be relied upon only in rare circumstances.

Section 32 does not proscribe particular kinds of behaviour or require proof of market power in the right holder, but instead seeks to ban uses of the intellectual property right leading to outcomes simply assumed to be undesirable whatever their effect on the competitive process. Section 32(1) provides that:

> In any case where use has been made of the exclusive rights and privileges conferred by one or more patents for invention, by one or more trade-marks, by a copyright or by a registered integrated circuit topography, so as to:
>
> (a) limit unduly the facilities for transporting, producing, manufacturing, supplying, storing or dealing in any article or commodity that may be a subject of trade or commerce,
>
> (b) restrain or injure, unduly, trade or commerce in relation to any such article or commodity,
>
> (c) prevent, limit or lessen, unduly, the manufacture or production of any such article or commodity or unreasonably enhance the price thereof, or
>
> (d) prevent or lessen, unduly, competition in the production, manufacture, purchase, barter, sale, transportation or supply of any such article or commodity.

---

[67] Competition Act RSC C-34, s 32(1).

[68] There is of course no stated equivalent for copyright, since under the Berne Convention for the Protection of Literary and Artistic Works 1886 the existence of that property right does not depend on registration.

[69] See *CCB Intellectual Property Guidelines* (2000), n 11 above, at para 4.2.2, and discussion at 8.7.1 below.

Despite its ostensibly wide scope, the effectiveness of section 32 remains limited in several ways. First, it has no application outside the listed rights, and can thus not be applied to a refusal to license a trade secret. Secondly, a quantitative or qualitative focus on the meaning of 'unduly' might in future cases provide a mechanism for reading the section down. Thirdly, only those rights deriving directly from the statutory grant can be abused. Thus deliberately-engineered technical incompatibility would not be covered. This would remain the case even if, as discussed above,[70] Canada enacts its proposed Copyright Modernisation Bill creating protection for TPMs, since these second-order rights, while still creatures of statute, are outside the first-order terminology of the statutory grant. Lastly, section 32 requires the existence of a tradeable 'article' or 'commodity'. While these terms are unlikely to be interpreted as restricted to a 'product' as in section 75 ('commodity', for example, is probably wide enough to include such an intangible item as electronically-distributed software, provided it is tradeable), it is difficult to envisage either expression being extended to such things as the extended distribution system in *Oscar Bronner*,[71] or the advertising services at the centre of *Tele-Direct*[72] or the *IMS* brick structure.[73]

As well as these inherent limitations,[74] the usefulness of section 32 is curtailed in two other ways. The first is that proceedings under the section have to be initiated by the Attorney-General and the standard of proof appears to be the higher criminal one of beyond reasonable doubt.[75] The second barrier to effective enforcement is the apparent view of some regulators (on whose advice the Attorney-General is assumed to act) that section 32 should be invoked in refusal to license cases only if there is likely to be no real or adverse effect on innovation as a result.[76] While none of this is necessarily fatal to the effective enforcement of

---

[70] See 8.4 above, nn 43 and 44.
[71] See *Oscar Bronner*, n 35 above.
[72] See *Tele-Direct*, n 49 above.
[73] See *IMS*, n 56 above.
[74] A further possible constraint on the operation of s 32 is to be found in s 32(3). This prohibits the making of an order that would be at variance with intellectual property treaties to which Canada is a party. In the light of the express saving of competition rules in Art 8.2 of the TRIPS Agreement, this may not matter as much as it once did.
[75] This is not universally accepted by Canadian legal scholars; see Wong, S, 'Competition Act Implications for the Licensing of Intellectual Property Rights: 2002 Update', paper presented at the Conference *Intellectual Property License Agreements*, Canadian Institute, Vancouver, 24–25 June 2002 (as cited by Cameron and Tomkowicz, n 45 above). Cf the standard of proof required in relation to civil reviewable matters which is on the balance of probabilities, see *Draft Updated Enforcement Guidelines*, n 48 above, at fn 8.
[76] Eg, Gwilliam Allen (representing the Canadian Competition Bureau), in considering the use of s 32 to address intellectual property expansion via copyright anti-circumvention laws, observed that 'the architecture of the law can change [so that] intellectual property [objectives] are actually being undermined by their very use, and as a marker that that may be happening would be the effects on competition.' Panel at the Hearing on Competition and Intellectual Property Law and Policy in the Knowledge-Based Economy hosted by the US Department of

section 32, the fact remains that no case has as yet been brought to trial under it or its predecessor provisions.[77]

8.6 THE PATENT ASSIGNMENT CASES

Mention should be made here of two decisions concerning patent assignments which, while not directly bearing on refusals to license, are nevertheless symptomatic of the degree of confusion prevailing among Canadian judges as to how intellectual property and competition law should properly intersect. The cases in question were brought under section 45 of the Competition Act, one of several criminal provisions in the Canadian competition statute. Both alleged an anti-competitive conspiracy (widely defined in section 45 so as to catch most agreements or arrangements unduly restraining competition).

The first of the patent assignment cases, *Molnlycke AB v Kimberly-Clark of Canada*,[78] arose out of an attempt by Molnlycke, the defendant in a patent infringement action, to counterclaim under section 45 by alleging that the original patent holder, an American company, had deliberately divested itself of the patent and conveyed it to its Canadian subsidiary (which had previously competed with the defendant without the benefit of the patent) in order to thwart competition in Canada. The counterclaim was not supported by any direct evidence as to the United States company's motives and might ultimately have failed on that ground. The Federal Court of Appeal, however, preferred to debate the case on the basis that, as a matter of law, no exercise of its rights by the patentee could ever be an undue impairment of competition as required by section 45. As the Court pointed out[79]:

> Certainly the existence of a patent is apt to limit, lessen, restrain or injure competition—monopolies do—but its issuance and the inherent impairment of competition has been expressly provided for by an act of Parliament, which has made provision for compulsory licensing in circumstances where it has considered the ordinary incidence of the statutory monopoly to be contrary to public policy. It is the existence of the patent, not the manner in which issue was obtained or how and by whom its monopoly is agreed to be enforced and defended that impairs competition.

As in *Warner*,[80] this was an explicit endorsement of the 'no implied revocation of grant' fallacy, and again, as in *Warner*, it was present as a justificatory principle of

---

Justice Antitrust Division and the US Federal Trade Commission, Washington DC, 22 May 2002) at 141–42, available at <www.ftc.gov/opp/intellect/020522trans.pdf>.

[77] The earliest of these predecessor provisions dates from 1910, see Combines Investigation Act 1910, s 22. For a history of these provisions see Trebilcock *et al*, n 51 above.
[78] *Molnlycke AB v Kimberly-Clark of Canada* [1991] 36 CPR 3d 493.
[79] *Ibid*, at 498.
[80] See *Warner*, n 31 above.

wide application to read down liability-creating words of an apparently open-ended nature, a seemingly unqualified invitation to take the scope of grant exit from the interface problem. Alternative exits, however, may be discerned in less all encompassing language elsewhere in the Court's decision indicating that this was really an evidentiary problem (here again anticipating *Illinois Tool*[81]) that anti-competitive motives cannot be inferred from the exercise of patent rights 'alone'.[82] Certainly it was this aspect of *Molnlycke* that was fastened on in *Eli Lilly and Co v Apotex Inc*,[83] a later decision of the Federal Court of Appeal. Like *Molnlycke*, this also involved an attempt to invoke section 45 as a shield against a patent infringement action. Unlike the situation in *Molnlycke*, which involved the transfer of a single patent which may not have conferred market power but, if it did, certainly did not *increase* anyone's market power, *Eli Lilly* involved allegations that the plaintiff, who had already held several patents relating to the process of making the antibiotic Cefaclor, had in effect, by its 'killer portfolio', foreclosed the whole of the market by also acquiring the only other known remaining and commercially viable patents over the drug. (It seems to have been assumed for the purposes of the case that Cefaclor had no substitutes, that is to say that the legal and economic monopolies coincided.)

This time, the Federal Court of Appeal was prepared to accept that trial judge had erred in holding the situation was not one in which an assignment could unduly lessen competition under section 45(1) of the Competition Act. In allowing the matter to be reconsidered for summary judgment,[84] the Federal Court of Appeal depicted the assignment as being 'evidence of something more than the mere exercise of patent rights' and, as such, not beyond the application of the Act's conspiracy provision. Uneasy, however, about overruling *Molnlycke* outright, the Court drew a distinction between cases in which market power[85] was *increased* by the assignment in question and those in which the assignment merely *transferred* power that was already inherent in the patent assigned.[86] This is not a distinction inherent in the words of the statute, and it does not have any obvious basis either in economic theory or in the law applied in other jurisdictions,[87] not even under Canada's own dominance provision, section 79. The obvious flaw in this mode of reasoning is that it invites us to ask (as indeed the

---

[81] See *Illinois Tool*, n 57 above.
[82] See *Molnlycke*, n 78 above, at 499.
[83] *Eli Lilly and Co v Apotex Inc* 2005 FCA 361 (2005).
[84] The case involved a rather tortuous procedural path.
[85] The stress on 'market power' is interesting since s 45, unlike s 79, does not speak in terms of dominance.
[86] See *Eli Lilly*, n 83 above, at paras 14 and 18.
[87] In Europe, Australia and New Zealand it is accepted that the acquisition of market power is controlled only via the merger process, while in the United States, as we have seen, although the acquisition of market power may be enjoined under § 2 of the Sherman Act, this can occur only when the mode of acquisition, not simply its outcome, is anti-competitive.

patent acquirer's counsel did ask) what would have happened if all the patents had been granted all at once to a single patentee rather than acquired separately through purchase over time. To this the Court could only rather lamely reply that the grant of a patent (or in this case patents) was a unilateral act and could thus not be the conspiracy or agreement required to establish a breach of section 45.[88] While the structure of the Canadian competition statute, as with most countries' competition laws, does legislate an enforcement divide between multilateral and unilateral practices, this simply provokes speculation as to what would have occurred had the patents been granted and immediately sold on as a bundle.[89] Fortunately for the logical coherence of the court's ruling, this was not a speculation on which the parties invited it to embark.

The Federal Court of Appeal was on firmer ground when it dismissed scope of grant arguments that would see the exclusive right to assign bestowed on patentees under section 50 of the Patent Act prevail over section 45 of the Competition Act in all circumstances. It explained that the former provision does not immunise an assignment of a patent from the operation of the latter 'when the assignment increases the assignee's market power in excess of that inherent in the patent rights assigned'.[90] The Court stated that section 50 of the Patent Act and Section 45 of the Competition Act do not conflict because section 50 merely authorises but does not compel assignment of a patent. Accordingly, with the provisions able to 'operate harmoniously in accordance with the ordinary meaning of [their] statutory language',[91] the Court found the 'assignment of a patent may, as a matter of law, unduly lessen competition.'[92]

The Court also pointed out that the existence of section 79(5) demonstrated that the legislature was perfectly capable of drafting an exempting provision similar to the defence available under section 45, had it so wished, and thus it must be assumed that it had deliberately refrained from doing so.[93] The Court was further fortified in this view by the fact that it appeared to be consistent with the *Intellectual Property Enforcement Guidelines* (2000) issued by the regulator,[94] and it is to these Guidelines that we now turn.

---

[88] See *Eli Lilly*, n 83 above, at para 30. The court presumably meant by this the process of applying for and obtaining the patents rather than the grant considered as a form of State action.

[89] It may also have been the case that Eli Lilly already had an exclusive licence over the patents it later acquired. The Federal Court had felt constrained from pursuing this point by the summary nature of the proceedings. Attempts to explore whether Eli Lilly had ever asked for a licence were similarly rebuffed.

[90] See *Ely Lilly*, n 83 above, at para 21.

[91] *Ibid*, at para 22.

[92] *Ibid*, at, para 28.

[93] *Ibid*, at paras 26–27.

[94] *Ibid*, at para 34, where the Federal Court found the IPEG Guidelines, at para 4.2.1, particularly relevant. See 8.7.2 below.

228   CANADA: INCOMPLETE STATUTORY SOLUTIONS

8.7   THE COMPETITION BUREAU'S ENFORCEMENT GUIDELINES

The *Intellectual Property Enforcement Guidelines* (IPEGs) (2000), like all other administrative interpretations, are not, and do not purport to be, legally binding, neither are they determinative of the meaning of the Competition Act.[95] Nevertheless they may be considered by the Court as an aid to the Act's interpretation,[96] especially since the *Guidelines* were released only after extensive consultation.

8.7.1   *Intellectual Property Enforcement Guidelines* (2000)

It is clear from the IPEGs (2000) that that a mere exercise of an intellectual property right would cause the regulator no or little concern under the general provisions of the competition statute, no matter what degree of competition is affected[97]; and if it were to cause such concern, it would only be under section 32. That provision, it will be recalled, provides for special remedies for abuse of intellectual property rights, and requires proof of lessened competition or undue restraint of trade. As far as unilateral conduct is concerned, the mere exercise of an intellectual property right is defined as an owner's exclusion of others from using it or non-use.[98]

The IPEGs propose a two-step test before an enforcement action under section 32 is triggered. First, the Bureau requires the refusal to affect competition adversely to a substantial degree in a relevant market, different or significantly larger than the subject matter of the intellectual property or the products or services which result directly from the exercise of the right. The Bureau sees this happening only where the right holder is dominant in the relevant market and the intellectual property is an essential input or resource for firms participating in that market. In other words, the IPEGs require a right owner's refusal to prevent another firm from competing effectively in the relevant market. Only where this is the case would the Bureau proceed to the second stage, to see if a special remedy is justified. This involves finding that the refusal to license the intellectual property is stifling further innovation (and this does not simply mean preventing replication of existing products). This step requires it to be shown that 'invoking a special remedy against the IP right holder would not adversely alter the incentives to invest in research and development in the economy'[99]. The

---

[95]   *Canada (Commissioner of Competition) v Superior Propane Inc* 2001 FCA 104, at para 124. Although, strictly speaking, the Guidelines referred to in the case were *Merger Guidelines* (this being a bank merger dispute), the same principle stands.
[96]   *Nowegijick v The Queen* [1983] 1 SCR 29 at 37.
[97]   *Intellectual Property Enforcement Guidelines* ('IPEGs'), n 11 above, at para 4.2.1.
[98]   *Ibid*, at para 4.2.1.
[99]   *Ibid*, at para 4.2.2.

regulator plainly expects its prerequisites for a special remedy under section 32 to be able to be satisfied only in very rare circumstances, but concedes this might occur in a network industry where intellectual property protection in combination with substantial positive effects associated with the size of the network are able to create or entrench market dominance. Thus the IPEGs indicate[100] that intellectual property incorporated in a network could merit less protection under some circumstances, such as when intellectual property rights and network externalities interact to create *de facto* industry standards, and where the resultant standardisation means that protected technology is essential for a competitor to produce viable alternative products. It is only in such a situation that the IPEGs expressly recognise that intellectual property protection may effectively exclude others from entering and producing in a market.

The IPEGs also address conduct such as patent trolling, and indicate that unilateral refusals to license associated with such conduct may not be treated benignly as a mere exercise of an intellectual property right. Where a firm has acquired market power by systematically purchasing a controlling collection of intellectual property rights (such as a patent thicket), and then has refused to license the rights to others, thereby substantially lessening or preventing competition in markets associated with the rights, the Bureau could view the acquisition of such rights as anti-competitive and review the matter under either the general abuse of dominance or mergers provisions of the Competition Act (sections 79 and 92 respectively).

8.7.2 *Draft Enforcement Guidelines on Abuse of Dominance*

The regulator has sought to clarify when actual and constructive refusals to deal or license may raise concerns under sections 78 and 79 of the Competition Act. It first addressed the issue in the 2001 *Abuse Guidelines*[101] and revisited it in its 2009 *Draft Updated Abuse Enforcement Guidelines*.[102] Generally speaking, the regulator is of the view that denial of access to a facility or service (that is, some sort of

---

[100] *Ibid.*
[101] See Canadian Competition Bureau (2001) *Enforcement Guidelines on the Abuse of Dominance Provisions (Sections 78 and 79 of the Competition Act)* ('*Abuse Guidelines*'), available at <www.competitionbureau.gc.ca/eic/site/cb-bc.nsf/eng/01251.html>.
[102] See Canadian Competition Bureau (2009) *Draft for Public Consultation: The Abuse of Dominance Provisions (Sections 78 and 79 of the Competition Act)* ('*Draft Abuse Guidelines*'), Appendix IV on 'Denial of Access to a Facility or Service'. The approach adopted is on all fours with the Bureau's *Information Bulletin on the Abuse of Dominance Provisions as Applied to the Telecommunications Industry*, Final Version, 6 June 2008. The 2009 *Draft Abuse Guidelines* are available at <www.competitionbureau.gc.ca/eic/site/cb-bc.nsf/eng/02942.html>, and the 2008 Information Bulletin re applicability to the Telecommunication Industry at <www.competitionbureau.gc.ca/eic/site/cb-bc.nsf/eng/02690.html>.

input) is common practice, raising competition concerns only in limited circumstances. Both the 2001 *Abuse Guidelines* and the 2009 *Draft Abuse Guidelines* concede that denial may be outright, or constructive if a prohibitively high access price is set or a prohibitively poor quality of service is offered for the input. Both also address non-supply of an input by an upstream supplier to a downstream customer with whom that supplier also competes.[103] (That said, one wonders what would happen were a factual situation like the one in *Boosey v Hawkes*,[104] to arise in Canada. Would the Bureau consider the denial of supply to be immune from its scrutiny, simply because it did not involve a refusal to a *competitor*?)

The 2009 *Draft Abuse Guidelines* represent a significant positional shift on the part of the Bureau.[105] The 2001 *Abuse Guidelines* not only required the refusing party to be dominant in the upstream market,[106] but also stipulated that it had to be 'established that the dominant upstream firm [had] a profit motive for extending its market power to a subsequent stage of production', a requirement able to be met by demonstrating that the dominant firm's ability to exploit its market power was limited.[107] The 2009 *Draft Abuse Guidelines* abandon that approach, placing much less emphasis on upstream market power, although its role is an important consideration when downstream market power is taken into account. The focus is more on downstream market power and the likelihood of its enhancement as result of denial of an input by a vertically-integrated firm.

---

[103] Csorgo, L, 'The Canadian Abuse Provisions and the Denial of a Facility', presented at the 2010 Annual Fall Competition Law Conference (30 September–1 October 2010) Gatineau, Québec, available at <www.crai.com/Publications/Default.aspx>.

[104] *Boosey v Hawkes* [1987] OJ L286/36, [1988] 4 CMLR 67. The General Court found abuse of dominance under Art 102 TFEU where discontinuance of supply on the part of a dominant firm was intended as a reprisal against a customer who had associated itself with a potential competitor of the dominant firm. See 6.3.1 above.

[105] See Csorgo, n 102 above, for a detailed exposition of the differences between the two sets of *Guidelines*.

[106] As one Canadian commentator has pointed out, there are flaws in this requirement in the 2001 *Abuse Guidelines*. On its face, the requirement seemed perfectly reasonable. If a downstream competitor could readily replicate the needed source or facility then it was unlikely that an access problem would arise in the downstream market. But, as she notes, the requirement disregarded the possibility that A (a firm without a significant presence in the upstream market) might have been the only source of supply to a downstream rival. This, she posits, could have happened if the upstream firm had created a product such as software for which there were several sources of supply, but had then tailored it for a particular industry. According to Walker's hypothesis, if, in reliance on that input, a downstream rival sold into that niche market, and Firm A then integrated downstream and refused to sell to its competitors, A's refusal would not be caught as A would not be dominant if the upstream market was defined broadly and without reference to the downstream buyer's perspective. See Walker, S, 'Refusals to Deal Under Canada's Competition Act', American Bar Association Panel (Washington, 7 April 2011), available at <www.fmclaw.com/upload/en/publications/2011/0411_Walker_Sandy_Refusals_To_Deal_Under_Canada_Competition_Act.pdf>. Walker notes, however, in relation to her hypothetical, that there would be no substantial lessening of competition if other downstream competitors did not require access to Firm A's input as well. *Ibid*, fn 7.

[107] 2001 *Abuse Guidelines*, n 100 above, at 10–13.

The 2009 *Draft Abuse Guidelines* set out a three-step test to ascertain whether a denial raises an issue under the Competition Act. The first question is whether a vertically-integrated firm has market power in the downstream (or retail) market for which the denied facility is an input in the time period following the denial. If the answer is yes, then it would proceed to ascertain whether the denial has occurred for the purpose of excluding competitors from entering or expanding in the downstream market, or otherwise negatively affecting their ability to compete, and determine whether the refusal has had, is having or is likely to have the effect of substantially lessening or preventing competition in the downstream market.

8.8 COMPULSORY LICENSING UNDER INTELLECTUAL PROPERTY STATUTES IN CANADA

Another impediment to obtaining a special remedy under section 32 of the Competition Act is that that there must be no remedy available under the relevant intellectual property statute. The Patent Act[108] provides for a special remedy for would-be-but-thwarted patent licensees in relation to abuse of patent rights, but only after the expiration of three years from the date of the grant of the patent for which the licence is sought. Section 66 of the patent statute provides that the Commissioner of Patents may grant a licence where there has been an abuse of exclusive patent rights,[109] while section 65(2) deems exclusive rights under a patent to have been abused under a list of illustrative examples[110]:

a) under section 65(2)(c), 'if the demand for the patented article in Canada is not being met to an adequate extent and on reasonable terms'; or

b) under section 65(2)(d), 'if, by reason of the refusal of the patentee to grant a license or licenses on reasonable terms, the trade or industry of Canada or the trade of any person or class of persons trading in Canada, or the establishment of any new trade or industry in Canada, is prejudiced, and it is in the public interest that a license or licenses should be granted'; or

c) under section 65(2)(e), 'if any trade or industry in Canada, or any person or class of persons engaged therein, is unfairly prejudiced by the conditions attached by the patentee, whether before or after the passing of [the Patent Act] to the purchase, hire, license or use of the patented article or to the using or working of the patented process'; or

d) under section 65(2)(f), 'if it is shown that the existence of the patent, being a patent for an invention relating to a process involving the use of materials not protected by the patent or for an invention relating to a substance

---

[108] Patent Act 1985, RSC, c P-4, s 65(1).
[109] *Ibid*, s 66(1)(a)–(c).
[110] *Ibid*, s 65(2)(c)–(f). The list has been abbreviated for present purposes.

produced by such a process, has been utilised by the patentee so as unfairly to prejudice in Canada the manufacture, use or sale of any materials'.

These criteria were treated as entirely stand-alone in *Puckhandler Inc v BADS Industries Inc*,[111] in which the Commissioner of Patents awarded a licence on the basis that the criteria in section 65(2)(c) were satisfied, although it could not also be shown that it was in the public interest for a licence (or licences) to be granted under section 65(2)(d). In one of the few other cases dealing with these provisions, *Torpharm Inc v Canada (Commissioner of Patents)*,[112] the Federal Court allowed an appeal from a decision of the Commissioner of Patents who had refused Torpharm's application for a compulsory licence to enable it to acquire a bulk chemical, lisinopril, subject at the time to a patent owned by Merck, for the purpose of manufacturing tablets in Canada for export. The Court found the Commissioner of Patents had erred in law by concluding that the list of illustrative abuses set out in section 65(2) was exhaustive. This has been interpreted by some commentators[113] as lowering the bar for granting compulsory licences under section 65(2)(c) and suggesting that any time an applicant offers reasonable terms and is refused, it would be entitled to obtain a compulsory licence based on the grounds laid down in section 65(2)(c). If so, this is a significant change from earlier cases, where patentees' exclusive rights were much more vigorously protected.[114]

---

[111] *Puckhandler Inc v BADS Industries Inc* [1998] 81 CPR 3d 261 (Patent Appeal Board), available at 1998 CPR LEXIS 143.

[112] *Torpharm Inc v Canada (Commissioner of Patents)* [2004] FC 673.

[113] Brown, DJ and Martino, P, 'Intellectual Property Licensing by the Dominant Firm: Issues and problems—A Canadian Perspective' (2006) 55 *De Paul Law Review* 1247 at 1265.

[114] *Ibid.* Eg, *Sarco Co Inc v Sarco Canada Ltd* [1969] 2 Ex CR 190, a case that dealt with earlier statutory counterparts of ss 67 and 68 of the Patents Act.

9

Reintegrating Law and Economics: Perfecting the Art of the Possible

9.1 THE CASE FOR NEUTRALITY RESTATED

Both lawyers and economists must bear some responsibility for the refusal to license impasse. The latter because the economics on this subject is empirically deficient, and the former because they continue to cling both to the notion that intellectual property is so special that it requires a bright-line protection denied to other potential sources of market power and that inaction is inherently more virtuous in competition terms than action. Rather than trying to find special solutions to special non-problems, it might be more fruitful to apply to them the fact-specific, right-blind approach argued for in chapter two. Under such an approach the court's or regulator's only task would be to determine the effect of a proposed regulatory intervention on incentive to innovate in a particular case. Whether or not innovation was protected by an intellectual property right would then be beside the point. Essentialness, exceptionality and rights to refuse would be treated as the irrelevant distractions that they really are.

9.2 INTELLECTUAL PROPERTY AND COMPETITION POLICY: REBUILDING THE INTERFACE

As we have stressed throughout this book, the relationship between intellectual property and competition policy cannot properly be understood by looking only at one of the two halves of the problem. Thus, while neither sub-discipline can wholly cure the imperfections of the other, neither do they exist in splendid isolation from each other. If over-intensive regulation poses difficulties from a property rights perspective, the fact of over-protection in a given case cannot be entirely ignored by regulators either. Competition rules are not a substitute for intellectual property law reform, but neither can the interface between the two be constructed entirely from the inadequate materials available on the intellectual property side of this artificial and exceedingly rickety fence. Nor can the interface be successfully rebuilt unless the choices facing judges and regulators are clearly set out.

9.2.1 Setting limits to competition policy

While economic analysis seldom figures directly in the jurisprudence of intellectual property enforcement, this is not due to a dearth of such analysis in the ongoing academic debate over rationales for, and the proper scope of, intellectual property rights. Commentary abounds, articulating and defending a law and economics perspective on both issues. That there are many welfare-reducing and inefficient aspects of intellectual property law as presently constituted is undoubted, but they are for most purposes beyond the reach of competition regulators unless and until they arise in competition proceedings. The expansion of the scope of intellectual property protection over the last half century may be a good or bad thing, but rolling it back or cheering it on is a matter for legislators not regulators. None of this means that courts and regulators in competition cases are required to treat intellectual property dealings as a regulatory no-go zone. Nor is competition policy a way of smoothing over trans-jurisdictional variations in the content of intellectual property rights. Intellectual property can be both the source of market power and the vehicle for its misuse, and regulators are in no way required to stop their inquiries at the boundaries of the right when these issues are properly raised in the case before them. Nor is it possible or desirable to ignore the existing contours of the intellectual property right in question when assessing future losses of innovative efficiency that might flow from a refusal to license if that is necessary to make the analysis work. Competition policy is more than a residual safety-net to be invoked only after intellectual property has done its job.

9.2.2 The inadequacy of intellectual property's internal controls

If competition policy is not an appropriate tool for fixing a broken intellectual property regime, the reverse is also the case. Intellectual property's internal controls on over-protection cannot act as a surrogate for a coherent (and neutral) competition policy. It is true that competition values are not entirely absent from the intellectual property side of the equation. Fair use rules and public interest defences sometimes provide hooks on which to hang a competition argument with or without a legislative prompt. It is also true that in the United States, the parallel structure of abuse of rights jurisprudence, although not formally part of antitrust law in a jurisdictional sense, shadows much of its content while operating formally as a defence to infringement. Again, where user lobbying groups are strong, they may be able to secure highly specific defences to infringement in the interests of their members. Such cases are rare, as we have seen. This partial internalising of competition values by intellectual property law is too weak and unfocused, however, to provide either a counterweight to, or substitute for, competition policy.

9.2.3 The choices for courts and regulators

When courts and regulators are asked to assess the allegedly anti-competitive behaviour of intellectual property owners, they may respond in any one of the following ways:

a) Permit right owners to exercise without interference any power granted to them by or under the relevant intellectual property statute, but carefully to scrutinise for anti-competitive intent or outcome any attempts to extend or enhance those powers. This is the scope of grant argument, one which allows the boundaries of the intellectual property right to define the limits of regulatory intervention.

b) Reverse the previous assumption and presume (or worse deem) all attempts by right holders to step outside what the intellectual property statute allows to be anti-competitive. This is the scope of grant turned upside-down, and while once widely prevalent, as we have seen, has few current backers among either lawyers or economists.

c) Accept that there may be occasions on which the court or regulator has to invade the four walls of the intellectual property right by prohibiting the exercise of rights granted by the intellectual property statute in question, but to marginalise such happenings by treating such occasions as rare or exceptional departures from a scope of grant starting point. Because it dresses up a prophecy as a rule, exceptionality is hard to pin down. Its scope of grant starting-point gives rise to a great many questions as well.

d) Treat intellectual property no differently from other legal rights or privileges, even if this sometimes means forbidding right owners to exercise powers given to them under the intellectual property statute. This is the viewpoint for which we have argued consistently in this book, since it places fewest obstacles in the path of a case-by-case economics-based approach.

9.3 FAILED BLACK-LETTER EXITS FROM THE REFUSAL TO LICENSE IMPASSE

A preference for legal certainty over the vagaries of economic discourse will often push judges in the direction of black-letter solutions to the refusal to license problem. While these seem to leave the rule of reason approach intact, they are in fact the antithesis of it. They are also apt to spawn a host of sub-rules and exceptions that are often illogical and unworkable, even on their own black-letter terms.

9.3.1 Essential facilities, the right to refuse and exceptional circumstances: non-solutions to non-problems

The essential facilities doctrine originated, as we saw in chapter five, as a corrective to the over-enthusiastic earlier adoption by courts in the United States of the notion that there is such a thing as a *right* to refuse to deal. The doctrine was not originally formulated with intellectual property transactions in mind. Never very easy to apply, it has been effectively abandoned on its home ground, not by returning to the rule of reason but again by effectively putting the right to refuse back on top while efforts continue to be made to balance a presumptive right to refuse against the essentialness of the thing refused. In the European Union, where the doctrine is alive and well, the attempt to apply both these ideas simultaneously has sent courts and regulators off in search of an ever-receding principle of exceptionality, the role of which seems to be to ensure that the right to refuse is disturbed only occasionally. If the American vice is the doctrine of atomisation, it comes with an abundance of unreconciled precedents; that of the Europeans is the opposite, trying to erect a rule of general application on the facts of a small number of cases. In neither jurisdiction has any serious attempt been made to find an economic justification for the various solutions put forward in the cases.

9.3.2 The ranking of rights: unworkable and distracting

The idea of a hierarchy of rights marching in lockstep with a spectrum of greater or less regulatory intervention is deeply seductive. The problem, as we saw in chapter four, is that there is more than one hierarchy and the ranking is anything but clear-cut. Pitting 'strong' against 'weak' rights, for example, is a very different kind of conceptual contest from that taking place when 'clear' and 'unclear' rights are placed in opposition to each other. There is the added difficulty that hierarchies can themselves be further subdivisible. Thus, we have 'hard to get' versus 'hard to keep' rights arising by express grant as against self-constituting rights, and 'high-tech' versus 'low-tech' rights. Alternatively, patents are claimed to be 'earned' because of the duty of disclosure and description attached to their grant, whereas copyright and trade secrets are said to be 'unearned' because they carry no such price tag. This kind of infinite regression does not make for a particularly useful analytical tool. Nor do the categories hold constant across jurisdictions (for example, patents for computer programs, business methods and processes relating to medical treatment are easier to obtain in some jurisdictions than others). The real difficulty with all of these hierarchies, however, is that they take the scope and content of the rights as givens. Once a right is classified in a particular way, it is assumed to deliver an identical dose of social utility and innovative efficiency as all of the other rights placed in the same category. For all these reasons, hierarchies are better ignored.

9.4 THE PERILS OF LEGISLATIVE INTERVENTION

One way of cutting through the confusion surrounding refusals to license is to seek clarity through the legislative process. In the United States and the European Union this has not been a realistic option given the formidable political obstacles facing any would-be amendment of section 2 of the Sherman Act or Article 102 TFEU. In other jurisdictions, notably Canada and New Zealand, legislators have been rather more proactive, placing on the statute book provisions that on their face seem to address the problem directly. The prospect of legislative rescue, thus held out, has proved to be largely illusory, however. In Canada, this is because while the competition statute contains discrete provisions regulating both 'abuse' of intellectual property rights and refusals to deal, the former is walled-off from ordinary regulatory processes in a quasi criminal ghetto all of its own, while the latter has been held to apply to everything but refusals to license intellectual property, thus leaving them to be dealt with under the competition statute's general abuse of dominance section (albeit with a forceful legislative nudge in the direction of a presumption of virtue). In New Zealand, the promise of legislative rescue has been largely unfulfilled due to the use of the statutory language, language so opaque that it can embrace most of the theoretical positions discussed in the preceding chapters. In both jurisdictions, the position is further complicated by the existence of limited compulsory licensing provisions in their patent legislation.

What do these legislative tinkerings tell us? Two things: first, intervention makes sense only where it is intended to move a rule of reason to a *per se* rule; and, secondly, one should do the latter only when the economics points unequivocally in that direction. Provisions that merely echo the uncertainties and obscurities of existing case law serve no useful purpose. Legislating outside the economic consensus is dangerous because it freezes the economic debate at a particular moment in time, and closes off avenues for judicial and regulatory retreat.

In the context of the issues discussed in this book, the choice available to legislators is simple: To privilege or de-privilege intellectual property? While few economists would now opt for de-privileging, there is no similar consensus in relation to bestowing on refusals to license either actual or presumptive immunity from competition scrutiny. Legislators should therefore stay their hand.

9.5 THE SHIFTING OF COMPETITION LAW'S INTERNAL MARKERS

Traditionally the world's competition regimes have drawn lines of greater or less rigidity between different types of behaviour, and analysed those behaviours largely within the lines so drawn. Thus the acquisition of market power was dealt with differently from its use. Unilateral behaviour was scrutinised separately from multilateral dealings and, crucially for the subject of this book, analysis of action parted company from the analysis of inaction. These internal divisions partly reflect the ways in which competition statutes are structured in our various jurisdictions (a structure usually, but not entirely, traceable to United States antitrust law), but they also owe something to judicial preference for thinking within internally-referenced categories. What they have in common is that they owe little or nothing to economics. They are almost entirely legal constructs.

These formerly rigid boundaries have been eroding in all of our five jurisdictions as courts search for overarching principles and economists focus on the effects of particular activities rather than activities for their own sake. None of this blurring of boundaries can be traced in detail within a book such as this. It is relevant to our topic only in so far as it points up the non-wisdom (and in some cases, the futility) of privileging refusals *qua* refusals.

9.6 REDUCING THE EMPIRICAL DEFICIT

Can the economics of refusals to license be rescued from its current indeterminate state (on both the intellectual property and competition law sides of the fence) by a greater attention to empirical attention and analysis? Yes, provided one very important limiting factor is kept clearly in mind: the larger the question being asked, the less immediately verifiable the answer obtained with the empirical tools currently available to economists. Unfortunately, it is precisely such large questions that judges and academic lawyers often want to ask as they pursue their traditional legal task of turning past factual findings into precedents for the future.

Four such large and interconnected questions hover over the issues raised in this book. In descending order of generality they are:

a) Are intellectual property rights innovatively efficient within their present boundaries?
b) Is inaction more benign in competition terms than action?
c) Is intellectual property more vulnerable to regulatory intervention than other forms of property (or indeed technological or business advantages in general)?
d) Will coerced licensing inhibit innovation and creativity?

Providing a definitive answer to these questions would bring closure to the refusals to license debate. Answering any one of them would greatly assist regulators and judges. Can either be done? Regrettably, no. There are simply too many variables and no fixed control groups. Harmonisation of competition rules and intellectual property law across borders over time makes 'with' and 'without' counterfactuals hard to test. Assessing the impact of regulatory intervention postulates a world of either/or choices facing judges and regulators that is at odds with the remedial flexibility that most would see as desirable. The innovative efficiency of paths not taken requires an ability to see into the future that few judges and regulators possess. Measuring the downside of coerced licensing is problematical when the fact that so few such orders are made keeps sample sizes small and unrepresentative.

Does this mean that empirical analysis is undoable and unnecessary? On the contrary, reducing the empirical deficit is, as we argue in the preceding chapters, the key to making rules of reason work effectively. This is best done incrementally: case by case, micro issue by micro issue. Context is all in the pursuit of these limited case-specific objectives. In this regard it is important that economists should not over-promise and lawyers not over-expect. Only if both disciplines appreciate the limits of their respective methodologies can their interaction continue to be effective, both in the setting of competition policy and in the shaping of intellectual property law.

Bibliography

ABRAHAMSON, S, 'Making Sense of the Copyright Merger Doctrine' (1998) 45 *University of California Law Review* 1125.
ADAM, M and MAIER-RIGAUD, F, 'The Law and Economics of Article 82 EC and the Commission's Guidance Paper on Exclusion' (2009) 1 *Journal of Competition Law* 131.
ADHAR, R, 'Escaping New Zealand's Monopolisation Quagmire' (2006) 34 *Australian Business Law Review* 260.
AHLBORN, C, Evans, DS and Padilla, AJ, 'Competition Policy in the New Economy: Is European Competition Law Up to the Challenge?' (2001) 22 *European Competition Law Review* 156.
—— 'The Logic & Limits of the 'Exceptional Circumstances Test' in *Magill* and *IMS Health*' (2005) 28 *Fordham International Law Journal* 1109.
AKMAN, P, 'Consumer Welfare and Article 82 EC: Practice and Rhetoric' (2009) 32 *World Competition* 71.
ALESE, F, *Federal Antitrust and EC Competition Law Analysis* (London, Ashgate, 2008).
ALLISON, JR and LEMLEY, MA, 'Empirical Evidence on the Validity of Litigated Patents' (1998) 26 *American Intellectual Property Law Association (AIPLA) Quarterly Journal* 185.
ANDERMAN, S, 'The IP and Competition Law Interface: New developments' in S Anderman and A Ezrachi (eds), *Intellectual Property and Competition Law: New Frontiers* (Oxford, Oxford University Press, 2011).
ANDERMAN, S and EZRACHI, A (eds), *Intellectual Property and Competition Law: New Frontiers* (Oxford, Oxford University Press, 2011).
ANDREANGELI, A, 'Interoperability as an "essential facility" in the *Microsoft* case—encouraging competition or stifling innovation?' (2009) 34 *European Law Review* 584.
AREEDA, P, 'Predatory Pricing' (1981) 49 *Antitrust Law Journal* 897.
—— 'Essential Facilities: An Epithet in Need of Limiting Principles' (1990) 8 *Antitrust Law Journal* 841.
AREEDA, P and HOVENCAMP, H, *Antitrust Law: An Analysis of Antitrust Principles and Their Application* (Boston, Aspen Publishers, 1995).
—— *Antitrust Law*, 2nd edn (New York, Aspen, 2002).
AREEDA, P and TURNER, DF, 'Predatory Pricing and Practices under Section 2 of the Sherman Act' (1975) 88 *Harvard Law Review* 697.
AREZZO, E, 'Intellectual property rights at the crossroad between monopolization and abuse of dominant position: American and European approaches compared' (2006) 24 *John Marshall Journal of Computer & Information Law* 455.
ARORA, A, 'Refusals to License: A Transaction Based Perspective' (2002), available at <www.ftc.gov/opp/intellect/020501arora1.pdf>.

ARROW, K, 'Economic Welfare and the Allocation of Resources for Inventors' in *The Rate and Direction of Inventive Activity: Economic and Social Factors* (Report for National Bureau of Economic Research, Princeton, 1962).

AUSTIN, GW, 'Copyright Across (and Within) Borders: Jurisdictional Issues and Choice of Law' in CER Rickett and GW Austin (eds), *Intellectual Property in the Common Law World* (Oxford, Hart Publishing, 2000) 105.

AUSTRALIAN INTELLECTUAL PROPERTY and COMPETITION LAW REVIEW COMMITTEE (the 'Ergas Committee'), *Review of Intellectual Property Legislation under the Competition Principles Agreement*, available at <http://www.ipaustralia.gov.au/about/ipcr.shtml#final>.

BAIN, J, *Barriers to New Competition: Their Character and Consequences in Manufacturing Incentives* (Boston MA, Harvard University Press, 1956).

BAKER, JB, 'Market Definition: An Analytical Overview' (2007) 74 *Antitrust Law Journal* 129.

BALGANESH, S, 'Hot News: The Enduring Myth of Property in News' (2011) 419 *Columbia Law Review* 422.

BARNETT, TO, 'Section 2 Remedies: What to do after Catching the Tiger by the Tail?' (2009) 76 *Antitrust Law Journal* 31.

BATCHELOR, B, 'The Fallout from *Microsoft*: the Court of First Instance Leaves Critical IT Industry Issues Unanswered' (2008) 14 *Computer and Telecommunications Law Review* 17.

BAUER, J, 'Refusals to Deal with Competitors or Owners of Patents and Copyrights: Reflections on the *Image Technical Services* and *Xerox* Decisions' (2006) 55 *De Paul Law Review* 1211.

BAUMOL, WJ and SIDAK, JG, 'The Pricing of Inputs Sold to Competitors' (1994) 11 *Yale Journal of Regulation* 171.

BAXTER, WF, 'Legal Restrictions on the Exploitation of the Patent Monopoly: An Economic Analysis' (1966) 76 *Yale Law Journal* 267.

BENTLY, L, et al, 'Opinion: Creativity stifled? A Joint Academic Statement on the Proposed Copyright Term Extension for Sound Recordings' (2008) 30 *European Intellectual Property Review* 341.

BERGMAN, M, 'The *Bronner* Case—A Turning Point for the Essential Facilities Doctrine?' (2000) *European Competition Law Review* 59.

BLAIR, RD, 'The Economics of the Roberts Court: An Introduction' (2008) 53 *Antitrust Bulletin* 1.

BLUMENTHAL, W, 'The Challenge of Sovereignty and the Mechanisms of Convergence' (2004) 72 *Antitrust Law Journal* 267.

BOLDRIN, M and LEVINE, DK, 'Growth and Intellectual Property' (2007) *NBER Working Paper No 12769*, available at <www.nber.org/papers/w12769.pdf>.

—— *Against Intellectual Property* (New York, Cambridge University Press, 2008).

BORK, RH, *The Antitrust Paradox: A Policy At War With Itself* (New York, The Free Press, 1993).

BOYER, M, Trebilcock, M and Vaver, D (eds), *Competition Policy and Intellectual Property* (Toronto, Irwin Law, 2009).

BREAKY, H, 'Natural Intellectual Property Rights and the Public Domain' (2010) 73 *Modern Law Review* 208.

BREYER, S, 'The Uneasy Case for Copyright: A Study of Copyright in Books, Photocopies and Computer Programs' (1970) 84 *Harvard Law Review* 281.

BRODLEY, JF, 'The Economic Goals of Antitrust: Efficiency, Welfare and Technological Progress' (1987) 62 *New York University Law Review* 1020.

BROWN, DJ and MARTINO, P, 'Intellectual Property Licensing by the Dominant Firm: Issues and problems—A Canadian Perspective' (2006) 55 *De Paul Law Review* 1247.

BRUNT, M, 'Antitrust in the Courts: The Role of Economics and Economists' in M Brunt (ed), *Economic Essays in Australian and New Zealand Competition Law* (The Hague, Kluwer, 2003) 356.

BURR, SL, 'Artistic Parody: A Theoretical Construct' (1996) 14 *Cardozo Arts & Entertainment Law Journal* 65.

CALABRESI, G and MELAMED, AD, 'Property Rules, Liability Rules and Inalienability: One View of the Cathedral' (1972) 85 *Harvard Law Review* 1089.

CALHOUN, D and BROWN, B, 'New Zealand: Interface Between Misuse of a Dominant Position and the Exercise of Intellectual property Rights' (1990) 12 *European Intellectual Property Review* 437.

CAMERON, A and TOMKOWICZ, R, 'Competition Policy and Canada's New Breed of Copyright Law' (2007) 52 *McGill Law Journal* 291.

CANADIAN COMPETITION BUREAU, *Intellectual Property Enforcement Guidelines* (2000), available at <www.competitionbureau.gc.ca/eic/site/cb-bc.nsf/eng/01286.html>.

—— *Enforcement Guidelines on the Abuse of Dominance Provisions (Sections 78 and 79 of the Competition Act)* (2001), available at <www.competitionbureau.gc.ca/eic/site/cb-bc.nsf/eng/01251.html>.

—— *Information Bulletin on Merger Remedies in Canada* (2006), available at <www.competitionbureau.gc.ca/eic/site/cb-bc.nsf/eng/02170.html>.

—— *Information Bulletin on the Abuse of Dominance Provisions as Applied to the Telecommunications Industry* (Final Version, 6 June 2008), available at <http://www.competitionbureau.gc.ca/eic/site/cb-bc.nsf/eng/02690.html>.

—— *Draft for Public Consultation: The Abuse of Dominance Provisions (Sections 78 and 79 of the Competition Act)* (2009), available at <www.competitionbureau.gc.ca/eic/site/cb-bc.nsf/eng/02942.html>.

CANDEDUB, A, '*Trinko* and Re-Grounding the Refusal to Deal Doctrine' (2005) 66 *University of Pittsburgh Law Review* 821.

CARROLL, L, *Through the Looking Glass and What Alice Found There*, Millenium Fulcrum Edition 1.7, available at <www.gutenberg.org/files/12/12-h/12-h.htm>.

CAVANAGH, ED, '*Trinko*: A Kinder, Gentler Approach To Dominant Firms Under the Antitrust Laws?' (2006) *St John's University Legal Studies Research Paper Series 06–0058*, available at SSRN <http://ssrn.com/abstract=940398>.

CENTRE OF EUROPEAN POLICY STUDIES, *Treatment of Exclusionary Abuses under Art 82 [Art 102 TFEU] of the EC Treaty: Comments on the European Commission's Guidance Paper* (Final Report, 2009).

CHAMBERLIN, EH, *The Theory of Monopolistic Competition*, 8th edn (Boston MA, Harvard University Press, 1962).

CLOUGH, D, 'Misuse of Market Power: "Would" or "Could" in a Competitive Market' (2001) 29 *Australian Business Law Review* 311.

COMANOR, WS, 'The Problem of Remedy in Monopolisation Cases: The *Microsoft* Case as an Example' (2001) 46 *Antitrust Bulletin* 115.

CORNISH, W, Llewelyn, D and Aplin, T, *Intellectual Property: Patents, Copyrights, Trademarks & Allied Rights*, 7th edn (London, Sweet & Maxwell, 2010).

CORONES, S, 'Technological Tying in the Computer Industry: When Does it Contravene Section 46 of the Trade Practices Act?' (2003) 3 *Queensland University of Technology Law and Justice Journal* 47.

COTTER, T, 'Patent Holdup, Patent Remedies, and Antitrust Responses' (2008) *Minnesota Legal Studies Research Paper No 08–39*, available at <http://ssrn.com/abstract=1273293>.

CRANDALL, RW, 'The Failure of Remedies in Sherman Act Monopolisation Cases' (2001) 80 *Oregon Law Review* 109.

CRANE, DA, 'Chicago, Post-Chicago, and Neo-Chicago' (2009) 76 *University of Chicago Law Review* 1911.

—— 'Bargaining in the Shadow of Rate Setting Courts' (2010) 76 *Antitrust Law Journal* 307.

CROCIONI, P, 'Leveraging of Market Power in Emerging Markets: A Review of Cases, Literature and a Suggested Framework' [2008] *Journal of Competition Law and Economics* 449.

CSORGO, L, 'The Canadian Abuse Provisions and the Denial of a Facility', presented at the Annual Fall Competition Law Conference (30 September–1 October 2010), at Gatineau, Québec.

CURLEY, D, 'Interoperability and Other Issues at the IP Antitrust Interface' (2008) 11 *Journal of World Intellectual Property* 296.

CZAPRACKA, KA, 'Where Antitrust Ends and IP Begins—On the Roots of the Transatlantic Clashes' (2006–2007) *Yale Journal of Law and Technology* 44.

—— 'Antitrust and Trade Secrets: The US and EU Approaches' (2008) 24 *Santa Clara Computer and High Technology Law Journal* 207.

DEMSETZ, H, 'Barriers to Entry' (1982) 72 *American Economic Review* 47.

DERCLAYE, E, 'Abuses of Dominant Position and Intellectual Property Rights: A Suggestion to Reconcile the Community Courts' Case Law' in C Graham and F Smith (eds), *Competition, Regulation and the New Economy* (Oxford, Hart Publishing, 2004) 55.

—— 'The *IMS Health* Decision: A Triple Victory' (2004) 27 *World Competition* 397.

—— *The Legal Protection of Databases: A Comparative Analysis* (Cheltenham, Edward Elgar, 2008).

DEVLIN, A, Jacobs, M, and Peixoto, B, 'Success, Dominance and Interoperabilty' (2009) 84 *Indiana Law Journal* 1157.

DEVLIN, A and JACOBS, MS, 'Microsoft's Five Fatal Flaws' (2009) *Columbia Business Law Review* 67.

DINWOODIE, G, Reichman, J and Samuelson, P, 'A Reverse Notice and Takedown Regime to Enable Public Interest Uses of Technically Protected Copyrighted Works' (2007) 22 *Berkeley Technology Law Journal* 981.

DOGAN, SL and LEMLEY, MA, 'Antitrust Law and Regulatory Gaming' (2009) 87 *Texas Law Review* 685.

DOLMANS, A, 'Restrictions on Innovation: An EU Antitrust Approach' (1998) 88 *Antitrust Law Journal* 455.

DONOGHUE, RO and PADILLA, AJ, *The Law and Economics of Article 82 EC* (Oxford, Hart Publishing, 2006).

DRAHOS, P, 'BITS and BIPS: Bilateralism in Intellectual Property' (2001) 4 *Journal of World Intellectual Property* 791.

—— (ed), *Death of Patents* (Witney, QMC and Lawtext, 2005).

DREYFUSS, RC, FIRST, H and ZIMMERMAN, DL (eds), *Expanding the Boundaries of Intellectual Property: Innovation Policy for the Knowledge Society* (Oxford, Oxford University Press, 2001).

DUSOLLIER, S, 'Electrifying the Fence: Legal Protection of Technological Measures for Protecting Copyright' (1999) 3 *European Intellectual Property Review* 285.

EAGLES, I, 'Of Ports, Pilots and Predation: New Zealand Courts Reassess Some Competition Fundamentals' (1996) 17 *European Competition Law Review* 462.

—— 'Of Firms, Families and Fair Trading' [1998] *New Zealand Law Journal* 241.

—— 'Intellectual Property and Competition Policy: The Case for Neutrality' in CER Rickett and GW Austin (eds), *International Intellectual Property Law and the Common Law World* (Oxford, Hart Publishing, 2000) 285.

—— 'New Zealand Moral Rights Law: Did Something Get Lost in Translation?' (2002) 8 *New Zealand Business Law Quarterly* 26.

—— 'Copyright and the Sequel: What Happens Next?' in F Macmillan (ed), *New Directions in Copyright Law*, vol 6 (Cheltenham, Edward Elgar Publishing, 2007) 35.

—— 'Regulating the Interface Between Competition Law and Intellectual Property in New Zealand' (2007) 13 *New Zealand Business Law Quarterly* 95.

EAGLES, I and LONGDIN, L, 'The *Microsoft* Appeal: Different Rules for Different Markets?' (2001) 7 *New Zealand Business Law Quarterly* 296.

—— 'Competition in Information and Computer Technology Markets: Intellectual Property Licensing and Section 51(3) of the Trade Practices Act 1974' (2003) 3 *Queensland University of Technology Law and Justice Journal* 1.

—— 'Refusals to License Intellectual Property: The Limits of Law and Economics' presented at the 3rd Law and Economics of Intellectual Property and Information Technology Conference at Queen Mary College Centre For Commercial Legal Studies, University of London, 5–6 July 2007.

—— 'Microsoft's Refusal to Disclose Software Interoperability Information and the Court of First Instance' (2008) 5 *European Intellectual Property Review* 205.

EASTERBROOK, FH, 'Insider Trading, Secret Agents, Evidentiary Privileges and the Production of Information' (1981) *Supreme Court Review* 309.

—— 'The Limits of Antitrust' (1984) 63 *Texas Law Review* 1.

ECONOMIC ADVISORY GROUP FOR COMPETITION POLICY (EAGCP), *Report on an Economic Approach to Article 82 EC*, available at <http://ec.europa.eu/dgs/competition/economist/eagcp_july_21_05.pdf>.

ECONOMIDES, NS, 'The Economics of Trade Marks' (1988) 18 *Trademark Reporter* 523.

EDWARD, K, 'The Nature and Function of the Patent System' (1977) 20 *Journal of Law and Economics* 265.

ELHAUGE, E, 'Defining Better Monopolisation Standards' (2003) 56 *Stanford Law Review* 253.

—— 'Disgorgement as an Antitrust Remedy' (2009) 76 *Antitrust Law Journal* 79.

—— 'Tying, Bundled Discounts and the Death of the Single Monopoly Theory' (2009) 123 *Harvard Law Review* 397.

—— 'The Failed Resurrection of the Single Monopoly Profit Theory' (2010) 6 *Competition Policy International* 155.

EPSTEIN, R, 'Intellectual Property: Old Boundaries and New Frontiers' (2001) 76 *Indiana Law Journal* 803.

ERICKSON, S, 'Patent Law and New Product Development: Does Priority Claim Basis Make a Difference' (1999) 36 *American Business Law Journal* 327.

EUROPEAN COMMISSION, *14th Annual Report on Competition* (1984), available at <http://bookshop.europa.eu/>.
—— *22nd Annual Report on Competition Policy* (1992), available at <http://bookshop.europa.eu/>.
—— *Communication: Guidance on the Commission's Enforcement Priorities in Applying Article 82 [EC now Article 102 TFEU] to Abusive Exclusionary Conduct by Dominant Undertakings* [2009] OJ C45/7, available at http://ec.europa.eu/competition/antitrust/art82/index.html <http://eur->.
EUROPEAN COMMISSION DG COMPETITION, 'Discussion paper on the application of Article 82 of the Treaty [now Article 102 TFEU] to exclusionary abuses' (2005), available at http://ec.europa.eu/competition/antitrust/art82/discpaper2005.pdf>.
—— *Final Report: Pharmaceutical Sector Inquiry (adopted 8 July 2009)*, available at <http://ec.europa.eu/competition/sectors/pharmaceuticals/inquiry/>.
EUROPEAN PATENT OFFICE, *Comments on the European Commission's November 2008 'Preliminary Report: Pharmaceutical Sector Inquiry'*, available at <http://ec.europa.eu/competition/consultations/2009_pharma/european_patent_office.pdf>.
EVANS, DS, NICHOLS, AL and SCHMALENSEE, R, 'An Analysis of the Government's Case in *Microsoft*' (2001) 46 *Antitrust Bulletin* 163.
EZRACHI, A, 'The European Commission Guidance on Article 82 EC—The Way in which Institutional Realities Limit the Potential for Reform' (2009) *Oxford Legal Studies Research Paper No 27/2009*, available at <http://ssrn.com/abstract=1463854>.
FAME, EF and LAFFER, AB, 'Information and Capital Markets' (1971) 44 *Journal of Business* 289.
FIRST, H, '*Microsoft* and the Evolution of the Intellectual Property Concept' (2007) 39 *Intellectual Property Law Review* 711.
—— 'Netscape is Dead: Lessons from the *Microsoft* Litigation' (2008) *New York Law and Economics Working Paper No 166*.
—— 'The Case for Antitrust Civil Penalties' (2009) 76 *Antitrust Law Journal* 127.
FITZGERALD, BF and GAMERTSFELDER, L, 'Protecting Informational Products Including Databases Through Unjust Enrichment Law: An Australian Perspective' (1998) 20 *European Intellectual Property Review* 244.
FORSYTH, M, 'The Digital Agenda Anti-circumvention Provisions: A Threat to Fair Use in Cyberspace' (2001) 82 *Australian Intellectual Property Journal* 12.
FOX, E, 'The 1982 Merger Guidelines: When Economists are Kings?' (1983) 71 *California Law Review* 281.
FRIEDMAN, M, *Essays in Positive Economics* (Chicago, Chicago University Press, 1975).
FRISCHMANN, B and WALLER, SW, 'The Essential Nature of Infrastructure or the Infrastructural Nature of Essential Facilities' (unpublished paper, 2007), available at <www.luc.edu/law/academics/special/center/antitrust/pdfs/frischmann_waller_article_31107.pdf>.
—— 'Revitalising Essential Facilities' (2008) 75 *Antitrust Law Journal* 1.
FROOMKIN, AM, 'Flood Control on the Information Ocean: Living with Anonymity, Digital Cash and Distributed Data Bases' (1996) 15 *Journal of Law and Commerce* 395.
FURSE, M, 'The Essential Facilities Doctrine in Community Law' (2005) 8 *European Competition Law Review* 469.
GAVIL, A, 'Thinking Outside the Illinois Brick Box: A Proposal for Reform' (2009) 76 *Antitrust Law Journal* 167.

GERADIN, D, 'Pricing Abuses by Essential Patent Holders in a Standard Setting Context' (2009) 76 *Antitrust Law Journal* 329.
GERMAN BUNDESKARTELLAMT and THE GERMAN MINISTRY OF ECONOMICS and TECHNOLOGY, *Written Statement on the DG Competition discussion paper on the Application of Article 82 of the Treaty to exclusionary abuses (Bonn, 2006)*, available at <www.bundeskartellamt.de/wDeutsch/download/pdf/Stellungnahmen/0703_Stellungnahme_DE_Art82_e.pdf>.
GHIDINI, G, *Intellectual Property and Competition Law* (Cheltenham, Edward Elgar, 2006).
GHOSH, S, 'When Exclusionary Conduct Meets the Exclusive Rights of Intellectual Property: *Morris v PGA* and the Limits of Free Riding as an Antitrust Business Justification' (2006) 37 *Loyola University of Chicago Law Journal* 723.
GILBERT, RJ and SUNSHINE, N, 'Incorporating Dynamic Efficiency Concerns in Merger Analysis: The Use of Innovation Markets' (1995) 63 *Antitrust Law Journal* 569.
GLADER, M and LARSEN, S, 'Excessive Pricing—An Outline of the Legal Principles Relating to Excessive Pricing and their Future Application in the Field of IP Right and Standard Setting' [2005] *Competition Law Insight* 3.
GOLDFINE, D, and Vorassi, K, 'The Fall of the *Kodak* After Market Doctrine: Dying a Slow Death in the Lower Courts' (2004) 72 *Antitrust Law Journal* 209.
GOLDSTEIN, P, *Copyright's Highway: From Gutenberg to the Celestial Jukebox* (New York, Hill and Wang, 1994).
—— *Copyright*, 2nd edn (Cornell, Legal Information Institute, 1996).
GORDON, WJ, 'An Inquiry Into the Merits of Copyright: The Challenges of Consistency, Consent and Encouragement Theory' (1989) 41 *Stanford Law Review* 1343.
—— 'Asymmetric Market Failure and the Prisoner's Dilemma in Intellectual Property' (1992) 17 *University of Dayton Law Review* 853.
—— 'On Owning Information: Intellectual Property and the Restitutionary Impulse' (1992) 78 *Virginia Law Review* 149.
—— 'A Property Right in Self-Expression: Equality and Individualism in the Natural Law of Intellectual Property' (1993) 102 *Yale Law Journal* 1533.
—— 'On the Economics of Fair Use: Systemic Versus Case by Case Responses to Market Failure' (1997) 8 *Journal of Law and Information Science* 1620.
GORMSEN, LL, 'Why the European Commission's Enforcement Priorities on Article 82 EC Should be Withdrawn' (2010) 31 *European Competition Law Review* 45.
GOWERS, A, *Gowers Review of Intellectual Property (December 2006)*, available at <http://www.official-documents.gov.uk/document/other/0118404830/0118404830.pdf>.
GRAHAM, C, 'All Hail the European Union: Implications of *Microsoft v Commission* on Global Antitrust Enforcement' (2008) 21 *Pacific McGeorge Global Business & Development Law Journal* 285.
GRAHAM, C and SMITH, F (eds), *Competition, Regulation and the New Economy* (Oxford, Hart Publishing, 2004).
GREENE, H, 'Guideline Institutionalisation: The Role of Merger Guidelines in Antitrust Discourse' (2006) 48 *William and Mary Law Review* 771.
GRIFFITHS, J and SUTHERSANEN, U (eds), *Copyright and Free Speech: Comparative and International Analyses* (Oxford, Oxford University Press, 2005).
GRONOW, A, 'Restitution for Breach of Confidence' (1996) 10 *Intellectual Property Journal* 222.
HARGREAVES, I, 'Digital Opportunity: A Review of Intellectual Property and Growth' (2011), available at <www.ipo.gov.uk/ipreview-finalreport.pdf>.

HARRIS, JW (ed), *Property Problems: From Genes to Pension Funds* (London, Kluwer, 1997).
HART, M, 'Getting Back to Basics: Reinventing Patent Law for Economic Efficiency' (1994) 8 *Intellectual Property Journal* 217.
HAY, G, 'The Quiet Revolution in US Antitrust Law' (2007) 26 *University of Queens Law Journal* 27.
HEINER, D, 'Single Conduct Remedies: Perspectives from the Defence' (2009) 75 *Antitrust Law Journal* 871.
HELLSTRÖM, P, Maier-Rigaud, F and Bulst, FW, 'Remedies in European Antitrust Law' (2009) 76 *Antitrust Law Journal* 43.
HESSE, RB, 'Section 2 Remedies and *US v Microsoft*: What is to be Learned?' (2009) 75 *Antitrust Law Journal* 847.
HEYER, K, 'A World of Uncertainty and the Globalisation of Antitrust' (2005) 72 *Antitrust Law Journal* 375.
HOVENCAMP, H, *Hornbook on Federal Antitrust Policy: The Law of Competition and Its Practice*, 2nd edn (Minnesota, West Publishing, 1999).
—— *The Antitrust Experience: Principle and Execution* (Cambridge MA, Harvard University Press, 2005).
—— 'Innovation and the Domain of Competition Policy' (2008) 60 *Alabama Law Review* 103.
—— 'The Harvard and Chicago Schools and the Dominant Firm' in R Pitofsky (ed), *How the Chicago School Overshot the Mark: The Effect of Conservative Economic Analysis on US Antitrust* (New York, Oxford University Press, 2008) 109.
—— 'United States Competition Policy in Crisis: 1890–1955' (2009) 94 *Minnesota Law Review* 311.
—— 'Patent Deception in Standard Setting: The Case for Antitrust Policy' (2010) *University of Iowa Legal Studies Research Paper*, available at <http://ssrn.com/abstract=1138002>.
HOVENCAMP, H, Janis, MD and Lemley, MA, 'Unilateral Refusals to Licence' (2006) 2 *Journal of Comparative Law and Economics* 1.
HURT, RM and SCHUHMAN, RM, 'The Economic Rationale of Copyright' (1966) 56 *American Economic Review* 421.
INDUSTRY COMMISION, *Report on Vehicle and Recreational Marine Craft Repair and Insurance Industries* (Industry Commission, Australia, April 1994).
INTERNATIONAL COMPETITION NETWORK UNILATERAL CONDUCT WORKING GROUP (ICNUCWG), *Report on the Analysis of Refusal to Deal with a Rival under Unilateral Conduct Laws*, presented at the 9th Annual Conference of the ICN, Istanbul, April 2010.
KAHN, J, 'The Origins of the Tort of Appropriation of Identity Reconsidered' (1996) 2 *Legal Theory* 301.
KALLAUGHER, J, 'Existence, Exercise and Exceptional Circumstances for a more Economic Approach to IP Issues under Art 102 TFEU' in S Anderman and A Ezrachi (eds), *Intellectual Property and Competition Law: New Frontiers* (Oxford, Oxford University Press, 2011) 113.
KATZ, ML and SHAPIRO, C, 'Network Externalities, Competition and Compatibility' (1985) 75 *American Economic Review* 424.
—— 'Systems Competition and Network Effects' (1994) 8 *Journal of Economic Perspective* 93.
KITCH, EW, 'The Nature and Function of the Patent System' (1977) 20 *Journal of Law and Economics* 265.

KOBAK, JB, 'Antitrust Treatment of Refusals to License Intellectual Property' (2009) 22 *The Licensing Journal* 1.

KOBAYASHI, BK, 'Spilled Ink or Economic Progress: The Supreme Court Decision in *Illinois Tool v Independent Ink*' (2008) 53 *Antitrust Bulletin* 5.

KOHLER, P and PALMER, N, 'Information as Property' in N Palmer and E McKendrick (eds), *Interests in Goods*, 2nd edn (London, Lloyd's of London Press, 1988) 3.

KORAH, V, 'The Interface Between IP and Antitust: The European Experience' (2002) 69 *Antitrust Law Journal* 801.

KRIER, JE, 'The (Unlikely) Death of Property' (1990) 13 *Harvard Journal of Law and Public Policy* 75.

KRIER, JE and SCHWAB, SJ, 'Property Rules and Liability Rules: The Cathedral in Another Light' (1995) 70 *New York University Law Review* 440.

KU, RSR, SUN, J and FAN, Y, 'Does Copyright Law Promote Creativity?' (2009) 62 *Vanderbilt Law Review* 1669.

LANDES, WM and POSNER, RA, 'An Economic Analysis of Copyright Law' (1989) 18 *Journal of Legal Studies* 325.

—— *The Economic Structure of Intellectual Property Law* (Boston MA, Harvard University Press, 2003).

LANDIS, RC and ROLFE, RS, 'Market Conduct under Section 2: When Is It Anti-Competitive?' in FM Fisher (ed), *Antitrust and Regulation: Essays in Memory of John T McGowan* (Cambridge MA, MIT Press, 1985).

LANG, JT, 'Compulsory Licensing of Intellectual Property in European Antitrust Law' (2002) *Department of Justice/Federal Trade Commission Hearings*, Washington DC.

LANGE, DL, 'At Play in the Fields of the Word: Copyright and the Construction of Authorship in the Post Literate Millennium' (1992) 55 *Law and Contemporary Problems* 139.

LAYNE-FARRAR, A, Padilla, AJ and Schmalensee, R, 'Pricing Patents for Licensing in Standard Setting Organisations: Making Sense of FRAND Commitments' (2006), available at <http://econpapers.repec.org/paper/cprceprdp/6025.htm>.

LEE, M, 'Beyond Safety? The Broadening Scope of Risk Regulation'[2009] 62 *Current Legal Problems* 242.

LEMLEY, MA, 'Beyond Pre-emption: The Law and Policy of Intellectual Property Licensing' (1999) 87 *California Law Review* 113.

—— 'The Economic Irrationality of the Patent Misuse Doctrine' (1990) 78 *California Law Review* 1599.

—— 'A New Balance between IP and Antitrust' (2007) 13 *Southwestern Journal of Law and Trade in the Americas* 1.

LÉVÊQUE, F, 'Innovation, Leveraging and Essential Facilities: Interoperability, Licensing and the EU *Microsoft* Case' in F Lévêque and HA Shelanski (eds), *Antitrust, Patents and Copyright: EU and US Perspectives* (Cheltenham, Edward Elgar, 2005).

LEVINSON, J, Romaine, RC and Salop, SC, 'The Flawed Fragmentation Critique of Structural Remedies in the *Microsoft* Case' (2001) 46 *Antitrust Bulletin* 135.

LIANOS, I, 'Competition Law and Intellectual Property: Is the Property Rights Approach Right?' [2005–2006] *Cambridge Year Book of European Legal Studies* 153.

—— 'Lost in Translation? Towards a Theory of Economic Transplants' (2009) 62 *Current Legal Problems* 346.

—— 'Judging Economists' in I Lianos and I Kokkoris (eds), *The Reform of EC Competition Law* (The Netherlands, Kluwer, 2010) 185.

—— Lichtman, DG, 'The Economics of Innovation: Protecting Unpatentable Goods' (1997) 81 *Minnesota Law Review* 693.
LIEBOWITZ, SJ and MARGOLIS, SE, *Winners, Losers and Microsoft: Competition and Antitrust in High Technology* (Oakland CA, Independent Institute, 1999).
LIM, D, 'Redefining the Rights and Responsibilities of Database Owners under Comparative Law' (2006) 18 *Singapore Academy of Law Journal* 418.
LIM, PH and LONGDIN, L, 'Fresh Lessons for First Movers in Software Copyright Disputes—A Cross Jurisdictional Convergence' (2009) 4 *International Review of Intellectual Property and Competition Law* 374.
LIND, RC and MUYSERT, P, 'Innovation and Competition Policy: Challenges for the New Millennium' (2003) 24 *European Competition Law Review* 87.
LITMAN, JD, 'Copyright Legislation and Technological Change' (1989) 68 *Oregon Law Review* 275.
LONG, C, 'Patent Signals' (2002) 69 *University of Chicago Law Review* 625.
LONGDIN, L, 'The New Zealand Communications Industry: The Worst of Two Worlds' (1995) 1 *Computer and Telecommunications Law Review* 26.
—— 'Computerised Compilations: A Cautionary Tale from New Zealand' (1997) 5 *International Journal of Information Technology Law* 249.
—— 'Fair Dealing and Markets for News: Copyright Law Tiptoes Towards Market Definition' (2001) 7 *New Zealand Business Law Quarterly* 10.
—— 'Parallel Importing Post TRIPS: Convergence and Divergence in Australia and New Zealand' (2001) 50 *International and Comparative Law Quarterly* 54.
LUNNEY, G, 'Re-examining Copyright's Incentives Access Paradigm' (1996) 49 *Vanderbilt Law Review* 483.
MACMILLAN, F (ed), *New Directions in Copyright Law*, vol 6 (Cheltenham, Edward Elgar Publishing, 2007).
MANNE, GA and WEINBERGER, S, 'International Signals: The Political Dimension of International Competition Harmonization' (2009) *SSRN Paper Series*, available at <http://papers.ssrn.com/sol3/papers.cfm?abstract_id=1448223>.
MANNE, GA and WRIGHT, JD, 'Innovation and the Limits of Antitrust' (2010) 6 *Journal of Competition Law and Economics* 153.
MCCARTHY, JT, 'Dilution of a Trademark: European and United States Law Compared' (2004) 94 *Trademark Reporter* 1193.
MCCHESNEY, FS, 'Easterbrook on Errors' (2010) 6 *Journal of Competition Law and Economics* 11.
MCCLURE, DM, 'Trademarks and Unfair Competition: A Critical History of Legal Thought' (1979) 69 *Trademark Reporter* 309.
MCCORMICK, E, 'The Future of Comparative Advertising' (1998) 20 *European Intellectual Property Review* 241.
MCGOWAN, D, 'Innovation, Uncertainty and Stability in Antitrust Law' (2001) 16 *Berkeley Technology Law Journal* 729.
MCKENZIE, R, *Trust on Trial: How the Microsoft Case is Reframing the Rules of Competition* (Cambridge MA, Perseus, 2000).
MCKEOGH, J, *Intellectual Property in Australia*, 2nd edn (Sydney, Butterworths, 1997).
MEINERS, RE and STAAF, RJ, 'Patents, Copyrights and Trademarks: Property or Monopoly?' (1990) 13 *Harvard Journal of Law & Public Policy* 911.
MELAMED, AD, 'Afterword: The Purposes of Antitrust Remedies' (2009) 76 *Antitrust Law Journal* 359.

MERGES, RP, 'Who Owns the Charles River Bridge? Intellectual Property and Competition in the Software Industry' (1999) *UC Berkeley Public Law and Legal Theory Working Paper Series No 15*, available at <http://www.law.berkeley.edu/files/criver.pdf>.

MERGES, RP and NELSON, RR, 'On the Complex Economics of Patent Scope' (1990) 90 *Columbia Law Review* 839.

MESTMÄCKER, EJ and SCHWEITZER, H, *Europäisches Wettbewerbsrecht* (Munich, CH Beck, 2004).

MEURER, MJ, 'Commentary: The Social Costs of Rent Seeking by Intellectual Property Owners' in M Boyer, M Trebilcock and D Vaver (eds), *Competition Policy and Intellectual Property* (Toronto, Irwin Law, 2009) 156.

MIALON, HM and WILLIAMS, M, 'What is a Barrier to Entry?' (2004) 94 *American Economic Review* 461.

MILLER, R, 'Common Law Protection for Products of the Mind: An Idea Whose Time Has Come' (2006) 119 *Harvard Law Review* 703.

MINCKE, W, 'Property: Assets or Power? Objects or Relations as Substrate of Property Rights' in JW Harris (ed), *Property Problems: From Genes to Pension Funds* (London, Kluwer, 1997) 78.

MINDA, G, 'Antitrust Regulatability and the New Digital Economy: A Proposal for Integrating Hard and Soft Regulation' (2001) 46 *Antitrust Bulletin* 439.

NELSON, RR, 'The Simple Economics of Basic Scientific Research' (1959) 67 *Journal of Political Economy* 297.

NETANEL, NW, 'Copyright in a Democratic Civil Society' (1996) 106 *Yale Law Journal* 283.

—— 'Copyright and the First Amendment: What Eldred Misses and Portends' in J Griffiths and U Suthersanen (eds), *Copyright and Free Speech: Comparative and International Analyses* (Oxford University Press, 2005) 151.

NEWBERG, JA, 'Antitrust for the Economy of Ideas: The Logic of Technology Markets' (2000) 14 *Harvard Journal of Law & Technology* 83.

NOLL, R (ed), *Regulatory Policy in the Social Sciences* (Berkeley, University of California Press, 1985).

NORDLANDER, K and SPINKS, S, 'The Interplay of Patenting Strategies and Competition Law in the Pharmaceutical Sector Inquiry' (2009), available at <www.competitionpolicyinternational.com/file/view/5840>.

NORTH, DC, *Institutions, Institutional Change and Economic Performance* (New York, Cambridge University Press, 1990).

ODDI, A, 'The International Patent System and Third World Development: Reality or Myth?' 1987 *Duke Law Journal* 831 (1987).

OLSEN, M, *The Logic of Collective Action* (Boston MA, Harvard University Press, 1971).

ONG, B, 'Anti-competitive Refusals to Grant Copyright Licences: Reflections on the IMS Saga' (2004) 26 *European Intellectual Property Review* 505.

—— 'Building Brick Barricades and Other Barriers to Entry: Abusing a Dominant Position by Refusing to License Intellectual Property Rights' (2005) 26 *European Competition Law Review* 215.

OSWALD, LJ, 'Tarnishment and Blurring under the Federal Trade Mark Dilution Act 1995' (1999) 36 *American Business Law Journal* 255.

OVERD, A and BISHOP, B, 'Essential Facilities: The Rising Tide' (1998) 4 *European Competition Law Review* 183.

PAGE, WH, 'Mandatory Contracting Remedies in the American and European Microsoft Cases' (2009) 75 *Antitrust Law Journal* 787.

PALMER, N, and McKendrick, E (eds), *Interests in Goods*, 2nd edn (London, Lloyd's of London Press, 1988).
PALMER, TG, 'Intellectual Property: A Non Posnerian Law and Economics Approach' (1989) 12 *Hamline Law Review* 261.
PARR, N and HUGHES, M, 'The Relevance of Consumer Brands and Advertising in Competition Inquiries' (1993) 14 *European Competition Law Review* 157.
PENNER, J, 'Hohfeldian Use Rights in Property' in JW Harris (ed), *Property Problems: From Genes to Pension Funds* (London, Kluwer, 1997) 164.
PERITZ, RJR, 'Competition Within Intellectual Property Regimes' in S Anderman and A Ezrachi (eds), *Intellectual Property and Competition Law: New Frontiers* (Oxford, Oxford University Press, 2011).
PETIT, N, 'From Formalism to Effects?—The Commission's Communication on Enforcement Priorities in Applying Article 82 EC' (2009) 32 *World Competition* 485.
PETRUCCI, RA, 'Parallel Trade of Pharmaceutical Products: The ECJ Finally Speaks. Comment on *Glaxo Smith Kline*' (2010) 35 *European Law Review* 275.
PICKERING, CDG, *Trade Marks in Theory and Practice* (Oxford, Hart Publishing, 1998).
PIGOU, AC, *The Economics of Welfare*, 4th edn (London, MacMillan, 1960).
PITOFSKY, R, 'Antitrust and Intellectual Property: Unresolved Issues at the Heart of the New Economy' (2001) 16 *Berkeley Technology Law Journal* 535.
—— *The Essential Facilities Doctrine under United States Antitrust Law*, Paper submitted to the European Commission in support of National Data Corporation in its essential facilities case against IMS (2002), available at <www.ftc.gov/os/comments/intelpropertycomments/pitofskyrobert.pdf>.
—— (ed), *How the Chicago School Overshot the Mark: The Effect of Conservative Economic Analysis on US Antitrust* (New York, Oxford University Press, 2008).
PLANT, A, 'An Economic Theory of Patents' (1934) 1 *Economica* 30.
—— 'The Economic Aspects of Copyright in Books' in A Plant (ed), *Selected Economic Essays and Addresses* (London, Routledge & Kegan Paul, 1974).
POSNER, RA, *Antitrust Law*, 2nd edn (Chicago, University of Chicago Press, 2001).
—— *Economic Analysis of Law*, 6th edn (New York, Aspen, 2003).
—— *A Failure of Capitalism: The Crisis of '08 and the Descent into Depression* (Cambridge MA, Harvard University Press, 2009).
PRIEST, GL, 'What Economists Can Tell Lawyers About Intellectual Property: Comment on Cheung' (1986) 8 *Research in Law and Economics* 19.
RAMELLO, GB, 'Copyright and Antitrust Issues' in W Gordon and R Watt (eds), *The Economics of Copyright* (Cheltenham, Edward Elgar, 2003) 118.
REY, P and TIROLE, J, 'A Primer on Foreclosure' in M Armstrong and RH Porter (eds), *Handbook of Industrial Organisation*, vol III (Oxford, North Holland, 2007).
RICHARDSON, M, 'The High Court of Australia Revisits Misuse of Market Power: Implications for Intellectual Property Right Holders' (2002) 24 *European Intellectual Property Review* 81.
RICHMAN, BD, 'The Antitrust Reputation Mechanisms: Institutional Economics and Concerted Refusals to Deal' (2009) 95 *Virginia Law Review* 325.
RICKETT, CER and AUSTIN, GW (eds), *International Intellectual Property Law and the Common Law World* (Oxford, Hart Publishing, 2000).
RIDYARD, D, 'Essential Facilities and the Obligation to Supply Competitors under UK and EC Competition Law' (1996) 8 *European Competition Law Review* 438.

RITTER, C, 'Refusal to Deal and Essential Facilities: Does Intellectual Property Require Special Deference to Tangible Property?' (2005) 28 *World Competition* 281.

ROACH, K and TREBILCOCK, MJ, 'Private Enforcement of Competition Laws' (1996) 34 *Osgoode Law Hall Law Journal* 461.

ROBERTSON, D, 'Taking Advantage of Market Power in the Modern Economy' (2004) 10 *New Zealand Business Law Quarterly* 26.

ROE, M, 'Chaos and Evolution in Law and Economics' (1996) 109 *Harvard Law Review* 641.

ROSE, C, 'The Comedy of the Commons: Custom, Commerce and Inherently Public Property' (1986) 53 *University of Chicago Law Review* 771.

ROUND, D and SMITH, R, 'Strategic Behaviour and Taking Advantage of Market Power: How to Decide if the Competitive Process is Really Damaged?' (2001) 19 *New Zealand Universities Law Review* 427.

ROWLEY, FA, 'Dynamic Copyright Law Its Problems and a Possible Solution' (1998) 12 *Harvard Journal of Law & Technology* 481.

RUTHERFORD, M, *Institutions in Economics: The Old and the New Institutionalism* (New York, Cambridge University Press, 1994).

SALOP, DC, 'Economic Analysis of Exclusionary Vertical Conduct: Where Chicago has Overshot the Mark' in R Pitofsky (ed), *How the Chicago School Overshot the Mark* (New York, Oxford University Press, 2008) 141.

SCASSA, T, 'Extension of Intellectual Property Rights' in M Boyer, M Trebilcock and D Vaver (eds), *Competition Policy and Intellectual Property* (Toronto, Irwin Law, 2009) 17.

SCHERER, FM, 'Antitrust Efficiency and Progress' (1987) 62 *New York University Law Review* 998.

—— 'Does Antitrust Compromise Technological Efficiency?' (1989) 15 *Eastern Economic Journal* 1.

—— 'Efficiency, Fairness, and the Early Contributions of Economists to the Antitrust Debate' (1990) 29 *Washburn Law Journal* 243.

—— 'The Innovation Lottery' in RC Dreyfuss, DL Zimmerman and H First (eds), *Expanding the Boundaries of Intellectual Property: Innovation Policy for the Knowledge Society* (Oxford, Oxford University Press, 2001).

—— 'The Effect of Conservative Economic Analysis on US Antitrust' in R Pitofsky (ed), *How the Chicago School Overshot the Mark* (Oxford, Oxford University Press, 2008) 30.

SCHMALENSEE, R, 'Ease of Entry: Has the Concept Been Applied Too Readily?' (1987) 56 *Antitrust Law Journal* 41.

—— 'Thoughts on the Chicago Legacy on Antitrust' in R Pitofsky (ed), *How the Chicago School Overshot the Mark* (New York, Oxford University Press, 2008) 11.

SCHOEN, FX, 'Exclusionary Conduct after *Trinko*' (2005) 80 *New York University Law Review* 1625.

SCHUMPETER, JA, *Capitalism, Socialism and Democracy* (London, Unwin University Books, 1942).

SCOTT, P, 'Abuse of Judicial and Administration Processes—An Antitrust Violation?' (1993) 21 *Australian Business Law Review* 389.

SELZNICK, P, 'Focusing Organisational Research on Regulation' in R Noll (ed), *Regulatory Policy in the Social Sciences* (Berkeley, University of California Press, 1985).

SEMERARO, S, 'Property's End: Why Competition Law Should Limit the Right of Publicity' (2011) 43 *Connecticut Law Review* 753.

SHELANSKI, HA, 'Unilateral Refusals to Deal in Intellectual and Other Property' (2009) 76 *Antitrust Law Journal* 369.
SIDAK, JG, 'Abolishing the Price Squeeze as a Theory of Antitrust Liability' (2008) 4 *Journal of Competition Law & Economics* 279.
STERK, SE, 'Rhetoric and Reality in Copyright Law' (1996) 94 *Michigan Law Review* 1205.
STIGLER, G, '*United States v Loews Inc*: A Note on Block Booking' (1963) *Supreme Court Review* 152.
—— *The Organisation of Industry* (Chicago, University of Chicago Press, 1968).
STROTHERS, C, 'Refusal to Supply as an Abuse of Dominant Position: Essential Facilities in the European Union' (2001) 22 *European Competition Law Review* 256.
—— 'The End of Exclusivity? Abuse of IPRs in the EU' (2002) 24 *European Intellectual Property Review* 86.
SULLIVAN, L, 'Economics and More Humanistic Disciplines: What are the Sources of Wisdom for Antitrust?' (1984) 125 *University of Pennsylvania Law Review* 1214.
TACKABERRY, P, 'Look What They Have Done to My Song Ma: The Songwriter's Moral Right of Integrity in Canada and the United States' (1989) 10 *European Intellectual Property Review* 356.
TAYLOR, CT and SILBERSTON, ZA, *The Economic Impact of the Patent System: A Study of the British Experience* (London, Cambridge University Press, 1973).
TEECE, D and COLEMAN, M, 'Meaning of Monopoly' (1998) 43 *Antitrust Bulletin* 801.
TEECE, D and SHERRY, EF, 'Standards Setting and Antitrust' (2003) 87 *Minnesota Law Review* 1913.
TEMPLE LANG, J, 'Defining Legitimate Competition: Companies' Duties to Supply Competitors and Access to Essential Facilities' (1994) 18 *Fordham International Law Journal* 437.
TEYERMAN, B, 'The Economic Rationale for Copyright Protection for Published Books: A Reply to Professor Beyer' (1971) 18 *University of California Law Review* 1100.
THAMBISSETT, S, 'Property as Credence Goods' (2007) 27 *Oxford Journal of Legal Studies* 707.
THOMAS, JR, 'New Challenges for the Law of Patents' in CER Rickett and GW Austin (eds), *Intellectual Property in the Common Law World* (Oxford, Hart Publishing, 1999) 165.
—— 'Of Proprietary Rights and Personal Liberties: Constitutional Responses to Post Industrial Patenting' in P Drahos (ed), *Death of Patents* (Witney, QMC and Lawtext, 2005) 110.
TREBILCOCK, M, Winter, RA, Collins, P and Iacobucci, EM, *The Law and Economics of Canadian Competition Policy* (Toronto, University of Toronto, 2002).
TROY, DE, 'Unclogging the Bottleneck: A New Essential Facilities Doctrine' (1983) 83 *Columbia Law Review* 441.
TURNEY, J, 'Defining the Limits of the EU Essential Facilities Doctrine on Intellectual Property Rights: The Primacy of Securing Optimal Innovation' (2005) 3 *Northwestern Journal of Technology & Intellectual Property* 179.
US ANTITRUST MODERNIZATION COMMISSION, *Report and Recommendations* (April 2007), available at <http://govinfo.library.unt.edu/amc/report_recommendation/toc.htm>.
US DEPARTMENT OF JUSTICE and THE FEDERAL TRADE DIVISION, *Antitrust Guidelines for the Licensing of Intellectual Property* (6 April 1995) available at http://www.ftc.gov/bc/0558.pdf.

—— Panel at the Hearing on Competition and Intellectual Property Law and Policy in the Knowledge-Based Economy (22 May 2002), available at <www.ftc.gov/opp/intellect/020522trans.pdf>.

US DEPARTMENT OF JUSTICE ANTITRUST DIVISION, *Antitrust Guide for International Operations* (Antitrust & Trade Regulation Report BNA No 799, Jan–June 1997).

—— *Competition and Monopoly: Single-Firm Conduct under Section 2 of the Sherman Act* (2008), available at <www.justice.gov/atr/public/reports/236681.pdf>.

VAN DEN BERGH, RJ and CAMESASCA, PD, *European Competition Law and Economics: A Comparative Perspective*, 2nd edn (London, Sweet & Maxwell, 2006).

VAN MELLE, A, 'Facing the Music: Liability for Musical Plagiarism in Contemporary Popular Music' [1997] *New Zealand Intellectual Property Law Journal* 160.

—— 'Refusals to License Intellectual Property Rights: The Impact of RTE v EC Commission (Magill) on Australian and New Zealand Competition Law' (1997) 25 *Australian Business Law Review* 4.

VAN ROOIJEN, A, 'The Role of Investments in Refusals to Deal' (2008) 31 *World Competition* 63.

VAN ROY, Y, 'Taking Advantage of Market Power: Should New Zealand Adopt the Approach of the High Court of Australia?' (2005) 11 *New Zealand Business Law Quarterly* 319.

VAVER, D, *Intellectual Property Law* (Ontario, Irwin Law, 1997).

VELJANOVSKI, CG, 'EC Antitrust in the New Economy: Is the European Commissioner's View of the Network Economy Right?' (2001) 22 *European Competition Law Review* 115.

—— 'Competition Law Issues in the Computer Industry: An Economist's Perspective' (2003) 3 *Queensland University of Technology Law and Justice Journal* 48.

VON WEIZSACKER, C, 'A Welfare Analysis of Barriers to Entry' (1980) 11 *Bell Journal of Economics* 399.

WALDRON, J, 'From Authors to Copiers: Individual Rights and Social Values in Intellectual Property' (1993) 68 *Chicago Kent Law Review* 841.

WALKER, S, 'Refusals to Deal Under Canada's Competition Act: Paper presented to the American Bar Association Panel (Washington, 7 April)' (2011), available at <http://www.fmc-law.com/Publications/0411_Walker_Sandy_Refusals_To_Deal_Under_Canada_Competition_Act.aspx>.

WALLER, SW, 'Past, Present and Future of Monopolisation Remedies' (2009) 76 *Antitrust Law Journal* 11.

WEINRIB, EJ, 'Two Conceptions of Remedies' in CER Rickett (ed), *Justifying Private Law Remedies* (Oxford, Hart Publishing, 2008) 3.

WEISS, LW, 'The Structure–Conduct Performance Paradigm and Antitrust' (1969) 127 *University of Pennsylvania Law Review* 1104.

WERDEN, GJ, 'Remedies for Exclusionary Conduct Should Preserve the Competitive Process' (2009) 76 *Antitrust Law Journal* 65.

WHINSTON, MD, 'Tying, Foreclosure and Exclusion' (1990) 80 *American Economic Review* 837.

WITT, AC, 'The Commission's Guidance Paper On Abusive Exclusionary Conduct: More Radical Than It Appears?' (2010) 35 *European Law Review* 214.

WONG, S, 'Competition Act Implications for the Licensing of Intellectual Property Rights: 2002 Update', presented at the *Conference on Intellectual Property License Agreements*, Canadian Institute, at Vancouver, 24–25 June 2002.

WORTHINGTON, S, 'Art, Law and Creativity' (2009) 68 *Current Legal Problems* 168.

(**Note:** All hyperlinks checked and functioning as at 20 June 2011.)

Index

Abuse of market power
  Australia
    anti-competitive conduct, 184, 187
    counterfactual test, 184–6, 202
    economic analysis, 185, 186
    hostile intent, 184
    legitimate business reason, 187, 188
    market power, 184, 189, 203
    material facilitation test, 186, 189
    property defence, 202–5
    purpose test, 187
    refusal to licence, 181, 182, 197–200, 203–5
    unfair abuse, 183–7, 189
  Canada
    anti-competitive behaviour, 210, 217
    barriers to entry, 217
    dominant undertakings, 217
    intellectual property rights, 210, 218–22
    margin squeeze, 217
    negative effect on competition, 217
    pre-emption of scarce facilities, 217
    prevention of competition, 217
    refusal to licence, 219–22
    statutory provisions, 217
    trade mark licences, 219–23
    trade secrets, 218
    tying, 219, 220, 222
  meaning, 5
  New Zealand
    anti-competitive behaviour, 189–91, 195
    comparative exercise, 190–2
    counterfactual test, 190–2, 195
    economic analysis, 192
    efficient components pricing rule, 193–5
    intellectual property rights, 205
    market power, 190
    refusal to licence, 181, 182, 196
    telecommunications market, 190–4, 207, 208
    unilateral exercise of market power, 197
Anti-competitive intent
  competition enforcement, 57
  evidence, 57, 58
  guide to outcome, 57
  inferred intent, 57
  malign intent, 57
  statutory liability, 57
Anti-competitive leveraging
  see **Leveraging**
Anti-competitive outcome
  economic effect, 57
  inculpatory, 57
  malign intent, 57
  proscribed purposes, 57
  refusal to licence, 41
Anti-trust law
  meaning, 5
Australia
  abuse of market power
    anti-competitive conduct, 184, 187
    counterfactual test, 184–6, 202
    economic analysis, 185, 186
    hostile intent, 184
    legitimate business reason, 187, 188
    market power, 184, 189, 203
    material facilitation test, 186, 189
    property defence, 202–5
    purpose test, 187
    refusal to licence, 181, 182, 197–200, 203–5
    unfair abuse, 183–7, 189
  anti-competitive behaviour
    abuse of market power, 184, 187
    anti-competitive leveraging, 43
    breach of confidence, 208, 209
    proof and presumption, 40
    restraint of trade, 208
  competition law
  connection issue, 183
    eliminating competition, 183
    excessive pricing, 183
    restricting market entry, 183
    inferred conduct, 183
    intervention, 84
    legislation, 181–9
    margin squeeze, 183
    preventing competition, 183
    purpose issue, 183, 187
    threshold issue, 183
  competition regime
    abuse of market power, 181–3
    economic elements, 26, 27
    per se rules, 26
    rule of reason, 26
  compulsory licensing, 92
  intellectual property
    anti-competitive agreements, 196
    assignment, 196
    competition legislation, 196
    licences, 196
    refusal to licence, 203, 204
    unilateral exercise of market power, 197, 202, 203

intellectual property rights
  copyright, 198–201
  database rights, 199
  enforcement, 84
  exclusive dealing, 197
  parallel imports, 119, 201
  protection, 196
  scope of grant, 196
  tying, 197
legal/economic monopolies
  after-markets, 202
  barriers to entry, 201
  consumer perceptions, 202
  copyright protection, 201
  economic analysis, 202
  intellectual property protection, 201
  legitimate business reason, 202
  parallel imports, 119, 201
refusal to licence
  absence of legislation, 196, 197
  abuse of market power, 181, 182, 197–200, 203–5
  access equals confiscation, 204
  accumulated rights, 197, 198
  conditional refusals, 198, 199
  constructive refusal, 197
  copyright infringement, 198–200
  database rights, 199
  intellectual property, 203, 204
  judicial approach, 197
  multiple/conflicting purposes, 199, 200
  multiple markets, 199
  primary/secondary markets, 203
remedies
  civil pecuniary remedies, 74
  structural remedies, 64

Barriers to entry
behavioural barriers, 100
competitive scrutiny, 100, 101
deterrent effect, 99, 100
economic approach
  categories/categorisation, 59, 98, 99
  cost equality arguments, 59, 60
  measurement, 59
  quantifiers, 59, 60, 98, 99
entry costs, 58
importance, 58
inefficient behaviour, 58
innovative efficiency, 100
intellectual property rights
  defeating/by passing, 98, 99
  litigation costs, 98, 99
  strong case, 99–101
  weak case, 98, 99
market power, 60
  see also **Market power**
market segmentation, 99

new markets, 99
simultaneous entry, 100
strategic barriers, 60
structural barriers, 60, 100
unique costs/new market entrants, 59
Bibliography, 240–55
Breach of confidence
abuse of rights, 94, 95
intellectual property rights, 86
public interest defence, 94, 95

Canada
abuse of market power
  anti-competitive behaviour, 210, 217
  barriers to entry, 217
  dominant undertakings, 217
  intellectual property rights, 210, 218–22
  margin squeeze, 217
  negative effect on competition, 217
  pre-emption of scarce facilities, 217
  prevention of competition, 217
  refusal to licence, 219–22
  statutory provisions, 217
  trade mark licences, 219–23
  trade secrets, 218
  tying, 219, 220, 222
anti-competitive behaviour
  abuse of dominant position, 210, 211
  abuse of market power, 210, 217
  adverse effect on competition, 223, 228
  adverse effect on innovation, 245, 228
  civil reviewable practice, 210
  criminal behaviour, 210
  prevention of competition, 217
  refusal to licence, 210
  statutory provisions, 210
civil pecuniary remedies, 74
competition law
  abuse of dominant position, 210, 211
  abuse of market power, 210
  adverse effect on competition, 223, 228
  adverse effect on innovation, 224, 228
  enforcement policy, 217
  enforcement powers, 210, 211
  essential facilities, 210
  refusal to deal, 210, 211
  refusal to licence, 210, 211
competition policy, 53
competition regime
  economic elements, 26, 27
  per se rules, 26
  rule of reason, 26
compulsory licensing
  patent rights, 231, 232
  special remedy, 231
copyright
  electronic works, 218
  fair use, 218

licences, 216
  paracopyright provisions, 218
  technological protection measures, 218, 224
Draft Enforcement Guidelines on Abuse of Dominance, 229–31
  see also **Draft Enforcement Guidelines on Abuse of Dominance (2009)**
efficiency defence, 53
Intellectual Property Enforcement Guidelines, 223, 227–9
  see also **Intellectual Property Enforcement Guidelines (2000)**
intellectual property rights
  abuse of market power, 210, 218–22
  adverse effect on competition, 223, 228
  adverse effect on innovation, 224, 228
  copyright, 218
  effective enforcement, 224, 225
  initiation of proceedings, 224
  market power, 223
  prohibited activity, 223
  refusal to licence, 224
  remedial orders, 223, 228
  statutory provisions, 223, 224
  trade marks, 219–23
  trade secrets, 218, 224
patent assignments
  anti-competitive motives, 226
  market power, 226, 227
  restraint of competition, 225, 226
  right to assign, 227
patent rights/abuse, 231, 232
refusal to deal
  abuse of market power, 219–22
  adverse effect on competition, 212–5
  anti-competitive intent, 217
  copyright licences, 216
  inability to obtain adequate supply, 211, 212
  insufficient competition, 212, 213
  intellectual property considerations, 216
  justification, 212–4
  market definition, 215
  market power, 215
  meeting trade terms, 212, 216
  purpose of refusal, 212, 214
  regulatory intervention, 216
  statutory enforcement, 211, 212
  statutory provisions, 211
  submarkets, 215

Coerced licensing
  confiscation, 15, 16
  design laws, 92, 93
  freedom of contract, 13, 14
  hierarchy of rights, 16, 96
  innovation/creativity, 18–20, 238, 239

ongoing supervision, 67
patents, 92, 93
presumption against coerced licensing
  evidentiary rule, 14
  remedial rule, 14, 15
regulatory intervention, 238, 239
  see also **Regulatory intervention**
remedial issues, 61, 65, 67
Competition cases
fact/law distinction, 36, 37, 39, 40
  see also **Fact/law distinction**
proof and presumption, 36–40
  see also **Proof and presumption**
Competition enforcement
anti-competitive intent, 57
  see also **Anti-competitive intent**
enforcement policy, 25
investment displacement theory, 6
regulatory neutrality, 6, 7
under/over-regulation, 17, 23, 32, 76
Competition law
bright-line rules, 7
conduct-based approach, 58
conflict of laws, 21
economic influences, 8, 21
  see also **Economic analysis**
European Union
  see **European Union**
evidentiary uncertainty, 34
failure to intervene, 32
false negatives, 32, 33
false positives, 32, 33
harmonisation, 21, 239
high-technology markets, 8
issues of scale, 32, 33
market outcomes, 10
market power, 32
  see also **Market power**
meaning, 5
private law rights, 7
protection of competitive process, 10
regulatory outcomes, 9
regulatory perfection, 34
remedies, 33
  see also **Remedies**
rule of reason, 7, 9
  see also **Rule of reason**
statutory interpretation, 20
strict liability, 9
substance/form, 7
super dominance, 32
transaction costs, 7
under-regulation/over-regulation, 17, 23, 32
Competition policy
bright-line rules, 23
consumer welfare, 52–4, 78
  see also **Consumer welfare**
economic efficiency, 52, 53

economic rationality, 23
efficiency defence, 53
empiricist approach, 23
fluctuations, 76
formalist approach, 23
freedom of contract, 170
globalisation, 20–2
intellectual property rights, 92, 233
justiciability, 23
limits, 234
non-economic values, 24
over-protection, 110
process of competition, 77
prohibited activity, 23
regulatory responses, 23
special rules/special markets, 48
transaction costs, 23
under-regulation/over-regulation, 23

Competition regimes
action/inaction analysis, 147, 238
anti-competitive behaviour, 238
Australia, 26, 27
　see also **Australia**
Canada, 26, 27
　see also **Canada**
economic analysis, 24
　see also **Economic analysis**
enforcement policy, 25
erosion of boundaries, 238
European Union, 25
　see also **European Union**
harmonisation, 239
internally-referenced categories, 238
market power, 238
　see also **Market power**
New Zealand, 26, 27
　see also **New Zealand**

Competition rules
anti-competitive intent, 36
anti-competitive outcomes, 36
collective misconduct, 36
economic analysis, 36
　see also **Economic analysis**
economic input, 35
evidentiary rules, 36
intellectual property rights, 92
legal taxonomies, 35
liability-creating rules, 35
liability-denying rules, 35
per se rules, 35
rule of reason, 35
　see also **Rule of reason**
substantive rules, 36
unilateral acts/omissions, 36

Compulsory licensing
　see **Coerced licensing**

Computer software
copyright/protection, 111, 116, 146

software products
　interoperability, 51, 52
　spare parts, 141

Conflict of laws
applicable law, 21
lex fori, 21

Consumer welfare
competition policy 52–4, 78
consumer gain, 54, 55
consumer harm, 56
consumer surplus, 55, 56
economic definitions, 52, 54, 55
efficiency
　objectives, 55
　productive/innovative efficiency, 55
European Union, 26
intermediate/downstream producers, 56
jurisdictional distinctions, 56
lower prices, 55
producer benefit, 55, 56
producer surplus, 55
protection, 78
total surplus, 55

Copyright
collective copyright licensing, 93
computer software, 111, 146
copyright misuse, 94, 144–7
exemptions, 91
fair dealing, 82, 91
fair use rules, 91, 146
idea/expression dichotomy, 111, 112, 116
obtained by unlawful means, 144
originality thresholds, 115
protection
　access to protected material, 120
　adaptations, 116, 119
　anti-competitive behaviour, 91
　compilations, 116
　computer software, 116
　degree of protection, 97, 98
　derivative works, 116, 119
　duration, 117, 118
　evidentiary presumptions, 115
　exhaustion of rights, 119, 120
　gaming opportunities, 115
　geographical extent, 117
　indirect copying, 115
　infringement net, 115, 116
　new markets, 117
　paracopyright protection, 91, 146
　rights to view, 120
　statutory protection, 83
　subconscious copying, 115
　substantial similarity, 115
refusal to licence, 141–3
right to exclude, 143, 144
technological protection measures, 91, 146

INDEX 261

see also Technological protection measures
Creativity
see Innovation and creativity

Delimiting rights
compulsory licensing, 92, 93
question of law, 41
Design laws
design right, 86, 88
Draft Enforcement Guidelines on Abuse of Dominance (2009)
access to facility/service, 229
market power, 230, 231
prevention of competition, 231
refusal to licence
constructive denial, 230
outright denial, 230
vertically-integrated firms, 230, 231

Economic analysis
absorbing economics, 31
competition rules, 36
see also Competition rules
content of legal rules, 31
deductive reasoning, 27
false negatives, 32, 33
false positives, 32, 33
forensic use of models, 27, 28
indeterminate/discordant economics
empirical deficit, 27, 28, 233, 238, 239
judicial response, 29–31
lack of consensus, 28
proof and presumption, 38, 39
standard capture/setting, 51
inductive reasoning, 27
innovation/creativity, 101, 102, 104
innovative efficiency, 28
intellectual property rights, 77–9
judicial deference
deference to business expertise, 30
deference to regulator, 29, 30, 31
judicial thought processes, 31
objective justification, 30
standard of proof, 30
legitimate business reason, 30
reversibility issue, 33
rule of reason, 27
see also Rule of reason
uneven reception, 24
Economic efficiency
competition policy, 52, 53
economic definitions, 52
European Union, 26
market behaviour, 53
statutory recognition, 53
Economics of rights expansion
comparative studies, 103

cross-border studies, 104
duration of protection, 104
empirical studies, 103, 104
entrenched rights, 103
innovation, 103
investment, 103
negative arguments, 104, 105
Economics of rights justification
copying/imitation, 101
economic analysis, 101
general property right, 102
innovative/creative goods, 101, 102
long-term efficiencies, 101
short-term adverse effects, 101
third-party capture, 102
under-production, 102
Efficiency
see also Economic efficiency
allocative efficiency, 53, 54, 117
efficiency gains, 54
innovative efficiency, 20, 28, 53, 54, 78, 79, 100, 117, 118, 238, 239
productive efficiency, 53
Enforcement
see Competition enforcement
Essential facilities doctrine (EU)
Colgate principle (right to deal), 154
competitive pricing, 179
concept, 153, 154
economic factors, 154
economic justification, 236
exceptionality tests, 155
facility/infrastructure, 154, 155
intellectual property rights, 155, 166
judicial approach, 154–6
recognition, 153, 154
right to refuse, 236
situation-dependent rules, 156
Essential facilities doctrine (US)
abolition/abandonment, 134, 236
anti-competitive intent, 136, 137, 149
Colgate principle (right to deal), 131, 132, 135
constructive refusal, 130, 137
continued dealing obligation, 133, 135
cross-market leveraging, 129
denial of access, 129–31
essential facility concept, 128–30, 236
expansion/refinement, 127–31
fair dealing, 132–4
indispensability, 127
intellectual property, 130, 131, 133, 135, 137
judicial limitations, 136
judicial responses, 134–6, 148
legitimate reason for refusal, 134, 137
non-discriminatory access, 130
origins, 126, 127, 236
parallel regulatory structure, 134

public interest, 127
refusal to deal, 128, 132, 133, 236
requirements
  control of essential facility, 129, 130
  denial of use, 129, 130
  feasibility of providing access, 129
  inability to duplicate essential facility, 129, 130
  shared facilities, 132, 133, 136
  two market factor, 129, 130
  unilateral refusal, 128, 132
European Commission Guidance (Abusive Exclusionary Conduct)
  anti-competitive foreclosure, 178
  constructive refusal, 178
  consumer harm, 177, 178
  disruption of previous supply, 177
  effects-based approach, 177, 178, 180
  elimination of competition, 177
  excessive pricing, 178, 179
  justification for refusal, 178
  necessary product/service, 177
  prior case law, 177
  refusal to licence, 176, 177
  soft law, 150–2, 180
  transparency, 178
  verification of competitive harm, 178
European Union
  abuse of dominant position
    Article 102 (TFEU), 150, 151, 154, 156, 159, 161–4, 166, 169, 173, 174, 180
    exceptional circumstances, 162–4
    intellectual property rights, 152, 153, 161
    refusal to licence, 168–70
  competition cases
    fact/law distinction, 36
    proof and presumptions, 40
    presumption of legality, 175, 180
  competition law
    abuse of dominant position, 150, 151, 154, 156, 159, 161–4, 166, 169, 173, 174, 180
    abusive unilateral conduct, 150, 151, 152
    anti-competitive behaviour, 25, 150
    Commission Guidance, 150–2, 176–80
    consumer choice, 175
    consumer welfare, 26
    economic efficiency, 26
    economic influences, 25, 26
    effects-based approach, 26
    elimination of competition, 165, 168, 169
    judicial deference, 151
    market power, 156
    refusal to deal, 150, 152
    refusal to licence, 150
  competition regime, 25
  economic analysis, 152
    see also **Economic analysis**

economic methodology, 152, 179
essential facilities doctrine, 153–6, 166, 179
  see also **Essential facilities doctrine (EU)**
exceptional circumstances test
  abuse of dominant position, 162–4
  basis, 153
  elimination/foreclosure of competition, 165, 169
  emergence
  exceptional circumstances, 163, 164
  hierarchy of rights, 174
  indispensability, 164, 165, 169, 171
  intellectual property rights, 161
  judicial refinement, 163–5
  new features test, 173
  new product requirement, 163–5, 169, 172, 173
  potential consumer demand, 162–4
  scope of exception, 163
  secondary/primary markets, 164, 165, 172
information asymmetries, 179
intellectual property rights
  abuse of dominant position, 152, 153, 161
  complex technology, 175
  copyright material, 162–4
  databases, 115
  exceptionality test, 161
  existence/exercise, 162
  interoperable systems, 170–4
leveraging
  anti-competitive leveraging, 46
  cross-market leveraging, 156, 157
  market power, 157
  secondary markets, 157
  viable commercial strategy, 156
refusal to licence/supply
  abuse of dominant position, 168, 169, 170
  abusive conduct, 161, 162, 166
  anti-competitive behaviour, 158, 159
  anti-competitive intent, 158
  competition law defence, 166
  consumer benefit, 159
  consumer demand, 162–4
  continued supply, 157, 159
  copyright material, 162–4
  denial of access, 171
  disruption of previous level of supply, 171
  dominant undertakings, 170
  duty to supply, 159
  efficiency considerations, 159
  elimination of competition, 165, 168, 169
  indispensible service, 160
  intangibles, 160, 161, 176
  interoperable systems, 170–4
  justification, 158–60, 164, 168, 173
  limiting production, 163
  limiting technical development, 173
  market power, 170, 171

INDEX   263

national treatment, 166, 167, 168
parallel trade, 158
  spare parts, 158, 162
  tangibles, 159, 160, 176
  unilateral refusals, 166, 167
structural remedies, 64
supervisory structures, 69, 175, 180
Exceptional circumstances test
  abuse of dominant position, 162–4
  basis, 153
  elimination/foreclosure of competition, 165, 169
  emergence
  exceptional circumstances, 163, 164
  hierarchy of rights, 174
  indispensability, 164, 165, 169, 171
  intellectual property rights, 161
  judicial refinement, 163–5
  new features test, 173
  new product requirement, 163–5, 169, 172, 173
  potential consumer demand, 162–4
  scope of exception, 163
  secondary/primary markets, 164, 165, 172

Fact/law distinction
  civil law, 36
  common law, 36
  European Union, 36
  judicial law-making, 37
  presumptions, 36, 37, 39, 40
  private law rights, 36
  United States of America, 36
Fair dealing
  copyright usage, 82
  essential facilities doctrine, 132–4
  protection of information, 89, 90, 113
Fair, reasonable and non-discriminatory terms (FRAND)
  licensing, 68, 69
Freedom of contract
  competition policy, 170
  presumption against coerced licensing, 14
  see also **Coerced licensing**

Globalisation
  competition policy, 20–2
  effects, 121
  intellectual property protection, 121

Hierarchy of rights
  coerced licensing, 16, 96
  see also **Coerced licensing**
  degree of protection, 16, 17
  drawbacks, 236, 237
  intellectual property rights, 96, 97
  network systems, 17

Innovation and creativity
  barriers to entry, 100
  see also **Barriers to entry**
  coerced licensing, 18–20, 238, 239
  see also **Coerced licensing**
  competition enforcement, 18, 19
  competitors, 78
  economic analysis, 101, 102, 104
  see also **Economic analysis**
  efficiency, 20, 28
  follow-on innovation, 116, 117
  incentives, 118
  innovative efficiency, 20, 28, 53, 54, 78, 79, 100, 117, 118, 238, 239
  intellectual property rights, 77, 78, 84
  protection, 20, 116
  regulatory intervention, 18, 19
Intellectual property
  boundaries, 82, 90, 105, 110
  competition policy/interface, 233
  competition rules, 92
  digital anarchists, 109
  economic analysis, 77–9, 234, 235
  see also **Economic analysis**
  economic input, 76, 77, 101
  economics of rights expansion
  see **Economics of rights expansion**
  economics of rights justification
  see **Economics of rights justification**
  electronic dissemination
  blogosphere, 109
  cybertopia, 109
  internet, 109
  exercise of powers/rights, 235
  expansion, 76
  expansionist thinking, 105–8
  fair dealing, 82, 89, 90, 113
  game theory, 109
  incentive theory, 106, 108
  independent discovery defence, 82
  inexhaustible right, 119
  innovation/creativity, 84, 101, 102, 104, 106, 107, 116, 117
  innovative efficiency, 20, 28, 53, 54, 78, 79, 100, 117, 118
  internal competition controls
  see **Internal competition controls**
  interoperability
  see **Interoperability**
  investment, 103, 106, 109
  investment displacement analysis, 109, 110
  juristic analysis, 83
  law reform, 233
  market power, 76, 109
  see also **Market power**
  monopolies
    economic monopolies, 84, 85

legal monopolies, 84, 85
new technologies, 76
originality threshold, 82
ownership, 10, 11, 76, 78, 84
privilege, 76
property rights
  see **Intellectual property rights**
protection
  allocative efficiency, 117
  arbitrary extensions, 118
  choice of law, 121
  commercial morality, 113
  copyright, 97, 98
  databases, 115
  degree/extent, 77, 97
  economic rationale, 98
  effort/investment expended, 113, 114
  exhaustion of rights, 119, 120
  expansion, 101, 105–8
  extended terms, 118, 119
  fair dealing, 82, 89, 90, 113
  fashion design, 97
  fixed terms, 118
  free-riding, 114
  globalisation, 121
  harmonisation, 121
  justification, 97
  liability rules, 102
  lobbying, 117, 118
  mere possession of information, 114
  new markets, 117
  over-protection, 97, 121
  parallel imports, 119, 120
  pharmaceuticals, 97
  pirated copies, 119
  property rights, 102
  protectable ideas, 111
  purchaser's rights, 119
  regulated privilege, 102
  scope, 234
  State-directed investment, 115
  temporal boundaries, 117, 118
  territoriality principle, 121
  transaction costs, 98
  value equals property, 114
public choice theory, 109, 110
public interest considerations, 82
regulatory intervention, 235
  see also **Regulatory intervention**
regulatory neutrality, 76
social constraints, 82
terminology
  monopoly, 79
  property, 79, 80
  regulation, 79, 80
trade agreements, 76
under/over-protection, 76

Intellectual Property Enforcement Guidelines (2000)
adverse effect on competition, 228
adverse effect on innovation, 228
aid to interpretation, 228
dominant undertakings, 228
enforcement action, 228
market dominance, 229
market power, 229
patent trolling, 229
prevention of competition, 228, 229
protected technology, 229
refusal to licence, 229
special remedy, 228, 229
Intellectual property rights
see also **Intellectual property**
absolute right, 10, 11
anti-competitive behaviour, 235
anti-competitive intent, 88
boundaries between rights, 90
breach of confidence, 86
competition policy, 92
competition values
  conflict, 2
  interaction, 1
consumption, 82
copyright, 82, 83, 86, 88, 97, 98
  see also **Copyright**
creators, 77–9
degree of protection, 34
design right, 86, 88
dispersed contributors, 79
economic analysis, 77–9, 234
  see also **Economic analysis**
economics-based approach, 235
enforcement, 234
exercise of powers/rights, 235
exploitation, 1, 107
fair dealing, 82, 89, 90
fair trading, 86
hierarchy of rights, 96, 97
immunity/privilege for right-holders, 87
inexhaustible right, 119
industry standard, 50, 51
innovation/creativity, 88
innovative efficiency, 20, 28, 53, 54, 78, 79, 100, 117, 118
inventors, 77–9
jurisdictional differences, 90
legal monopoly, 12
meaning, 4
misaligned rights, 90
monopoly rents, 106
nature/characteristics
  anti-competitive substance, 87
  judge-made rules, 85
  juristic term, 85, 86
  obligation/property divide, 86, 87

registration-based rights, 86, 87
self-constituting rights, 86, 87
statutory rights, 85
underlying rationales, 85
vulnerability to regulation, 85
ownership, 10, 11, 76, 78, 84
passing off, 86
patents, 86, 88
  see also **Patents**
pharmaceuticals, 97
private rights, 83
property rights
  allocation, 81
  assignment, 81
  bundle of rights, 80
  categorisation, 81
  competition enforcement, 81
  distinctions, 82, 83
  exclusivity, 81
  justifications, 82
  meanings/context, 80
  natural rights, 82
  property status, 11
  recognition/creation, 81
  regulation, 83, 84
  severability, 81
  tangible property, 82
proprietary/non-proprietary rules, 4
public law objectives, 83
regulatory intervention, 235
  see also **Regulatory intervention**
reputational rules, 88, 89
  see also **Reputational rules**
scope of grant, 12, 13, 46, 47, 235
  see also **Scope of grant principle**
simultaneous enjoyment, 82, 83
social value, 79
standard capture, 50, 51
State registration, 86
technological protection measures
  see **Technological protection measures**
trade marks, 86, 87
trade secrets, 82, 87
  see also **Trade secrets**
unfair competition, 86
Internal competition controls
  abuse of rights doctrines
    breach of confidence, 94
    copyright misuse, 94
    patent abuse, 93, 94
    principles of construction, 93
    public interest defence, 94, 95
    undesirable development, 95
    United States of America, 93, 95
  collective copyright licensing, 93
  competition values, 234
  compulsory licensing, 92, 93
    see also **Coerced licensing**

core concept, 95, 110
economic rationale, 95
effects, 96
erosion, 96, 110
fair use, 234
inadequacy, 234
over-protection, 234
public interest defences, 234
self-correcting mechanisms, 96
Interoperability
industry standard, 50
mandated interoperability, 51, 52
partial interoperability, 52
reverse engineering exception, 51, 52
software products, 51, 52
technological protection measures, 52
  see also **Technological protection measures**
Investment displacement theory
competition enforcement, 6
intellectual property, 109, 110

Leveraging
anti-competitive leveraging, 43
Australia, 43
condition precedent/regulatory intervention, 46
cross-market leveraging, 43, 129
European Union
  anti-competitive leveraging, 46
  cross-market leveraging, 156, 157
  market power, 157
  secondary markets, 157
  viable commercial strategy, 156
evidential issues, 45
forensic gaming, 46
intellectual property rights, 45
judicial recognition, 45
monopoly profits theory, 43–5
New Zealand, 43
prescribed behaviour, 43
scope of grant principle, 46, 47
  see also **Scope of grant principle**
self-destructive outcomes, 44
vertical leverage, 43, 44
Licensing
  see also **Coerced licensing**
fair, reasonable and non-discriminatory terms (FRAND), 68, 69
reasonable and non-discriminatory terms (RAND), 67, 69

Market power
barriers to entry, 60
  see also **Barriers to entry**
concentrations, 109
intellectual property, 76, 109, 140
leveraging, 157

see also **Leveraging**
markets
  role of markets, 40, 41, 43, 47, 49, 50
  special rules/special markets, 49
patents, 140, 142, 144
refusal to licence, 6, 170, 171
spare parts, 140

Markets
anti-competitive behaviour, 42
anti-competitive outcomes, 41
downstream market, 43
geographic markets, 41
leveraging, 43–7
  see also **Leveraging**
market definition, 40, 41
market power, 40, 41, 43, 47, 49, 50
  see also **Market power**
product markets, 41
rights
  multiple rights/markets, 42, 43
  right/market confusion, 41, 42
  separate/single markets, 42
special rules/special markets
  anti-trust analysis, 50
  competition policy, 48
  digital technology, 47
  emerging economy, 47
  high-technology markets, 47–50
  market differentiation, 47
  market power, 49
  network effects, 47, 48
  new/innovative industries, 47, 48
  product function, 47
  regulation, 49
submarkets, 43
substitutability, 40, 41
tying, 42
  see also **Tying**
upstream market, 43

New Zealand
abuse of market power
  anti-competitive behaviour, 189–91, 195
  comparative exercise, 190–2
  counterfactual test, 190–2, 195
  economic analysis, 192
  efficient components pricing rule, 193–5
  intellectual property rights, 205
  market power, 190
  refusal to licence, 181, 182, 196
  telecommunications market, 190–4, 207, 208
  unilateral exercise of market power, 197
anti-competitive behaviour
  abuse of market power, 181–3
  anti-competitive leveraging, 43, 183
  breach of confidence, 208, 209
  connection issue, 183

  eliminating competition, 182
  preventing competition, 182
  proof and presumption, 40
  purpose issue, 183
  restraint of trade, 208
  restricting market entry, 182
  threshold issue, 183
civil pecuniary remedies, 74
competition cases, 40
competition law
  abuse of market power, 181–3, 189
  anti-competitive behaviour, 189–91, 195
  anti-competitive leveraging, 43, 183
  eliminating competition, 182
  preventing competition, 182
  restricting market entry, 182
competition policy
  efficiency considerations, 53
  parallel import restrictions, 119
competition regime
  abuse of market power, 181, 182
  economic elements, 26, 27
  per se rules, 26
  rule of reason, 26
intellectual property
  anti-competitive agreements, 196
  assignment, 196
  competition legislation, 196
  licences, 196
  unilateral exercise of market power, 197
intellectual property rights
  abuse of market power, 205
  enforcement of rights, 205–8
  evidential perspective, 205, 206
  exclusive dealing, 197
  immunity/rights holders, 205
  protection, 196, 205, 207
  scope of grant, 196
  statutory interpretation, 205–7
  technological protection measures, 205
  tying, 197
refusal to licence
  absence of legislation, 196
  anti-competitive intent, 206
  enforcement of rights, 205, 207, 208
structural remedies, 64

Parallel imports
restrictions, 119, 120
Patents
assignment, 225–7
compulsory licensing, 92, 93
market power, 140, 142, 144
  see also **Market power**
misuse, 123, 144, 145, 147
non-obviousness, 164
novelty, 164
patent acquisition, 82

patent abuse, 93, 94
procedural flaws, 142
process patents, 111, 120
protection
    fraud, 100, 141, 142
    protectable ideas, 111
    term of protection, 117
    right to exclude, 141
    United States of America, 123, 124
    see also **United States of America**

Per se rule
    competition regimes
        Australia, 26
        Canada, 26
        New Zealand, 26
    competition rules, 35
    proof and presumption, 38
    regulatory intervention, 237
    see also **Regulatory intervention**

Precedent
    stare decisis, 31

Pricing coerced access
    abandoned past access, 69
    access price, 68
    competitive price, 68, 69
    expert opinion, 68
    fall-back process, 68
    imprecise price setting, 69
    judicial reluctance, 67
    RAND/FRAND formula, 67–9

Proof and presumption
    anti-competitive harm, 38, 39
    Australia, 40
    burden of proof, 38, 39, 40
    competitive virtue, 38
    European Union, 40
    indeterminate economic theory, 38, 39
    judge-made presumptions, 36, 37, 39, 40
    New Zealand, 40
    per se rule, 38
    presumption against regulatory intervention, 38
    rule of reason, 38
    United States of America, 40

Public choice theory
    effects, 109, 110

Public interest defence
    abuse of rights, 94, 95
    breach of confidence, 94, 95
    competition controls, 234

Reasonable and non-discriminatory terms (RAND)
    licensing, 67, 69

Refusal to licence
    anti-competitive outcomes, 41
    black-letter solutions, 235
    competition cases, 6
    see also **Competition cases**
    competition scrutiny, 237
    economic issues, 3, 233, 238, 239
    see also **Economic analysis**
    empirical analysis, 233, 238, 239
    essentialness, 233
    see also **Essential facilities doctrine (EU)**; **Essential facilities doctrine (US)**
    exceptionality, 233
    see also **Exceptional circumstances test**
    fact/law distinction, 36, 37, 39, 40
    see also **Fact/law distinction**
    guiding principles, 2
    importance, 2
    legal certainty, 235
    market power, 6, 170, 171
    see also **Market power**
    markets
    see **Markets**
    meaning, 4
    potential conflict
        competition policy, 2
        intellectual property law, 2
    presumptive immunity, 237
    regulatory intervention, 237
    see also **Regulatory intervention**
    remedies, 61, 66
    see also **Remedies**
    right to refuse, 233
    rule of reason, 235
    see also **Rule of reason**
    trans-jurisdictional analysis, 2, 3
    unilateral refusal, 6

Regulation
    intervention
        see **Regulatory intervention**
    meaning, 5
    regulatory neutrality, 6, 7, 76
    regulatory outcomes, 9
    under-regulation/over-regulation, 17, 23, 32, 76

Regulator
    meaning, 5

Regulatory intervention
    coerced licensing, 238, 239
    see also **Coerced licensing**
    economic consensus, 237
    exclusion, 12
    hierarchy of rights, 16, 17, 236
    impact, 239
    innovation and creativity, 18, 19
    see also **Innovation and creativity**
    justification, 16, 17, 19
    legislative clarity, 237
    legislative rescue, 237
    per se liability, 237
    see also **Per se rule**

268 INDEX

privileging/de-privileging (intellectual property), 237
restraint, 237
rule of reason, 237
  see also **Rule of reason**
scope of grant principle, 12
  see also **Scope of grant principle**
under-regulation/over-regulation, 17, 23, 32
Remedies
behavioural remedies, 61, 62, 64–6, 71
coerced licensing, 61, 65, 67
  see also **Coerced licensing**
competition proceedings, 61, 62
court-appointed entities
  compliance monitoring, 66
  costing access, 66
  supervisory regimes, 66
damages, 71, 73, 74, 75
deterrence, 61, 62, 70, 71, 74
discretionary remedies, 74
disgorgement, 71, 74
efficacy, 61
fairness, 71
fines, 71, 73, 75
forward-looking, 71
future compliance, 73
harm done, 73, 75
hierarchy of remedies, 65
injunctive relief, 70
interlocutory relief, 71
judicial concerns
  behavioural remedies, 66
  extended judicial supervision, 66, 67
  flexibility, 67, 69
  intellectual property rights, 67
  judges acting as quasi-regulators, 66
  legal certainty, 67, 69
  pricing coerced access, 67
judicial decision-making
  existence of wrong, 72, 73
  mental sequencing, 72
  reasoning backwards, 72, 73
liability-enhancing, 72
liability-restricting, 72
mandated contractual remedy, 70
market repair, 62, 73, 74
monetary remedies, 74, 75
pricing coerced access, 67–9
  see also **Pricing coerced access**
profits gained, 73
refusal to licence, 61, 66
remedial failure, 61
remedial objectives, 62
retrospective assessment, 70, 71
retrospective efficacy, 71
structural remedies
  Australia, 64

behavioural remedies/relationship, 62, 64, 65
coerced licensing, 65
corporate restructuring, 62–5
deterrence, 61, 62
effectiveness, 63
European Union, 64
jurisdictional differences, 63
multiple markets, 65
New Zealand, 64
United States of America, 63, 64
substantive liability, 61
supervisory structures
  intermediate structures, 69
  jurisdictional limitations, 70
Reputational rights/rules
business connection, 112
competition, 113
consumer protection, 88, 112
origin of goods, 88
signifier/reputation link, 112, 113
trade marks, 88, 89, 112, 113
Rhetorical exaggeration/distortion
coerced licensing, 15, 16
  see also **Coerced licensing**
competition scrutiny/parallel regulatory regime, 18
compulsory licensing/innovation, 18–20
freedom of contract, 13, 14
freedom to choose, 13–15
right to exclude others (ownership), 10, 11
regulatory intervention, 16, 17, 19
  see also **Regulatory intervention**
scope of grant principle, 12, 13
  see also **Scope of grant principle**
under-regulation/over-regulation, 17, 23, 32, 76
untested assumptions, 10
Rule of reason
anti-competitiveness, 24
competition law, 7, 9
concept, 24
economic analysis, 27
  see also **Economic analysis**
fault-based liability, 24
freedom of contract, 24
judicial decision-making, 24
proof and presumption, 38
refusal to licence, 235
regulatory intervention, 237
  see also **Regulatory intervention**
United States of America, 24, 25

Scope of grant principle
anti-competitive leveraging, 46, 47
  see also **Leveraging**
common law jurisdictions, 13
competition scrutiny, 12

enforcement difficulties, 12
exclusion of regulatory intervention, 12
judicial support, 13
legal monopoly, 12
market power, 12
  see also **Market power**
Singapore
  parallel imports, 119
Soft law
  influence, 31
Spare parts
  after-markets, 139, 140
  anti-trust liability, 139
  copyright protection, 141, 142
  denial, 138
  judicial approach
  lock-ins, 139, 140
  market power, 140
  patent protection, 140, 141
  refusal to supply, 158, 162
  software products, 141
Standard capture
  anti-competitive behaviour, 51
  discordant economics, 51
  intellectual property rights, 50, 51
Standard setting
  anti-competitive behaviour, 51
  collective monopsony, 51
  discordant economics, 51
  high-technology industries, 50
  industry standard, 50
Substitutability
  delayed substitution, 42
  demand side, 41
  future substitution, 42
  past substitution, 42
  probable substitution, 42
  SSNIP tests, 42
  substitutable alternatives, 42
  supply side, 41

Technological protection measures
  abuse of rights, 146
  intellectual property rights, 91, 146, 205, 218, 224
  interoperability issues, 52
Terminology
  abuse of market power, 5
  competition law, 5
  difficulties/distractions, 3, 4
  intellectual property rights, 4
  monopolisation/monopoly, 5, 79
  property, 79, 80
  refusal to licence, 4
  regulator, 5
  regulation, 5, 79, 80
Trade marks
  licences, 219–23

protection, 88, 89, 112, 113
Trade secrets
  abuse of market power, 218, 224
  independent discovery defence, 82
TRIPS Agreement
  inward investment, 21
  national licensing practices, 21
  restraint of trade, 21
  state aids, 21
  technology transfer, 21
Tying
  anti-competitive behaviour, 42, 147, 148, 197, 219, 220, 222

United States of America
  abuse of rights
    anti-trust law, 145
    copyright misuse, 144–7
    doctrine, 93, 95
    fair use, 146
    parallel jurisprudence, 144–7
    patent misuse, 144, 145, 147
    technological protection measures, 146
  anti-trust law
    absolute immunity, 148
    abuse of rights, 145
    action/inaction distinction, 147
    anti-competitive conduct, 122
    coerced licensing, 148
    fragmentation, 122
    freedom to licence, 148
    gaming the system, 148
    intervention, 84
    market power, 122
    per se liability, 122, 125
    prescriptive approach, 125
    refusal to deal, 147, 148
    regulatory neutrality, 122, 125, 126
    rule of reason, 24, 25, 122, 147
    Sherman Act, 25, 122, 124, 126, 127, 138
    sub-rules, 122
    tying, 147, 148
  competition cases
    fact/law distinction, 36
    proof and presumptions, 40
    remedies, 74
    rule of reason, 24, 25, 122
    submarkets, 43
  compliance officers, 69
  constructive refusal, 130, 137
  copyright
    computer software, 146
    fair use, 146
    misuse, 144–7
    obtained by unlawful means, 144
    paracopyright rules, 91, 146
    protection, 116, 141, 142
    refusal to licence, 141–3

right to exclude, 143, 144
technological protection measures, 146
essential facilities doctrine, 126–37, 148, 149
  see also **Essential facilities doctrine (US)**
intellectual property rights
  anti-trust claims, 124
  anti-trust laws, 123, 124
  enforcement, 84, 124
  hierarchy of rights, 123
  licensing, 124, 125
  market power, 140
  misappropriation, 114
  over/under-enforcement cycles, 123
  patents, 123, 124
  process patents, 111
  protection, 114, 123, 124
  quasi-property, 114
  social bargain, 123
  unjust enrichment, 114
legal/economic monopolies
  absolute immunity, 126
  access costs, 138
  judicial assumptions, 125
  margin squeeze, 137, 138
  market power, 125
  'Nine No-Nos', 125, 126
  per se liability, 125
  presumption of illegality, 125

presumption of virtue, 125, 149
presumptive immunity, 126
price squeeze, 137, 138
unreasonable terms/conditions, 130, 137
vertical integration, 137
patents
  anti-trust liability, 124
  dissemination, 123
  ex ante disclosure, 123
  fraud, 141, 142
  legislation, 124
  market power, 140, 142, 144
  patent misuse, 123, 144, 145, 147
  procedural flaws, 142
  protection, 123, 140, 141
  right to exclude, 141
refusal to deal, 137
regulatory neutrality
  emergence, 125, 126
  uneven approach, 126
remedies
  damages, 74
  monetary remedies, 74
  structural remedies, 63, 64
spare parts, consumables, services, 138–42, 148
  see also **Spare parts**